Passivity, Resistance, and Collaboration

孤岛上海

布灵题

Passivity, Resistance, and Collaboration

Intellectual Choices in Occupied Shanghai, 1937–1945

Poshek Fu

STANFORD UNIVERSITY PRESS, STANFORD, CALIFORNIA

Stanford University Press, Stanford, California © 1993 by the Board of
Trustees of the Leland Stanford Junior University
Printed in the United States of America
Published with the assistance of a special grant from the
Stanford University Faculty Publication Fund to
help support nonfaculty work originating at Stanford
CIP data appear at the end of
the book

●

Stanford
University Press
publications are distributed
exclusively by Stanford University Press
within the United States, Canada, Mexico,
and Central America; they are distributed exclusively
by Cambridge University Press throughout the rest of the world.

For
Jin Qiang and my parents
with love

Acknowledgments

I began the research that led to this book eight years ago in Shanghai. Inspired by the moral courage of two friends who persevered in their fight against social injustices despite great adversity, I had long been fascinated with the issue of moral choices under oppressive conditions. But I was unsure how to develop this into a doctoral dissertation, especially at a time when I was afflicted by severe financial and political troubles, not knowing whether I could return to my scholarly life at Stanford University. I owe many debts of gratitude to the people who made it possible for me to complete first the dissertation and then the book.

Although I had never met Ke Ling, an 85-year-old survivor of the Japanese Occupation, he wrote me letter after letter explaining in vivid detail the complexity of intellectual life in occupied Shanghai. He also graces my book with his calligraphy. Qian Jinxi, another survivor, gave me several long interviews despite his busy schedule. For their generosity I am deeply grateful. It is my fortune to have had two wonderful advisors who complemented each other. Constantly challenging me to think the impossible, Harold Kahn guided me through the writing and revising of my dissertation. He never once failed me when I needed his help. Lyman Van Slyke, always understanding, allowed me freedom to be creative.

For his love and trust, my heartfelt thanks to William Lyell. The comments of Sherman Cochran, Paul Cohen, Bryna Goodman, Theodore Huters, Andrew Nathan, Sun Lung-kee, Makoto Ueda, Frederic Wakeman, and Bernard Wasserstein prompted me to reformulate some of the issues discussed here. I also appreciate the support of Polly Duxbury, Paul Jankowski, Philip Kafalas, Mark Tam,

viii   ACKNOWLEDGMENTS

Steven Van Zoren, Wang Ke-wen, and Yeh Wen-hsin, who in various ways contributed to my work. I am grateful to my colleague
at Colgate University Jill Harsin for her unfailing support of my
research; to Thomas Gold, whose enthusiasm made me feel at home
during my post-doctoral stay at Berkeley; and to Ming Chan, who
convinced me to pursue a doctoral degree at Stanford. At Stanford University Press, the editorial care of Muriel Bell, the insight-
ful copyediting of Peter Dreyer, and the polite thoughtfulness of
John Feneron have made the publication process a joyful experience
for me.

I also thank the Center for East Asian Studies and the Center for
International Studies of Stanford University, the Huadong Normal
University (Shanghai), the Mabelle McLeod Lewis Fund, the John D.
and Catherine T. MacArthur Foundation, the Center for Chinese
Studies of the University of California at Berkeley, and Colgate
University for their generous financial support of my research and
writing.

Two friends gave me help at critical times of my life, and to
them I owe deep gratitude. William Li Kwok-wai lent me the
money that allowed me to return to the United States in 1986 and
continue my academic life; and Larry Robinson made it possible for
me to refocus my energy on writing after going through a period of
political anxiety.

My deepest debt of gratitude is to my family. My parents, Fu
Ming-sun and Liu Yuk-chun, have given me all their love and support, but never once imposed their will on me, although I was the
first in my extended family to have a university education. Siu-pak,
Chun-kau, and Yat-mui, my brothers and sister, demanded so little
from me but gave so much during my long absence from home.
Words cannot express my gratitude to my wife, Jin Qiang, whose
commitment to me in adversity, whose sacrifice for our love during
these many years, and whose intelligence and inner strength in the
face of challenges have inspired and sustained me. Her influence per-
vades the book. Our baby son Chunmin, with his alternate show of
affection and demand for attention, is my best teacher of life who
challenges me to appreciate the existential truism No pain, no gain.
This appreciation has helped make my years of writing a great joy.

                                                      P.F.

Contents

Preface *xi*

Abbreviations *xix*

Prologue:
Toward Occupation 1

1
Passivity:
Wang Tongzhao and the Ideal of Resistance Enlightenment 21

2
Resistance:
Li Jianwu and the Theater of Commitment 68

3
Collaboration:
The "*Gujin* Group" and the Literature of Anachronism 110

Epilogue 155

Notes *169*

Bibliography *221*

Glossary *241*

Index *249*

(maps follow page xix; eight pages of photographs follow page 67)

Preface

This is a study of the moral and political choices of Chinese intellectuals under the Japanese Occupation during World War II. In contrast to the impressive scholarship devoted to the human condition in Nazi-occupied Europe, especially Vichy France, Chinese historians have yet to pay attention to the problem of human responses to occupation. The extant historiographical literature on occupied China—both in China (Mainland and Taiwan) and in the West—is parochially political. It concerns itself either with the politics of collaboration or with unraveling the "enigma" of individual political collaborators: Why did Wang Jingwei or Zhou Fohai work for the Japanese? What was the political-diplomatic context of Chinese collaboration? What were the relations between Chiang Kaishek and the Wang regime? Alternatively, the literature contributes to the ongoing ideological debate as to whether the Nationalists or the Communists led the war against Japan: Who was responsible for the resistance in occupied areas?[1]

The only exception to this approach is Edward Gunn, who, in his pioneering work *Unwelcome Muse: Chinese Literature in Shanghai and Peking, 1937–1945*, discovers the literary quality of occupied Beijing and Shanghai by identifying its "antiromantic" thrust. But as he is interested primarily in locating Occupation literature within the modern Chinese tradition and in evaluating its literary merit (besides providing a general, informative introduction to the political condition of the two cities), Gunn makes little effort to relate the literary texts to their historical context. Hence the moral situation of writers under the Occupation and their various responses to it remains an untold story.[2]

Focusing on intellectual life in Shanghai, the major cultural, commercial, and financial center under Japanese occupation and the largest city controlled by the collaborationist regime of Wang Jingwei, my book aims to redress this historiographical imbalance by explicating the moral and political responses of writers to foreign occupation. The intellectuals studied here are not a cluster of abstract intellects in isolation from history; rather they represent thinking individuals with a conscious grasp of their historical situation. Their lives and thought, in other words, provide us with a privileged position from which we can delve into the prevailing mood and mind of occupied Shanghai. For this emphasis I choose to focus on one group of intellectuals—writers—who are sensuously expressive of their emotions and inner feelings and are especially capable of articulating them in vivid, powerful images. Given the cherished tradition of using literature as a political medium, Chinese writers are prone in times of crisis to see themselves as the social conscience of China, a moral elite interpreting the people's needs and speaking out on their behalf against the unjust conditions. Literary texts, then, become the primary vehicle for our exploration of the human drama unfolded in occupied Shanghai.[3]

Shanghai fell to the Japanese after three months of fighting from August 13 to November 12, 1937; and until its liberation on August 15, 1945, the city underwent two phases of occupation, the first being from 1937 to December 1941 and the second from then until 1945. This temporal division was a result of the spatial-political structure of Shanghai. Lying at the confluence of Suzhou Creek and the Huangpu River, which runs into the eastern estuary of the Yangzi River, Shanghai was a hybrid city made up of Chinese and foreign areas. The two areas were run by different governments, each acting in accordance with its own laws, and enjoyed disparate levels of economic prosperity.

Under Western administrations, with their self-proclaimed neutral status in the War of Resistance, the foreign areas (the British-dominated International Settlement and the French Concession) remained intact, while the Chinese part of the city—the 320 square miles comprising the Shanghai Special Municipality, which included Jiangwan, Zhabei (Chapei), Nanshi (Nantao), Yangshupu (Yangtzepoo), and Pudong—and its hinterland fell under the Japanese Occupation in November 1937. The tiny foreign town of less than ten square miles between Suzhou Creek to the north (just 60 yards from the occupied zone), Xujiahui (Siccawei) Creek, which bordered Nanshi to the south, and the ambiguous Extended-Settlement Areas to the west, then, created a haven for all the Chinese who for various reasons did not flee to British-run Hong Kong or into the unconquered interior. Known as the Gudao (Solitary Island), this foreign-proffered haven, a privileged city within an occupied metropolis, set the Shanghai experience apart from its European and Asian counterparts during World War II. But this distinction needs to be qualified. Although free from direct (and indirect) Japanese control, the Gudao had only limited freedom of expression. Throughout this period, the city was engulfed in a gangland-style terror—assassination, kidnapping, and extortion—engineered by the Japanese secret services and underground Nationalist agents. The lives of both patriots and collaborators were in jeopardy. This partial occupation was soon cut short with the disappearance of the Gudao following the outbreak of the Pacific War.

On December 8, 1941, following the attack on Pearl Harbor, the Japanese army extended its occupation to the foreign areas. Now, for the first time since 1843, when Shanghai became a treaty port, the whole city was again unified under one administration, albeit a foreign one. But the price was too high. Systematic repression and economic bankruptcy turned Shanghai into what people at the time called a "dark world" (heian shijie). Not until the afternoon of August 14, 1945, after the broadcast of Emperor Hirohito's surrender at the racecourse on Nanjing Road, was the city liberated.

During the eight years of the Occupation, intellectuals in Shanghai found themselves confronted by the dilemma of the conflicting demands of private and public morality: on the one hand, survival, concern for one's family, and pursuit of one's own interests; on the other, patriotic commitment and dignity. This moral dilemma was all the more haunting because most writers were tormented by a pervading sense of guilt for choosing to live under the enemy rather than uproot their families to eke out a new and uncertain life in the economically backward Chinese-controlled interior. Should they continue to compromise? How could they maintain their human dignity and patriotic ideals in the teeth of the Occupation? And if compromise was inevitable, what should they do?

In postwar China, moral choices during the Japanese Occupation were telescoped into clear-cut, idealized polarities: the prevalent perception was of a Manichean world in which, heroes versus villains, selfless resisters fought shameless collaborators. In fact, however, wartime Shanghai exhibited a complexity and ambiguity of moral choices that defies such simplistic stereotyping. Ambiguous response was only natural in an extreme situation of dehumanizing terror, which Primo Levi aptly calls the "grey zone" of existence: a situation in which weaknesses, inevitable inconsistency of behavior, and even a degree of compromise, as well as dignity and moral courage, were involved for anyone trying to survive in the face of the enemy.[4] Few Shanghai writers openly resisted, and those who did were often also fearful, hesitant, and wavering; conversely, many literary collaborators lived through the latter part of the war in a state of deep remorse and repentence. Hence, in place of the postwar binary stereotype, my book proposes a tripartite mode of intellectual responses to the "grey zone" of the Japanese Occupation.

Echoing the archetypal behavior of traditional literati in times of moral and political upheaval—eremitism, loyalism, and collaboration[5]—writers in occupied Shanghai conceived a triad of responses to the Occupation: passivity, resistance, and collaboration. Each of these choices entailed a discourse that involved philosophical concepts, familiar (self-)images, historical analogies, and stylized postures with respect to the dilemma of choosing between personal survival and patriotic ideal. This echo of history should not, however, be read as a "return to history" or a "resurgence of tradition." Rather, it presupposes a hermeneutic dialogue, a mutual communication between the past and present. The relation between these two temporal horizons is, in other words, one of productive fusion rather than of binary opposition: the present is often illuminated in the light of the past, while the past can be grasped only in terms of the concerns and assumptions of the present. Indeed, the three modalities of traditional response, as we shall see, were invested in occupied Shanghai with meanings and ideologies sensuously peculiar to the cultural context of post–May Fourth China.

It is important to note at this point that human constructs are not historical realities. These three modalities are merely heuristic concepts and narrative categories, which highlight, but do not exhaust, the ambiguity of intellectual choices in occupied Shanghai. They are useful to the extent that they avoid the rigid moralism of the postwar Chinese stereotype without succumbing to the poststructuralist tendency to particularism and amoralism, which reduces all human intentions to matters of pure difference, utter indeterminacy, and historical insignificance by conceiving texts, to borrow the apt phrase of Edward Said, "as existing within a hermetic, Alexandrian textual universe" with no grounding in actuality.[6] By recognizing a certain role for human will in the form of confrontation with a specific historical dilemma, a situation fraught with confusion and moral uncertainty, my tripartite categorization makes possible value judgments while remaining sensitive to the Levian notion of complexity of responses under foreign domination.

To achieve the balance between moral judgment and historical relativism, this tripartite scheme of intellectual choices calls forth a set of definitions as flexible as possible in order to heighten our sensitivity to the "grey zone" of moral ambiguity of occupied Shanghai. According to these definitions, many writers chose to live a reclusive life as a means of harmonizing the conflicting demands between private and public morality. They saw in *passivity* a symbolic voice of protest, a way toward "dignified survival" that saved one's skin without sacrificing much of one's ideals. The few who *resisted* slighted personal concerns and championed the notion of moral integrity in the heroic tradition of loyalism in order to mobilize a revolt against compromise. In their minds, though not always in their actions, collective interests transcended the private realm. At the same time, there were many literary *collaborators* seeking to assuage their moral guilt over betrayal. They emphasized the banality of human needs; they portrayed themselves as human "anachronisms" who clung to an existence totally at odds with the present, representing their feeling of alienation in nostalgia. Thus, while the passivists chose to withdraw to preserve their sense of human dignity, the resisters defined humanity in terms of moral defiance and the collaborators justified their will to live as all too human.

These three modes of intellectual response were respectively illustrated by the novelist and poet Wang Tongzhao (1897–1957), the playwright Li Jianwu (1906–1982), and a group of essayists associated with the collaborationist magazine *Gujin*. Together their Occupation experience forms the narrative structure of this study. The book is divided into three main chapters, with the Prologue serving as an introduction to the intellectual life of Shanghai on the eve of the Occupation. It describes the passion and frustration of intellectuals in the Battle of Shanghai from August to November 1937. Each of the three chapters is then devoted to one specific mode of response to the Occupation. The writers examined here gave personal voice to the complexity and ambiguity of intellectual choices, thereby symbolizing life in occupied Shanghai.

This biographical approach raises the problem of typicality. I choose Wang Tongzhao, Li Jianwu, and the *Gujin* group not so much because they were typical in any statistical, classifying sense as because their Occupation experience testified to the profound uncertainty of intellectual life under the Japanese Occupation. None of these writers were consistently selfless or invariably shameless, and neither did any of them play a central role in defining the political contours of the Occupation. Wang's passivity was an eloquent statement of patriotic protest, but beneath it lay a subtext smacking of alienation and political escapism. Li constantly wrestled with the conflict between the pursuit of scholarship and the demands of resistance. And he committed himself to fighting the enemy only when he was compelled to find employment in the theater, which represented the most important forum of anti-Japanese expression during the latter part of the Occupation. The *Gujin* essayists, on the other hand, refused to glorify the occupying force, yet enjoyed the rewards and privileges that went along with their compromise. Thus, if these intellectuals were typical of anything, they typified, on a human level, the "grey zone" of moral ambiguity involved in surviving the dark days of Occupation.

Another reason for my choice of Wang Tongzhao, Li Jianwu, and the *Gujin* group is that they engaged in different forms of writing: prose poetry and short stories, modern theater, and lyrical essays. Although there exists no automatic or absolute kinship between genres and ideology, just as passivists (e.g., Geng Jizhi) could also be playwrights while resisters (e.g., Ke Ling) also tried their hands at essays, a critical analysis of the ways these respective literary forms reflected and related to their authors' moral and political choices provides us with an extra dimension in which to apprehend the intellectual life of Shanghai under the Occupation.

It should be clear by now that I approach literature primarily as a "socially symbolic act," a mediated, symbolic response to a concrete historical situation.[7] By situating literary texts in their historical moment, my reading is based on a historically grounded reconstruction of the "affiliative" context from which a text was produced. This context entailed, among other things, the sociopolitical conditions of writing and publication, the life and (self-)perception of the author, values and ideas tacitly assumed in the process of textualization, a shared language of literary symbols and historical allusions, and a specific network of human relationships surrounding artistic production.[8]

This interpretative strategy is especially relevant to our understanding of literary texts from occupied Shanghai. Expressed in a highly disguised form for fear of retaliation, these texts are all distinguished by their ethical motif, strong political undertone, intensely personal, even autobiographical, texture, and profound sense of historical anguish. Indeed, to most of the writers under Japanese domination, literature, with its elaborate symbolism and codified language, represented precisely that limited "social space," to borrow James Scott's notion, in which "offstage dissent" to the occupying power could be safely defined and voiced. And as to be shown, this dissent was not limited only to intellectuals who overtly or symbolically defied the enemy, but was also found among some literary collaborators who refused to propagandize for the occupying forces. Thus my working assumption throughout this book is that many of the literary texts of this period should be read as "hidden transcripts," mediated responses of "disguising ideological insubordination," and a "veiled critique of power" expressed in the face of terror and death.[9] This complexity of resistance and compromise unfolds to us, in sum, the ambiguity of intellectual choices in occupied Shanghai.

Abbreviations

CCP Chinese Communist Party
CRB Central Reserve Note (*zhongchu juan*) of the Wang Jingwei
government (1 CRB = 2 Guomindang Chinese dollars, or
fabi)
GMD Guomindang
SGJ Shanghai shi gejie kangdi houyuan hui (All-Shanghai Feder-
ation for the support of Armed Resistance)
SWH Shanghai shi wenhua jie jiuwang xiehui (Shanghai Cultural
Circles National Salvation Federation)

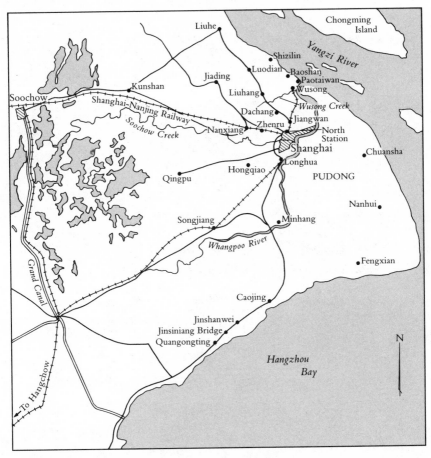

Shanghai and its hinterland. Based upon a map from *Four Months of War*
(Shanghai, 1937).

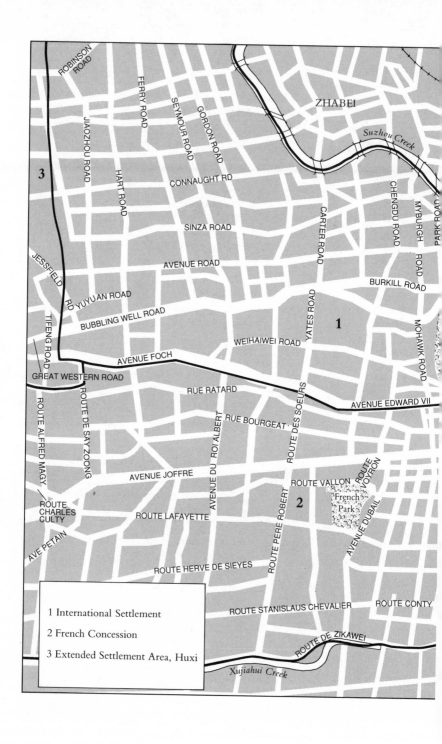

ROBINSON ROAD

FERRY ROAD

SEYMOUR ROAD

GORDON ROAD

JIAOZHOU ROAD

HART ROAD

CONNAUGHT RD

ZHABEI

Suzhou Creek

CHENGDU ROAD

MYBURGH ROAD

PARK ROAD

3

SINZA ROAD

CARTER ROAD

AVENUE ROAD

BURKILL ROAD

JESSFIELD RD

YUYUAN ROAD

TIFENG ROAD

BUBBLING WELL ROAD

YATES ROAD

1

MOHAWK ROAD

WEIHAIWEI ROAD

AVENUE FOCH

GREAT WESTERN ROAD

RUE RATARD

AVENUE EDWARD VII

ROUTE ALFRED MAGY

ROUTE DE SAY ZOONG

RUE BOURGEAT

AVENUE DU ROI ALBERT

ROUTE DES SOEURS

AVENUE JOFFRE

ROUTE VALLON

ROUTE VOYRON

French Park

2

ROUTE CHARLES CULTY

ROUTE LAFAYETTE

ROUTE PERE ROBERT

AVENUE DUBAIL

AVE PETAIN

ROUTE HERVE DE SIEYES

ROUTE STANISLAUS CHEVALIER

ROUTE CONTY

ROUTE DE ZIKAWEI

Xujiahui Creek

1 International Settlement

2 French Concession

3 Extended Settlement Area, Huxi

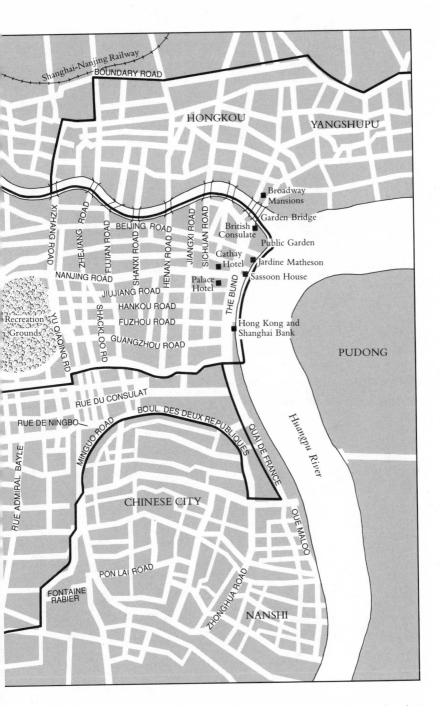

Solitary Island Shanghai. Based upon a map from Harriet Sergeant, *Shanghai*
(New York, 1990).

. . . the gap that exists and grows wider every year between things as they were "down there" and things as they are represented by the current imagination fed by approximative books, films, and myths. It slides fatally toward simplification and stereotype . . . this phenomenon is not confined to the perception of the near past and historical tragedies, it is much more general, it is part of our difficulty or inability to perceive the experience of others, which is all the more pronounced the more distant these experiences are from ours in time, space, or quality. We are prone to assimilate them to "related" ones, as if the hunger in Auschwitz were the same as that of someone who has skipped a meal, or as if escape from Treblinka were similar to an escape from an ordinary jail. It is the task of the historian to bridge this gap, which widens as we get farther away from the events under examination.

Primo Levi, *The Drowned and the Saved*

Prologue:
Toward Occupation

•

By the mid 1930s, China had entered a period of national crisis, a situation that bore out the popular catchphrase "domestic trouble and foreign invasion" (*neiyou waihuan*): incessant civil war between the Guomindang (GMD) and the Chinese Communist Party (CCP), and increasing Japanese encroachment in the northeast. In pursuing its appeasement policy of "first internal pacification, then external resistance," the Nationalist government had made repeated territorial concessions to Japan in order to direct all of its military force against the Communists. Most educated Chinese thought this unconscionable and championed a war to expel the Japanese invaders as the only means to end the national crisis.

Ever since the "Mukden Incident" of September 1931, in which the Japanese Kwantung Army occupied Manchuria, followed in March 1932 by the setting up of "Manchukuo" with Pu Yi as its puppet "head of state" through a combination of force and conspiracy, a heightened sense of anti-Japanese patriotism had been growing among the educated elite throughout urban China. Their protests against what they considered the Nationalist government's weak-kneed policy toward the enemy, and their pleas for an immediate effort to ward off Japanese aggression found their most dramatic expression in the 1935 "December Ninth Movement," which saw tens of thousands of patriotic students demonstrating in Tiananmen Square in Beijing.[1] Student protests soon caught on in other major cities. Goaded into action by the students' courage, intellectuals in many parts of the country began to organize themselves, along with the business community and labor groups, into national salvation unions (*jiuguo hui*) to put pressure on the government to engage in a national war of self-defense. In May 1936, 70 representatives of over 60 national salvation unions from 18 provinces and cities gathered together at the YMCA Building in Shanghai to found the Quanguo gejie jiuguo hui xiehui (All-China Federation of National Salvation Unions) whose manifesto criticized the GMD's continued pursuit of the civil war and appealed to all political parties to stop fighting each other and instead to form a united front of "mighty force against Japanese imperialism."[2]

To stem this rising tide of militant nationalism, the Chiang Kaishek government stepped up its suppression. The chief victims of this show of force were the seven outspoken leaders of the recently established Quanguo gejie jiuguo hui xiehui—Shen Junru, Shi Liang, Wang Zaoshi, Zou Taofen, Zhang Naiqi, Sha Qianli, and Li Gongpu. In November 1936, shortly after they had helped organize an anti-Japanese mass procession at the funeral of the writer Lu Xun, which marched through the heart of Shanghai, and given support to a strike involving 50,000 workers at seven Japanese cotton mills in Huxi, Pudong, and Yangshupu, the "seven gentlemen" (qi junzi), as they were dubbed by the press, were arrested despite massive protests.[3] This confrontation was, however, ameliorated by the dramatic kidnapping in Xi'an in December 1936 of Chiang Kaishek, whose equally dramatic release later paved the way for the second united front between the GMD and the CCP. The détente between these two arch-rivals brought China eventually to unity, symbolized by the freedom of the qi junzi in July 1937, against Japanese aggression.[4]

The Battle of Shanghai

The outbreak of hostilities in Shanghai on August 13, 1937, which precipitated the eight-year War of Resistance, was as much a tragic shock as a moment of fulfillment to the intellectuals.[5] The Battle of Shanghai started in the working-class district of Zhabei when Japanese marines crossed the Shanghai-Wusong Railway to attack Chinese troops stationed on the Bazi Bridge and Baoshan Road, near the North Station. The fighting quickly spread to Jiangwan, Pudong, Yangshupu, and Hongkou—"Little Tokyo." Millions of residents from the battle zone sought refuge in the foreign areas south of Suzhou Creek. The mass exodus at the beginning of the war, as the North-China Daily News reporter Rhodes Farmer witnessed it, was horrendous:

Never had I dreamed there could be a pilgrimage so sad.... The phalanx halted slowly but odd people pressed remorselessly on, like a filling being bedded down in a tooth cavity. Word had been passed back that barbed wire and Japanese sentries blocked all the approaches to Shanghai save Garden Bridge and the twenty-foot wide crossing that led to it over the stinking, garbage-filled [Suzhou] Creek. The mid-day sun scorched down pitilessly, for it was still the season of *tahsu*—the Great Heat ...the mass pressed on at snail's pace toward what was becoming the bridge of life....My feet [were] slipping...on blood and flesh. Half a dozen times I knew I was walking on the bodies of children or old people sucked under by the torrent, trampled flat by countless feet. A crowd of marines and *ronin* [wave men] stood beside the two Japanese sentries on the far side of the bridge. One of them bayoneted an old man and pitched his body into the creek.[6]

But what awaited many of these refugees who made it to downtown Shanghai was, ironically, only death. On Saturday, August 14, when the city was in the grip of a typhoon, a Chinese bomber failed in its mission to destroy the Japanese flagship *Idzumo,* which was tied up on the Huangpu River facing the Bund, and instead dropped its bombs on the foreign areas in desperation as it turned back. The first two bombs hit the Palace and Cathay hotels at the corner of the Bund and the Nanjing Road, the shopping district of the International Settlement. Over 700 people were killed instantly.

On the corner a decapitated Sikh policeman lay with his arms outstretched as though against oncoming traffic.

Yellow, slowly lifting, high explosive fumes exposed a terror scene in [Nanjing] Road. Flames from blazing cars were incinerating the bodies of their riddled occupants. In grotesque heaps where they had been huddling in doorways and annexes of the Cathay and Palace hotels were heaps of refugees whose blue coolie clothes were turning red. Heads, arms, legs lay far from mangled trunks. For the full long stretch of both buildings, pavements and roadway were littered with bodies.

The sticky-sweet stench of blood hung in my nostrils until I could almost taste it.[7]

The other two bombs, which landed among the refugees crowding the busy intersection of Yu Qiaqing Road and Avenue Edward VII outside the Great World Amusement Palace in the French Concession, which had only the day before been turned into a refugee camp, caused even more deaths and injuries—a total of over 3,000.

The whole scene was like hell on earth, blood flowing everywhere "just like a river," and fingers, arms, legs, and heads separated from the scorched, torn bodies lying around in heaps. Mutilated corpses lined the streets, emitting a stench that made downtown Shanghai smell like a "charnel house" for days. As a young French rescue worker told his friends later, "I didn't eat for a week afterwards."[8] August 14 came to be known as "Bloody Saturday," and it destroyed once and for all the myth of the invulnerability of the foreign areas.[9] Shanghai was now caught up in a total war, and no one could escape its brutality.

Most people in Shanghai at the time believed that the bombings had been perpetrated by the Japanese army, which was losing ground in the street fighting in Zhabei, Hongkou, and Yangshupu. In the first week of the battle, armed principally with big swords and hand grenades, Chinese troops frequently managed to push the enemy all the way back to the waterfront, only to be forced to retreat by the fire of the Japanese warships that held sway over the Huangpu River.

To win the war, Japan had to reformulate its strategy. On August 23, numerous reinforcements arrived at Shanghai under the command of General Iwane Matsui, who decided to take advantage of Japanese naval and aerial predominance and encircle the city from the direction of Hangzhou Bay and Wusong Creek. With Japanese landings at Shizilin, Paotaiwan, and Wusong in early September, the battlefront was extended northward for over 40 miles, from Zhabei all the way up to Liuhe. Japanese planes and warships subjected the front to incessant bombing; by now over 200,000 Japanese marines had joined the battle. Facing them, aside from an elite, German-trained corps of 25,000, were 500,000 poorly equipped Chinese soldiers (the Third Area Army under Chiang Kaishek and Gu Zhutong) who fought heroically, stubbornly holding on to their defensive line; when they lost a strategic position (e.g., Luodian and Baoshan), they took it back in hand-to-hand fighting at night, when the Japanese naval guns became less effective. However, after Japanese marines crossed Wusong Creek in late October and took Dachang, a strategic town just eight miles northwest of Jiangwan and Zhabei, the Chinese line was broken. The final blow to the defense of Shanghai came when the Japanese 10th battleship squadron mounted a surprise landing in Hangzhou Bay at Jinshanwei, Quangongting, and Jinsiniang Bridge on November 5 and proceeded to lay siege to Nanshi, the Chinese city bordering the French Concession. Attacked from front and rear, Shanghai fell on November 12, 1937 (see map 1). Although the courageous Chinese defense failed, the Battle of Shanghai helped destroy the Japanese hope of a quick victory in China. Instead of taking the whole of North China in a matter of months with a force of 300,000 as it had boasted it would do, Japan was forced to commit almost a quarter of a million men and hundreds of planes and warships to the Shanghai front alone.[10]

National Salvation Work

At the beginning of the war, when bullets and shrapnel shells flew all day, when buses and streetcars wound through the main streets of downtown Shanghai with posters calling for support of the war effort, and when the Chinese soldiers just across Suzhou Creek held out relentlessly against the aggressors, whose nonstop bombing turned the Chinese areas into shambles, a new age of heroism appeared to have dawned over China. This exhilarating mood is captured by the novelist Ba Jin:

That first roar of cannon was what I had long been praying for. It finally came as a surprise. That morning, many friends of mine were so excited that they jumped about like crazy; they called it the "holy roar of cannon.".... The roar of cannon in Shanghai removed all the doubts of many people. Some of them went so far as to assert that liberation [*da fansheng*]—smashing the shackles to pieces to secure freedom—had finally come. It was surely the happiest moment for humanity. The previous reservations and restraints were all gone. Everyone could now freely run about and shout at the top of their voices: "Down with Japanese imperialism!" Not only could they express this sentiment, but they could also act it out.[11]

With the new freedom to speak and to act, intellectuals in Shanghai promptly switched from urging military action to reinforcing the war effort. In a twist of language, they redefined their activity as a change from a "national salvation movement" (*jiuwang yundong*) to "national salvation work" (*jiuwang gongzuo*)—a shift from words to deeds. This turn to action gave the intellectuals a sense of worth and power, a renewed confidence in their spiritual leadership at a time of national crisis, something they had been seeking since the Mukden Incident. They were "emancipated" from the burden of alienation and self-doubt. Within the framework of the anti-Japanese united front, their *jiuwang gongzuo* was identified in terms prescribed by, or at least acceptable to, the Nationalist government.

In August 1937, the GMD's Central Executive Committee in Nanjing, primarily interested in mobilizing support for military operations around Shanghai, issued a list of projects to be carried out in rear areas. They included producing propaganda, fund-raising, soliciting contributions for the front, comforting and caring for wounded soldiers, and providing relief to the tens of thousands of war refugees in the city. To take charge of these activities, the GMD Bureau in Shanghai reorganized the Shanghai shi gejie kangdi houyuan hui (All-Shanghai Federation for the Support of Armed Resistance; hereafter SGJ), which had been established in July 1937 in response to the "Marco Polo Bridge Incident" outside Beijing, which marked the beginning of the war. The new SGJ brought together activists of all social backgrounds and political colorations. It was controlled by a combined leadership of Shanghai GMD unit chiefs and business leaders.[12] Headquartered in the neutral foreign settlements, it served as an umbrella organization, its various committees (i.e. fund-raising, nursing, supplies, and propaganda) overseeing more than 500 political and social groups in Shanghai.[13] As the largest and leading national salvation organization in the city, the SGJ's purpose was to give direction to the overall operation of civilian war work. It focused on two areas of service: providing military supplies to the front and rendering medical care to wounded soldiers.[14] By virtue of its semi-official status, the SGJ also became an intermediary between the various resistance groups and the foreign areas authorities with regard to anti-Japanese activities in their precincts. Hence when the Shanghai Municipal Council demanded all the political groups in the International Settlement register with it by October 1937, for example, the SGJ told them to ignore the order and protested on grounds that they had all previously registered with the Chinese government. And when it learned of the Shanghai Municipal Council's intention to escalate suppression of anti-Japanese propaganda in early November, it summoned all its members to keep their propaganda work "within bounds and respect given for law and order."[15] In sum, the SGJ represented a conduit through which the bulk of the national salvation work in Shanghai was funneled.

On July 29, 1937, the GMD formed a new association in order specifically to enlist intellectuals into war propaganda efforts. This was the Shanghai shi wenhua jie jiuwang xiehui (Shanghai Cultural Circles National Salvation Federation; hereafter SWH), meant as a collateral body to the SGJ. Under a board of 83 trustees, who included Mao Dun, the former Beijing University chancellor Cai Yuanpei, the GMD official Pan Gongzhan, and the movie producer Zhou Jianyun, the organization boasted a membership of 121 cultural societies and some 5,000 individuals in September. The SWH's organizational structure was as hierarchical as that of the SGJ: when it decided on a fund-raising goal, each of its affiliates would be given a quota to fulfill within a certain period. Most of these affiliates emerged from the prewar national salvation unions affiliated with the CCP.[16] As a result, although the SWH was a united front organization in which the GMD and CCP shared the top leadership, at the grassroots level it was dominated by CCP activists. The SWH's organ, *Jiuwang ribao* (National Salvation Daily), for instance, was under firm control of Communist writers, who succeeded in turning it into a political forum. The newspaper editors Xia Yan, A Ying, and Ba Ren, all veterans of the CCP cultural apparatus, made it a rule that the newspaper would publish no official news releases from the GMD Central News Agency; instead, it would assume the role of popular supervision, concentrating on political exposés and literary criticism, which were to provide guidelines for activists and exert pressure on the GMD regime to hold on in the fight against Japan.[17]

Aside from its publications, the SWH invested most of its energy in organizing artists and students into drama troupes to stage plays on the streets, in refugee centers, and in hospitals throughout Shanghai to drum up support for the war. In September two comforting corps were organized (by the prominent writer Guo Moruo) with 25 young artists each to visit the front, and a total of 13 drama troupes established through an SWH affiliate, the leftist-dominated Shanghai xiju jie jiuwang xiehui (Shanghai Dramatic Circles National Salvation Association), headed by Yu Ling.[18]

The plays, aptly termed "street drama" (*jietou ju*), originated in the mid 1930s as an experimental dramatic form to extend the national salvation message. They were all very short, generally consisting of no more than one episode, and required only simple props and few performers. Aimed at the illiterate or semiliterate, the messages of these plays were usually clear and straightforward. As war propaganda, all of them were concerned with exhorting people not to forget the havoc being wrought by the Japanese aggression, and not to become traitors for the sake of short-term material benefits. No one, they harangued the audience, should entertain the illusion that he or she alone might be able to stay aloof from the trouble. The performers applied little makeup and wore simple costumes, hardly looking different from the audience. Combined with a dramatic technique that stressed active interaction between the audience and the "stage," the performances created a sense of immediacy that was absent in more formal theatrical presentations.[19]

The most famous *jietou ju* was *Fangxia nide bianzi* (Put down your whip), a one-act play originally created by the Communist writer Chen Liting in 1931 aiming to mobilize the workers in Shanghai for revolution. Between 1932 and 1937 the play had been successively revised by many leftist dramatists, including Cui Wei, to suit the need of anti-Japanese propaganda. The scene was quickly set: an old man is going to whip his daughter in order to force her to sing on the street for money. She cries for help. A young worker comes forth from the audience shouting: "Put down your whip! How dare you!" Shamed, and in tears, the father goes to great length in explaining that they are refugees from the Japanese-occupied northeast and have no other means of surviving. The youth then turns to the crowd and cries: "Brothers and sisters! Suffering like this will fall upon each of us if we don't immediately stand up to save ourselves!" When someone in the audience expresses doubt about China's military power, the youth rebukes him: "Our fists are our weapons....If we unite our power will be insurmountable!" At this point the audience became so moved as to join in with the performers, chanting: "Down with Japanese imperialism! Down with traitors!"[20]

Because of this emotive identification between the stage and the audience, street drama became a very effective propaganda device in

Shanghai during the three months of fighting. Indeed, so successful was street drama in building popular enthusiasm that a large number of dramatic troupes sprang up in Shanghai and its suburbs. According to one source, there were altogether 110 troupes during the three months of fighting.[21] Since most of these new troupes were inexperienced, the SWH sent out short-term advisors to help improve their organization and performances.[22] In sum, the SWH represented the nerve center for intellectual involvement in *jiuwang gongzuo*.

Under the supervision and coordination of the SGJ, a multitude of resistance groups, generally called national salvation unions (*jiuguo hui*) or war-front service corps (*zhandi fuwutuan*), were drawn into rear services. Their members came from different walks of life. Some of the groups were made up of students and intellectuals, numbering anywhere from 30 to over 1,000 people.[23] Others included organized industrial workers, white-collar workers from commercial and industrial corporations (e.g., bank employees, public utilities technicians, etc.), educators and civil servants, and writers and artists organized by profession (e.g., film, Beijing opera, journalism). Their activities duplicated each other and largely reflected the guidelines prescribed by the GMD government, as noted above. Two cases illustrate this.

The Yi she (Ant Society), which had had a strong leftist coloration since its founding in 1936, was a powerful resistance group affiliated with the Shanghai zhiye jie jiuwang xiehui (Shanghai Vocational Circles National Salvation Association). Formed by over 1,000 college students, young white-collar workers, and store employees, many of whom were also members of the SWH, the Yi she centered its work throughout the Shanghai hostilities around propaganda, refugee relief, comforting wounded soldiers, and fund-raising for the front. For example, its popular drama troupe, the Yi dui (Ant Troupe), headed by Li Bolong and the Communist Zhang Geng, and its chorus, led by the famous composer Xian Xinghai, visited emergency hospitals and residential alleys on weekends, where they performed street drama and patriotic chorales. In September, many of its members organized themselves into a traveling troupe to carry propaganda to the interior.[24] Also in that month, according to a *Jiuwang ribao* report, the Ant Society managed to establish two refugee centers in the foreign areas, at which activists provided literacy classes and placement services for refugees. It also ran an infirmary for wounded soldiers carried down from the front, with a medical crew of 50 members, sponsored lectures and discussions by public figures to bolster soldiers' morale, and solicited 14,000 pieces of winter clothing and thousands of first-aid packages to send to the front through an arrangement made between the SWH and the military authorities.[25]

The Qingnian jiuguo fuwutuan (Youths' National Salvation Service Corps) was an exceptionally large resistance group, with a total membership of 2,000, whose alleged purpose was to "enlist all the young people engaged in different walks of life in wartime service."[26] The corps enjoyed close ties with the GMD, inasmuch as some of its leading members were connected with the Police Bureau of the Shanghai municipal government. By virtue of this connection, it had access to the front, which was otherwise closed to young volunteers. Over a period of several weeks in October, the corps dispatched some 660 members to assist the army in constructing fortifications and transporting the wounded to the rear.[27] In the city, on the other hand, corps members devoted themselves to soliciting funds and creating propaganda against traitors. To achieve these ends, some of them went so far as to visit dancing halls, bordellos, and movie houses to force contributions from the clientele. They also staged *jie-tou ju* in different refugee centers to exhort their audiences to forsake betrayal of the country for material rewards. They distributed pamphlets door to door calling for the boycotting of Japanese goods and detailing how to track down traitors, urging Shanghai's citizens to be always alert. And in the event that they were successful in arresting suspects, they should send them without delay to the Chinese authorities rather than to the foreign areas police, who were criticized as too lenient to traitors.[28]

Aside from routine relief and medical services, the SGJ and SWH launched various kinds of propaganda campaigns on commemoration days. Most of the SGJ's campaigns strike one as political rituals serving to command loyalism and summon the Shanghai populace's support for the government's wartime policy. On October 10, 1937, just three days after the Japanese crossed Wusong Creek and attacked Dachang, for example, the SGJ called for a "peaceful demonstration and oath-taking ceremony" to commemorate the twenty-sixth anniversary of the National Day. According to the intelligence reports of the foreign areas police, over 1,000 activists took part in the demonstration.[29]

The demonstration turned out to be a carefully orchestrated one, involving little violence and disorder. At 12 P.M. that day, a loudspeaker set up in a highrise building at the crossing between Nanjing and Xizang roads, the busiest intersection of the International Settlement, which led to the Bund, broadcast the GMD anthem and a speech by a local party chief. The party chief urged the public to pledge loyalty by boycotting Japanese goods and subscribing to GMD-issued "national salvation bonds." No sooner had the broadcast begun, than hundreds of activists, who had earlier assembled in small groups, thronged together near the building and repeated the speech verbatim. When the broadcast stopped, a procession of eighteen taxicabs came to a stop near the protesting crowd; from these cars emerged many youths, each waving a national flag, who lost no time in handing out pamphlets and chanting anti-Japanese slogans, while the crowd joined in singing patriotic songs. Moved by this outburst of nationalistic passion, passersby joined in chanting slogans and shouting. All of this happened in a very short time. As soon as the Shanghai Municipal Police broke in and began to make arrests, however, the demonstrators and spectators dispersed.[30] Many such political rituals were carried out, but few attempts were made to mobilize the Shanghai populace for more active resistance.

The SWH intellectuals were more subtle, and ideological in their propaganda drive. Sensitive to the power of cultural symbols, they sought to point out historical continuities with the present national resistance. They wove these historical events into a mythology of revolutionary tenacity, thereby giving them a potent voice. Historical dates and names were transformed into symbols loaded with nationalistic significance. Past and present merged into a unified image of China's ceaseless struggle toward national emancipation. The preeminent examples of these creative efforts involved the 1911 Revolution and the recently deceased writer Lu Xun.

On the same National Day in October 1937, for example, publications connected with the SWH, including the *Jiuwang ribao*, *Kangzhan sanrikan* (Resistance Triweekly), edited by Zou Taofen, and *Fenghuo* (Beacon), edited by Mao Dun and Ba Jin, published special issues to celebrate the historical significance of the day. All the contributors concurred that the twenty-six years since the overthrow

of the Manchus in 1911 constituted a tragic period of "national humiliation," during which thousands of martyrs had failed in their
struggle to secure independence for the country. Their unfinished
task was left to be fulfilled in the present resistance against Japanese
imperialism.[31]

No one captured the symbolic power of the 1911 Revolution as
poignantly as the author Yang Dongchun. In an article published in
Wenhua zhanxian (Cultural Front), he argued that the Revolution
had been a mixed blessing to modern China. Although it had failed
disastrously to deliver the country from the joint evils of imperialism
and feudalism, it had succeeded in inaugurating an era of heroic revolutionary idealism. This idealism, Yang asserted, sought to create a
free independent China through immense sacrifices. Indeed, various
revolutionary movements, including the Northern Expedition (an
anti-warlord campaign mounted in 1926 by the Nationalist army
under Chiang Kaishek, which brought China nominal unity in
1927), were launched after 1911, but to Yang all had been abortive
because of their failure to mobilize the masses. And now, in the face
of Japanese aggression, China was at a "critical juncture of life and
death" (*shengsi cunwang de zuihou guantou*). It would become a
"giant" able to "settle the 43 years of blood debts with the Japanese
imperialists," or it would perish as a nation-race. The key to China's
survival, Yang proclaimed, lay in mass mobilization, as Sun Yatsen
had emphasized again and again after 1911.[32]

Lu Xun, the most celebrated Chinese writer of this century,
whose funeral in 1936 occasioned a massive anti-Japanese protest,
was another example of such symbolic transformation. On October 19, 1937, the first anniversary of Lu Xun's death, Guo Moruo
and Zheng Zhenduo called upon the Shanghai literary community
to organize commemorative publications and public conferences to
honor his spiritual legacy. To shape the propaganda drive, the SWH
put forth a document known as the "Outline of Propaganda in
Commemoration of Lu Xun's Death," in which it described the intellectual odyssey of the writer as "from an anti-feudal and anti-
imperialist fighter to an active proponent of the War of Resistance."[33] According to the document, before the Mukden Incident
of 1931, Lu Xun was a warrior against feudal habits of mind, which
he believed to be the intrinsic cause of China's servility. After 1931,

he became a committed patriot, calling for armed resistance to Japanese imperialism. What distinguished Lu Xun's legacy, then, was not merely his patriotism but, more important, his "uncompromising spirit" (*bu tuoxie jingshen*). Lu Xun was hailed for his relentlessness in fighting for the good of China; be it against feudal evils or imperialist marauders, he would never give up the fight until his enemies submitted. So if China lacked artillery and planes, the SWH authors asserted, it could more than make up for these deficiencies by fighting as unremittingly as Lu Xun. At the end of the document, therefore, all Chinese were called upon to internalize and emulate the "uncompromising spirit" of Lu Xun in order to win the war against Japan.[34] In sum, Lu Xun was made, along with the Revolution of 1911, into a symbol system whose core was a grand optimism that China would win the war as long as the masses were mobilized.

Yet optimism quickly gave way to disappointment. Amidst the passion and action of *jiuwang gongzuo*, a widespread feeling of embitterment and alienation soon seized many intellectuals in Shanghai. Their misgivings were centered around the problem of "having no access to save the nation" (*jiuguo wumen*),[35] a formulation of misgiving in ways strikingly similiar to that expressed by the intelligentsia prior to the war. But whereas prewar intellectuals were disgusted with traditional habits of mind or indignant at the GMD government's reluctance to lead the country (and themselves) in fending off the Japanese invasion, they now became frustrated at being barred from involvement in the political work of mass mobilization.

Frail and inadequate for fighting the enemy at the front as they were, these intellectuals argued that mass mobilization at the rear would be as critical as military operations to winning the war, because this was a total war involving all the social forces in the country. Hence their organizational skills and pedagogical expertise could in fact be as important as frontline combat to national resistance. "Cultural work in the war," the SWH activist Zhang Wozhou proclaimed, "meant nothing but mass education and mass organization."[36] Anxious to leave their mark on the "Great Age" of resistance to Japan, intellectuals in these early months found few opportunities in Shanghai for political engagement. They blamed this phenomenon on the GMD government's continued hostility toward mass mobilization, such as organizing each alley (or village) into a self-governing body or setting up new channels for facilitating democratic expression on national issues, as a means of supporting the war. According to this view, the GMD had fallen prey to what one writer sarcastically termed "traitor paranoia" (*kong hanjian bing*), a political delirium that identified grassroots activism with treasonable disturbances on the grounds that it would destabilize the political situation. As a result, the government looked upon "national salvation" work as merely a "tool" to serve the interests of the overall military operation.[37] It restricted all national salvation groups to performing such "marginal" and "mechanical" work as fund-raising, refugee relief, and medical aid. Political concern with mass mobilization was prohibited. Moreover, according to these critics, most national salvation unions shared the GMD hostility to grassroots politics, because they worried that such activities would incur disfavor from the government and undermine national unity. So they did their best to exclude intellectuals whose social radicalism they distrusted. In this hostile situation, the intellectuals charged, they were being denied opportunities to serve their war-torn country. Moreover, as the war reached a climax in October, many more young intellectuals left the war zones (along with other war refugees) to seek safety and freedom in Shanghai. This constant influx of patriotic youths aggravated the problem of *jiuguo wumen*.[38]

Indeed, there were so many stories and letters to editors grumbling about such political prejudice that Zou Taofen, the outspoken editor of the *Kangzhan sanrikan*, exclaimed: "Now a lot of people have nothing to eat and nothing to do; and they have no idea whatsoever how to work to save the country....It has almost become a common outcry today that people are desperate for [national salvation] work"; he told readers to stop sending in letters requesting placements or making complaints, because he was as impotent to improve the situation as they.[39] Hu Sheng, on the other hand, voiced the feeling of some intellectuals by claiming with a touch of self-pity that "once the war began, culture became useless." Underlying this frustration was the intellectuals' loss of confidence in themselves as the spiritual leaders of the national Resistance. Although their hope of defending the country against the Japanese was fulfilled, they felt once again forced to the sidelines, made spectators rather than heroes in the "Holy War of Resistance."

At the same time, a few military leaders lamented that the masses around Shanghai, unlike those they had encountered during the Northern Expedition of 1926-27, were hopelessly disorganized and did not cooperate with the army. According to Song Xilian, the commander of the 88th Army's 36th Division defending Jiangwan, the masses were so uncooperative that his army was unable to obtain even a packet of salt from them. General Song was disgusted with the peasants' apathy and attributed it to the lack of grassroots organization in the hinterland.[40] Discontented intellectuals in Shanghai always cited this to justify their criticism of the GMD government's reluctance to undertake mass mobilization while leaving idle so many educated youths who were eager to undertake grassroots organization. On this basis, the head of the SWH organization, Qian Junrui, a Communist who later joined the New Fourth Army, concluded with despair that national salvation work thus far had been a political fiasco, where "some people had nothing to do, and there were some things nobody cared to do."[41]

To alleviate these problems—the overabundance of manpower in Shanghai and the political apathy of the masses around it, the SWH leadership encouraged intellectuals who were not presently engaged in rear-area services to "return to the countryside" (huanxiang), with the countryside here referring to the vast territory of China's interior. They called this movement "cultural guerrilla warfare." Qian Junrui, for one, challenged intellectuals to relinquish their familiar world of "classroom and garret" for uncomfortable rural lives. The SWH claimed that in the countryside of China, where little national salvation work had been done, intellectuals could put their cultural knowledge to good use by combating the feudal mentality of servility of the rural masses and by organizing them into support for the war.[42] Rather as in the May Fourth period, intellectuals from the city were portrayed as conveyors of political enlightenment to the "backward" countryside; indeed, in order to win the war, Qian Junrui and other SWH activists exhorted, rural China had to be aroused, and this was surely a task for the educated youth of the day.[43]

In an attempt to launch the huanxiang movement, starting in early September, the SWH dispatched its eleven drama troupes along with the Ant Troupe to conduct war propaganda in various

parts of China's interior.[44] One of these troupes, the "Wartime Mobile Dramatic Troupe Number 2," led by the eminent playwright
Hong Shen and the actor Jin Shan, set out for Hebei and Suiyuan.
When asked their reason for traveling inland by the audience in
Suzhou, Hong replied that there was nothing for them to do in
Shanghai; other troupe members invoked motives that involved re-
forming the countryside.[45] Many artists and writers who were
equally fed up with the frustration of seeking wartime involvement
in the city appear to have followed suit. The SWH announced in
mid-September that all its members should register with it as soon as
possible, because in the confusion of recent weeks, when so many
intellectuals had left Shanghai, many cultural groups had disappeared,
even though their names remained on record.[46]

   If some intellectuals left for the interior in September and October out of frustration, the fall of Shanghai in November 1937 forced
many others to flee the city in order to escape the perils of the Occupation. In early October, the strategic towns of Luodian, Nanxiang, and Dachang (seven miles northwest of the International Settlement) fell successively to the Japanese. These military losses led to
the collapse of the Zhabei-Liuhe line on the 26th. By then the Chinese army had suffered over 200,000 deaths. After the November 5
landing by General Yanagawa Heisuke's 30,000 marines in Hangzhou Bay at Jinshanwei and Quangongting and the critical fall of
Songjiang, less than twenty miles from the city, the Chinese government ordered a general retreat from the Shanghai front and the formation of a new line along the Suzhou-Hangzhou railway to defend
Nanjing. On November 11, after three months of bloody fighting,
the Japanese Shanghai Expeditionary Force took over Greater Shanghai, except for the foreign areas, which claimed to be neutral.[47]

   Shortly before the occupation of Greater Shanghai, however, the
SGJ and SWH leadership strove to sustain the resistance spirit of the
Shanghai public. Stressing that Shanghai was too important to be
abandoned and that the present retreat was only a switch in offensive
strategy, the SGJ called on everyone to continue rear echelon support of the war.[48] In order to ensure continued loyalty from the
city's populace in the face of military loss, it launched several anti-
traitor campaigns in early November, in which activists were dispatched to distribute patriotic handbills to relatives and friends, conduct small-group discussions in residential alleys, and stage small-

scale demonstrations in front of shops accused of selling "enemy goods."[49]

On the eve of the collapse of the line of defense on October 26, 1937, the SWH intellectuals resolved to devote themselves to "more propaganda work in the form of writings."[50] So ensued a change from deeds back to words. The propaganda work referred to here, according to their program, "Baowei da Shanghai yundong xuan-chuan dagang" (Outline of propaganda for the defense of Greater Shanghai), was directed at stiffening the will of both the military and the civilian population.[51] This theme shaped the SWH's work in the latter days of Shanghai's war.

The 800-strong "Lone Battalion" (Gujun) furnished an excellent illustration of this propaganda drive. Under Colonel Xie Jinyuan, the battalion was part of the 88th Division, which was ordered on October 28 to serve as the rear guard for the Zhabei and Jiangwan troops in their retreat toward Suzhou. With the Japanese army in pursuit, this seemed to be a doomed cause. "Imprisoning" itself in the fortresslike Joint Savings Society Godown (warehouse) facing the Xin Laji Bridge on the northern edge of Suzhou Creek, a landmark that served as an informal boundary between the war zone and the foreign areas, the "Lone Battalion" held out heroically for four days against constant bombings and heavy Japanese machine-gun fire. In the meantime, sandbag emplacements and barbed wire, guarded by British troops and the Volunteer Corps, had been set up along the International Settlement border, but the Shanghai Municipal Council nonetheless feared that stray shells and bombs would land in its precinct, causing another "Bloody Saturday." It urged the battalion to surrender, promising sanctuary in the International Settlement. Still the Gujun refused to give up. None of its members expected to survive.

The Shanghai populace saw in this determination the unyielding spirit of the Chinese people, especially when the Gujun managed to raise a large Chinese flag over the warehouse, allegedly presented to it by a girl guide, Yang Huimin, who had swum in the dead of night across the creek from the Bund with the flag concealed in her clothes.[52]

This extraordinary resistance commanded respect from both Chinese and Western observers. The American journalist George Bruce reported from a hotel room over the Bund that "the roofs of buildings in the Settlement near the struggle are lined night and day with watchers."[53] It became so crowded that the whole section of the Nanjing Road east of Yu Qiaqing Road was blocked off to traffic. Besides watching this "real" street drama, the people of Shanghai also joined in the fight by contributing food, cotton clothing, medical supplies, and other daily necessities to the Gujun. These items were transported to the warehouse after dark by SGJ volunteers. Residents of Beijing, Guizhou, and Parker Roads, a residental area bordering the Bund, for example, held a day-long fast to raise money for the defenders. And many—both Chinese and foreigners—asked British soldiers to pass food and money to the battalion.[54] At the same time, all the city's newspapers wildly acclaimed the "Lone Battalion" in headlines; reverential reports appeared in every journal. The 800 soldiers became national heroes.

SWH intellectuals were quick to capitalize on the immense appeal of the Gujun, creating of it a historical legend. In three consecutive special issues of the *Jiuwang ribao*, they published poems and essays praising the uncompromising will of the "Lone Battalion." In these works, the 800 soldiers were construed as symbols of the Chinese spirit. Their self-sacrificial resistance symbolized the will of the Chinese nation to brave all adversity on the way to final victory. In a poem entitled "Babai chuangshi kangzhan xin" (The resistance spirit of the eight hundred warriors), Yi Guan wrote:

> In the spreading shade of dusk,
>   we pull up the shining national flag.
> It represents the unique holiness and purity
>   of our national uprightness.
> Inside our eight hundred lives is hidden
>   the spirit of China.
> We shall win one day.

As the Chinese spirit incarnate, the "Lone Battalion" became part of a complex legend together with other symbolic elements. One of these was, of course, the 1911 Revolution. Coincidentally, the 327 survivors dashed out of the Joint Savings Society Godown under Japanese bombardment into the safety of the International Settlement (as ordered by Chiang Kaishek) on October 31, the twenty-second anniversary of the death of Huang Xing, recognized as the

Revolution's most important leader, after Sun Yatsen. A *Jiuwang ribao* editorial eulogized Huang as a staunch patriot and fearless warrior, unwavering in his devotion to the freedom and independence of China. "We shall die whether we fight or not, so we should strike first," he was quoted as having asserted on the eve of the Revolution.[55] By evoking Huang's patriotism and his spirit of perseverance, the author construed a historical link between him and the Gujun. This connection was enhanced by the symbolic power of their spiritual affinity. Their moral strength and resoluteness became an ideal that the intellectuals hoped would shine through in the national struggle of the Chinese people.

In early November, following the retreat of the "Lone Battalion," a less dramatic but equally heroic resistance was mounted in Nanshi, bordering the French Concession, by the elements of the 55th Division. It lasted for only two days. In an effort to display their neutrality to the encircling Japanese troops, the foreign areas authorities stepped up their suppression of anti-Japanese activities in their precincts. They closed down the SWH (on November 5th) and the SGJ (on November 11th, the day the mayor of Shanghai, Yu Hongjun, announced the flight of the municipal government), and banned all prominent resistance publications.

When the war in Greater Shanghai came to an end in mid November 1937, with black smoke hovering over areas north of Suzhou Creek, most leaders of the national salvation movement were convinced that the war was over as far as the city was concerned. Before it was closed down, the SGJ had ordered that all propaganda work be moved immediately to Wuhan or into the interior, and civilian services restricted to such activities as fund-raising and refugee relief, which were still allowed in the foreign areas.[56] By the early weeks of December, just after the announcement of the retreat of the Nationalist government to Wuhan (and in late 1938 to Chongqing) and the fall of Nanjing (followed by the bestial "Rape of Nanjing" that claimed a total of at least 200,000 deaths), according to one source, only 8 out of a total of over 200 active members of the SGJ remained in Shanghai.[57] Simultaneously with this flight, meanwhile, came a mass exodus of SWH intellectuals, who took their newspapers and journals with them. Among them were such cultural figures as Mao Dun, Guo Moruo, and Zou Taofen. Before his departure for Hong Kong, while saying good-bye to his friends at a hotel cafe, Guo wrote a bit of doggerel expressing his continued confidence in the eventual victory of the Resistance:

> Shanghai's a hopeless island;
> sooner or later we must get out.
> From now on we'll live as soldiers,
> return, and put the Japs to rout.[58]

But those intellectuals who, unlike Guo, could not leave this "hopeless island" had to live through the war as a "conquered people" (wangguo nu).[59] Were they guilty of treason for not "living as soldiers" in Free China? When would the enemy be "put to rout"? When that day came, would they remain uncompromised, like the heroic Gujun? How to stand up for patriotic honor without harming the ones you loved? What should be done if survival came into conflict with integrity? If the uncompromising spirit failed to defend Shanghai, did the spirit need a new interpretation, and would that be any more effective under the Occupation? Above all, what was to be the role and status of intellectuals under the new dispensation? How would they sustain the resistance spirit of the Shanghai populace?

Different writers responded differently to these various questions within the moral and political discourse of Chinese culture. They might withdraw to preserve their integrity, they might resist in the tradition of spiritual heroism, or they might even collaborate in the name of human anachronism. But whatever choices they made, their lives during the eight years of the Japanese Occupation constituted a drama of fear, suffering, survival, and moral ambiguity, to which we now turn.

I

Passivity:
Wang Tongzhao and the Ideal of
Resistance Enlightenment

When stones have rotted, the sea dried up,
My lonesome heart, one fleck of loneliness.
Wang Fuzhi,
"Expressing My Feelings"

•

During the eight years of occupation that followed the fall of Greater Shanghai to the Japanese in November 1937, intellectuals in the city experienced the war as captives and victims. As a writer lamented, "We who remain in Shanghai are deprived of the protection of our country, and the evil hand [*moshou*] of the aggressor is constantly hovering over us."[1] The "evil hand" is an apt image, epitomizing the prevailing feelings of fear, agony, and humiliation among these intellectuals. Finding themselves caught in a moral dilemma between the need to survive on the one hand and the patriotic call for integrity on the other, some of them withdrew into silence, stopped publishing, and went into seclusion. By being passive they sought to escape Japanese persecution while symbolically resisting the enemy.

One of these passivists was Wang Tongzhao (1897–1957), a veteran May Fourth novelist and poet who remained in Shanghai throughout the Occupation. In the face of the conflict between nationalist commitment and self-preservation, he formulated an ethical ideal that I would call "Resistance enlightenment." It was in effect a moral reinterpretation of the May Fourth scheme of ideas embracing universalistic humanitarian values that celebrated the potential of individual autonomy. Building upon an apocalyptic vision of the war as a vehicle of universal rebirth for China, Wang reaffirmed the liberal values of reason and freedom in the wartime context. Yet the terror, poverty, and collectivist mood of the war crushed his ideal, resulting in his withdrawal into silence from 1941 on, during which time he devoted himself entirely to the ethics of personal integrity.

The Making of a May Fourth Humanist

Wang Tongzhao was born in February 1897 into a declining gentry family in Zhucheng, Shandong.[2] When he was nine his father died. Brought up along with his two sisters by his widowed mother, whom he later recalled as an exemplar of devotional virtues, the frail and sensitive boy early on developed a sense of duty toward others. His childhood experience helped shape his personality. He was known among his friends as a reserved, mild-mannered scholar, unfailingly loyal to his friends as well as to his work. Shy and inhibited by perpetual self-doubt, he also throughout his life displayed prominent traits of introversion and, with it, a propensity to depression.[3]

In 1918, after an arranged marriage to an illiterate Shandong girl, Wang left for Beijing to enter Zhongguo University, majoring in English literature. In Beijing, infected by the youthful activism of the time, he became involved in student propaganda and took part in the demonstration that heralded the May Fourth Movement in 1919. Although Wang was too temperate and cautious to take a leading role in the student demonstration, the political experience was a moral revelation to him. It was a rite of passage that gave shape to his worldview and self-image. He thereafter saw himself as a May Fourth veteran, with a lifelong commitment to enlightenment and the humanistic ideals of the movement.[4]

Like the various cultural movements of the European humanist tradition from which it drew inspiration, the May Fourth Movement, with its patriotic subtext, aimed to effect simultaneous national renewal and universal progress by liberating human potential from the dead weight of tradition. The humanistic ideals of individual autonomy and self-development that grew out of the Western bourgeois economy were hailed as the centerpiece of the Chinese "enlightenment." To achieve this cultural enterprise, May Fourth intellectuals set out to revolutionize the traditional mentality of servility and self-denial, supplanting it with the Western (bourgeois) "culture of criticism." Under the banner of "Mr. Democracy and Mr. Science," they celebrated the "natural rights" of men to assert critical reason as a way of liberating their innate capacity for changing both their inner and outer worlds. (This "cultural pro-Westernism" was indeed, as Lucien Bianco points out, "compatible" with their "anti-Western nationalism.")[5] These intellectuals conceived of themselves as a spiritual elite, acting alone to save the country by liberating their fellow compatriots from what Lu Xun called the "Iron House" of self-deception.

This elitism and apparent idealism gave the May Fourth Movement a touch of impracticality. More articulate in what they opposed than in what they championed, and trying in so short a time to change a China whose realities and people they little knew, the cultural radicals risked easy disillusionment. Indeed, when they came face to face with the social realities beyond the campus, many fell prey to depression and some surrendered to the establishment. Social inertia and pressure for conformity (not to mention political suppression and the prevalent agrarian economy) was simply overwhelming.[6] Also characteristic of the movement was its tendency to bring together ideas and concepts that were not normally in harmony with each other. For example, despite its stress on skepticism and critical reason, May Fourth thinking was pervaded by a vision of apocalyptic fulfillment. It "created an abstract and rosy dream and deposited that dream in a paradise [which was supposed] to arrive in the near future."[7] All these May Fourth traits, as we shall see, remained with Wang at the time of the Japanese Occupation.

By temperament Wang was not a social activist. He remained on the periphery of the May Fourth movement. He frequently took part in discussions on the new culture and Russian Revolution in the future CCP founder Li Dazhao's Beijing University Library office, adding his voice to the call for patriotic mobilization.[8] But he did not join the iconoclastic assault on tradition. Instead, he took up literature to voice his yearning for a humane society. In 1921, shortly before his graduation from Zhongguo University, where he was to be appointed lecturer in 1922, he joined eleven other aspiring writers, including Mao Dun, Zheng Zhenduo, Geng Jizhi, and Ye Shengtao, all to become lifelong friends, in founding the Society for Literary Research (Wenxue yanjiu hui), championing a new

aesthetic of cultural and social criticism. They sought to spread the
May Fourth gospel of enlightenment by literature.

Typical of most writers of his generation, Wang's creative and
critical writings during the May Fourth period were permeated with
a highly subjective perception of reality and an obsessive concern
with self-expression and aesthetic exploration.[9] Behind this artistic
sensibility was a faith in man's potential creative power and a devotion to the humanistic values of Love and Beauty. He also followed
Rabindranath Tagore, whose lecture trip in China in 1924 was
facilitated by his (and the poet Xu Zhimo's) services as interpreter,
in embracing a deistic view of human self-actualization. In Wang's
conception, romantic love and natural beauty represented the sole
avenues to happiness, the supreme virtues that could unlock the latent moral qualities of man and as such harmonize individual interest
and common good.[10] In this vein, adopting W. B. Yeats's metaphysi-
cal ideal of "criticism of life," Wang conceived of literature as a
means of changing Chinese moral perceptions and thus revitalizing
China. He hoped to accomplish this through the creation of a "little
world" of affectionate personal relations and aesthetic sensibility
placed within the larger world of moral depravity, thereby enlightening his readers as to their human potential.

Concomitant with this humanistic view was a liberal belief in
pacifism.[11] True to his belief in freedom and liberty, Wang lauded as
"just" the kind of war (*yizhan*) championed by Mazzini and Byron,
fought for national autonomy. All other wars he condemned as unjust and inhuman—expressions of the bestiality of man. As he wrote
in 1919, "War is barbarity, love is humane. Should barbarity prosper,
humanity would diminish."[12] Thus, while he extolled such nationalist movements as the "May 30 Movement" for their resistance to
imperialist violence, he urged all writers to use literature as a vehicle
of "pacifism" (*feizhan*), opposing war with their spirit of "righteous"
defiance.[13] This liberal-humananistic vision, as we shall see, was to
govern Wang's thought during the Occupation.

Equally significant to the development of his wartime thinking
was the psychological tension between social involvement and a self-
absorbed mode of personal existence. In 1937, on the eve of Shanghai's fall, Wang owned that he had a split personality: "Sometimes [I
am] too detached; sometimes too passionate"; he attributed it to
genetic and childhood influences.[14] Indeed, Wang's emotional and

intellectual life before 1937 can be neatly divided into three phases: he switched from social engagement to withdrawal, then to patriotic activism. From his participation in the May Fourth demonstrations until 1926, he took an active part in the Wenxue yanjiu hui in Beijing and Shanghai and through these connections published several volumes of poetry and short stories.[15] This active involvement ended in 1926–27, however, following the death of his beloved mother in Qingdao and the political calamity of the White Terror, a counterrevolutionary coup in which Chiang Kaishek massacred tens of thousands of Communists and trade unionists in central China (April 1927). This conjunction of personal and historical tragedies shattered his hopes for a better life—both for himself and his country. As Wang later recalled: "The violent change of realities dashed all our dreams. Besides struggling for sheer survival, all the flower and light in abstraction had been lost in darkness."[16] In a manner reminiscent of traditional mourning practices (which were related to Confucian eremitism),[17] the young Wang resigned from Zhongguo University and moved his family to Qingdao. That city, incidentally, held an ironic significance for him, as its loss to the Japanese in 1919 was the raison d'être of the May Fourth Movement with which he identified. Now, however, inflicted with a sense of futility, he withdrew from the social world (aside from teaching at a local high school in Qingdao).[18]

This period of self-imposed isolation was broken by a trip to the northeast in the spring of 1931. Wang went to teach for four and a half months at a high school run by a friend in Jilin. Between school breaks he traveled extensively in the region. This firsthand experience of life under Japanese subjugation revived his sense of nationalist duty. As he wrote in a poem after the trip:

> Danger—as I reflect on the present,
> a lost way—as my past reveals;
> I regret those youthful writings
> and am distressed that I have no means to save the country.[19]

In calling the whole of his literary past into question, the poet reveals his guilt about his self-absorbed, escapist existence.

Wang began to speak out against imperialist encroachment and the problems of rural poverty after he returned to Qingdao in the summer of 1931. With the connections afforded by his former

Society for Literary Research friends (many of whom, including Ye Shengtao, had also just emerged from their political despair), he brought out two novels and five collections of essays between 1932 and 1937. Strident in tone, all these works were informed by the theme of patriotic urgency. True to his liberal-humanist beliefs, Wang appealed to the notion of freedom and conscience in urging his compatriots to join the struggle for national autonomy. Because of his advocacy of national salvation, Wang's most famous 1933 novel, *Shanyu* (Mountain Storm), which depicted the ruin of rural life under imperialist domination, was blacklisted by the GMD censors. In 1934, partly to avoid persecution, he sold most of his land to take a year-long trip to Europe.[20]

In 1936, having returned to China, Wang left Qingdao for Shanghai, then the center of the national salvation movement, to devote himself to patriotic writing (though he went back to visit his family every once in a while). There he joined Zheng Zhenduo, Ye Shengtao, Mao Dun, and several leftists to found the Zhongguo wenyijia xiehui (Federation of Chinese Writers and Artists) to promote unity in the literary community, and became a member of the Shanghai wenhua jie jiuguo hui (Shanghai Cultural Circles National Salvation Union), which included all prominent writers in the city. In July, Wang accepted an invitation to become the chief editor of the left-leaning journal *Wenxue* (Literature).[21] This episode was to prove significant to his later political response to the Japanese Occupation. Despite his initial enthusiasm to make *Wenxue* a forum for cultural enlightenment and national salvation, he soon found the editorial work too taxing and uncongenial to his personality. His sensitive, high-minded character was ill-suited to practical chores, especially when they required him to guide a prominent journal through the quarrelsome world of modern Chinese letters. Although he was generally detached from organized politics and never involved in politicized literary debates (e.g., the "Two Slogans" debate in 1936 about the relationship between writing and patriotic mobilization),[22] which at the time absorbed the creative energy of most writers, he found himself in a situation at once isolated and embittered. He often complained to his close friends about his inability to handle personal relations and told them how sad this made him.[23] Moreover, it was a time of increased GMD suppression of literary dissent, and as an editor who constantly urged his authors to take up the theme of national salvation, Wang was in a constant state of anxiety over the possibility of sudden attack. (He kept the iron gate of his editorial office locked at all times and reminded his friends not to make his address known.) Already a frail, hypersensitive person, Wang began to develop symptoms of asthma and insomnia, which seriously impaired his health.[24]

When the War of Resistance broke out in the north in July 1937, Wang rushed back to Qingdao and brought his family to join him in Shanghai. Ironically, they escaped the Japanese occupation of Qingdao (where Wang left all the valuable books he had collected since 1919) only to settle in a city doomed to the same fate.

Fenghuo and the Battle of Shanghai

Shortly after Wang returned to Shanghai with his family, the war broke out there. With the onset of the war, despite a feeling of exhilaration among individual writers, the literary world of Shanghai as a whole was plunged into a state of inactivity. As all publishing companies and printing shops—most of which were located in the war zone—had either been destroyed by bombs or were preoccupied with moving to safer places, the publishing industry came to a standstill.[25] All literary journals were forced to cease publication; no new literary works were issued. Without further supplies of literature, the few bookstores that remained open displayed only maps and war pictures for sale.[26]

By late August, however, following the publication of *Jiuwang ribao*, the organ of the SWH, a few new literary journals began to appear. The first venture was *Fenghuo* (The Beacon; originally entitled *Nahan*, or Call to Arms), a slim weekly review that, in its editor Mao Dun's words, was dedicated to rallying support for the national Resistance, a task he aptly termed "cultural work" (*wenhua gongzuo*).[27] Along with Mao Dun, its editorial committee included such May Fourth liberals as Ba Jin and Zheng Zhenduo; Wang also became one of its members.

There were two reasons for Wang's involvement with the *Fenghuo* group. In the first place, he was on very good terms with all the editors of *Fenghuo*. According to the publisher, Zhao Jiabi, they lived in the same neighborhood on Jessfield Road, in Huxi, the western section of Shanghai. These writers frequently visited each other, sharing literary gossip and discussing political issues. With the outbreak of the war, all of them joined the SWH, and they met more often, focusing their discussions increasingly on their personal futures as well as their proper response to the national crisis.[28] After the closing of *Wenxue* in July 1937, this community of friendship afforded Wang a forum in which he could devote himself to "cultural work."

Ideologically, moreover, Wang identified himself with the group's liberal humanism. In line with the May Fourth tradition, they conceived of the War of Resistance as a just war, because its ultimate object was freedom and liberty. Contrary to the "unjust aggression" of Japanese imperialism, in their view, the Chinese Resistance was not only a righteous (*zheng*) act of national self-defense but also a virtuous (*yi*) struggle to defend "human civilization." Its aim was to eliminate the violators of international political and cultural order by spurring the Japanese people on to overthrow their militarist dictatorship.[29] With this liberal view, Wang and the other editors saw no conflict between their respect for the ethics of peace and their intense nationalism. Their beliefs were exactly expressed in an aphorism by another *Fenghuo* editor, Jing Yi: "Only war can diminish war." By defining the war in terms of a struggle between "us" and "them," between good and evil, the group found a source of optimism in a moral interpretation of the military situation. As Wang paraphrased two classical sayings, "An army with a just cause enjoys high morale" (*shi zhi wei zhuang*), while the "army without one is devoid of fighting will" (*shi chu wuming jun wu douzhi*).[30] In other words, moral qualities would dictate the outcome of the war. That was why Wang and all his *Fenghuo* friends (as well as the SWH) celebrated the moral integrity and "uncompromising spirit" of Lu Xun. His "unyielding dignity," according to these writers, was a shining example of Chinese strength.[31] Thus when all its people devoted themselves to it completely, China's just war would ultimately lead to triumph over Japan, despite China's apparent military weakness. This humanitarian vision of the Chinese Resistance and consequent moral faith in China was to remain the central motif of Wang's thought throughout the war.

It was in *Fenghuo* that Wang published most of his writing during the Battle of Shanghai (August–November 1937). The writer Guo

Tianwen later commented that "all writers were poets at the beginning of the war, because poetry was the most direct form for expressing excitement."[32] This generalization was particularly true in Wang's case. Since 1927, the year he retreated to Qingdao, Wang had given up poetry, as he found himself unable to make sense of a changing world.[33] But the poet in him awoke as the war broke out. His literary output during the three months of battle in Shanghai consisted entirely of verse, a total of sixteen poems. All these poems reveal a well-defined perception that China's survival as a race-nation was at stake, its defense a morally superior cause for which all intellectuals should transcend their "elitism" and individual concerns in order to struggle together.[34]

An elegant example of this theme is the poem "Yi Jinsiniang qiao" ("Remembering Lady Golden-Threads Bridge"), which epitomizes Wang's early enthusiasm for the war. The Lady Golden-Threads Bridge was a famous scenic spot near Jinshanwei, between Shanghai and Hangzhou, which Wang had visited in the autumn of 1936, an area devastated by heavy bombing on November 5, 1937, as the Japanese fought to land at the Hangzhou Bay. In a tone at once strident and sentimental, the verse evokes the interplay of natural beauty and human brutality. These contrasts bring to the simple imagery of the scenic bridge a density of moral and political meanings. The last stanza is particularly revealing:

> This dream world for poets also changes
>   into an image of horror;
> now Lady Golden-Threads Bridge is crisscrossed
>   with threads of blood.
> What's the use of remembering? Paddy field, a sparse grove,
>   straw cape and hat,
> the willow bank, the shallow pond, the cattail reeds
>   swaying in one's face.
> No! No! That memory has already been painted over
>   with a gallant image.
> I would rather paint blood over that beautiful corpse.
> Only a brave battle would fit this graceful scenery.[35]

Beauty and harmony have been destroyed. The bridge, an innocent victim, has been ravaged by Japanese bombings. Resistance becomes both necessary and righteous.

The Occupation of Greater Shanghai and the
Rise of Foreign-published Newspapers

Shortly after the publication of "Remembering Lady Golden-Threads
Bridge" in November 1937, Chinese Shanghai fell. The Japanese
Occupation that followed threw the cultural world of Shanghai into a
panic. Within weeks, all national salvation organizations and anti-
Japanese publications were closed down, and rumors arose of the im-
minent persecution of activists. All users of the Garden Bridge link-
ing the Bund and Hongkou had to bow and show respect to the
Japanese sentries, or they could be beaten up or killed on the spot.
There were also incidents involving harassment and assassination of
prominent writers and educators.[36] Anxious for their own lives and
freedom of expression, a great number of intellectuals escaped to
British-run Hong Kong or into the Chinese-controlled interior.[37]
Wang did not join this intellectual exodus. He was then forty-one
years old and was at the height of his literary fame. He remained in
Shanghai because he had no connections elsewhere to find him employment and housing. Moreover, as most transportation was disrupted by the war, traveling was not only costly but also exhausting.
Wang's family obligations and failing health made such a long trip
seem impossible. In addition to the old problems of asthma and
insomnia, he contracted typhoid when Shanghai fell. So after sending his eldest son (then twenty years old) to Sichuan with the aid of
Mao Dun, he stayed behind to live with his wife and remaining
two sons.[38]

Following the mass exodus of refugees from the Chinese areas in
Shanghai, in late 1937 Wang and his family moved from Jessfield
Road in Huxi to a small apartment on Avenue Dubail, a nice, quiet
neighborhood in the French Concession. The foreign areas com-
prised about 8,100 acres at the heart of Shanghai under the administration of Western powers, by virtue of whose extraterritorial rights
and neutral status in the Sino-Japanese hostilities they remained
largely unoccupied until the commencement of the Pacific War in
December 1941.[39] This unusual situation was aptly expressed by the
contemporary metaphor Gudao (Solitary Island), which vividly invoked a privileged island at the center of Shanghai, cut off from the

Chinese hinterland by an ocean of Japanese occupiers. But the isolation was actually not as complete or hermetic as the metaphor suggested. Throughout the Occupation, as we shall see, the Gudao was closely interconnected with the unoccupied regions. A secret but vast network of intelligence operations, trade activities, political maneuvers, propaganda work, and escape routes existed between the two zones. Without these connections, it would have been impossible for the Resistance to operate in Shanghai.

It was therefore in this relatively free, isolated foreign zone that resistance to the Occupation began to take shape. This made Shanghai's wartime experience prior to 1942 rather different from that of Europe, where resisters had to fight the Nazi occupiers face-to-face, and circulating antifascist leaflets and publishing clandestine newspapers (e.g., the French *Combat* and *Défense de la France* and the Dutch *Vrij Nederland*) were highly risky activities, in which all the participants "took their lives in their hands with every sheet which they delivered to a neighbour."[40] (But, similarly, the difference should not be exaggerated, inasmuch as all major, successful European Resistance movements were seriously dependent upon protected bases overseas—notably in London—for propaganda broadcasts, military supplies, financial assistance, and so forth.)

In the Solitary Island, intellectuals were among the first resisters to emerge during the early months of 1938. They took advantage of the neutrality claimed by the Western powers to pursue legal propaganda activities. The legal status they enjoyed helped expand their circle of influence. Yet their freedom of expression was severely limited; they were in constant danger of discovery and reprisal (from both the Japanese army and the foreign areas authorities). This danger was most clearly manifested in the terrorism that eventually threatened the very existence of those intellectuals involved in Resistance journalism. It was under these circumstances that Wang acted out his commitment to resist.

Indeed, the press in Shanghai was one of the first targets of suppression after the fall of the city. The foreign areas authorities made it clear in late 1937 that because of the need to maintain their "neutral status," they would not tolerate anti-Japanese propaganda activities in their precincts.[41] Thus, in November alone, the Shanghai Municipal Police closed down a total of 11 newspapers and periodicals (while 30 others stopped publication of their own accord) in the International Settlement for "publishing invalid information," and issued over 45 warnings to 3 others.[42]

After seizing control of three foreign cable companies, the Japanese military authorities took over the former GMD Press Censorship Bureau, located on Nanjing Road in the International Settlement, on November 28, and renamed it the Shanghai Press Censorship Bureau. The new bureau was jointly controlled by the Japanese Expeditionary Forces in Central China and the local Japanese consulate; but its day-to-day operation, according to one report, "lay rather in the hands of a number of Chinese assistants."[43] At different times, these Chinese assistants included propaganda agents of the early collaborationist regimes: the Dadao shi zhengfu (Great Way Government) in Pudong, created in December 1937 to administer the occupied suburbs of Shanghai; and later the Weixin zhengfu (Reform Government) under Liang Hongzhi in Nanjing, which was established in March 1938 to take nominal charge of all occupied territories in the Yangzi Delta. The main duty of these agents was to censor Chinese news items concerning their respective regimes.[44]

In the wake of the bloody massacre at Nanjing of hundreds of thousands of Chinese civilians and prisoners of war on December 13, 1937, the Japanese censors in Shanghai demanded that all Chinese newspapers published in the foreign settlements be submitted to them for examination. Since submission to Japanese censorship symbolized recognition of the legitimacy of the Occupation, the choice seemed to be between resistance or collaboration. Most newspapers resisted by immediately ceasing publication, and some of them moved out of Shanghai altogether.[45]

The only overt challenges to Japanese censorship were the two small evening newspapers—Huamei wanbao (Chinese-American Evening News) and Damei wanbao (Great American Evening News, the Chinese version of the Mercury and The Evening Post)—which had been both registered under U.S. sponsorship (originally to escape GMD harassment). These two papers ostentatiously ignored the Japanese order, continuing operations, as the latter's publisher Randall Gould announced, without "submitting to censorship from anybody."[46]

Their sales increased remarkably at the beginning of the Occupation,[47] but these two American-registered papers were inadequate to the needs of the Solitary Island's reading public. Steeped in anger and uncertainty, many readers found the occupied city a "cultural wilderness," within which little inspiring and reassuring news about China's struggle against Japan circulated.[48] Most newspapers contained little news and were politically ambivalent in tone, if not downright pro-Japanese. In the safety of anonymity, the Shanghai public expressed their patriotism by boycotting those Chinese newspapers that gave in to Japanese censorship and by refusing to subscribe to the Japanese-sponsored newspaper, *Xin shen bao* (New Shanghai Daily), the Chinese edition of *Shanhai godo shimbun*, which was soon compelled to distribute copies gratis in streets adjacent to the occupied area.[49]

In view of this situation, a group of displaced intellectuals, among them newsmen who had quit their jobs to protest their managements' submission, decided in early 1938 to launch a daily of their own, *Wenhui bao* (The Standard), which they hoped would provide them with both a livelihood and a forum for patriotic expression.[50] Inspired by the tactical success of the two American-published papers in evading Japanese censorship by claiming foreign neutrality, the group paid an Irish businessman, H. M. Cumine, a high salary to serve as managing publisher. Since his sole duty was to ensure that the newspaper would be "protected" from Japanese harassment, Cumine was nicknamed the "foreign bodyguard."[51]

Wenhui bao opened an office at the intersection of Fuzhou and Fujian Roads, the Chinese Fleet Street, and commenced publication in January 1938, printing government proclamations (obtained from underground GMD agents) and war news from all over the country among other items. Its strikingly nationalistic stance and inflammatory language won it immediate popularity in the Solitary Island, and sales went up quickly from 20,000 copies during the first days of publication to 100,000 five months later, in March 1938.[52] This figure is especially remarkable when we consider that its circulation was restricted to the two foreign areas, while previously newspapers had been sold throughout Shanghai and all its environs along the Shanghai-Hangzhou and Shanghai-Nanjing rail lines. *Wenhui bao*'s great success marked the creation of a special genre soon to become widely practiced in Solitary Island journalism—the "foreign-published newspaper" (*yangshang bao*). All of these newspapers, although completely under Chinese management, employed American,

British, or other European publishers to represent them and thereby
acquired legal immunity from Japanese censorship. As the Communist critic Ba Ren described it, these *yangshang bao* "hung out foreign
shop-signs while expressing Chinese opinion."[53] They provided the
intellectual resisters in Shanghai with an institutional voice, which
rang, in the words of the literary editor, Ke Ling, with the "courage
of [the Chinese people] to struggle."[54]

Thanks to this unique foreign "protection" in an occupied city,
Shanghai experienced a boom in journalism. From mid 1938 on,
a large number of foreign-published newspapers emerged. Among
them were newspapers like *Shen bao*, which had originally moved
out of Shanghai in defiance of Japanese censorship.[55] According to a
contemporary observer, there were "probably more newspapers in
the Solitary Island than in any period before the war."[56]

Immensely popular, all the *yangshang bao* claimed to make the
Shanghai resistance part of the national Resistance. In an effort to lift
morale and to exhort the faint-hearted, they attacked collaborators in
the most virulent language and turned military and other events into
war propaganda.[57] They also published important government announcements (on all commemorative events including the October
10th Chinese National Day and July 7th "Marco Polo Incident")
and reports distributed to them in mimeograph by GMD agents. For
example, the special liaison officer of the underground Central Propaganda Department, the *Shen bao* reporter Jin Huating, was charged
with providing all Shanghai newspapers with "news" of GMD-
supported guerrilla movements around the city.[58] Leftist papers also
publicized news on behalf of the CCP, particularly regarding the
guerrilla war in central and northwestern China.

It is thus clear that the foreign-published newspapers were closely
linked to the continued underground presence of the GMD and the
CCP in the foreign areas. After the fall of Shanghai, both parties
maintained either clandestine party cells (the CCP's Jiangsu Provincial Party Committee) or secret departments (the GMD's Committee of United Coordination) to organize and to vie for control of
the Resistance there. They built up intelligence systems and secret
communication networks respectively with Yan'an and Chongqing,
which maintained a regular flow of information and personnel
throughout the Occupation. The GMD's Central Propaganda De-

partment (under Feng Youzhen), for example, directed a secret "Central News Agency" in the French Concession that transmitted official information to Shanghai and also supplied funds to newspapers and newsmen loyal to the party.[59] In January 1938 the CCP's Cultural Committee (under Sha Wenhan and Sun Yefang) issued a British-published newspaper *Yi bao* (Translation News) as its organ and relayed Yan'an materials to sympathetic newspapers.[60]

The Japanese army authorities were enraged by the popularity of Resistance papers being published under their noses. As a *Shanhai mainichi* (Shanghai Daily) editorial complained: "The Chinese newspapers, which had remained silent after the fall of Shanghai, have once more become exceedingly active in the publication of anti-Japanese articles. That anti-Japanese newspapers can still be allowed to publish, especially at this time, when Shanghai has been under Japanese occupation for more than six months, is indeed an extraordinary phenomenon, which should never have been permitted."[61]

The Japanese reacted vigorously. None of the *yangshang bao* were allowed to circulate beyond the foreign settlements. Military sentries were posted and postal censorship was enforced between the foreign zone and neighboring areas to prevent circulation of anti-Japanese papers in the occupied territories.[62] Above all, intellectuals in the foreign areas soon fell prey to political terror. Failing to bring Chinese journalism under control by legal means, the Japanese resorted to terrorism as a means of suppression.

Under the control of the Kempeitai (Military Special Services Section), the Japanese equivalent of the Gestapo, which was in charge of secret intelligence and anti-espionage activities, a terrorist organization called the Huangdao hui (Yellow Way Association) was formed in March 1938, allegedly by the collaborationist "Reformed Government." With a force of 1,000 Chinese hoodlums (under the notorious gangster Chang Yuqing), the Yellow Way Association was charged with destroying the Resistance in the foreign areas through terrorism.[63] Based at the New Asia Hotel on Hongkou's North Sichuan Road (where all the early collaborators resided and worked under Japanese protection), just across the street from Bridge House, the Kempeitai headquarters, which was synonymous with midnight arrest and savage torture,[64] these terrorists could easily escape arrest by fleeing into the occupied areas of Hongkou, Nanshi, or Huxi after committing crimes in the foreign settlements.

The brutal murder in February 1938 of Cai Diaotu, editor of the tabloid *Shehui ribao* (Society News), was the first in a series of assassinations and political threats, which continued in the ensuing months. Cai's head was chopped off and hung from a lamppost in front of the French Concession police station on Rue Chevalier with a note under it reading: "Look! Look! The result of anti-Japanese elements."[65] Within a few months, six victims had been decapitated and their heads put on display in different parts of the foreign areas. Many intellectuals reported having received decayed hands and bullets in the mail, along with letters of warning. Even the police officers in charge of the Cai case received fingers in the mail.[66] In this atmosphere of fear, as one newspaper editor later recalled, "everyone [in the Solitary Island] was anxious about his head or hand."[67]

Assailed by such fears, anti-Japanese intellectuals confronted the moral dilemma of having to choose between survival and preservation of a sense of human dignity. To some intellectuals, the choice was unequivocal. In the words of Ke Ling, "The road is clear: it is to struggle relentlessly [against the enemy]."[68] Burdened with a feeling of guilt about staying in the sheltered foreign areas rather than joining the national Resistance in the Chinese-controlled interior, they found in the terror of the Occupation rather an ordeal of redemption.[69] These intellectuals invariably identified humanness or human dignity (*renge*) with patriotic commitment and placed it above individual survival (*huoming*). "Certainly life is an important matter and survival is the starting point of everything," wrote the leftist writer Tang Tao, "but we must equate the life of our country with ourselves, identify our life with that of our posterity.... Those who think otherwise are certainly [not men] but slaves."[70] Thus to be human was to resist.

Reminiscent of the May Fourth intelligentsia, and not unlike the intellectuals in the French Resistance described by James Wilkinson, these writers saw themselves as a "moral elite" acting alone to save the country by exorcising the fears and hesitations of their fellow citizens.[71] As the literary scholar Zheng Zhenduo, a founder of the Wenxue Yanjiu hui, declared, in a tone redolent of May Fourth

elitism: "[The Writer] is a man of foresight, so he should be 'the first
to become concerned with the world's troubles and the last to re-
joice in its happiness,' holding up a torch until dawn for the country
and the numberless masses in this darkest and longest night."[72]

After months of enforced silence since late 1937, the literary supplements of foreign-published newspapers now provided these writers with a platform upon which they could unite to speak as the
collective voice of the intellectual Resistance. Calling their task
"beating war drums on the sidelines" (*qiao biangu*), a term reminiscent of Lu Xun's "cheering from the sidelines" (*nahan*), they set out
to "educate and constantly encourage the masses [to resist]" through
literature.[73]

The most popular of all the literary supplements in 1938–39 was
Wenhui bao's *Shiji feng* (Century Wind), which began publication
under the editorship of Ke Ling in February 1938 and folded in May
1939 with the closing of *Wenhui bao*. Ke, who was to become one of
the most prominent literary editors in occupied Shanghai, was an ac-
complished essayist in his own right. Born in 1910 in Shaoxing
(Zhejiang), he had long been active in leftist cultural circles. He remained in Shanghai after its fall because of financial considerations
and family obligations.[74] The job offered by *Wenhui bao* in February
1938 thus gave him both a secure living and a sense of purpose—
a way to prove to himself and others that he was still part of the
national Resistance.

By virtue of his personality and organizational skills, Ke Ling
quickly built up an intellectual community around *Shiji feng* that
brought together writers of different generations as well as people of
vastly different ideological persuasions and literary approaches.
Numbered among its contributors were the May Fourth veterans
Zheng Zhenduo and Chen Wandao, the middle-aged Communist
critics A Ying and Ba Ren, and the young leftists Tang Tao and
Zhou Muzhai. These writers were united by a common set of historical responses: aversion to the Japanese Occupation and estrangement from the old order. Most of them, like Ke Ling, sought to
forge literature into an arm of combat, a "bayonet" with which to
engage their enemies. As the essayist Wen Zaidao proclaimed: "In
destroying the enemy there is little distinction between weapon and
pen."[75] In pursuit of this objective, *Shiji feng* chiefly printed *zawen*

(the embattled genre of social critique popularized by Lu Xun in the early 1930s) aimed at combating the despair and uncertainty prevalent in the wake of China's repeated military setbacks in 1938 (i.e., the successive falling of Wuhan and Guangzhou in October).[76] In addition, because of Ke's leftist connections, this one-page supplement also serialized Agnes Smedley's *China's Red Army Marches* and other literary sketches of the Communist base areas.[77]

The Ideal of Resistance Enlightenment

Wang Tongzhao was one of *Shiji feng*'s writers. He was initiated into its community by Ke Ling, whom he met probably through his close friend Zheng Zhenduo. In early 1938, after several months of unemployment, Wang accepted an offer to teach Chinese literature at Jinan University, where Zheng Zhenduo was the dean of arts, a job he held until the Japanese overran the foreign areas in 1941.

Jinan University had relocated from Zhenru (which fell to the Japanese in October 1937) to a three-story apartment house on Rue Dolfus in the French Concession, and still later moved to the top floors of a Catholic church on Connaught Road. Although it had only 200 students, it was a center of underground Nationalist agitation counteracting the Japanese attempt to infiltrate Shanghai's institutions of higher education. Because of the GMD-CCP united front, Communist student organizations were also very active on the campus.[78]

Being a tough grader and a dry, monotonous speaker with a heavy Shandong accent, Wang was not a popular teacher. Few students enrolled in his lecture classes on Chinese fiction and classical poetry. But his literary fame, erudition, and devotion to his pupils commanded wide respect at Jinan. One student remembered:

I did not have a good impression of him at first. I can still recall that on the first day of my class with him, he said nothing to introduce himself but merely passed us the syllabus. Then he immediately started lecturing.... I could not understand even one single word of his Mandarin....But after a while, I began to make sense of his lectures, and each word was such an insight. Mr. Wang assigned a paper once every two weeks....And whenever I got my papers back they were all a mess as a result of his countless comments and correction. They showed me how ignorant I actually was. There were just too few professors as conscientious as Mr. Wang.

Another student recalled: "He looked pale and thin. He had a receding hairline, sported thick tortoise-shell eyeglasses, and always wore a long, brownish gown. It was hard to imagine that he had been to Europe....He looked just like a poor scholar who had never stepped out of the country."[79]

Wang was also a devoted father. Every morning and night, when off from work, he spent hours tutoring his two sons, one fourteen and the other eleven, whose education was disrupted by the war. The syllabus, according to his youngest son, consisted of patriotic poetry and short stories, both classical and modern, selected by Wang himself.[80]

For extra income, Wang took on a part-time teaching job at the Shanghai Music Conservatory, and in July 1938 he was offered the editorship of the literary supplement of *Daying yebao* (Great Britain Evening News), a British-published newspaper sponsored by the GMD. The offer came from a Jinan colleague, Weng Shuaiping, who edited the paper after his return from France. After much hesitation, Wang accepted, but only subject to unusual conditions: his position was to be unofficial, he would enjoy editorial autonomy, and he would never have to appear at the paper's office. Instead, he would hold meetings with the assistant editor, Qin Shouou, a young popular writer, at a nearby food stall. (The first editorial meeting was, however, held at Zheng Zhenduo's house at Yuyuan Road, where Wang had been a frequent visitor.) Despite this unusual arrangement, Wang managed to shape *Daying yebao*'s supplement, which he named *Qiyue* (July) in commemoration of the outbreak of the war, into a respectable forum for patriotic literature, with contributions from such May Fourth luminaries as Ba Jin and Zheng Zhenduo.

Just a month later, in August, Wang quit the job. It is clear that the hostile environment of the Occupation and his frequent conflict with the pro-GMD management over editorial policy reminded Wang only too well of his distressing experience with *Wenxue*.[81] This apprehension was aggravated by poor health (his typhoid lingered until 1939, while the insomnia and asthma had become worse) and concern for his family. Who else would support his wife, an illiterate housewife, and three teenage children? In the face of mounting danger, he reconciled himself to a less prominent role than that of Resistance newspaper editor.

The *Qiyue* episode demonstrates the extent to which Wang agonized over the predicament of choosing between personal safety and patriotic commitment: How was one to survive the Occupation without betraying one's country and oneself? How to redeem oneself for "objectively helping the enemy" by remaining in Shanghai, as claimed by some writers who had fled to the interior?[82] How was one to "survive like a human being"? In this situation, creative writing was the only form of resistance open to Wang.

Yet Wang's recourse to literature cannot be explained solely by concern for his personal safety. It was also owing to his belief in the power of literature, as conveyor of ideas and values, to change lives, inspire hope, and bring salvation to mankind.[83] This betrayed his allegiance to the May Fourth conception of an intellectual: a member of the moral elite who shaped social reality through the power of ideas and his command of reason and pen. Thus, despite his acute awareness of the prevalent mood favoring deeds over words, he continued to see the purpose of writing at a time of national crisis to be an act of self-affirmation and spiritual regeneration. As Wang explained: "In this age of overflowing blood, solemn writings would still have the effect of spiritual inspiration on [our readers]."[84] His choice of creative writing should thus be seen as a commitment to the humanistic ideal of enlightenment that he had embraced since the May Fourth period as much as to his desire for survival.

For whom did Wang write? Whom did he hope to inspire? His writings seem to have been aimed at the young readers of Shanghai. The May Fourth discourse on "new youth," that extraordinary faith in the young people as the agents of moral and cultural transformation, still influenced him. He was part of the moral elite, dedicated to enlightening the country. In fact, some of his most ardent works were popular among college and high school students, who found them "a glittering light in the dark night." His students recalled that Wang was especially generous of his time in advising and encouraging them on matters of literature and moral character.[85]

Wang believed, throughout the Occupation, that if he were to spread his hope of spiritual regeneration, it was his task as an intellectual to formulate a humanistic ideal opposed to both collaboration and doctrinaire nationalism. For want of another name, I shall call this ideal *Resistance enlightenment*. It was in effect a reformulation of the May Fourth goal of enlightenment, which Wang fashioned into a scheme of moral reason and humanitarian pacifism in the new historical context of the Resistance.

With many young readers praising his writing, and thereby affirming its value, Wang embraced the cause of Resistance enlightenment with great optimism in 1938, but the terror and moral degeneration engendered by the worsening conditions of the Occupation, together with the logical inconsistences of his moral ideal, shattered his hopes and drove him into profound despair, leading to his withdrawal from political engagement in the latter part of the war.

In 1938, under the collective title *Liangyu zhong de huohua* (Sparks in purgatory), Wang published a series of prose poems in *Shiji feng* that gave shape to his ideal of Resistance enlightenment. The highly personal, subjective tone and intensely metaphorical language of prose poetry gave him a fitting vehicle of expression, in which lyrical self-examination and moral exhortation fused harmoniously. In these poems, like many European intellectuals under Nazi domination seeking to overcome their feeling of helplessness by planning for the future,[86] Wang gave artistic expression to an ideal world of liberty and universal harmony, which he held up as the guiding principle for the Resistance. The work draws its poetic intensity from a powerful imagination of moral transcendence and delicate evocation of the author's emotional turmoil. Presented in a series of inner conflicts between fear and hope, vacillation and commitment, anticipation and reflection, personal concern and moral ideal, *Liangyu zhong de huohua* reaffirms the triumph of individual morality over the inhumanity of war. An example of this moral transcendence is a piece titled "Meigui se zhong de liming" (Dawn in rose shades), which earned Wang wide recognition among the young generation in Shanghai:

> In the dim light, look closely at the figure you cut;
>   see how it magnifies the roaming and soaring of your soul,
>   strengthening your pure, firm faith.
> The majestic and heroic rhythm of the rainstorm announces a
>   revelation to move you even more.
> The rose shades of dawn that you have long awaited are even
>   now sifting through flake of wind and thread of rain.[87]

The Dantean title of the collection bore testimony to the apocalyptic vision underlying Wang's moral ideal. Conceiving of the Occupation as a "purgatory" that the Chinese people were forced to endure, he stressed the importance of individual willpower in overcoming the ordeal. By releasing their courage and character, the trial might actualize their human potential. Thus the spiritual rebirth of China would be represented by the ascendancy of reason: "It is in such a time of social turmoil and human suffering that...because of the pressure from outside devastation and the urge from the moral conscience within, human reason will grow and develop much more quickly than in normal times" (p. 21). This celebration of reason echoed the call of the May Fourth cultural movement. Indeed, most of the concepts embodied in Wang's Resistance enlightenment can be found in the May Fourth scheme of ideas: freedom of thought, individual liberty, and the defense of human dignity. Wang was not unique in this continuous commitment to the humanistic ideal of enlightenment. His good friend Ba Jin, who was then working on *Qiu* (Autumn) in seclusion, held a similar belief: "They all say that anything and everything is for the sake of the War of Resistance. Instead, I give more thought to the question of what to be done after the war. We should fight against feudalism during the war. And we should hold on to our anti-feudal struggle after the war."[88]

Yet the different historical context gave rise to differences in tone, assumptions, and configurations of values. The May Fourth intelligentsia had placed their ideals within an iconoclastic framework, rejecting morality in toto as a "feudal" sham and replacing it with the aesthetics of self-expression. In the context of the Occupation, where every Shanghai man and woman was forced to go through a test of loyalties in the "juncture of life and death" (*shengsi guantou*), Wang now subsumed the values of reason and individual autonomy under the ethical imperatives of public welfare. Assuming that human behavior followed upon value judgments derived from conscience, Wang quoted John Locke to the effect that human reason was subject to moral principle. But how to define morality? In answering this question, Wang betrayed his Confucian stress on social ethics and as such moved farther from the May Fourth concept of rationality. He now no longer claimed to subject traditional habits of

mind to critical scrutiny. Instead, he pointed up the distinction between the essence and the historical expression of morality. Thus
while different moral standards developed over time, basic principles
governing human conduct remained the same. In China these basic
principles were grounded in the Confucian ideals of loyalty and sincerity (*zhongxin*) and the sense of shame (*lianchi*). On another occasion, he claimed that there was a universal ethic made up of the European Enlightenment ideals of freedom, humanity, and rational
individuality as well as the Christian notions of brotherhood and
personal sacrifice. Although he never attempted to differentiate between or to integrate these two sets of moral values, it seems safe
nonetheless to assume that these values represented to Wang all con-
stitutive virtues within an immutable and universal norm of human
behavior. From these socially orientated values we know that, under
the force of political exigencies, Wang was concerned more with
moral behavior than with moral character. He elevated morality to
universal maxims.

Wang's strong emphasis on moral action was in harmony with
the intellectual community in Shanghai, which was pervaded by a
sense of humiliation and guilt. The sentiments of *Shiji feng*'s editor
Ke Ling were typical: "We are all slaves...hiding under foreign protection. What's the use of writing? Using our pens, have we ever
fulfilled our responsibility as human beings?"[89] These intellectuals
lived in a Manichean world and attached absolute value to morality.
As one Shanghai author, Wei Zheng, proclaimed: "Human conduct
is dictated by moral values....In the old days, loyal ministers and
martyrs [*zhongchen lieshi*] died for the principle of integrity because
they had high moral standards. In contrast, traitorous ministers and
unfilial sons [*luanchen zeizi*] ingratiated themselves to foreign invaders
because they had no sense of morality. So it is today."[90]

What distinguished Wang's ideal was his effort to integrate private and public morality. He resolved this dialectic with the conception of "renewed social contract" (*gengxin de minyue*). Like the European humanists who conceived of the theory of social contract as
a way to combine personal freedom and social obligation, Wang
aimed to formulate a moral matrix within which individual autonomy was defined. In this framework, he envisioned a moral community formed by free and responsible people, who governed their

social relations via individual moral principles. As such the "renewed social contract" was actually a projection of individual morality onto the social and political realm.

But how to ensure correspondence between personal and public interests? Wang formulated his argument as an antidote to the anti-individualist tendency of the Resistance. He reiterated the liberal-humanistic premise that the individual personality lies at the center of the human universe. Invoking the Mencian and Mohist concepts of commiseration and universal love (*jian'ai*), he further assumed that man's instinctive aim was to pursue happiness and avoid misery, and thus sympathy for others and regard for their happiness was as natural in a human being as self-love. It needed nothing more than education to bring this latent potential to realization. Hence his frequent invocation of Locke's dictum "Knowledge is morality." In the "renewed social contract" all people were rational in the sense that they held within themselves "moral self-discipline" (*daode de zilu-xing*). Adopting the utilitarian distinction between "sublime" and "vulgar" pleasures, he described these rational individuals as being able by their own moral capacity to channel their "vile" impulse of self-interest into the "lofty" realm of public good: "The meaning of life lies not in outward aggression but in trying one's very best to bring joy and happiness to others...and in striving for one's peace of mind by serving the public good.... Upon this basis moral values are formulated. Altruism and the unselfish spirit of devotion to public affairs originate in the sense of self" (p. 35).

By formulating a binary mode of moral action, Wang was able to vindicate the primacy of individual autonomy on the one hand and to condemn egoism and self-indulgence on the other. Yet in stressing the imperative of public welfare, he ran into a logical fallacy. For if there was but one path to individuality, how could man be free? Could he ever achieve "authentic" autonomy if he felt morally constrained to serve the public?

Failing to consider these problems, Wang held the concept of "renewed social contract" to be not only the end but also the means of Chinese Resistance. If every individual were a morally responsible person in society, nations would also treat one another according to moral principles within the world community. Following the liberal view of interest politics, he attributed the source of international violence to the egoistic pursuit of national interests and the subsequent rise of nationalist fanaticism. From this premise he pointed up the distinction between nationalism, a rational passion that inspired struggle for national autonomy, and thus a lasting peace, and doctrinaire nationalism. In his conception the Chinese Resistance was to be a just war of self-defense. It was a moral crusade to rid the world once and for all of the terror and injustice caused by a handful of egoistic Japanese militarists. Because the masses of Japanese people were as much victims of these militarists as the Chinese, Wang took pains to urge the Resistance not to lose sight of its just cause, guiding its nationalist passion by moral reason.

Wang held out an ideal that integrated individual freedom and collective interests within the Chinese Resistance in Shanghai. Yet this humanitarian ideal, with its vague expression and moralistic tone, lacked a coherent plan that might have led to its realization. His only concrete proposal was the education of public opinion; to *enlighten* mankind in general, and Chinese and Japanese youth in particular, as to the ethics of humanitarianism. He had faith in the moral potential of mankind, which would ultimately prevail over injustice and aggression. Thus, unlike most Shanghai writers, who strove to incite the Chinese people to fight with bravery, Wang saw himself as a philosopher-king who counseled restraint and sought to inspire hope for a rational postwar society: "In this age when our common blood gushes forth as a result of foreign invasion, we are all feverish, and have lost our heads. But we must not lose our human reason; we should not be so stupid as to 'answer violence with violence,' losing our respect for justice....We are still looking forward to enjoying with all mankind the warmth and brightness that will follow the storm clouds" (p. 29).

But was moral assertion enough to defend national autonomy? How to shape the community of free beings into a historical force? What was the a priori authority behind all these moral maxims?[91] How to realize the ideal of rational individualism as long as the occupiers inflicted brutality on the Chinese people? How else to mediate the contradictory ideals of universal peace and national resistance besides such vague notions as "education" or "personal examples"? And, above all, how to achieve freedom without binding individuality to collective interest? Failing to resolve any of these conflicts,

Wang's Resistance enlightenment remained a vision, an ethical absolute rather than a program, a viable means of political action. His humanistic ideal as such represented only an "ethics of ultimate ends," serving as his own self-affirmation, an individual protest, and, at best, as a moral encouragement to others who sought dignified survival through passivity.

The Disillusioned Enlightened Resister

From 1939 to 1941, the year the foreign areas fell to Japan, both political and living conditions in the Solitary Island deteriorated significantly. The military domination of Europe by Nazi Germany during this period and its pact with Japan in September 1940 compelled the Western powers in Shanghai to make "gradual surrenders" to the occupying forces there. The foreign areas authorities were steadily losing political autonomy and administrative control over their precincts. Since late 1939 the Japanese army had mounted an economic blockade of the city that deprived it of rice and other important resources normally obtained from the hinterland and overseas, and inflation spiraled upward. At the same time, the Japanese escalated their terrorist offensive in order further to disrupt the political situation in Shanghai.[92]

Shanghai's economy had experienced a brief period of prosperity before 1940. But this prosperity was deformed (*jixing*), built mainly "upon the loose sand" of cheap labor (supplied by war refugees) and the new markets in Southeast Asia. The rapid development of light industry in this period, for example, was poorly equipped and relied heavily on imported raw materials.[93] So when Shanghai lost its overseas market and supply of raw materials as a result of the Japanese blockade, its economy faltered, and its plentiful cheap labor became a liability. The cost of living went up rapidly.

The Shanghai Municipal Council index of rice prices is particularly revealing of the resulting inflation. With one picul (133.3 lbs.) of second-grade native rice in 1936 as the reference point, the index witnessed a sharp rise from 130 in 1938 to 1,030 in 1940, and to 1,221 in March 1941. To translate this into actual prices, one picul of second grade native rice cost Ch. $107 in 1940 and $127 in March

1941, more than a tenfold increase over the 1938 figure of Ch. $12.[94] Although the foreign areas authorities tried to alleviate the problem by importing Saigon rice in January 1940 and by commissioning 100 grain shops to sell this *yangmi* (foreign rice) at a lower price, these efforts had little effect except to create long queues everywhere. Much of the "cheap rice," which officially cost Ch. $89–116 in July 1941, went to the black market.[95] In this situation, even the fortunate people who were employed could not maintain minimum subsistence in "the majority of cases."[96] Thus the editors of a magazine devoted to the self-education of young low-income white-collar workers suggested a diet mixing 70 percent rice with 30 percent red beans and cutting out breakfast as the "healthiest" way to get by the hard times.[97]

This economic crisis gave rise to serious social polarization. This polarity was certainly not so much a new inequality as an old one perpetuated. So while the survival of the poor was at stake,[98] a few profiteers made easy fortunes through speculation and profiteering. Between 1940 and 1941, a total of Ch. $5.3 billion in idle capital moved into Shanghai from the war-torn interior and Hong Kong as a result of political instability in the Pacific region. Yet no more than 40 percent of this capital was absorbed into the banking system; the rest went to different quick-buck schemes.[99] People with big capital took advantage of what was then called the "national calamity" (*guonan*) to hoard practically all kinds of foreign exchange as well as commodities: from rice to meat, gold, and other metals. Black markets flourished, and the stock market went wild. Speculation became so rampant that when upper- and middle-income people greeted each other, they said, "What have you hoarded recently?" instead of the usual "How are you?" Many among the lower middle class also joined in the hoarding craze, vainly hoping to keep up with price hikes.[100]

Coincident with this, there was a mood of hedonism among the populace as they searched for a return to normality or, perhaps more probable, for a way momentarily to escape from the miseries of wartime lives. As the newspaper publisher Randall Gould commented on the city's popular mood: "Notwithstanding bad business conditions, the Great World and other amusement resorts seem to thrive as hitherto maybe on the theory that man wants amusement most when he has big worries" (September 1938). Indeed, prostitution, opium dealing, and gambling "prospered." In desperate need of funds for terrorist operations, the gangsters associated with the Japanese army turned the occupied area of Huxi and Nanshi into a land of vice. Known to the Shanghainese as the Badlands (Daitu), this area between Yuyuan, Jessfield, and Great Western Roads was full of casinos and opium dens (with evocative names such as "Hollywood" and "Good Companion"), all heavily guarded and crowded day and night. Inside the foreign settlements, moreover, brothels under various disguises, movie houses, and nightclubs all had to extend their business hours.[101] Even college students who prided themselves on being "progressive" and wrote anti-Japanese tracts and articles during the day went dancing and gambling at night.[102] One result of this "escapist" lifestyle was that one in twenty youths in Shanghai had syphilis.[103]

Terrorism only accentuated these economic difficulties and moral corruption. Wang Jingwei arrived in Shanghai in May 1939, and the "return" of his "Reformed Nationalist government" to Nanjing took place in March 1940. His arrival in Shanghai goaded the underground GMD to disrupt this "Peace Movement," while the Japanese occupiers and their puppets stepped up their campaign of terror and propaganda.

The GMD secret services in the foreign areas, the "Shanghai District Office" of the Military Bureau of Statistics and Investigation, then under Chen Gongshu (who was soon to join the Wang group), had a large force of over 1,000 agents, made up of members of the Green Gang (the largest criminal organization in Shanghai) and educated youths who had undergone military intelligence training in Guizhou. Aiming to discredit the Wang Jingwei regime, these underground agents engaged in military sabotage and assassination that resulted in a total of 160 deaths between 1940 and 1941.[104] Besides publishing newspapers in the foreign settlements to promote peace with Japan and anticommunism (see also Chapter 3), the collaborators created the much better equipped and far more brutal "Secret Service Headquarters" (Tegong zongbu; better known in Shanghai as "No. 76," a euphemism derived from its location at 76 Jessfield Road in Huxi), which superseded the Yellow Way Association.

Headed by Li Shiqun and Ding Mocun, both former members of the CC Clique, a conservative GMD faction adamantly loyal to Chiang Kaishek, and Central Bureau of Statistics and Investigation, No. 76 was an organized apparatus of terror composed of gangsters and GMD turncoats.[105] Operating on the simple principle of "an eye for an eye," No. 76 engaged the underground GMD secret services in a "Middle Ages horror" of reprisals and counterreprisals. Bombings, political kidnappings, and murders occurred "almost daily."[106]

Resistance intellectuals in the Solitary Island, particularly foreign-published journalists, became the prime victims of such atrocities. As spokesmen of patriotic conscience, intellectuals risked their lives with every piece they wrote or edited. Starting with the murder of Zhu Xinggong, the literary supplement editor for *Damei wanbao*, over 20 journalists were either assassinated or kidnapped by No. 76 terrorists between 1939 and 1941. Among these, Samuel Zhang of *Damei wanbao* and Jin Huating of *Shen bao* were leading GMD agents in charge of the Shanghai press; they were killed in retaliation for the murder of two well-known editors of the puppet regime (see Chapter 3).

Besides engaging in political assassination, No. 76 terrorists constantly raided newspaper offices. Between 1939 and 1941, more than seven foreign-published newspaper offices were bombed, each at least three or four times; after publishing an abrasive GMD denunciation of Wang Jingwei, for example, the GMD's CC Clique organ *Zhongmei ribao* (Sino-American Daily) was bombed in July 1939 by 20 terrorists, causing 3 deaths and 23 injuries.[107] In the circumstances, many Resistance newspapers had to cease publication; those remaining were compelled to fortify themselves by installing several layers of iron fences and sandbags outside and inside their buildings, and all editors and reporters moved into the offices for shelter. For example, the *Wenhui bao* office on Fuzhou Road was completely fenced in, with only a small hole left at the front for business transactions.[108] The Shanghai Municipal Police also stationed armored cars and security guards around these offices 24 hours a day.[109] Because of such security measures, in the words of the editor Bao Mingshu, visiting a newspaper office was like "visiting a prison."[110] Indeed, many intellectuals in occupied Shanghai felt like prisoners, as much physically as ideologically.

In their anxiety to stamp out the collaborationist threat, both the
GMD and the CCP took extreme ideological measures to whip up
national sentiment and mobilize direct action. In 1939 the warlord
Wu Peifu died. His widely publicized refusal to find refuge in the
foreign settlements during the war or to work for the Japanese had
won him widespread admiration. The GMD press in Shanghai capi-
talized on this by eulogizing Wu as a "paragon" of Chinese morality and organized a fund-raising campaign to build a statue in his
honor.[111]

While dismissing the whole Wu Peifu myth as an expression of
"feudalistic mentality," some young CCP militants on the other
hand glorified what they called "progressive passion"[112] and declared
war on what they considered "individualistic tendencies" in art and
literature. This led to such a restrictive mood that, as Ke Ling noted,
one was subjected to criticism if one expressed any sentiments other
than militant optimism about the Resistance.[113] In this climate of ideological intolerance, attacks on the May Fourth values of reason and
individuality naturally surfaced. In early 1940, after denigrating the
May Fourth ethos of "more doubts and less faith" as a "nihilistic attitude," the Communist critic Ba Ren took the lead in railing against
the "silence of the old generation of writers" as responsible for the
depressed state of Shanghai's Resistance literature. With token
appreciation for their "inner endurance," he denounced their passivity, their failure to represent the world of fighting, as utterly
irresponsible and divorced from the Chinese masses (which implied,
of course, their being unpatriotic).[114] Similarily, several May Fourth
men of letters, including Feng Zikai and Ye Shengtao, good friends
of Wang's who had recently escaped to the interior, and whose writings were widely circulated in Shanghai, were vilified as weakening
the Chinese Resistance because they dwelt upon personal sensibili-
ties (like their sensuous description of the exquisite scenery during
their escape) at such a time of national crisis. As the essayist Wen
Zaidao (who, as we shall see in Chapter 3, soon compromised) declared in his scathing critique of eremitism (which was lauded by
many leading Resistance writers, such as A Ying and Ba Ren) that
there was but one road open to Chinese: armed resistance. Passivity
was little different from collaboration; any appeal to an abstract ethic
was no more than a rationalization of intimidation and selfishness.[115]

With his fixed salary, Wang must have felt hard-pressed by inflation. Ideologically, too, although he had never been singled out
for assault, his prose poetry, *Liangyu zhong de huohua*, met with open
suspicion. The editor of *Shiji feng*, Ke Ling, found it necessary to defend his works, along with those of Feng and Ye, by underlining
their moral import and imaginative power. But to no avail.[116] It is
thus no accident that Wang at this time described Shanghai as a
"prison city" (*laocheng*), a "city of death" (*sicheng*) where every person, living in captivity, was infected with the "plague" of moral corruption.[117] He was disillusioned and on the point of abandoning his
earlier optimism about human potential and giving in to a sense of
the futility of human affairs. He now realized that resistance and enlightenment were actually unconnected, even antithetical. In his
perception, the Chinese Resistance in Shanghai, being dictated by
the logic of what he characterized as "answering violence with violence," was engaged in an equally unjust war of brutality and ven-
geance, totally relinquishing its ethical purpose. Its cult of patriotic
passion and direct action and its celebration of violence and collective discipline were morally reprehensible.

Wang thus found himself torn between patriotism and moral authenticity. His commitment to the cause of China's national autonomy led him to identify with the Resistance, yet he was deeply repelled by its betrayal of the humanistic ideal of universal justice.
How to resolve this conflict of values? In an essay written in 1939,
he began formulating his solution by way of a symbolic journey toward self-realization. Rejecting both violence and escapism (represented by a soldier and an old man respectively) as immoral modes
of existence, the hero finds freedom in the eternal quest for self-
perfection. "[Happiness] lies within one's unselfish quest. It is to be
assiduous and just while pressing along on one's eternal journey."[118]
By stressing the virtue of self-cultivation to the exclusion of social
relevance, Wang saved himself from total despair only by embracing
a kind of moral self-righteousness. This idea encouraged the belief
that the inner life, even when lived for its own sake, was far superior
to social action that was not morally pure. But how effective could
the ideal of moral purity be in counteracting the corrupt state of
human affairs? Was such an inner quest effectual in resisting the Japanese Occupation? If not, was this not another form of escapism, a

covert way of justifying private concerns? His solution seemed to raise more questions than it was supposed to have answered.

When terror and economic pressure reached an alarming point in 1940, Wang felt compelled to confront these psychological and emotional conflicts in a series of short stories. Choosing one art form over another is never a purely formal decision, but rather, as Roland Barthes points out, a moral choice, a "morality of form."[119] Wang chose short fiction rather than the prose poetry he had employed in 1938, probably because, as Suzanne Ferguson has shown, modern short stories provide the best medium for articulating an author's sense of alienation and isolation. Dwelling upon the "subjectivity of reality," with its compactness and limited point of view, the short story brings into sharp focus the moral anguish of "outsiders" searching for a reliable, interpersonal knowledge of the world that threatens to overcome them.[120] Indeed, all four of Wang's short stories in 1940, reminiscent of the May Fourth obsession with tragic alienation (e.g., Lu Xun and Yu Dafu), represented and explored the dilemma of moral authenticity and social futility from an outsider's perspective.

The most distinctive piece in this genre was "Lei yu yi" (Tears and wing), a story published in June 1941 in an anthology that included three other stories. Written in highly reflective prose laden with Catholic metaphors, and plotted in a framework of moral pessimism informed by the Miltonian motif of *Paradise Lost,* the story has an undeniably autobiographical ring to it. This narrative condition, with its biblical dualities of original sin versus redemption, grace versus the fall, revelation versus knowledge, allowed Wang to oppose his different conceptions of the tension between moral cultivation and social engagement.[121]

The story aims to defamiliarize what is considered familiar in war. In a tombstone city ravaged by war, the Statue of Peace, "lonely, depressed, and weak," finds herself suspended between an urge to pursue harmony and beauty and the desire to become involved in ending the human tragedy of "self-destruction." By contrast, the goddess Sister Moon is indifferent to the war. Representing divine revelation, she affords the Statue of Peace a glimpse of the solemn harmonies that could be hers, and then reveals to her that war is the result of man's fall from grace and is thus inevitable. Man can find redemption only in death. Even the few sage-poets who strive to bring salvation to humanity by invoking their moral idealism cannot change this condition because they are numerically and spiritually too insignificant to survive the overwhelming force of man's evil:

> Just think about it. The first man was born on earth; he would therefore die on earth. And earth is the source of evils. Right? Thus man is born in evil and dies in evil....There are too few "perfect men." They are too weak to change their sinful and cruel kind. They—these spirits from the heaven—are like a tiny bit of light in a dark ocean, extinguished and submerged immediately by the great storm of ridicule and attack. What remains is nothing but the overflow of blood, the expansion of evil desires.[122]

In her agonizing confusion, the Statue of Peace deplores the sinful condition of human existence. Her "tears of benevolence," falling upon the dead at her feet, awaken the "desire for life," but all of them rise up only to kill. "To kill all the enemies," wrote Wang. "Let's dig out blood from their chests / Let's make their posterity pay." In a grotesque image calling to mind Pieter Brueghel's painting *The Triumph of Death* (ca. 1562), the city turns into a spectacle of horror. Equally ironic is the destruction of the Statue of Peace by bombs during the war of the risen dead. "The Statue's chaste body [*zhenjie*] falls on the ground right after a moment of absolute silence...what remains is an expanse of red blood underneath her body."[123]

Thus the familiar metaphor of enlightenment in the May Fourth literature—awakening the dead (as, for example, in Lu Xun's "Iron House")—is here given a new, ironic interpretation. The enlightened resister's (Statue of Peace's) struggle to save mankind through power of moral reason produces only increased brutality. This irony spells out that enlightenment not only fails to prevail over the human tendency to violence but in fact aggravates the doctrinaire nationalism inherent in the Resistance. Wang's moral vision of universal peace engenders only the kind of nationalistic war that turns out to be as unjust as aggression: "a fight between monsters," he lamented. The ironic ending of the heroine's death in a war for which she is partly responsible epitomizes Wang's total pessimism about man's moral potential. As the narrator psychologizes the Statue of Peace shortly before her demise: "She has lost all her mercy, her sympathy, as well as her tears of tenderness." Indeed, if man was utterly unable to aspire to the highest excellence, all efforts to elevate the human condition were doomed to futility and self-destruction. Thus the only alternative left for an enlightened resister was to choose the cultivation of one's inner life over social engagement.

To what extent was self-cultivation meaningful as a mode of response to the Occupation? Was it solely a kind of escapism, little different from collaboration, as many resisters claimed? In early 1940, apparently to resolve this tension, Wang wrote "Huating he" (The crane of Huating), which was first published in a popular magazine edited by his neighbor and close friend Zhao Jiabi and later became the leading story of the 1941 collection.

"Huating he" is seemingly based on the true story of an old artist in Suzhou, a long-time friend of Wang's, who lived in seclusion after the Japanese occupied the city and eventually killed himself in 1939. In an earlier essay dedicated to the recluse, Wang interpreted his suicide in terms of the Neo-Confucian concepts of *qijie* (moral integrity) and *xingji you chi* (self-consciousness of shame) and praised him as a man of the highest virtue.[124] By transforming his story into a literary work, Wang invested the suicide with a set of moral-political values related to the issue of self-cultivation. Zhu Laoxian (literally the Immortal Zhu) is a "stubborn old man" who, no longer a cultural rebel as in his youthful days, indulges himself in a self-absorbed mode of existence during the Occupation. He feels morally repulsed by the decadent society around him, so he contents himself with a life of contemplation, finding solace in classical Chinese poetry and friendship. His ideal of *qijie* remains an assertion rather than an action. As he describes himself to a friend after a few drinks: "All my problems are because of books. No matter. I can say this: I have been living with my spine straight ever since the age of fifteen! And I won't change, not until I die. You, you don't believe [in my integrity], right?" Zhu's test of loyalty comes when his only son, a "young, smart returned student," joins the puppet regime as a high-ranking official. He tries to change him, but to no avail. "Twenty-five years ago, [Zhu Laoxian] had spent several hours every night after work teaching his son classical maxims on moral cultivation. But now....He could not but ask himself: why was his son so diametrically opposite to his own youthful idealism. Was it a matter of personality or of education?"[125] This personal tragedy forces him to confront the dilemma between private and public morality. Unable to save his own son or bring himself to put righteousness above kinship (a concept that was very important to many Resistance writers) and to compromise his moral ideals, he chooses to kill himself. He leaves his son his favorite poem by the Song poet Su Shi, the last couplet of which summarizes the reason for his suicide:

> Do you know that I cry for you?
> Since eternity the crane of Huating has flown away alone.[126]

The "crane of Huating" is an allusion to Lu Ji, the poet-general of the Eastern Jin (A.D. 317–420), whose uncompromising loyalty became an allegory of moral rectitude. Thus the old recluse's suicide represents a voice of passive protest. Although self-cultivation was surely ineffective in opposing the Occupation, it was not a surrender of moral commitment. It was a defense of purity and dignity in the face of the impossible. Not unlike "Lei yu yi," the tragic ending here spelled out a symbolic challenge to the May Fourth faith in enlightenment. If the younger generation—to whom Wang dedicated his *Liangyu zhong de huohua*—was worse than the older one in spite of more and a modern education, wasn't it a sad testament to misguided faith in the "new youth," the futility of reason and progress?

The deaths of both Zhu Laoxian and the Statue of Peace were thus clearly symbolic of Wang's choice of the inner life over social engagement. Disillusioned of his earlier optimism about man's moral potential and the power of critical reason to realize itself through the Resistance, he went to the other extreme, total pessimism. As he lamented:

> Living in the sea of humanity goes against my grain,
> The calamities of these several years have deeply grieved me.[127]

The sense of despair registered in this classical poem—which he wrote, significantly, on the cover of the collection *Huating he* as a token of his appreciation of his publisher, the essayist Lu Yi—

marked the beginning of the end of Wang's social involvement. He launched himself into a new phase of self-cultivation, comparable to that of 1927–31, stressing the virtue of *qijie* over *qimeng*. Thus began his life of seclusion.

Eremitism Under Complete Japanese Occupation

On the morning of December 8, 1941, following the bombing of Pearl Harbor, Japan extended its military occupation to the foreign areas of Shanghai. The whole city was now occupied, and all Westerners were sent to internment camps. The Solitary Island disappeared. Shanghai's "deformed prosperity" vanished forever, to be replaced by what a popular metaphor of the time called the "dark world" (*heian shijie*), a world in which political suppression, extreme economic deprivation, rampant political corruption, and fin-de-siècle decadence constituted an accepted way of life (see also Chapter 3).[128]

Patriotic intellectuals became particular victims of Japanese suppression. As soon as the Japanese army entered the city, it closed down all foreign-published newspapers and important publishing companies and ordered the confiscation of anti-Japanese books so as to purge "enemy culture" (*tekisei-bunka*).[129] Press censorship and political surveillance were now universally enforced. The Japanese authorities also required all resisters, if they hoped for "political amnesty," to register with "No. 76" in order to show allegiance to the new authorities.[130] At the same time, starting with the arrest of Xu Guangping (Lu Xun's widow) in mid December 1941 and with the tragedy of the publisher Lu Yi, who, recently remarried, presented himself at the Kempeitai office hoping to arrange the early release of his company's books and disappeared forever, the Japanese Thought Police began a systematic persecution of Resistance writers.[131]

In this atmosphere of terror, many intellectual resisters who were associated with the GMD and CCP, such as A Ying, Ba Ren, and Zhao Junhao, fled Shanghai. Most writers who could not leave, as Kong Lingjing testified, "saw little hope of [active] resistance, so some of them retired into seclusion while others changed professions."[132] Whether it was withdrawal into self-cultivation or becoming a street merchant or a used book dealer in order to survive,[133] this passive mode of resistance was reminiscent of what Frederick Mote calls "compulsory eremitism" in traditional China, when some Confucian literati opted for symbolic protest of a new dynasty through passivity and noncooperation. Indeed, eremitism provided a culturally sanctioned mode of resistance by which recluses could preserve their lives in the face of danger and uncertainty without sacrificing their moral principles. It was both a quest for purity and a symbolic statement of patriotic defiance.[134] Although the Shanghai writers expressed themselves in Neo-Confucian terms of loyalty to legitimate authority, *esi shixiao shijie shida* (To starve to death is a very small matter; to lose one's integrity is a grave matter),[135] they gave them a modern nationalist interpretation. They refused to compromise, not because they were faithful to the Nationalist government or to its leader, but because of their moral commitment to the nation as a whole.[136] Thus they heaped scorn on those intellectuals who justified their collaboration with the enemy in terms of sheer survival, *Shijie shixiao shiye shida* (Losing one's job is graver than losing one's integrity),[137] and bitterly denounced them as lacking *qijie* and for being dictated to solely by appetite.

In order to avoid the connotations of escapism and hypocrisy that accompanied modern images of traditional recluses,[138] however, these passivists justified their withdrawal in terms of *zheju*, literally, "hibernation." Redefining the concept of the recluse in a metaphor of biological necessity, they tended to see themselves as being forced to lie low, to remain silent while awaiting the ultimate victory of China. Thus "waiting for dawn" or "hoping for spring" or "flowers will blossom soon" became the code imagery of art and literature among resisters in occupied Shanghai. "Silence is...the beginning of courage," as the essayist Tang Tao put it. "Human history is indeed a record of silences. Short-sighted people have tried every selfish way to create History. But History awaits in silence, waiting for these people to vanish into ashes."[139] Despite their faith in China, these writers withdrew in the face of deprivation and agony. Their withdrawal demanded great moral endurance.

This moral endurance was buttressed by mutual support among these symbolic resisters. Bound by a common patriotic urge, these intellectuals became ever more intimate as the Occupation proceeded.[140] This experience of being alone together was summed up by a code widely used in contemporary writing, which originated in the Daoist classic *Zhuangzi*: "The fish are left stranded on the ground, they spew each other with moisture and wet each other down with spit."[141] Seeing themselves in the image of stranded fish desperate for water of some sort, these writers sought affection and affirmation from one another in order to survive the Occupation in silence.

The most common practice of mutual reinforcement was a support group of close friends and relatives (usually three to ten people) who met, for safety's sake, at a private home or irregularly at private parties. In a group effort to sustain each other's moral commitment, participants in these informal gatherings shared news inimical to the Japanese occupiers that they had heard on the wireless or in rumors. More important, the sense of community and emotional intimacy provided a context for mutual support of their choice of passivity and one in which they could safely vent their distress and frustration. These private meetings constituted what James Scott has called the "social space" for offstage defiance of the Occupation.[142]

There were also institutional forms of support. Among writers the most popular were publishing houses, their major hangouts, and financial backers. Located in the International Settlement, the Kaiming shudian (Enlightenment Book Company), for example, furnished eminent liberal men of letters in occupied Shanghai with a steady though meager income and, above all, a sense of true community. Founded in 1925, Kaiming had become the liberal voice of Chinese literature by 1937. With the eruption of the war, Kaiming moved part of its business to Guilin and Chongqing, while the Shanghai office on Fuzhou Road coordinated the whole company.[143] The Shanghai office was shut down by the Japanese army in December 1941, but in mid 1942 it was allowed to reopen, along with other big publishing companies, on the condition that they published no anti-Japanese or anti-Manchukuo materials.

To resist Japanese cooptation prudently, Kaiming concentrated on reprinting the Chinese classics in popular editions and compiling reference works and dictionaries. Whereas the former venture was aimed at nourishing the patriotic identity of the Shanghai reading public, the latter served to provide its personnel with a meaningful long-term project to enable them to endure the Occupation while waiting for ultimate liberation. For the compilation project, Kaiming engaged several eminent old scholars and writers who had no means of livelihood yet were steadfast in their moral resistance to the occupiers. The times were hard, but these editors found some fulfillment in the affection and mutual support afforded by the Kaiming community of recluses.[144] The editorial staff of Kaiming and their friends also received encouragement from writers in Chinese-controlled areas through the company's business network.[145]

Wang was one of the Kaiming editors. He joined the staff after Jinan University voluntarily closed down on December 8, 1941. On the last day of class, as two of his students recalled, Wang for the first time talked about his personal life after the lecture. In an emotional tone he told the class at the end:

This is our last class. Our school will move to the interior. Whether you can move along [with us] will depend on the situation of your own family. Our school will not force it upon you. Indeed, the critical question is not whether you choose to stay or to leave Shanghai. The question is rather which road you will take from now on. In both action and spirit, will you continue to resist or surrender to the enemy? All of you should prepare for this [ultimate choice].

This statement turned out to be prophetic of Wang's own future.[146] Sick, poor, and depressed, he did not follow the university to its new location in Fujian but remained in Shanghai, where he presently changed his name to Xunru, in part to avoid harassment by the Japanese, who were now desperately seeking the services of famous intellectuals.[147]

Aside from going to Kaiming irregularly, which was about a half-hour bus ride from his home, he lived in seclusion. Thus most of his friends and students did not even know Wang was in Shanghai throughout the Occupation.[148] In retirement, like the fictional Zhu Laoxian, he devoted himself to the compilation of an English-Chinese dictionary for Kaiming and found brief solace in classical poetry and friendship. Among the few friends with whom he remained in close contact were the famous writers Geng Jizhi, Xia Mianzun, and Zheng Zhenduo, who often had lunch with Wang at the Cantonese restaurant Da Sanyuan on Nanjing Road or at the famous Lao Ban Zhai Restaurant on Hankou Road, both within walking distance of the Kaiming office, before visiting the bookstore together.[149] Like Wang, they all changed their names after the Occupation to

avoid harassment. All May Fourth veterans, they had known one another as students in Beijing in the 1920s, when they had worked together on various new cultural projects, but their friendship became
intimate only during the Occupation, and especially so after 1941.[150]
    Since the fall of Shanghai in 1937, Xia and Geng had both led
reclusive lives. A famous linguist and liberal educator who had studied in Japan, Xia Mianzun was unable to escape into the interior
allegedly because of his family obligations. With a meager income
from his high school teaching, at times complemented by book
royalties, he was in constant financial straits; his own grandchildren
could not afford schools. Always in a bad mood, which greatly affected his health, Xia turned to Mahayana Buddhism for solace,
becoming a lay monk (jushi). His deep interest in Buddhism also
stemmed from a soteriological orientation. In his view, occupied
Shanghai was a world of spiritual decay in which only Buddhist wisdom could enlighten people and lift them out of decadence. In 1939
he had been commissioned by a Shanghai monastery to undertake
the sustained, systematic editing and collating of various Buddhist
scriptures for publication. Aloof from organized politics though he
was, Xia nevertheless helped his activist friends, including the Communist literary organizer Lou Shiyi, to skirt political harassment by
including them (nominally) in his project.[151]
    Geng Jizhi, the preeminent Chinese translator of Russian litera-
ture and a career diplomat, had to remain in Shanghai, where good
medical facilities were available, because of a heart problem and high
blood pressure. He sought to create a structure of meaning for his
life of passivity by devoting himself to the project of translating Dostoyevski's collected works (which he planned to publish after the
Occupation), an ambition he had entertained since the May Fourth
Movement. Besides working on translations for several hours in the
morning, Geng also opened a small used bookstore on Rue de Ray
Zoong, about ten blocks from Wang's house, to help support his big
family, which included his parents and his brothers' children. This
bookstore, with its convenient location and book-lined walls, soon
became his friends' favorite meeting place. The business setting also
made it safe from Japanese intervention.[152]
    On the other hand, the literary historian Zheng Zhenduo, whose
energy, resourcefulness, and erudition made him unacknowledged

leader of the liberal intellectuals in Shanghai, saw himself in the image of the Ming loyalist Huang Zongxi, turning his bibliomania into a means of upholding national culture. In 1938, invoking the memory of a Late Ming literati group famed for its fearless commitment to integrity, he founded the Fu she (Restoration Society) with twenty other former associates of the SWH, including the Communist writer Ba Ren, Lu Xun's widow, Xu Guangping, the banker Sun Ruihuang, and the *Shen bao* editor Hu Zhongchi, with the aim of keeping alive the spirit of tenacious defiance. To achieve this, through a secret distribution network, the Fu she published the first edition of Lu Xun's collected works and a Chinese translation of Edgar Snow's *Red Star over China*.[153] From 1940 to 1941, with the help of Zhang Yongni (president of Guanghua University) and Xu Shenyu (curator of the Palace Musuem), Zheng devoted himself to the acquisition of rare books and cultural artifacts on behalf of the GMD's Ministry of Education and the National Central Library in order to prevent their appropriation by Japanese and Manchukuo agents. The Pacific War started soon after he shipped some of these rare books to Hong Kong and hid the others (probably with Xia Mianzun's help) in a Buddhist temple on Rue de Ray Zoong, close to Geng's bookstore. With his visibility and intellectual stature, Zheng felt compelled to go quickly into hiding in a tiny room on the quiet Route Charles Culty. Yet he refused to give up on the "cultural war," only he now fought all by himself, with no government funding. Every afternoon, disguised as a bookstore buyer, Zheng continued to search for rare books around Fuzhou Road, and he soon filled his room with them. At night he worked on compiling a multivolume anthology of Ming surviving loyalists' writings in between learning to cook and to wash dishes himself (his mother, wife, and children remained in the Yuyuan Road house).[154] Thus, the solidarity of these May Fourth veterans with Wang was clearly a result both of their common intellectual background and shared patriotic commitment.

   When these friends met, usually at Kaiming or at Xia Mianzun's bookstore, or at the home of Zheng Zhenduo or Geng Jizhi or Zhang Xisheng, a veteran Kaiming editor, they drank, gossiped, shared meals (Mrs. Geng's Russian cuisine and Zheng's newly learned Fujian dishes), sometimes played mah-jongg, brewed coffee together over an alcohol burner,[155] complained to each other about their difficult lives, discussed literature and politics, or exchanged poems expressing their commitment to China despite their personal sufferings. They also tried to affirm themselves by lashing out against former friends who had compromised.[156] As Wang was to remember later: "Whenever we got together, we talked about the adverse circumstances and economic difficulties. We could not help but sigh and groan, or even at times glower and glare at each other. Although we placed our hopes in the future, it was nonetheless impossible not to be depressed at the time."[157]

This community was also a network for patriotic publications. Zheng Zhenduo arranged for Geng Jizhi to sign his book contract for the Dostoyevski translations with Zhao Jiabi, who lived right next door to Wang, for example, and Wang kept in touch while in seclusion with younger writers, including Ke Ling and Fan Quan, a newspaper supplement editor who came regularly to Kaiming to solicit manuscripts and seek editorial advice.[158]

It was indeed through this personal connection that Wang soon published his last novel. In February 1943 the embattled editor of *Shiji feng,* Ke Ling, accepted an offer from Ping Jinya, a famous tabloid writer and publisher of pirate editions, to edit his popular magazine *Wanxiang* (Phenomena). He did this at a time when most men of letters had retired to avoid direct confrontation with the occupiers and to avoid being identified with the cultural world dominated by collaborators. Ke, a self-styled idealist (who had hid for months when "No. 76" tried to coerce him to change sides) sought instead to preserve the voice of conscience and to provide Shanghai's readers with a literary magazine that would give vent to their patriotic sentiments.[159] With his editorial autonomy, resourcefulness, and intimate connections with Kaiming, which he referred to as "the information center for writers in Shanghai and the interior,"[160] Ke Ling succeeded within a few months in turning *Wanxiang* from an apolitical Mandarin Ducks and Butterfly publication catering to the popular taste for amusement into a forum for symbolic resistance. Many writers in seclusion, including the famous translator Fu Lei, the senior Kaiming editor Xu Diaofu, and the young writers Shi Tuo and Tang Tao, contributed to *Wanxiang;* the magazine thus gave an institutional voice to the passivists in occupied Shanghai.[161]

To avoid Japanese censorship, Ke improvised creative ways of conveying patriotic sentiments, which were later adopted by other magazines of similiar political bent. For example, in 1944 he published a special issue on the Kaiming coterie's celebration of Xia Mianzun's fortieth wedding anniversary (a party with wine and good food, which Wang later recalled as "a rare occasion for happiness and fulfillment" in occupied Shanghai),[162] to which prominent writers and editors, including Wang, from both Shanghai and the interior (such as Zhu Ziqing and Ye Shengtao) dedicated poems. All the poems were classical in form, heartfelt in tone, and demonstrated a skillful transformation of wishes for continued commitment between the old couple into metaphors expressing their unwavering loyalty to China as a nation.[163] Ke also published private letters or intimate reports about and writings of authors in the Chinese-controlled areas like Ye Shengtao, Feng Zikai, Ba Jin, and Mao Dun (which he claimed to obtain from Kaiming) in every issue. All this careful blending of private life and political messages was intended to show that all Chinese were in solidarity while awaiting liberation.

Despite this tactical ingenuity, Ke had to pay a price for his courage. In June 1944 and again in June 1945, he was arrested by the Kempeitai. The first arrest (when he was detained for six days) cost him his editorship, as Ping Jinya soon closed *Wanxiang* for fear of persecution; the second left him disabled for months. Throughout nine days of brutal beating and torture on the rack, Ke remained defiant, refusing to betray his friends. Not wanting to take any more chances, he fled Shanghai shortly after his release in mid June 1945.[164]

It was in Ke Ling's *Wanxiang* that Wang serialized his last piece of wartime writing, a novel, *Shuangqing* (The two virtues), between July 1943 and June 1944. According to Ke, Wang agreed to write mainly because he needed the extra income to support his family and also because of their friendship.[165] Important too, perhaps, was the renewed optimism inspired in Wang by the apparent, if limited, success of noncooperation as a mode of moral resistance. Although the intellectuals of Shanghai were unable to fight or to defeat the enemy, noncooperation had at least shown them their own integrity and unyielding pride. In fact from 1942-43 on, the occupiers had repeatedly expressed discontent with the current literary scene, which consisted solely of minor writers and hacks and was characterized by the apolitical theme of nostalgia (see Chapter 3). The Japanese were visibly frustrated by their failure to recruit well-known figures, whose services and cooperation were, in their eyes, essential to a "literary renaissance" in the occupied areas. The legitimacy of the Occupation was thus at stake.[166]

Wang's serialized novel is incomplete. The plot and several of the main characters need further development, yet the major structuring theme of the narrative seems to have been fully developed. Thus, although Wang probably stopped writing out of fear of implication after Ke's first arrest, the vague ending of the novel makes one wonder if the unfinished form bespeaks Wang's own state of mind, his deep sense of uncertainty about the future. Indeed, the doubtful tone seems to represent a fitting summation of his experience during the war years.

Indeed, *Shuangqing* is a literary rendering of Wang's recent reflections on his Occupation experiences. Couched in historical allegory, it is the story of a singsong girl's quest for enlightenment. Its setting in North China under warlord rule parallels the political situation of occupied Shanghai. The singsong girl suggests the symbolic resister.[167] This choice was an obvious one. The post–May Fourth literary construction of women as weak and helpless and usually pure figures victimized by men's social and sexual abuses matched in symbolic terms the dismal situation of passive resistance under Japanese domination.[168] By creating the figure of a "chaste" prostitute, therefore, Wang connotes committed patriots striving to maintain their moral integrity in the face of extreme danger.

Xiaoqian is a "beautiful, determined and noble" singsong girl from the northeast who was sold as a child into prostitution but has managed to maintain her chastity despite tremendous pressure. She dreads becoming the concubine of "militarists or bureaucrats," and her longing for a dramatic change in her life is realized with the eruption of the Northern Expedition. She falls in love with a young revolutionary whom she has saved from persecution, but the affair is brief and futile. He sees her as merely an "unusual prostitute," and she resents his condescending, moralizing attitude, saying: "You should not despise this tiny and fragile flower."

The ensuing turmoil drives Xiaoqian away to the country, where she is adopted by an old "recluse," Gao Da (literally, Lofty). A frustrated scholar widely respected in the local community for his moral cultivation, Gao helps Xiaoqian to get to know the Confucian classics as well as to appreciate the beauty of nature. She soon begins to enjoy her new life of idyllic tranquility. Yet the image of "that strong and handsome young man often comes to her mind," evoking in her "a strange, vague feeling of discontent." Soon the political turbulence caused by the civil war disrupts the peace of the countryside. The bucolic world is turned upside down; banditry becomes rampant, and there is chaos everywhere. Xiaoqian is sent by Gao to a remote Catholic church for sanctuary, where she finds fulfillment in helping the Chinese nun there run its orphanage. Her intelligence is appreciated, and she enjoys working with the orphans. Yet she is troubled at the same time by a deep sense of anxiety and loneliness. The story abruptly ends in this mood of uncertainty.

Harking back to Wang's 1939 essay on the absolute of self-cultivation, the young revolutionary, who justifies violence as the necessary means to a noble goal, "a nightmare to be easily forgotten," and the old recluse Gao Da in *Shuangqing* represent the two ends of a complex spectrum of moral responses to the Occupation. Violent resistance and hermetic escapism, in Wang's view, were extreme expressions of public and private morality. Xiaoqian's rejection of both, and her choice of dedication to the spiritual regeneration of humanity, as symbolized by her work in the orphanage, reveals Wang's reaffirmation of his ideal of enlightenment. But this reaffirmation was derived from his mature understanding of human nature through his encounter with the reality of resistance. No longer was he optimistic (as indicated by the uncertain tone of the story's "end"), as he had been at the beginning of the war; nor was he pessimistic, as when he realized that his moral ideal had been crushed. The incompleteness of the story may thus be indicative of his acceptance of the ambiguity of human life. One could do only what one could. The future was open insofar as it was unknown.

But this openness was not without its existential ironies. How much did Wang's symbolic defiance contribute to the future? Was passivity an effective means of changing the course of history? What had he done for the country after all? Was withdrawal an "empty gesture," placating one's sense of morality rather than serving the public good?[169] And to what extent was enlightenment feasible in a country torn by war and occupation? Even back in 1940, Wang was aware of these questions: "[From my own writings] I of course acquire some sort of comfort, but they also increase my feeling of shame....How much have I done for my country?"[170] The unfinished journey of Xiaoqian is therefore a fitting end to the story of Wang Tongzhao in Shanghai during the eight years of the Occupation. In July 1945, only one month before the Japanese surrender, he left with his family for Qingdao. Wang finally decided to leave Shanghai because he could no longer afford the high prices there, and probably, with U.S. bombers in sight every day in the spring of 1945, he also feared that the Allies would carpet bomb Shanghai, as was rumored, which led to a massive evacuation to the suburbs that summer.[171]

Although he was only 48, the years of suffering, distress, and despair under foreign occupation had turned Wang into a sick old man.[172] Yet he survived, and notwithstanding that his struggle for enlightenment failed as a historical force, the ideal helped articulate the moral values and patriotic commitment of a group of symbolic resisters in occupied Shanghai whose voices might have otherwise gone unnoticed. And although the Resistance failed as a vehicle of universal rebirth, Shanghai was liberated, and China survived as a nation.

If Wang had demonstrated the pride, honor, and dignity of the occupied by remaining morally defiant, refusing to serve the enemy, however, to what extent did his passivity contribute to the city's liberation? Did his noncooperation help overcome foreign domination? If not, was passivity just a dignified way of self-preservation? Wang was only too conscious of the ambiguity. Hence the sentimental poem he dedicated to his close friends, including Ke Ling, Xia Mianzun, and Zheng Zhenduo, at his farewell party. In a pensive mood, and with simple idyllic imagery, he contemplates his life, realizing that in a time of historical uncertainty a reclusive existence is best for him:

> Letting ten years slip by, I have failed the Lower Yangzi delta;
>   my sideburns have merely taken on the color of snow.
> While I dreamt of fishing and singing at the seashore,
>   violence and destruction have finally come to an end in
>   gardens, woods, and my hometown.

Drifting in shame, I can only envy the bliss of free and
  unfettered wandering [*xiaoyao you*];
I well know that my dream could only be realized with great
  difficulty.[173]

Indeed, Wang also opted for a reclusive existence throughout the
ensuing Civil War (1945–49). Although utterly disgusted with the
postwar moral and political turmoil, he avoided direct resistance to
the GMD government. As under the Japanese Occupation, he remained steadfast to his ideal of moral integrity, refusing to work for
the returned regime despite poverty and distress. He found some solace in classical poetry and scholarship and in remembrance of his
close friendships in occupied Shanghai, not unlike the committed
Confucian literati who also chose to live out dynastic crisis by way
of eremitism, waiting for "the Way to prevail" once again in the
state. In 1949, with the founding of the People's Republic, he
emerged from his long silence to take up a senior cultural post in the
new Shandong government despite his bad health. As if to redeem
his reclusive past, Wang devoted himself wholeheartedly to the task
of creating a "new China" until his death in early 1957, just a few
months before the onset that June of the Anti-Rightist Campaign, a
campaign of political suppression aimed at prominent liberal intellectuals just like him.

On August 12, 1937, thousands of refugees from Greater Shanghai streamed into the foreign settlements through the Garden Bridge to escape the Japanese. (Randall Gould Papers, Hoover Archives)

Two scenes of horror on "Bloody Saturday," August 14, 1937, in front of the Great World Amusement Palace in the French Concession. (Randall Gould Papers, Hoover Archives)

The burning of Zhabei in November 1937 after a Japanese air raid, as viewed from the International Settlement. (George Bruce, *Shanghai's Undeclared War*)

As the Japanese army laid siege to Nanshi in November 1937, refugees swarmed around the gate to the French Concession. (*Four Months of War*)

The Joint Savings Society godown along the Suzhou Creek, where 800 soldiers of the "Lone Battalion" held out against the Japanese army toward the end of the battle. (*Four Months of War*)

People in the International Settlement lining up to buy "cheap rice" in 1940. (Robert Barnett, *Economic Shanghai*)

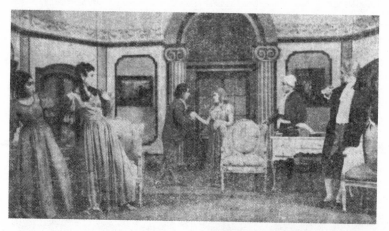

Above: Le Jeu de l'Amour et de la Mort, adapted by Li Jianwu as *Ai yu si de bodou* in 1938. (*Wenxian*)

Right: Li Jianwu's *Zhe buguo shi chuntian,* performed by the Shanghai juyishe in 1939. (*Juchang yishu*)

Below: A Ying's popular historical play *Bixue hua,* of 1939. (*Shanghai shenghuo*)

Above left: Wang Tongzhao in 1930. *Above right:* Wang Tongzhao in 1949. (Feng Guanglian and Liu Zangren, *Wang Tongzhao*)

(From left to right) Li Jianwu, Tang Tao, Zheng Zhenduo, unknown, and Ke Ling, 1949. (*Xin wenxue shiliao*)

Zhou Lian in 1943. (*Fengyu tan*)

When Japan extended its occupation into the foreign settlements on the morning of December 8, 1941, a group of Japanese sailors blocked a strategic point on the Nanjing Road. (*The XXth Century*)

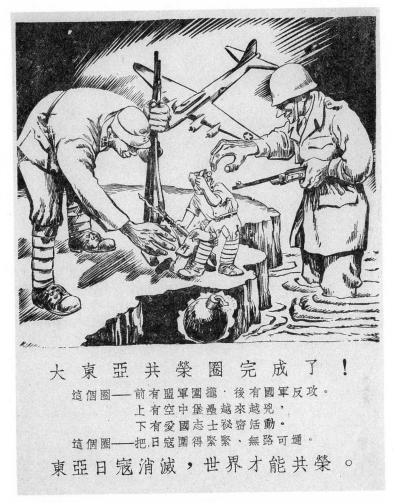

大東亞共榮圈完成了！

這個圈——前有盟軍圍攏．後有國軍反攻。
上有空中堡壘越來越兇，
下有愛國志士秘密活動．
這個圈——把日寇圍得緊緊．無路可通。

東亞日寇消滅，世界才能共榮。

Toward the end of the Occupation, an Allied leaflet circulated in Shanghai, reading (in block letters): "The completion of the Greater East Asia Co-Prosperity Sphere! The world can live in Co-Prosperity only with the destruction of the Japanese bandits."

2

Resistance:
Li Jianwu and the
Theater of Commitment

I rebel, therefore we exist.

Albert Camus,
The Rebel

•

In occupied Shanghai, Wang Tongzhao's "prison city," many intellectuals fought back. The resources they needed to resist the Japanese Occupation were the tenacity and recalcitrance of a "prisoner." The will to rebel, the courage to refuse to accept unjust conditions, became as critical for the liberation of Shanghai and the country as military campaigns elsewhere in China. "Human lives in times of trouble are like weeds," wrote Ke Ling in 1937. "Yet we have the freedom to choose between being self-determined or slavish, loyal or traitorous, virtuous or mean.... The War of Resistance will be a protracted one; we should spiritually prepare ourselves for it."[1]

Resistance was perceived by these intellectuals as inseparably linked with freedom and human dignity. To resist was a matter of moral commitment. In this frame of mind, they called for persistent revolt against both the enemy within oneself and the enemy without. Self-interest and a desire for compromise were seen as being as detrimental to the national cause as military defeat. Indeed, the War of Resistance was interpreted as at once an act of spiritual cleansing, whereby the self ascended to a higher plane of public interest and all national humiliations were overcome, and the gateway to a new era of Chinese history. The intellectual who best typified this stance of active resistance was the playwright, translator, and literary critic Li Jianwu

(1906–1982), and like Wang Tongzhao, whom he had known since the 1920s in Beijing, he lived in Shanghai throughout the eight years of the Occupation.

During the Occupation, Li leapt from being an obscure, politically aloof academican to become a Resistance hero—a leader of the modern theater, which, along with the foreign-published newspapers, formed the principal instrument of Shanghai Resistance. But unlike many of his comrades, Li remained largely on the fringe of the Resistance, because he refused to succumb to the collectivistic trend of patriotic mobilization, insisting on the continued relevance of individuality and creative freedom. In his wartime plays he combined drama and a model of humanistic values to explore the dialectic between history and freedom. To Li, political choice was also moral choice, and politics was an extension of personal morality; accordingly, resistance and self-transcendence were intertwined and integral to the liberation of the country. Yet throughout the Occupation, he vacillated constantly between political engagement and scholarly contemplation, and he resolved the moral dilemma only after he could no longer hold on to his academic position.

The Son of a Revolutionary Martyr

Li Jianwu came from "a revolutionary family." He was born in 1906 in Yuncheng County in the province of Shanxi, and his childhood was largely spent in flight. His father, Li Qishan, had been one of the most colorful of the military leaders responsible for the liberation of Yuncheng in the 1911 Revolution. Coming into conflict with the new Shanxi military governor, Yan Xishan, the strong-willed, outspoken Li Qishan was accused of treason and thrown into jail. Immediately after his release in 1913, he moved his family to Xi'an (Shaanxi), where he helped organize a revolt in concert with the Second Revolution campaign against the military dictator Yuan Shikai. For safety during the rebellion, Li Jianwu, the youngest of the three children, was sent to live with his father's military comrades at various places in and around Tianjin. He rejoined the family only after the rebellion was over and Li Qishan had obtained a post with the War Office in Beijing. This did not last long, however. Yan Xishan soon conspired to have Li Qishan incarcerated again;

and after his release in 1919, he was assassinated by Yan's ally, the military commander of Xi'an, while traveling on a political mission there.[2]

Li was thirteen years old when his father died. The family was left to struggle on the monthly interest from a meager "widow's fund" established by a few political associates of his father's. Living in a seedy Shanxi guildhall near the Nanxiawa slums in northern Beijing, Li began writing while in high school. One of his pieces attracted the notice of Wang Tongzhao, then a newspaper supplement editor, who offered the young boy both literary advice and introductions.[3] In 1925, the already widely published Li entered Qinghua University, and when he graduated with a degree in Western literature in 1930, he was recommended by his teachers Zhu Ziqing, the famous May Fourth essayist, and Wang Wenxian (or John Wong-Quincy), a London-trained theater scholar, for the post of tutor at Qinghua. A year later, in 1931, when Yan Xishan lost power, Li was awarded a special scholarship by the new Shanxi governnnor, Shang Zhen, who had been a good friend of Li Qishan's, to do graduate work at the University of Paris. In Paris, Li worked hard and enjoyed the social life. His friends at the time remembered him fondly as a tireless chatterbox, open, cheerful, and lovingly generous.

Li returned to Beijing in the summer of 1933, where he shortly afterward married You Shufen, a Qinghua economics graduate whom he had met in 1931. In the same year, the groom won a government fellowship to write a critical biography of Flaubert. Despite his reputation as a promising young scholar of French literature, with the gift of an elegant, witty style, and an incisive critic championing the impressionist approach of critical subjectivity, he could not secure a permanent academic job in Beijing.[4] Thus, in 1935 when he was offered a faculty position at Jinan University by Zheng Zhenduo, whom he had known through Wang Wenxian and Zhu Ziqing, he left for Shanghai to teach French literature. And in Shanghai he was to stay until 1954.[5]

In retrospect, his father's assassination had a twofold effect upon Li's intellectual development. First, the incident became a memory invested with symbolic significance as he grew up. He was obsessed throughout his adult life with the memory of his father as a heroic figure, a paragon of courage and moral commitment, who refused to compromise his conscience.[6] This image, as we shall see, provided Li with a primitive myth of heroism, an inner urge to defiance, that gave an underlying structure to all of his later writings.

Secondly, the loss of paternal authority provided him with the freedom to develop his own interests. Soon after his father's death in 1919, discovered and coached by Feng Zhimo and the Japan-returned Chen Dabei (who later worked for the Japanese in Shanghai), Li became involved in the emergent modern theater. Although he was still only in primary school, his charm, his liveliness, and especially his knack for crying tempestuously, made him a celebrity, a popular female impersonator at a time when no women were allowed on stage.[7] When he entered high school in 1921–22, however, females began to appear on stage and he consequently lost his roles. Yet his passion for drama remained. He began writing plays.[8]

Known in Chinese as *huaju* (spoken drama), modern drama was introduced from the West via Japan in the 1900s and 1910s as a vehicle of cultural enlightenment.[9] Toward the middle of the 1930s, when China was beset by partisan strife and the imminent threat of Japanese invasion, *huaju* was developed along with other Western-style literary genres into political theater, especially the "theater of national defense" (*guofang ju*), which was dominated by such leftist playwrights as Tian Han, Xia Yan, and Yu Ling, and liberal dramatists, including Hong Shen. Yet their efforts to shape modern theater into patriotic propaganda had limited political impact. In addition to GMD suppression, most practicing dramatists were amateurs with little knowledge of the theater. Their political zeal notwithstanding, most if not all of their performances were based on awkward translations of Western plays and were poorly staged. Moreover, unlike traditional drama (e.g., Beijing or Shaoxing opera) and modern cinema, *huaju* enjoyed circumscribed popularity. From its very inception, its foreign form, overt didacticism, and platitudinous dialogue appealed only to a narrow circle of like-minded intellectuals in the big cities. Few plays ran for more than two shows. Even in Shanghai, the center of *huaju*, there was no permanent theater for their performance. Drama enthusiasts had to make do with odd hours in rented movie houses or school or guildhall auditoriums in inconvenient locations.

Thus, up to the eve of the war, modern drama remained largely amateurish and was saddled with the problem of reaching beyond a limited audience of urban intellectuals.[10]

It was in this atmosphere of isolation that Li embarked upon his career as a playwright. While constantly complaining about the poor reception of and prejudice against *huaju* in China, he viewed theatrics and dramatic writing as a "spiritual revolt," a test of will, revolting against society and the philistinism it spawned. It was a lonely occupation engaged in by people of unusual character. "[Writing plays in China] requires courage, a supremely spiritual value," he wrote in 1934, "Those who persevere in fighting alone are heroes of words."[11] This intense language of defiance bespoke Li's obsession with his father's image. Theater became the arena in which he explored and defined his vision of heroism.

Before the war, Li had written several plays; but all, with one exception, were closet dramas, read but not staged. The sole exception was *Zhe buguo shi chuntian* (This is only spring), a play about love and revolution that was first put on in 1934, with only one performance by a group of Bridgeman Girls' Secondary School students in Beijing. It was later restaged in occupied Shanghai.

A common theme that runs through all of Li's early dramatic works is the search for redeeming possibilities in the human condition. This existential anxiety grew directly from Li's feeling of betrayal and disappointment as he matured. "I have discovered certain human weaknesses...that I am at a loss as to whether to ridicule or sympathize," he revealed in 1935. "The older I have gotten...the more depressed I have become and the more I have turned in on myself."[12] And, indeed, writing to him represented a refuge of fulfillment, a defense against depression: "If there is no perfection in human life, might it not exist in the Kingdom of Art [?]...[So] I took it that only in the arts could we ever achieve spiritual victory."[13] This explained Li's political aloofness prior to 1937. He was a marginal man, or, as his old friend Ba Jin described him, a "bystander," a "pedant," who "sits in his study, and at times turns to look at Flaubert on the left and at others looks at Zola and George Sand on the right."[14] He wrote only to express himself.

Li was deeply disillusioned. He had been a hero-worshipper, worshipping his father and his father's military comrades, with whom he spent his roving childhood. But, aside from his father, who fought against injustice until his death, all these "heroes" either died young or degenerated into minor warlords, drug addicts, or petty thieves, bragging about or trying to hide their pasts. They lacked the perseverance to hold on to their ideals. They were a "myth" demystified by the challenge of time. Along with this disillusionment came Li's realization that he was no hero either. He could not even find himself a job in his beloved Beijing, much less save the country or change the world.[15] Man, he concluded, was limited by his own nature—he was susceptible to weakness and compromise.

But he found the contrary in his own creation—a "spiritual revolt." This flight into words was most evident in his plays *Zhe buguo shi chuntian* and *Shisan nian* (Thirteen years), which was written in 1936 but first performed in 1939. Both plays are set in Beijing on the eve of the Northern Expedition and depict the dramatic escape of revolutionaries (without indication of their ideological allegiance) from warlord persecution. In *Zhe buguo shi chuntian*, set in Beijing in the 1920s, a police chief's wife, repelled by her materialistic life, sets free her former lover, a rebel "from the south." Similarly, *Shisan nian* portrays a police agent who releases two of his victims (both supposedly comrades of the Communist martyr Li Dazhao's), when he discovers that one of them was his high-school sweetheart. Before his suicide, Huang Tianli, the warlord agent, says to his former lover: "Let me tell you. Although you call me a dog, I have actually only been able to live this long because of that vague dream [love]."[16]

Li claimed that the two plays allegorized the dawning of a new age, but more significant is his portrayal of the two characters—in his words, "ordinary people," destroyed by life but able to redeem themselves somewhat by remaining loyal to their love. They pass the "final test" despite themselves, grasping their "last chance to shine through." To the playwright, they were not "heroes" in the ordinary sense, because they acted out of "despair and remorse." In fact, they represent just the opposite of Li's fallen heroes: whereas the former reclaim their better selves, the latter lose theirs.

Unbeknownst to Li, his own "last chance to shine through" his life was soon to come. His search for the meaning of heroism arrived at the "final test" of political reality—the Japanese Occupation—when the war began in August 1937.[17]

The Solitary Island and the Rise of Resistance Theater

Li, then aged 31, seemed to regard the outbreak of the war with a mixture of aloofness and naïveté. Under heavy machine-gun fire and bursting shells, he went on with his secluded life, preparing lecture notes and taking daily walks around the western suburbs of Shanghai with his good friend Bian Zhilin, the impressionist poet (who, however, soon left for the interior), while chewing sugarcane and discussing French literature.[18]

It was only in September that Li began to sense the urgency of the situation. Jinan University was obliged that month to relocate from Zhenru, a suburb northwest of Shanghai, to the city's French Concession, and Li followed. He moved his family—his wife and two infant daughters—to a cramped little room on the quiet Rue Ratard, not far from the Jinan campus on Route Dolfus. It was here that he lived through the war.

During the Battle of Shanghai from August to November 1937, *huaju* showed itself for the first time as a potent instrument for patriotic mobilization. Under the aegis of the SWH, as described in the Prologue, the Shanghai xiju jie jiuwang xiehui (Shanghai Association of the Theatrical Circle for National Salvation), headed by the Communist playwright Yu Ling, was founded in the French Concession in August 1937 to bring together artists and writers for the theater and cinema to serve the war cause. The association sponsored several collective projects to produce "Resistance plays" (*kangzhan ju*), especially street dramas, which were simple and direct in plot structure. All of them were highly clichéd and stereotyped, calling for armed resistance. Amid the rising nationalistic fervor of the Shanghai public, political theater became very popular. The association also organized thirteen drama troupes, with over twenty members apiece, to perform in emergency hospitals and refugee centers and to visit the front. Soon many national salvation organizations in both the Chinese and foreign areas, including the Ant Society and the Banking and Finance Employees' Club, followed suit, setting up drama troupes to lecture and stage patriotic plays at street corners and in hospitals. In late October, with the Chinese army losing ground in Shanghai, the association dispatched eleven of these troupes to travel inland to mobilize the masses for the national cause.

Like most patriotic intellectuals of the time, Li was excited by the War of Resistance while at the same time troubled by the problem of his personal life. Surely the best way to contribute to the war effort was to fight at the front. Yet "I cannot abandon my personal responsibility. Heroes make sacrifices; but I can't do that. Once I see my children innocently running to me, my heart softens," he lamented. "Then I sit down and see in my mind's eye the heroic scene at the battlefront.... We men of letters are all weaklings. We live in a house [future] built on the ground of reality. Now what collapses is not the house but the ground. So whenever I meet a wounded soldier on the street, I feel as if my own scars were torn open. I feel at once ashamed and thankful [to the soldier]."[19] This moral conflict and self-abhorrence became more acute after Greater Shanghai fell to the Japanese in November 1937 and the Nationalist government moved to the southwest.

On November 12, the SWH closed down and dissolved into several small underground offices, hoping to carry on its patriotic work under different circumstances.[20] While most writers and theater people affiliated with the Shanghai xiju jie jiuwang xiehui fled to the interior in the following weeks, Li chose to stay in occupied Shanghai. Aside from his family, which he had to support by teaching at Jinan, lacking other financial resources, the fact that he had a lame leg (owing to a childhood illness) also contributed to his decision. Couched in clichés and no doubt self-justifying, his reasons for staying were nonetheless genuine and compelling.[21] As most transportation was disrupted by the war, travel throughout the war was not only expensive but also arduous and dangerous. Moreover, the large exodus of intellectuals to the materially backward interior created immense employment and housing problems. The right connections were usually necessary to relocate there. In fact, not a few writers died of hunger and exhaustion in the attempt, and some were killed en route.[22] Li dreaded moving his two infant daughters under such conditions. He seemed to have at times considered escaping alone, leaving his family in Shanghai, but to whom could he entrust them and how would he support them?

As discussed in Chapter 1, intellectual life was in great turmoil in Shanghai immediately after its fall to the Japanese. The authorities in the foreign areas, the only part of the city that remained unoccupied, thus becoming known as the Solitary Island, banned all patriotic propaganda. All national salvation organizations were closed down (or went underground) and patriotic publications were suspended. Rumors of imminent Japanese persecution were rife. There were some anti-Japanese incidents (in December 1937, for instance, a Chinese shouting "Long Live China" hurled himself from a highrise building on Nanjing Road into the Japanese victory parade, and a small group of Chinese youths were arrested on Bubbling Well Road a week later while meeting to plan a propaganda campaign),[23] but these were sporadic and ineffective. Intellectuals who remained found a city of oppressive silence. Moreover, the damage wrought by the war (with a total loss of Ch. $30 billion and 73.5 percent of all Chinese-owned factories destroyed)[24] and the large flow of refugees into the city since 1937 gave rise to widespread unemployment and acute shortages of housing and food. No one was as forceful in articulating the pessimism prevalent among intellectuals during the early months of the Occupation as the editor Ke Ling, who created a vivid parallel by juxtaposing two stock phrases, "No gate to save the nation, no path to survival" (*Jiuguo wumen, qiusheng wulu*).[25]

The situation became less bleak by January 1938. Resistance movements began to take shape, and there was the related rise of foreign-published newspapers and Resistance theater. Both the Nationalists and the Communists in Shanghai made important contributions to this breakthrough. Aside from the underground Nationalist agencies, as noted in Chapter 1, the CCP Jiangsu Provincial Committee (founded in November 1937 under Liu Xiao, Liu Changsheng, and Zhang Aiping) operated a clandestine cell in the Gudao. With a membership of about 100 in 1938, and working closely with the Eighth Route Army Office (under Liu Shaowen), its main purpose was to take advantage of the United Front to mobilize the Shanghai populace as covertly as possible for continued resistance (as well as to support the New Fourth Army in Anhui). Much of the work was propaganda, which fell to its cultural committee, led by Sha Wenhan and Sun Yefang, later to be an eminent economist.[26]

One mobilization strategy the Communist literary organizers discovered, probably inspired by the success of street drama as propaganda during the battle of Shanghai, was the use of *huaju*. As Eric

Bentley points out, unlike other art forms, theater is a powerful form of presentation: enactment before an audience. It lends itself to demagogy.[27] The ritual of performance, which involves the gathering of a large audience, an intense relation of dialogue between spectator and spectacle, a collective venture in production, and a complex dramaturgy that gives the events represented a more urgent reality, makes theater what Sartre aptly describes as "a great collective, religious phenomenon."[28] Done competently, drama can call forth "a maximum of eloquence and magic from those in charge," and the highly charged response of the audience in turn affirms the actors on stage. Theatrical engagement can, in sum, become a political demonstration without a political meeting. This was what it achieved in Europe under the Nazi Occupation; and what Resistance theater aspired to in Shanghai.[29]

Unlike its counterparts in occupied Europe, Resistance theater in Shanghai got off to a difficult start, relying on the immature and foreign-inspired *huaju* genre. Nonetheless, as we shall see, the political and social conditions of the Occupation brought it unprecedented popularity as the war wore on. In December 1937, the Communists Yu Ling and A Ying, both famous playwrights and senior members of the CCP's cultural committee, started the Qingniao jushe (Blue Bird Dramatic Society), an amateur group made up largely of members of the two dramatic troupes of the Shanghai xiju jie jiuwang xiehui who had not traveled inland (including Xu Xingzhi and Li Bolong, a Shanghai Municipal Government Chinese Employees' Club theater activist).[30]

The Qingniao jushe did not last long. After presenting a few shows (including Cao Yu's *Thunderstorm*) in January 1938, all in different theaters in the International Settlement, it closed down because of personal squabbling (typical of modern Chinese letters), and political dissension within the group, as well as terrorist bomb threats (one bomb was actually found inside the auditorium of the Xinguang Theater where the Qingniao jushe was scheduled to perform the next day).[31]

Some Qingniao jushe members, especially Yu Ling, insisted on the political imperative of putting on *huaju* as a means of resistance, however, and in early 1938 they went on to found another group. This was the Shanghai yishu juyuan (Shanghai Arts Theater). Among its members were Gu Zhongyi and Zhu Duanjun, both professors at Fudan University and amateur dramatists. After putting on one benefit performance for refugee children at the Lyceum Theater, on Rue Bourget, and while rehearsing for the second show, Li Jianwu's *Sahuang shijia* (an adaptation of William Clyde Fitch's *Truth*), however, the group was "expelled" by the French Municipal Government, which cited security reasons. It too thereupon dissolved,[32] but Yu Ling did not give up. With his characteristic tenacity and resourcefulness, he built up another group, the Shanghai juyishe (Shanghai Dramatic Arts Society). Its founding demonstrated the GMD-CCP united front in action, and it soon became the leading Resistance theater in the Gudao.

After failing to gain permission to perform in the International Settlement, the Shanghai juyishe applied for registration with the French Municipal Council to operate within its precinct, where most Nationalist agencies including the Central News Agency and the Propaganda Department had secretly relocated after the fall of Greater Shanghai. Its application was rejected, however, and the Shanghai juyishe was ordered expelled.

Inspired by the foreign-published press's success in surviving under the nominal protection of Western publishers (which began to emerge in January 1938 with *Wenhui bao*), however, Yu sought help from his senior colleague Liu Shaowen, an expert in "making friends" with the upper class, who in turn introduced him to Chinese directors of the Zhongfa lianyihui (Sino-French Friendship Club) like Zhao Zhiyou and Chu Minyi, who were affiliated with the Nationalist leaders. In July 1938 the Shanghai juyishe was thus officially registered as a subsidiary of the club, and to ensure its financial viability, Yu Ling enlisted the help of Cai Shuhou, a big entrepreneur and a secret CCP member, in securing bank loans and providing security for renting theaters.[33]

The Shanghai juyishe was a semi-professional company, but it brought together practically all the important playwrights and artists remaining in the Solitary Island. Its leading members, besides Yu Ling, included such famous dramatists as A Ying, Gu Zhongyi, Zhu Duanjun, Chen Xihe, Wu Rengzhi, and Hong Mo (a fellow traveler who enjoyed close ties with both the Nationalist and foreign areas police). In its pronouncements, the society proclaimed itself to be an educational organization devoted to the furthering of Sino-French cultural relations.[34] But its real intent was political. According to Gu Zhongyi, whose 1948 memoir remains the best source of information about wartime *huaju*, all its founders agreed that the theater should constitute a propaganda movement, working hand in hand with the national Resistance, that would serve to mobilize the Shanghai public to oppose the Occupation.[35]

Resistance theater in occupied Shanghai was plagued from its outset by both political and professional problems. Japanese terrorism—political assassinations, bombings, and threatening letters—had menaced activists since early 1938. Moreover, they could find no theaters in which to perform on a permanent basis and were short of money. They were also subject to harassing censorship by the foreign areas authorities, who imposed stringent registration requirements, including submission of scripts in translation for prior examination and permission before each performance. After 1938, censors even came to performances to check on content. No reference to anti-Japanese agitation was tolerated, under penalty of expulsion of the group in question from the foreign settlements.

Implementing *huaju*'s patriotic agenda under such circumstances called for tactical ingenuity,[36] and Li Jianwu, a founding member of the Shanghai juyishe, was one of the major figures involved in building the Resistance theater against these odds.

From "Spiritual Rebellion" to "Mythless Heroism"

After the Occupation, Li continued teaching at Jinan. Owing to severe cutbacks, which were prevalent at all universities in wartime Shanghai, the job did not provide him with a secure means of livelihood. So Li also taught part-time at Fudan University and held a research fellowship at the Zhongfa yanjiusuo (Institute of Sino-French Studies), where he was responsible for writing a history of French literature. He worked hard and continued, as in 1935 and 1936, to teach, to translate, and to write about Flaubert.[37] With these different jobs, he managed to give his family a decent life. But the shame of *tousheng* (ignoble existence) under foreign domination, rather than following the government into the harsh southwest (which then represented the motherland) confronted him with pointed questions:

am I loyal? am I a coward? and am I self-indulgent? Like many guilt-ridden intellectuals, such as Ke Ling, who defined writing in terms of "fulfilling human responsibility,"[38] Li responded by justifying survival under Japanese Occupation as a challenge, a test of moral character: living through it was what Confucius had said of a *junzi* (gentleman), *gu qiong* ([being] steadfast in hardship).

Consistent with this attitude was a tendency to be moralistic: everything was viewed in terms of moral condition. Thus when his two daughters, aged four and two respectively, suffered from high fever for several weeks in 1938, Li railed against what he called the "Twisted-branch Plum Syndrome" (*wanzhi meihua bing*) of people living in Gudao. Plum, a stock metaphor for China, was here twisted and withered in foreign surroundings devoid of freedom and vitality, the distinguishing features of his romanticized view of the Chinese-controlled interior. And illness took on the symbolic meaning of moral weakness. Together they invoked the image of a city dying of corruption and deprivation.[39]

If he did not want to remain a "weakling," useless and ashamed, and to get "sick," the alternative was action. To resist was at once existential and political. Existential because resistance freed one from moral anguish and degeneration; political because it liberated Shanghai, along with assuring China's victory. It was thus an act both of self-liberation and of national autonomy: "We ought to put our lives on the line and win back the freedom of our land in order to become men who are sound and strong, real men who are moving toward a better life in every area of their lives," Li wrote in 1938.[40]

This juxtapostion of patriotism and freedom explained Li's decision to resist;[41] and indeed he joined the Resistance without a specific ideology. What he committed to was only a vision of personal dignity and moral defiance, as articulated in his new definition of heroism. As discussed above, his disillusionment with his childhood idols, all larger than life but finally destroyed by life, led him to reinvent heroism in the "kingdom of art." Like Huang Tianli in *Shisan nian* or the police chief's wife in *Zhe buguo shi chuntian*, the heroes they represented were smaller than life, and were even detestable characters, but through their courage in facing the "final test" they transcended themselves. These dramatic creations found close proximity, or indeed fulfillment, in actual people and historical events in 1937.

During the Battle of Shanghai, almost at the same time as Li heard of the collaboration of one of his childhood heroes, now a village headman, he read about the martyrdom of his former classmate Niu Xiaoshan. The son of a migrant laborer who grew up to become a poor farmhand himself, Niu had long lived in humiliation. Because of his ugliness, his low class background and his apparent timidity, everyone including the young Li ridiculed him and enjoyed throwing dung at him as he cowered in frenzy to avoid the attacks. Yet he died in honor when he was shot after blowing up a strategic bridge and killing many Japanese. He had joined the army out of a vague sense of patriotism and because it offered him an opportunity to escape from the economic oppression of tenancy. To Li, his martyrdom "illuminated" his whole life as well as everyone in the village. It was this self-transcending patriotism that in Li's projection epitomized the true meaning of heroism. Reflecting the new age of "a gray and firm reality," the martyr was a "hero, but without name, without myth." He was mythless because up till his final moment of defiance he was as weak and colorless as (if not worse than) anyone else. Here Li's art seemed to fuse with history, and reality was more powerful than imagination. Indeed, more than his own fictional characters who similarly redeemed themselves as they grasped their "last chance to shine through," the mythless heroes were fighting for an ideal, and they fought with strength and dignity. According to Li, they were the very stuff of Chinese culture, a culture full of heroic deeds and aspirations. China would win the war. "I am now reading a great historical fiction. It is not about the past; it is our own age. I almost miss that [heroism without myth]."[42] The image of hero as a social victim also served Li well as a metaphor of self-justification. In the long-suffering, humiliated tenant could be seen an analogy to the situation of Chinese intellectuals in occupied Shanghai. Living under the shame of foreign domination, only their strength of commitment, their courage to rebel—to fight for freedom and human dignity—would redeem and affirm their own worth while at the same time contributing to the liberation of China. No longer escaping into the "kingdom of art" for solace, Li now saw himself confronting his "final test" of moral defiance in the image of his mythless heroes.

Li's philosophic stance and psychological outlook in some ways reflected the prevailing mood and feel of intellectual resistance in Shanghai. Permeating their highly ideological discourse was a moralistic tone, characterized by an outlook Paul Fussell terms the "versus habit." Confronted by an extreme situation where the pressure for compromise was pervasive, the resisters perceived their world as a Manichean universe, whose denizens were either human beings or beasts. It was a world that pitted total virtue against total evil. Ambivalence or ambiguity were utterly impossible in this limited field of perception. As the Communist critic Ba Ren declared: "Neutrality and aloofness are but alibis for surrender and selling out.... Those who resist, come here; those who collaborate, go there! Only when the two sides are clear can we fight on."[43]

Resistance writers of both the left and the right strove to dehumanize their enemies by drawing on the traditional lexicon of traitorous behavior and, on this basis, to set the agenda of purification. They characterized collaborators as demonic spirits, trash, and scum. The Chinese word for collaborators is *hanjian*. Its etymology goes back to Ming times (1368–1644), denoting a person so irredeemably subhuman as to forfeit all claim to being Chinese. Hence Wang Jingwei, the quintessential *hanjian* became an archtype of such degeneracy. And intellectuals serving him were all "prostitutes," soulless and shameless.[44]

Dehumanizing the "others" served to enhance "our" humanity. Resistance intellectuals defined human dignity largely within the Mencian framework of *haoran zhengqi* (natural spiritual élan). This perception appropriated the whole Neo-Confucian discourse of *zhongyi* (loyalty), *qijie* (moral integrity), and *qingcao* (sentiment)— terms that symbolized the inner freedom of individuals to pursue moral ideals at times of crisis. Consonant with this stance was an attack on greed, selfishness, and egoism. In this state of mind, resisters tended to conceive of the Occupation as above all a test of humanity. Those who passed it acquired dignity, and those who failed were beasts. Involved were both redemption and damnation. The resisters' task, then, was to inspire and lead the Shanghai public through this trial by constantly subjecting themselves to self-purification. A man/ hero would be born in this cleansing "furnace."[45]

The realization that the war would be a protracted one, coupled with the romanticization of the quiet tenacity of the peasantry by writers of both right and left gave impetus to ideas of collective struggle and survival. Thus, traditional values were reinterpreted in a new context. The Neo-Confucian notion of moral self-assertion was celebrated within a collectivist framework. As the Communist critic Ba Ren asserted: "Loyalty is defined not as an ethical obligation to any individual ruler, but rather to the nation. Filial piety is also not defined as an obligation to one's parents, but to the race as a whole. So if anyone ever runs counter to the benefit of the nation-race...we have to oppose and to eliminate [zhicai] him in the very name of loyalty and filial piety. This is the ethical grounding of collectivism." It was this emphasis on party politics and the collective imperative that, as we shall see, set Li's conception of "mythless heroism" apart from the beliefs of many of his comrades.[46]

This vision of the war and its attendant call for collective heroism was not limited to the Shanghai intellectual resisters. Chinese-controlled areas experienced a similar climate of thought, albeit with less overt concern about the trial of loyalty. This morally charged mode of feeling and thinking was best captured in the play Tuibian (Metamorphosis) by Cao Yu, a good friend of Li's. Although Cao was then living in Guilin, the play was staged in Shanghai. In its preface, which was to be repeatedly paraphrased by Shanghai writers, Cao proclaimed: "This chapter of blood-written history consists of numerous heroic and painful facts, which profoundly bespeak the difficulties of our national warriors' struggle, and the moan and groan of the corrupted class that is in the process of being eliminated."[47] Both the Nationalist and Communist leaderships, to varying degrees and with different emphases, made concerted efforts to formulate and popularize the collectivist ideal. Chiang Kaishek's slogan "Resistance and Nation-building" and Mao Zedong's theory of "New Democracy," with their critique of individualism and reaffirmation of traditional morality, both widely publicized in the Shanghai foreign-published press, exemplified such efforts.[48] This similarity of war rhetoric and moralistic tone helped created a unifying discourse that, along with other material and military connections,[49] strengthened the emotional, psychological, and political bonds between Shanghai and the national Resistance. As some of the Shanghai intellectuals aptly put it, Shanghai, the Solitary Island, was not solitary (*gudao bugu*); rather it was part of Free China. Indeed, there were constant contacts between intellectuals of the two zones. Cao Yu introduced the director Huang Zuolin to Li when he moved to Shanghai from Chongqing, for example, and Mao Dun sent all the manuscripts for his *Wenzhen* (Literary Front) to his brother-in-law in Shanghai, the essayist Kong Lingjing, via Hong Kong. After being printed, the magazines were to be shipped back to the interior.[50]

It was within this symbolic framework of patriotic commitment that Li, together with other Shanghai playwrights, sought to inspire the public to hold on to their fight for freedom, both national and individual.

The Past As Metaphor: Theater of Heroism

With his command of French and experience in drama, Li played an important role in the Shanghai juyishe in shaping *huaju* into a spectacle of patriotic commitment. He became involved through an intricate network of personal connections. After the fall of Greater Shanghai, besides renewing his contact with Wang Tongzhao at Jinan, he paid regular visits to Zheng Zhenduo, whose Yuyuan Road home was the hub of social and political life for patriotic liberal intellectuals. There, Li met A Ying, Xia Yan, Huang Xindi (a London-trained poet, whose father-in-law, Xu Shenyu, was then working closely with Zheng in acquiring rare books), and the dramatist Chen Xihe, who had recently returned from France. When Xia and A Ying wanted to launch a magazine in late 1937 on behalf of the CCP, they asked and were permitted by Li to use his penname, Liu Xiwei, for registration. This magazine was *Lisao* (Encountering Sorrow), in which Li published his article on mythless heroism, but it was suppressed after just one issue.[51] Still, the hitherto apolitical and unknown Li began to attract notice among the literary officials of the CCP, who were now open to a broad range of ideological alternatives, owing partly to the united front, and partly to the paucity of literary people still in occupied Shanghai.

In January 1938, when Yu Ling was trying to organize a new theater group, he hosted a party at the small Jinjiang Teahouse, a literary hangout at the intersection of Route Voyron and Avenue Joffre, for the remaining theater people in Gudao. Li was invited by his favorite student, Zhang Ke, a CCP activist who worked closely with Yu's wife, Bo Li, a Communist actress. It was at this party that the Shanghai yishu juyuan was born, launching Li's career in the Resistance theater.[52] But the new group was soon suppressed.

Indeed, from the very beginning, the major problems the Shanghai *kangzhan ju* faced, aside from the lack of permanent theater spaces and good scripts, were how to deal with Japanese terrorism and continual censorship by the foreign areas police.

To dodge these restraints, the Shanghai juyishe, the successor to the Shanghai yishu juyuan, sought to take advantage of its semi-official status. It was Li who wrote the application in French that won it approval in July 1938 (see above) as a wing of the Sino-French Friendship Club. In this capacity, it was allowed to present its first public performances in the French Municipal Council Auditorium free of charge by producing French masterpieces for the benefit of refugees. To most of the Shanghai juyishe's activists, however, in spite of the oppressive condition, it was their "human responsibility" to resist, producing "meaningful plays."

Hence one of the first performances was Romain Roland's *Le Jeu de l'Amour et de la Mort*, which was translated by Li Jianwu in October 1938 as *Ai yu si de bodou* (The struggle between Love and Death).[53] As he later remembered, he had been troubled by a correct translation of *jeu* (game); the correct Chinese translation is *youxi*, but Yu Ling persuaded him to change the word to "struggle" in order to highlight the play's political message.[54] Directed by the leftist Xu Xingzhi with the assistance of Chen Xihe, and starring Lan Lan and Zhang Jie, this play of revolution was reworked into a plea for self-transcendence. The translator aimed the play's main thrust at what he deemed the prevalent mood of despair and apathy in occupied Shanghai. He spoke of the mind of the Resistance when he proclaimed: "Yes, we live to struggle. The biggest enemy is no one but ourselves.... We are acting, and what we want is strength."[55]

The "strength" Li hoped to arouse in the audience was the

courage to struggle against one's inner limitations. Contrary to his prewar cynicism, he now found in Roland's play a celebration of the "unlimited hopefulness of human nature," a resonance with the Mencian imperative of moral assertion: "We live to struggle, and the greatest enemy is no one but ourselves."[56] In fact, he and other Shanghai resisters took the moral high ground by condemning others who, in those depressing times, wrote or produced "corrupted art" for money. They railed against these works—pornographic novels and apolitical movies—as creating a world of pusillanimous fantasy, "forgetting the War, forgetting the motherland," which helped to "pollute" the public's mind and sapped patriotic zeal. These works were expressions of moral irresponsibility, symptomatic of the "Twisted-branch Plum Syndrome" prevalent in Shanghai.[57]

Li's message was not missed by his fellow resisters. Ke Ling, for example, praised the translation and agreed that "at times of crisis like ours, we should subject ourselves to more stringent self-examination."[58] Wang Tongzhao, who went to see the play at Li's invitation, was so moved that he wrote a poem to celebrate the power of moral engagement. Even the French commissioner of education, Gnoisbois, was deeply impressed by the performance and went backstage to congratulate the cast, awarding them Ch. $200. Li was also soon invited to serve on the jury for the French Municipal Council's first Best French Translation prize, along with Yu Ling and Gu Zhongyi (the prize went, incidentally, to Zhao Zhiyou, head of the Sino-French Friendship Association).[59]

Ai yu si de bodou was not, however, a box office success at the time.[60] The idealistic and didactic message, intellectualized language and Western form (e.g., performers in French costumes) alienated the audience. It remained an intellectual excitement. For fun and entertainment after a day of stress, most people preferred, as before the war, to listen to storytellers at teahouses, or go to traditional opera, or the modern cinema, which was dominated by Hollywood motion pictures.[61] Their priority was survival. Reading foreign-published newspapers in private, grumbling about the difficulties of life in Shanghai, and sharing news or rumors of the war while queuing for rice or lunching at food stalls and restaurants were the sole outlets for their patriotism.[62]

While many writers continued to rail against apolitical cinema and "pornographic literature" for their "polluting" effects, some dramatists, in quest of a wider audience, began to search for a new representational language that would accommodate *huaju* to popular taste.[63] Following the Communist call for "Chinese style" (*Zhongguo qipai*) in art and literature in connection with the need for patriotic mobilization, Shanghai intellectuls blamed the "foreign form" of drama for their box office failures, and, with their revolutionary populist vision, identified Chinese style with popular culture.[64] But the resisters' attitude toward popular culture was purely ideological and utilitarian. Analogous to the historical practice of cultural elites appropriating popular entertainment forms for didactic purposes, they were to inject anti-Japanese nationalism into traditional formulas. One playwright called the approach "placing pedagogy within entertainment" (*yu jiaoyu yu yule*).[65] Hence from early 1939 on, Resistance theater started experimenting with various forms of the traditional performing arts and found inspiration for its subject matter in historical stories and figures that had long been part of the public's world of symbolic meaning.

One of the first playwrights to venture into this field was Li Jianwu. He was probably encouraged by the discussions among resistance writers and artists. Like Wang Tongzhao and the other passivists discussed in Chapter 1, intellectual resisters in Shanghai had their own "social site," a sequestered, intricate network of support and literary connections through which they could define and articulate their "hidden transcript" against oppression.[66] To evade Japanese suppression, they formed luncheon clubs, meeting once every week at the YMCA or YWCA, or they met irregularly in restaurants, street-corner cafes, private homes (often during mah-jongg games), and public bathhouses, and occasionally at birthday parties, marriage receptions, or funerals. Many young leftists also formed study groups at schools or offices, secretly and passionately discussing Lu Xun and the Communist base areas represented in *Red Star over China*.[67]

One of these discussion groups was held among playwrights of the Shanghai *juyishe*, which as an "experimental playhouse" managed to get a short-term contract to perform between 10 and 12 A.M. on Sundays in the Xinguang Theater, a small, seedy movie house on

Rue de Ningbo, from March to June 1939. They staged 1930s plays like Li's *Zhe buguo shi chuntian* and Yu Ling's *Nüzi gongyu* (Woman's dormitory), which were at least less Westernized in content than the French classics. The turnout was unsatisfactory, even though admission was only Ch. $0.60 ($1–2 less than a first-run movie ticket).[68] Financial difficulties continually threatened the Shanghai juyishe's survival. Writers and artists active in the Resistance theater, many of them Communists, gathered together backstage at the Xingguang or at restaurants or private homes after each weekly show to discuss ways to popularize *huaju*. Thus theatrical reform became as much a survival technique as a political necessity to the resisters.

It is therefore likely that Li got the idea of borrowing from popular entertainment forms for patriotic purposes from these discussions. Based on the Song-Yuan "southern play" style (*Nanxi*), he wrote the first part of *Fanma ji* (Horse-trading) in eight acts (*zhe*) in 1939. Unlike his prewar dramatic works, which are all impressionist in the sense of centering on the mental life of the chief character rather than on the objective reality, and are mostly what Sartre terms "theater of situation," characterized by an economy of language and an emphasis on situational responses rather than on plot and characterization, the new play followed a clear narrative line based on the unilateral development of the hero, with little psychological exploration, and was full of martial action typical of traditional dramaturgy.[69] In this fictional rewriting of his father's life, as in *Ai yu si de bodou*, Li sought to transform a political tragedy into a celebration of individual assertion, an unyielding will to rebel. The hero, Gao Zhenyi, is a poor *xiucai* (licentiate) who leads a military insurgence into a Shaanxi township only to discover that the revolution is over. "I have to go somewhere else to search for the truth. We can't make the revolution like enjoying a game....I will go to the ends of the earth, even if it means my death, to search for my dream, to search for a truly free body for the Chinese Republic. The 1911 Revolution is not a success; it is essentially a failure," he proclaims at the end.[70] Here the parallels between the Manchus and the Japanese and the 1911 Revolution with the Battle of Shanghai are all too clear. And the "hidden" message of a failed revolution echoed the SWH's political vision (see Prologue): a "truly free" China would only be created through *bu tuoxie jingshen*, tenacious defiance.

Fanma ji ended up as another closet drama. Its incompleteness, its loose plot, its weak characterization, its trite symbolism—redeemed somewhat only by Li's characteristically witty dialogues and evocative scene-setting—made it unstageable. Li had given a copy of the play to Ba Jin when he visited Shanghai in 1939, and Ba Jin later took the scripts with him to the interior, intending to publish it.[71] Although the play *Fanma ji* failed artistically, its experimentation with traditional stagecraft and its use of historical events as a political metaphor for the present situation marked a point of departure for Shanghai Resistance theater.[72]

Using the past as a metaphor for the present (*yi gu yu jin*), like imposing elite ideology upon popular culture, was a time-honored literary convention in China, widely practiced to evade political suppression. Educated in a culture that prized precedent and historical awareness, Chinese writers commonly drew parallels between past and present and textualized their political messages through the medium of historical allusion.[73] Along with the desire to make *huaju* accessible to the public, this appeal to history was the motive that spurred Li and his fellow playwrights to find dramatic expression in historical discourse. "Our circumstances give us no freedom of action," the dramatist Shu Yan explained. "History will not repeat itself, yet we should be aware of history's lessons. It is our task to magnify the points of similiarity between the past and present—the ethics of loyalty and the way we evaluate them."[74]

The metaphor of history itself, however, entailed a grammar of traditional values and imagery.[75] It is therefore no accident that the Resistance theater was fraught with traditional Chinese symbolism of loyalty—*zhongchen* (loyal ministers) and *lienü* (faithful women)—and glorified the stock virtues of *zhongyi* and *zhenjie* (fidelity). They invariably portrayed collaboration in such moralistic terms as *yinjian* (licentiousness) and *xialiu* (obscenity). The content itself was further mediated and tempered by a generally inept dramatics expressing the Resistance discourse of collective nationalism.

In August 1939, after months of negotiation, Yu Ling, the mastermind behind the Shanghai juyishe, arranged with a veteran secret Communist, Yang Zao, to rent his dance hall on Avenue Edward VII in the International Settlement for six months and remodeled it into a theater, the Xuangong. With relatively long-term command of a theater for the first time, the Shanghai juyishe proclaimed itself a professional company. The seven plays it staged from August to November 1939 (including Li Jianwu's *Zhe buguo shi chuntian* and Yu Ling's famous *Ye Shanghai* [Benighted Shanghai]), were mostly critically acclaimed but box office disasters. Attendance was in general as poor as 20 to 30 percent of seating capacity. The commercial failure engendered a huge debt for the Shanghai juyishe, and cancellation of its contract was threatened.[76]

These failures were followed by the unanticipated success of A Ying's experimental costume play *Bixue hua* (Flower of blood) in November 1939, which filled the Xuangong for over 35 days. For the first time in *huaju*'s history, all seats had to be reserved three days in advance. The immense popularity of the play stemmed largely from its simple moral theme and skillful juxtaposition of historical metaphor and modern sensibility. It also attracted playgoers by using the familiar title of a recent Beijing opera hit, *Mingmo yihen* (Sorrow of the Late Ming), to confuse the censors.[77] In addition, its production was a truly collective effort. A Ying, Gu Zhongyi, Wu Renzhi, Yu Ling, and Li Jianwu all helped with the direction (the director was A Ying's close friend, the leftist Wu Yonggang), while the whole cast, including the veteran actress Tang Ruoqing and the upcoming star Tu Guangqi, was passionately involved on the stage.[78]

Inspired by the story of the late Ming heroine Li Xianjun as portrayed in Ouyang Yuqian's contemporary Beijing opera *Mingmo yihen*, A Ying's *Bixue hua* is essentially a dramatized exposition of the Neo-Confucian doctrine of fidelity: *Lienü bu erfu, zhongchen bu erzhu* (Faithful women marry only one husband, loyal ministers serve only one master), in which the parallel between the past and present is symbolically drawn.[79]

Bixue hua is about a tragic situation analogous to that of occupied Shanghai. Centered around the life of a circle of literati and courtesans in Nanjing during the last days of the Ming dynasty, it portrays a polarized response to the crisis. The dramatis personae, as in traditional narration, are stereotyped, and their dialogue is made up of clichés or set phrases drawn from the Confucian lexicon. The unyielding integrity of Sun Kexian (Shu Yan) and his mistress Ge Nenniang (Tang Ruoqing), a famous courtesan, is set against the greed and selfishness of a traitorous Chinese couple and the lamentable passivity of two friends who vow to maintain their loyalty by with-drawal. In the climactic scene, after their capture in the wake of a failed attempt at armed resistance, Sun is executed for refusing to surrender, and Ge, after condemning the collaborator Cai Ruheng (Tu Guangqi), kills herself in order to maintain her fidelity. Their heroic self-transcendence, which they express in the famous Neo-Confucian dictum *Shijie shida* (Loss of integrity is exceedingly seri-ous), affirms their human values. As a counter to the personal trag-edy, A Ying gives the play an optimistic ending, implying that the occupation of Nanjing (read Shanghai) will soon end, because the militia (the New Fourth Army) is approaching.[80]

The sensational subjects of love and death and faithfulness in the play, all familiar themes presented in a traditional form, captured the imagination of the audience. The dramatic images invoked indigna-tion at the terror of the Occupation and a means for the audience to vent their patriotism. According to Ke Ling, many men and women who were new to *huaju* so identified with it that they cried or cursed on seeing the suicide of Ge Nenniang and hearing her curse Cai Ruheng and the Manchu general Bolo as "beasts." At the same time, the audience's passion raised the morale of the Shanghai juyishe. Holding each other's hands backstage, all its members felt a height-ened sense of solidarity and fulfillment; many movie stars and Beijing opera singers joined the production. The great success of the play, however, brought about its suppression.

Under Japanese pressure, the Shanghai Municipal Police demanded changes, and A Ying consequently made eight revisions. But in per-formance, the company continued to use the original version. When the censors made surprise visits to the theater, the performers simply switched to the revised script. The censors were also plied with ciga-rettes and cakes, both expensive items, to keep them from watching the play too closely. And on one occasion, a group of young uni-formed Japanese appeared in the auditorium and took all the front seats. The company refused to cancel the show as the theater owners suggested, however, and the performance became even more intense with these "Manchus" sitting in front. The audience went wild, and soon afterward the play was banned.[81]

Following the success of *Bixue hua* came a flurry of historical dra-mas. This phenomenon was as much a result of commercial necessity

as of "trendiness," which some critics readily railed against as characteristic of the Shanghai literary world. In December 1939, the Shanghai juyishe moved to the Lafayette Theater, a small and isolated
venue on Rue Lafayette in the French Concession, and staged the
popular French play *Patrie!* by Victorien Sardou. Despite all the
money and energy invested in the production, it was a box office
disaster.[82] So the society turned again to Chinese costume drama.
Among the 27 plays it staged between 1940 and 1941, as listed by
Gu Zhongyi, about half were historical.[83] And two of them, Wu Zuguang's *Zhengqi ge* (Song of uprightness) and Yang Hansheng's *Li Xiucheng zhi si* (The Death of Li Xiucheng), both originally written
in the interior, drew full houses for over a month.[84] These historical dramas were all *pièces à thèse*, exploring the familiar virtues of
heroic loyalty and self-sacrifice, varying only in matters of stress—
some opting for loyal ministers, some for chaste widows, and some
for both.[85]

Some Shanghai intellectuals, however, were ambivalent about
the political relevance of costume dramas. Although recognizing their
wide appeal, they expressed misgivings that the stress on the past,
and its portrayal of loyalists and faithful women, imparted a "de-
featist" view and "feudal" attitude to the public. Instead, they called
for a "realistic" approach, with which playwrights would strive to illustrate the present political and social evils of occupied Shanghai. In
the name of immortalizing "the era of Gudao," some critics advo-
cated tackling such "immediately relevant" subjects as rice prices,
high rents, and speculation.[86]

Li Jianwu was likewise ambivalent about historical plays. In artistic terms, he saw no difference between a costume drama and
a modern play. He adhered to the impressionist distinction between "reality" and "actuality," "essence" and "phenomenon," and
attached great importance to the philosophical import of textualization. Hence, to him, a "realistic" play was one in which, regardless
of its form or subject matter, the author succeeded in capturing the
"eternal truth" and representing it in a delicate, authentic language
that would inspire humans to transcend themselves.[87]

Ideologically, however, Li was repelled by the anti-individualist
tendency of the historical drama. Consonant with Resistance rhetoric, its stress on the Neo-Confucian virtues of loyalty and chastity,

although they were now situated within a new discourse of revolutionary nationalism, was in conflict with the May Fourth ethos of moral autonomy and critical reason, which was so much a part of the liberal-humanistic tradition with which Li identified himself. Indeed, he came under fire between 1939 and 1941 for his undue respect for artistic individuality. "[Li] is a supporter of the old society, and he is a preacher of rotten ideas," one writer, Ouyang Wenpu, wrote of his impressionist criticism, which he called "the critic's subjective response to a literary work." [88] Li's prewar plays, *Zhe buguo shi chuntian* and *Shisan nian*, with their refined prose and sensitive portrayal of human weaknesses, were singled out by some young resisters as examples of what is meant by "art for art's sake." They were, in brief, "irrelevant" to the War of Resistance. [89]

Yu Ling and Ba Ren, both senior Communists responsible for the united front policy in cultural circles, occasionally had good things to say about Li. [90] But Li knew that he was tolerated, rather than accepted, in the Resistance theater. He was in a minority. "The dramatic movement in Gudao opens its door wide, anyone can come in as long as they take the same line," he once said, describing his situation. "My so-called artistic stand is a headache to everyone. Yet they keep me in and no one [tries to] kick me out." [91] At times he became so annoyed that he returned blows, railing at his critics: "Aren't those great writers of chanted slogans also 'Twisted-branch Plums' waiting in the market to be sold for the right price?" [92] Still he felt constantly compelled to justify his literary and political views.

In 1940 Li wrote several essays to clarify his view of artistic autonomy. Invoking the authority of such French neo-romanticists as Jules Lemaître and Anatole France, he claimed as in prewar times that artists, including literary critics, were by definition individualists. They projected their individualities in and through their works. "What is the use of objectivity?" Li explained to his readers. "Everyone has his own interpretation of [life], and no one has any claim to truth. Why? It is because everyone is an individual self." Literary creation (including especially criticism) was therefore an expression of critical subjectivity. [93] But Li's sense of moral engagement after 1937 gave him a new definition of subjectivity. Like his good friends Wang Tongzhao and Zheng Zhenduo, and like Sartre or Marc Bloch in occupied France, he now elevated collective moralism to the status of "universal maxims."[94] Assuming that human beings were bound by "a shared sense of justice," he redefined the self rather vaguely as an entity of critical empathy. "It was not a selfish entity, neither sentimental nor frivolous...but rather it is a possible focus of all realities, and a concrete, specific small universe."[95] It was a small universe, in other words, determined by and responsive to history. In this perspective, contrary to his prewar apoliticism, he equated individualistic existence with tenacious defiance. A true individualist, he proclaimed, was, like Lu Xun or Balzac or Flaubert, fiercely "independent," listened to no one but his own inner voice, and was steadfastly committed to fight for justice. The individualist lived for humanity's sake, and he revered his own freedom as much as he respected that of others. Thus, as long as a writer "lives for the noble dream common to all humans" and "knows what he is doing," Li appealed to his critics, "we should then give him the rights of creative freedom."[96]

This appeal perhaps evoked only more suspicion among militants. So if Li had moved out from his anonymity after the occupation of Shanghai, he moved only to the sidelines of the literary stage. Indeed, until 1942, Li wrote little, and only his translation of *Le Jeu de l'Amour et de la Mort* attracted much notice. He also joined no political organization save the Shanghai juyishe. Even there, he seemed to play a respectable but not a leading role. They needed his talent but not his ideas. Li continued to devote most of his time to his family, teaching, and academic research. Aside from going to occasional rehearsals and production meetings, he remained very much a scholar in his social life; he found the company of academics (especially Chen Xihe, Chen Linrui, a Jinan literature professor, son-in-law of the famous anti-Manchu poet Liu Yazi, and Yang Jiang, the brilliant scholar-writer Qian Zhongshu's wife, another student of Wang Wenxian's) more congenial than that of militants, and he was busy supporting his former mentors—Wang Wenxian was now teaching at Shanghai's St. John's University, while Zhu Ziqing (who had moved to the interior) had entrusted his family in Shanghai to the care of Li.[97]

Despite Li's ambivalence, the success of costume plays, which the Japanese lumped together with foreign-published newspapers in the hostile category of "Foreign Settlements literature," led to an increase in the popularity of Resistance theater. The quick rise of amateur theater provided an index to such popularity. Since late 1938, *huaju* had become fashionable among the patriotic youth of Shanghai. Many amateur acting troupes grew out of schools and trade and public organizations. They chiefly performed one-act agitprop plays for a limited circle of friends and colleagues and were thus restricted mainly to the reaffirmation of patriotic fellowship. In order to become more effective in the Resistance movement, many troupes were brought together under the Shanghai xiju jiaoyishe (Shanghai Theater Friendship Club), a confederation organized by the CCP's cultural committee. By 1940, the club claimed a total of 120 participants. Working closely with the Shanghai juyishe, which theater people then called *da juchang* (large theater) to distinguish it from amateur groups (known as *xiao juchang*, or small theater), the club brought all these inexperienced troupes together, provided them with training in dramatics, supplied them with directors or scripts or costumes if needed, and arranged for them to perform every Sunday from 10 to 12 A.M. in theaters like the Lafayette, Xinguang, Lyceum, and Carlton, so that they could reach beyond their limited audiences.

With these institutional arrangements, amateurs and professionals met regularly, and each group brought to the other its experience and audience. From July 24 to July 30, 1939, for example, the club organized a six-day charity show involving almost twenty performances, with the participation of eleven amateur troupes (over 300 people). This large-scale performance was hailed as a "historic event" in Chinese theater and part of the take was secretly presented by the organizers, Li Bolong and Zhang Jusheng, both formerly involved with the Ant Society, to Liu Shaowen for the New Fourth Army. On the last day, to applaud the success, all Shanghai's major dramatists joined the participants for a morning of celebration at the Huangjin theater on Rue Consulat, including Li Jianwu, who, as if trying to distinguish himself from other militants, gave a scholarly lecture on Chekhov's stagecraft. According to one observer: "All the people attending encouraged one another to persist in the fight for Resistance theater, and the whole hall was filled with a lively spirit of comradeship." This kind of affecting camaraderie gave the Shanghai Resistance theater a sense of patriotic solidarity and an emotional intensity of performance that brought the audience to its feet several times.[98]

In March 1941, before they fled to Hong Kong because of increasing Japanese persecution, Yu Ling and Ba Ren came to bid farewell to Li and asked him to be more active in the Shanghai juyishe. Hard at work on his research project with the Institute of Sino-French Studies, however, and (probably) still resenting the ideological intolerance of his colleagues, Li rarely went there. He was soon to regret this.[99]

In October 1941, Cao Yu's *Tuibian*, a popular play written in the interior about the rebirth of China, was performed by the Shanghai zhiye jutuan (Shanghai Professional Company), which was close to the Shanghai juyishe. Directed by Huang Zuolin, a British-trained dramatist who was initiated into Shanghai theater by Li, the play ran to full houses for a month. According to one witness, the whole audience applauded and chanted patriotic slogans when the hero declared: "China, China, you should be strong," while the people backstage cried and embraced one another with emotion. The play was banned in November.[100] The suppression was surely an omen of the future, as one month later, in December 1941, the Japanese army extended its military occupation into the foreign areas and, with the shutting down of the Shanghai juyishe, the Resistance theater was crushed.

Complete Occupation and the Rise of Commercial Theater

When the Japanese army entered the foreign areas on December 8, it closed down all theaters, along with foreign-published newspapers, and demanded submission of lists of members from different dramatic companies. Military sentries were set up all over the city, and residential areas deemed politically suspicious were sealed off for weeks. The military command required all resistance materials to be summarily surrendered, and the Japanese army planned a citywide census. All these policies fed the rumor of imminent suppression of political resistance. Indeed, Xu Guangping was arrested by the Kempeitai in December 1941 and released only in March 1942, after suffering torture. The clandestine CCP cell quickly moved out of Shanghai, while the GMD leaders left for Anhui, Zhejiang, or Chongqing; intellectuals affiliated with the two parties also fled to the interior or to Southeast Asia. All Resistance groups were dissolved.[101]

For those who could not leave Shanghai, life was dreary and dangerous. After being informed by the leftist writer Tang Tao of Xu's arrest, for instance, Zheng Zhenduo immediately moved out of his home. Thereafter he lived in constant fear. "I had a lot of nightmares. I was frightened even by cars just passing by," he later recalled. "Sometimes I felt as though I was constantly being followed, but I dared not look back. At other times, when someone stared at me on the bus or tramcar, I would immediately get off at the next stop."[102] Huai Jiu, another writer, articulated the experience in terms of a moral dilemma: "We had to endure contempt and insults while seeking to preserve our pitiable existence."[103]

Li Jianwu was one of those intellectuals. Jinan, Fudan, and the Zhongfa Research Institute were all closed down in protest in December 1941. Unemployed, Li was troubled by the conflict between his need to pursue his personal livelihood and to remain *qingbai* (morally pure). His lame leg and family obligations, again, as he explained, prevented him from undertaking the long journey with Jinan to the interior, where he had few personal connections. He might in fact have withdrawn into seclusion, as Wang Tongzhao and the Kaiming group did, if he had had the financial resources and institutional support they enjoyed.[104] How was he to find a job that would not compromise his dignity?

In early 1942, the famous May Fourth writer Zhou Zuoren, who was believed to have worked for the enemy, wrote Li and offered him an administrative post at the Japanese-controlled Beijing University. Li declined the offer; instead, along with his Shanghai *juyishe* colleagues Huang Zuolin and Zhu Duanjun, he found a job in the theater business.[105]

After several months of enforced silence, the Shanghai theater made itself heard again. The reemergence of *huaju* in 1942 resulted largely from the Japanese banning of Anglo-American movies. Only very old German and French films were now shown, along with Japanese pictures and some Chinese productions. And each show was preceded by fifteen minutes of dull Japanese propaganda newsreels.[106]

This would not do for an alienated, entertainment-starved public. In order to maintain a veneer of normality, the occupiers therefore loosened their control over the performing arts. Theaters were re-opened. At the same time, the collapse of the manufacturing economy after the Occupation led some entrepreneurs to shift their investments to entertainment. Already a highly profitable venture because of the prevailing escapist mood, show business became even more profitable when the Japanese centralized the Shanghai film industry under their direct control in 1943. Some cinema owners, for both commercial and political reasons, turned their properties into live theaters and organized drama companies themselves. Meanwhile, many movie people took up *huaju*. All these factors combined to produce a flourishing theater in occupied Shanghai.[107]

Unlike the drama movement during the Solitary Island period, however, *huaju* under complete Japanese Occupation was essentially a commercial enterprise. Entertainment and profits took command. The "commercialization" of *huaju* brought about an unprecedented growth in the Shanghai theater; many writers and artists found employment in this burgeoning industry.[108] Between 1942 and 1945, there were at different times over 30 full-time companies, 16 theaters, and a total of over 500 people involved in the dramatic professions.[109] And while the average attendance rate was about 40 percent of seating capacity, the most popular plays, Qin Shouou's *Qiuhaitang* (Begonia), in 1942, and *Fusheng liuji* (A drifting life), directed by Huang Zuolin in 1943, ran to full houses for over five and four months respectively.

This commercial success was nonetheless criticized by writers of varying political outlooks as a betrayal of the didactic and artistic tradition of *huaju*. They charged that it was a surrender to philistinism, being guided by rather than guiding society. As one critic demanded in a patriotic magazine: "Stop pleasing the audience and letting yourself be controlled by them. Otherwise [*huaju*] will sooner or later be eliminated."[110] The collaborationist official Zhou Yuren, on the other hand, condemned the commercial theater: "In recent years the theater has catered to the vulgar taste, aiming to attract only the lowbrow audience.... All the companies today are concerned only with profit, they have moved steadily away from art."[111]

What the patriotic critics seemed to overlook was the ironic fact that occupied Shanghai was a world in which apparently apolitical art could become potently political.[112] The systematic Japanese persecution rendered overt defiance highly perilous. The Japanese Kempeitai and the collaborationist secret police kept a close eye on intellectuals and regularly visited, detained, and tortured suspected ones in the name of "thought reform." So for safety's sake, Resistance theater had to camouflage itself in order to become an effective arm of combat.[113]

Li seems to have had this in mind when he asserted after the war, with slight exaggeration (in light of Ke Ling's popular magazine *Wanxiang*), that theater was the "only cultural artifact" independent of Japanese ideological control. Its openly profit-making orientation and apolitical thrust, in which it was again comparable to *Wanxiang*, shielded it from political intervention.[114] Nonetheless, he explained, under the guise of commercial art, patriotic dramatists "fought to maintain national purity...by actively instilling resistance consciousness into their plays."[115] And in fact this seems to be borne out by some of Li's plays, which in significant ways reflected the mood, the aspirations, and mode of representation of Resistance playwrights under complete Japanese occupation.

In early 1942, Li had joined the Rongwei Theater Company as a writer-director. The company was owned by the grandson of Huang Jinrong, one of Shanghai's legendary underworld leaders, but it went bankrupt after three months of unprofitable operation, and from then until 1945, Li worked for other theater companies, all with the financial backing of wealthy investors whose political connections were ambiguous. During these four years Li directed, acted in, and wrote many plays.[116] These jobs gave him a secure livelihood, but he was troubled by his new career in commercial theater and by the dubious background of many of these companies. For example, he was hired in late 1942 to co-head the performance committee of the Huayi jutuan (Chinese Art Company) but found out after a while that the man who financed it (Fu Rushan) enjoyed a close connection with the Japanese. Li thereupon quit and joined the Shanghai yiguang jutuan (Shanghai Arts Light Theater), which turned out to be well connected with the notorious Shimbunhan (Press Bureau) of the Japanese Expeditionary Army in Central China. Li left with other members when the connection was disclosed in 1943.[117] At times Li compared himself to Li Guinian, the famous court jester to the Tang dynasty emperor Xuanzhong (r. 712–55), who wrote to please, to entertain whoever patronized him. "I am an ordinary person, without political ambition, but with a conscience always needing to be put at ease," he declared. As he was to recall his decision to join the theater business in 1946, not without a hint of defensiveness, "I leapt down from the ivory tower. I made my living in the theater...just because I tried to make a few clean dollars so as to survive in the best possible way. I had become an ignoble thespian [xizi] despised by the gentry."[118]

Li found some solace in friendship and scholarship. "Theater had sustained my life, and it was my outside identity. But my regular job at my desk every day was actually translation."[119] Every morning, after helping his wife stand in line for food, he spent several hours translating Flaubert's novels, hoping to publish them after liberation. This anticipation gave him the optimism to survive the Occupation. He also became closer to his liberal friends, including Chen Xihe, Chen Linrui, and Yang Jiang, all of whom had also started writing plays for a livelihood, and Qian Zhongshu, who came to Shanghai from Kunming in 1941 to be reunited with his wife. These good friends supported and constantly entertained one another, having dinners at Chen's or Yang's houses on Avenue Joffre, which were just a few minutes' walk from Li's, or enjoying mutton hot pot and wine in cheap restaurants. They gossiped, shared jokes, discussed theater and Western literature, introduced one another's plays to theater companies, and exchanged literary gossip and war news. One day, Qian Zhongshu gave Li "a whole afternoon of happiness" by finding him a footnote he had been seeking for weeks. In this congenial atmosphere, from 1942 to 1945, Li finished the translation of *Madame Bovary*, *Trois contes*, and *L'Education sentimentale* and revised *La Tentation de Saint-Antoine* (which he had translated in 1936) and *Salammbô*.[120]

But the greatest challenge to Li was how to hold on to his moral defiance in the teeth of Japanese terror. Although he had not joined the reemergent *huaju* for political reasons ("I joined the theater to earn my living not to engage in underground resistance"),[121] his patriotism and his deep anxiety to live up to his father's image ("The stern, tragic face of my father haunted me all the time and gave me inspiration to live on")[122] soon confronted him with the question: How to turn the commercial theater into a "hidden transcript" of resistance?

With his personal charm, dramatic versatility, and writing skills, Li had become what one critic called "arguably the most respected figure, the leader of Shanghai theater."[123] He was nonetheless not happy with most of his theatrical works. They gave him little opportunity to express his artistic and patriotic ideals. He complained at times about his sense of frustration, his inability to write what he wanted. "The human being is a species distinguished by regret, always hoping to do what he cannot necessarily do."[124]

In order to produce more plays for performance and to sustain the commercial viability of *huaju*, Li translated many French "well-made plays" (including Sardou's *La Tosca, Fernande,* and *Fédora* and Beaumarchais's *Le Mariage de Figaro*) and also adapted bestselling novels by the celebrated popular writer Zhang Henshui like *Tixiao yinyuan* and *Manjiang Hong.* This was in line with the trend in Shanghai theater, which, according to Ke Ling, also an active playwright then, was dominated by adaptations (there were few original native plays), comedies, and historical melodramas. Common among these subgenres was the theme of romantic love and social gossip.[125] The moral-political motif of *zhongchen* and *lienu* that characterized most dramatic works before 1941 had largely disappeared because of fear of retaliation. But in the hands of resisters, familiar love stories could become symbols of protest.

Indeed, Li gave most of his melodramatic adaptations a new, moral-political interpretation. But the subtle messages, often "hidden" beneath a dry, unpolished prose that showed a sloppy hand writing under the pressure of a deadline, were rarely recognized by the amusement-seeking audience.[126] For example, in *Hua xin feng* (originally Sardou's *Fernande*), Li makes the heroine, a rape victim, into a metaphor for occupied Shanghai. Her young fiancé, who resolves after much hesitation to marry her despite social pressure, symbolizes the resisters whose *haoran zhengqi* defines them as human beings. Yet this association of high moral-political purpose with the merely unconventional acceptance of a rape victim seems artificial at best. As a critic complained: "The characters of the play are all so unrealistic and the language so idealistic...[in sum] the play is full of problems."[127]

His other adaptation of Sardou, *Jin Xiaoyu* (a Chinese version of *La Tosca*), was better received, playing to a full house for two months. Produced by his friends Huang Zuolin's and Ke Ling's

Kugan jutuan (Struggle Company), and involving a formidable cast that included Shi Hui (nicknamed the "king of theater") and Dan Ni, the play was staged in the Carlton Theater at 21 Parker Road. Set in the Beijing of the 1920s, a favorite setting of Li's, it was about a female singer (Dan Ni) tortured by the warlord police (Shi Hui) into trading her body for the freedom of her former lover, a young revolutionary. The torture scene and the lead character, Shi Hui's masterful representation of the sadistic torturer, smoking cigars and speaking halting Cantonese on occasion, captured the hearts of the audience, none of whom could miss the parallels with the Kempeitai, "No. 76," and Wang Jingwei. But Li, who played a minor role himself, suffered not only from constant fear of Japanese suppression but also from inhaling the smoke of the stage cigars. He even passed out once backstage after finishing the show.[128]

It remained for Li's original play *Qingchun* (Youth), which he wrote and staged in 1944 for the Xinyi jutuan (New Arts Theater Group), to express his philosophic vision successfully. This play was a thematic reworking of his earlier work *Fanma ji*, stressing the romantic rather than the revolutionary aspect of the hero's life in order to evade Japanese suppression. This four-act play is the most eloquent statement of Li's wartime ideas. Like Sartre's *The Flies* (1943), *Qingchun* is essentially a political drama of resistance and the struggle for moral freedom. It insists on fortitude and commitment as the prerequisite for the redemption of humanity. To Li, as to Sartre, every political act was also a moral choice, because inner freedom is the precondition for political freedom. Only by freeing oneself from within could one change injustices without.

Written in vivid, fluent language spiced with slang and local dialect, evocative of Shansi country life on the eve of the 1911 Revolution, *Qingchun* is about the struggle of a poor farm laborer, Xier, to marry the village headman's daughter, Xiang. Despite her father's objections to the marriage and subsequent death threat, Xier's commitment to the girl and his faith in a "better tomorrow" spur him to defy the tyrant. After a futile elopement, however, Xiang is forced into a marriage with a rich eleven-year-old boy. This is a commonplace enough story of unfulfilled love in feudal society, but Li uses it to set the stage for a remarkable drama of human redemption. A year later, Xiang returns home with her in-laws, and Xier once again urges her to flee with him to freedom:

Xier: Have you really changed toward me?

Xiang: One day I know I'll just die.

Xier: You won't die....You married a child, that doesn't count as a marriage. One of these days I'll get power...there's a change of rule coming, and everything will change along with it...

Xiang: Dear Xier, I can't last out till that day comes.

Xier: Yes, you can, and it won't be long either...[129]

No one could have missed the meaning behind these lines. Here Li makes effective use of the metaphor of faithful love, a popular code in Resistance writings at that time, to summon up the audience's will to hold out until the liberation of Shanghai. But the dialogue also suggests a tone of uncertainty.

This second elopement plot is again discovered, and Xiang is divorced. Seeing the divorce as a disgrace, her father demands her suicide, and Xiang submissively prepares to comply. In the hands of most Resistance playwrights, this would have been a fitting ending.[130] Leaving Xier to wait for "tomorrow" consumed by wrath and hatred would have served to highlight the terror and absurdity of the Occupation. Li chose, however, to stress the redemptive power of engagement instead. Xier knows that Xiang is doomed, and that the village headman will kill him if he interferes. Yet he perseveres in fighting for the freedom of his love. Here a sharp distinction is made between the "beast"—who would kill his daughter—and the "human"—who devotes himself to saving his lover. Even Xier's strong-willed, sharp-tongued widowed mother (representing the beleaguered GMD government) comes to his help, despite her earlier objections to his love affair. She is converted by his unyielding commitment. Xier succeeds in defeating the village headman in a highly melodramatic manner and brings Xiang home. The play then ends in a mood of victory and hope: "A new shaft of sunlight falls on their retreating figures, as the evening draws in. The farmers have finished their work in the fields and are heard in the distance—their singing, their commands to their animals...the cawing of crows as darkness falls, weave together to make the music of the countryside."[131] Here the "music of the countryside" is an obvious symbol of the national Resistance in the interior, whose unyielding struggle will precipitate the collapse of the Occupation.

Echoing his earlier essay about the martyrdom of a poor farmhand (Niu Xiaoshan), Li reaffirms his belief in "mythless heroism."

The audacity of Xier in rebelling against feudal oppression (read the terror and injustice of the Occupation) suggests the possibility of redemption through engagement. The playwright shows that every living situation contains both a limitation (history) and a possibility (freedom); every political act is also a moral act. Only by freeing oneself, like Xier, from fear and intimidation can one help to free others from political oppression. Thus Xier's moral audacity delivers both Xiang and his widowed mother to freedom. Individual liberation is thus complementary to the liberation of China. In the face of death, it was the Resistance writers (the true "individualists") who should take on the role of political prophets, helping to dispel the illusion of weakness and futility within all people including themselves (and the government) and to empower them with the strength to fight for a "better tomorrow."

The political significance of Li's message comes into sharper relief when we put *Qingchun* into its immediate context. From 1943 to 1945, Japan was locked in a desperate struggle for raw materials and economic resources to bolster its war efforts after repeated military setbacks in the Pacific.[132] Besides the Ichigo offensive in 1944, which threatened the survival of the Nationalist regime in Chongqing, the Japanese Imperial Army tightened its political and economic grip on the occupied territories.[133] In Shanghai, all economic materials deemed militarily useful were confiscated and centralized. The material life of the city quickly went from bad to worse, and along with this, ruthless suppression of political dissent became a part of life. By 1943, the film industry was totally Japanese-run; the theater narrowly escaped a similiar fate, but censorship led to the frequent closing down of theaters and arresting of intellectuals. Many writers and playwrights were arrested; others disappeared. In this atmosphere of terror, collaboration by writers and artists increased, as did the general acquiescence and escapism of the public. For the few committed resisters, this situation was the ultimate trial of loyalty and dignity. As Ke Ling stated in his play *Henhai*: "Moral corruption has never been greater since the beginning of our Chinese history than it is today....A lot of people have degenerated; some of them have become beasts."[134]

It seems clear that in this context Li's *Qingchun* was meant in part to exorcise the fear and intimidation of the Shanghai intellectuals, reminding them of their moral responsibility to persevere in fighting for freedom on behalf of the people. Like Xier, they would prove their humanity only through tenacious engagement, and as in the case of Xiang, the fate of the Shanghai people was in their hands.

And soon Li was forced to confront his own "final test" of integrity. On April 19, 1945, at about 2 A.M., he was arrested by the Kempeitai. Displaying his political naïveté, as at the beginning of the war, when the three Kempeitai agents entered his house by the side door, he thought that the intruders were thieves and therefore slipped through the front door to call the police from a neighbor's house. But when he returned home later, he found a Kempeitai officer waiting for him. As he was led out into the street, he thought he was seeing his family for the last time. "My wife was crying and crying. On the bed were my two kids sleeping soundly, with one still in his crib. The pitch-dark night was not as dark as my heart." Still, luckily for Li, as he was soon to discover, his wife had saved his life by quickly putting away all his letters from friends in the interior under the bed.[135]

Li was taken to the Kempeitai station (originally the American Community Church) on Avenue Pétain in the French Concession (known euphemistically as the "Bei Mansion") and was put to interrogation immediately by the notorious Hagiwara Daikyoku, an ex-monk. The evilly handsome Hagiwara looked like a strange combination of "Machiavelli, Li Lianying (the Qing eunuch) and Xu Zhimo (the Romantic poet)," Li thought; unlike the imaginary torturer played by Shi Hui in Li's *Jin Xiaoyu*, he neither smoked a cigar nor spoke Cantonese.

After four straight hours of questioning, Li's answers did not satisfy the Kempeitai man. Li was then led through the kitchen (where he naïvely thought to himself that he would be fed) into a room containing a huge cement bathtub and rubber hoses, where he was instantly stripped naked, tied to a low bench, and subjected to water torture. Ice-cold water was poured into his mouth and nostrils continuously until the water come back out mixed with blood. Then the process started again. At times torturers would even sit or stand on his bloated belly in order to increase the pain. Throughout the torture, with the help of a Chinese interpreter, Hagiwara asked him question after question. Li, already reduced to what Jean Amery aptly calls "a flesh," "a whimpering prey of death," refused to name names. For someone who had fainted away because of inhaling cigar smoke on stage, Li's endurance clearly showed a "moral power of resistance to physical pain."[136]

To increase the psychological agony, Li was asked to leave a "will" for his family. "I was shivering and trembling all over, with cold water stuck inside my throat. My nostrils, my ears, and my teeth were all shaking. Although I even had difficulty breathing, I managed to burst forth a sentence: 'Tell my children that I have been a *good man*. Papa has died in bitterness, tell my children to behave better.'" Perhaps with his own father's martyrdom in mind, implied in this "will" was the affirmation of an honorable death, the fulfillment of one's humanity in a just cause.

With not much evidence against him, mainly a personal notebook of literary sketches, and with his stoic endurance yielding little information, Li was released after twenty more days of interrogation.[137] A close friend from his time at Qinghua University, Sun Ruihuang, now the associate manager of the Xinhua Bank and a former SWH and Fu she member, made the necessary connections and paid a CRB $500,000 ransom on his behalf. His life was saved.[138]

His survival gave Li a sense of pride as well as dignity. He felt like a hero, a "mythless hero" indeed, having come through the cleansing furnace, attesting to the redemptive power of moral engagement and, like his friend Niu Xiaoshan, redeeming his whole life as "an ordinary person, without political ambition, but with a conscience always needing to be put at ease." The torture provided him with that "final test" in which, as he wrote in *Shisan nian*, "his soul shone through."[139] Soon after his release in May 1945, he wrote again of his feeling of spiritual rebirth in two plays, *Wang Deming* and *Ashina*, adapted respectively from Shakespeare's *Macbeth* and *Othello*. In order to avoid censorship, Li resorted to historical metaphor to give voice to his political experience. The former play was accepted by the Kugan jutuan and was shortly afterward staged at the remote Lafayette Theater. Directed by Huang Zuolin and starring Dan Ni, Huang's wife, this self-revealing but hurriedly written play was lukewarmly received.[140]

Set in the chaotic Five Dynasties period (A.D. 907–60), *Wang Deming* is about a loyal official who chooses to live under an alien dynasty only to help overthrow it. Inspired by the moral theme of the Yuan drama *Zhaoshi guer* (The orphan son of Madam Zhao), the hero, Li Zhen, a high official under the usurper, sacrifices his only infant son to save the dethroned king's heir, thereby contributing to the eventual collapse of the usurping regime. (Aware of his earlier ambivalence to the dramatic motif of *Zhongchen lienü*, Li tried to distinguish his character by giving him a subtle touch of "individualism": Li Zhen neither belongs to any organized loyalist movement nor feels comfortable following instructions; he acts alone in accordance with his inner voice.) This individual act of self-sacrifice for the dynastic cause helps atone for the loyal official's sin of having served a foreign ruler; above all, it "illuminates" his whole life and redeems his humanity. Hence Li lets the hero quote at length the Mencian dicta about the integrity and *hongyi* (inner strength) that define and affirm man. He proves to himself as well as to others that he is truly human despite everything.[141]

The parallel between Li and his fictitious official is only too obvious. Li felt he had acquired humanity and "redeemed" his life of political aloofness through his struggle to maintain "national purity" (alone) in the face of an alien reign of terror. The pedantic, apolitical scholar had gone a long way toward becoming a Resistance hero, surviving one of the most brutal, dehumanizing Japanese tortures. And along with this, he escaped from anonymity into the center of Shanghai literary life.[142] From his own self-affirming experience, he was convinced that the war had brought a new era of spiritual strength to China. Like many of his comrades, such as Zheng Zhenduo, Ke Ling, Huang Zuolin, and Yang Jiang,[143] Li tended to equate politics with personal morality, to view the War of Resistance in terms of the moral regeneration of China. "We" were redeemed, while the subhuman "others" were damned. "[In the war], corruption gives way to vitality, old to new, and materialistic to spiritual....So the war is at once a destruction and a construction." However, this moralistic view soon led him, as well as other intellectual resisters, to bitter disillusionment in the face of the corruption and bureaucratic abuses of the Nationalist government when it returned in 1945. Like the hero in his play *Fanma ji*, he was to write after the war: "All those who had sacrificed their private desires for the public good changed for the worse amidst the indulgence of selfishness....Brightness has faded in the dark, a gray shadow....is enveloping the wounded land on which blood and tears are yet to dry."[144]

In May 1945, however, it was with his new sense of self-liberation that Li awaited national liberation. By the summer of 1945, the imminent defeat of Japan was obvious to the Shanghai public. The increasing appearance of U.S. B-29s over the city and the collapse of the Third Reich, publicized by a map hung outside the Russian Consulate at 2 Huangpu Road, along the Bund, showing the state of the European war, indicated the reversal of the military situation. But at the same time, the Japanese Kempeitai became more savage in dealing with the city's populace.[145]

A fortnight after his freedom, Li was obliged to see Hagiwara Daikyoku again, this time at a small cafe near his Rue Ratard home. Sporting a stylish suit and a felt hat, the Kempeitai man asked his victim whether he knew the famous Resistance playwright Tian Han, and, when Li gave him a vague answer, said in an intimidating voice (and in English), "He is on the road to Shanghai." The whole conversation seemed aimed at showing Li that the Kempeitai were still in control, well-informed, and well-connected, and that he had better behave. After half an hour, the meeting was over, and it was Li who paid for the coffee.[146]

This kind of harassment was too much of a psychological burden to bear. In late May, through the introduction of his friend Li Bo-lung, a drama activist, Li arranged with an itinerant trader to help him flee Shanghai through the smuggling network between the occupied zone and Free China. He was first taken to Hangzhou. After a reunion with his family, who arrived later, they traveled to Tunxi in Anhui province (the first city of Free China west of Shanghai).[147] As soon as Li's boat crossed over the demarcation line, he felt a sense of liberation. The "Twisted-branch Plum Syndrome" seemed to be cured at once: "In the land of freedom I breathed the air of freedom. As our boat was making a detour at Fuyang, oh, how undescribably free my mind had become. I was severely burnt by the fierce sun. But how happy I was for my sunburn! Good-bye! Good-bye for ever, Hagiwara Daikyoku!"[148]

Having found his freedom through resistance (Xier's tyrannicide), having overcome his feelings of guilt through his torture

(*Wang Deming*), and having become a leader of the Shanghai theater, Li now saw himself as an *écrivain engagé,* born of the war, a modern hero committed to the salvation of his people. In August 1945 Japan surrendered. Elated, impassioned, and full of hope, he immediately made his way back to liberated Shanghai, preparing to devote himself to the spiritual regeneration of China—"a phoenix reborn."[149]

3

Collaboration:
The "*Gujin* Group" and
the Literature of Anachronism

So many stalwart friends, men of high constancy;
And I, because I wavered at the crucial moment,
I hide in the reeds on borrowed time.

Wu Weiye,
"In Times of Sickness"

•

Collaboration in Shanghai started as a self-proclaimed minority revolt with very few intellectual followers. Under the leadership of
Wang Jingwei, the "Peace Movement" invoked an image of an enlightened handful of self-sacrificing patriots striving, in the face of
inept Nationalist politicans and an irrational and misled majority, to
negotiate peace with Japan so as to save China. After the complete
Japanese annexation of the foreign settlements in December 1941,
many more intellectuals joined the movement. But there was no
Marcel Déat or Robert Brasillach in occupied Shanghai; few Chinese
writers took the Japanese ideology of Tōa shin'chitsujo ("New
Order in East Asia"), the equivalent of Hitler's rhetoric of a "New
Order" in Europe, to heart. Most of them were unwilling to propagandize for the enemy; rather they opted for partial cooperation in
order to survive. Their writings were filled with set allusions to the
shame and anguish of compromise. As if to atone for their guilt,
these writers portrayed themselves as *yimin*, anachronisms.[1] Nostalgia,
rather than any aspiration for a "New Order," became the dominant
motif of collaborationist writings.

This anachronistic stance was embodied in *Gujin* (Reminiscences), a literary journal published and sponsored by several senior

leaders of the Wang Jingwei regime, whose endeavors to promote an early peace were constantly frustrated by the Japanese policy of military domination. *Gujin* provided many intellectual collaborators, including Wen Zaidao, Zhou Lian, and Ji Guoan, with space for atonement, becoming the vehicle of a self-pitying, self-justifying, and reclusive literature that befitted *yimin*. The contributors to *Gujin* thus voiced the otherwise unarticulated political ambivalence of collaboration in Shanghai.

Collaboration as a Revolt of the Minority, 1937–1941

After the loss of Greater Shanghai in November 1937, China was repeatedly defeated by Japan. Military fiascoes followed one after another. Xuzhou, Kaifeng, Wuhan, and Guangzhou fell in 1938. But the Japanese army failed to conquer China. It managed only to occupy what were then called "points and lines"—coastal cities and areas along the railroad. The Nationalist government installed itself securely in the southwest after its retreat there in mid 1938. Similarly, the Communists established large guerrilla bases in northwestern China. Resistance continued and the war reached a stalemate.[2]

In early 1938, in order to resolve the "China Problem," Prince Konoe Fumimaro, then Japan's prime minister, went against the wishes of the military to call for Sino-Japanese "cooperation" in building a "New Order in East Asia" free of "Communism and imperialism." He promised that his terms for peace would include no territorial appropriations or war indemnities. The charismatic Nationalist leader Wang Jingwei, second only to Chiang Kaishek in the GMD hierarchy, responded to the Japanese plan with enthusiasm. Pessimistic about continued Chinese resistance, Wang and a number of GMD bureaucrats centered in the so-called "Low-key Club" (Didiao julebu), most of whom belonged to his "Reorganization Clique" (Gaizu pai), sought negotiations with Japan. They charged that Chiang, whose "despotic capriciousness" precluded dissent within the government and ignored the military weaknesses of China, was being entrapped by the "Comintern-controlled Communists" into committing the country to a hopeless, disastrous war. After Wang had slipped through Kunming to Hanoi (where his long-time aide Zeng Zhongming was assassinated by GMD secret agents) and announced his endorsement of Prince Konoe's proposal in the "Twenty-ninth telegram" (Yandian) in December 1939, the group departed with Japanese assistance for Shanghai to launch the Peace Movement. The Chongqing government responded by renouncing the movement as traitorous and expelling Wang and his associates from the ruling party.[3]

When Wang arrived in Shanghai with his followers in May 1939, they found the city hostile to their Peace Movement.[4] A sense of militant patriotism prevailed. The Chinese press—notably the foreign-published newspapers—was relentless in condemning collaboration. Intellectuals who showed sympathy for Wang risked ostracism, if not death. Under the slogan of "eliminating traitors" (chujian), political assassination by the clandestine Nationalist secret services was rampant. Between 1939 and 1940, for example, a total of over 52 collaborators were "punished" (zhicai).[5] In this atmosphere, as Wang's lieutenant Zhou Fohai, the former acting GMD propaganda chief and Chiang Kaishek's advisor, bitterly noted, "the threat to life we suffer now is much worse than that under the Japanese bombing."[6] Yet the group did not want to base its operations in the occupied areas of Hongkou or Nanshi or Pudong for fear of appearing to be Japanese puppets. Hence they were compelled to stay in the ambivalent extended-settlement area, Huxi, where law enforcement was shared by the Shanghai Municipal Council (the streets) and the Japanese (the houses alongside). Wang Jingwei, Zhou Fohai, and their team all lived and worked in the well-fortified Lane 1136, Yuyuan Road.

In order to overcome their isolation, the collaborators took steps to expand their base of support. Two secret recruitment centers, one on Avenue du Roi Albert (French Concession) and the other in the Sun Court of Weihaiwei Road (International Settlement), were instantly established; all recruits—mostly with personal connections—were given a monthly allowance of Ch. $30–100 while awaiting assignments.[7] In order to lend the movement a show of legitimacy, on August 29 and 30, 1939, the Wang group, having proclaimed itself the orthodox Guomindang, convened the Sixth National Congress at 76 Jessfield Road, Huxi. Under heavy Japanese protection, the congress sought to graft the Peace Movement onto Sun Yatsen's legacy of national liberation. It presented the movement as the direct heir to the Revolution of 1911 and, in this vein, confirmed Wang Jingwei's claim as the heir apparent of Sun Yatsen. In a logic analogous to Marshal Pétain's rhetoric of *don de ma personne* (gift of my person), the Wang group described their advocacy of peace with Japan as an act of patriotic faith, a desperate struggle to deliver China from crisis. They claimed that continued resistance would be disastrous, not only because it was militarily impossible, but because politically it would invite the Communists to destroy the Chongqing Guomindang from within by way of the united front. A new alternative was thus in order. It was to negotiate for peaceful cooperation with Japan in emancipating China through the creation of a "New Order in East Asia." In fact, the earlier the armistice was to conclude, the better the terms China (under Wang Jingwei) would obtain. "Pacifism" toward Japan, rather than being capitulation, was thus a "revolutionary act," a patriotic quest for "a just peace" (*heyu zhengyi zhi heping*).[8]

This "just peace," according to Wang Jingwei, was actually a better means than war to achieve the end of national salvation. Accordingly, the Sixth Congress distinguished itself from the Chongqing Guomindang (which called for *kangzhan jianguo*, or "resistance and national construction") by delineating the objectives of the Peace Movement as a struggle for "peace, anticommunism, and national construction" (*heping fangong jianguo*). It then set forth its political agenda in terms of "promoting a revolution" of the national consciousness (*xinli gaizao*)—from anti-Japanese sentiment to cooperative spirit. The congress urged all Chinese to forsake chauvinistic war rhetoric as government propaganda and, instead, to embrace the internationalistic ideal of a "New Order in East Asia."[9]

To this end, the Wang group took steps to organize propaganda in the foreign settlements. They also formalized the terrorist organization created by the Kempeitai in early 1939 to replace the Yellow Way Association under two former Nationalist secret servicemen, Li Shiqun and Ding Mocun. Organized along the line of the GMD secret police (specifically Dai Li's "Military Statistics Bureau"), the "Secret Service Headquarters" at 76 Jessfield Road (thus its nickname "No. 76") boasted a striking force of over 300 terrorists, all in green uniforms but without insignia, made up of GMD turncoats as well as former Shanghai municipal police and underworld figures, mostly associated with the Green Gang boss Ji Yunqing. It was charged with "safeguarding" the peace cause.[10]

Propaganda work for collaboration in the Solitary Island was, indeed, difficult and dangerous. The publication industry there was dominated by the Resistance. Under a secret sixteen-member "editorial committee," which included Zhao Shuyong, Fan Zhongyun, and Zhu Pu, a long-time disciple of Wang Jingwei's and the future publisher of the literary magazine *Gujin* (Reminiscences), the Wang group had little success in disseminating its propaganda. Controlled by the Nationalist underground, most newspaper dealers and printing shops in the foreign zone boycotted their publications. In mid 1939, the group was able to publish only one newspaper, Lin Bosheng's *Zhonghua ribao* (China Daily), the Peace Movement's official organ, along with the Japanese-sponsored *Xin shen bao* (New Shanghai News) and a few small magazines, among them the former SWH leader Zhu Qinglai's *Shidai wenxuan* (Times Selection). But sales were bad; *Zhonghua ribao*, for instance, had a monthly sale of only 500 copies. As a result, the committee switched its attention to bribing (a monthly allowance of Ch. $20–100) and bullying anti-Japanese newsmen, as well as to buying over such influential newspapers as *Wenhui bao* (The Standard) and *Huamei wanbao* (Sino-American Evening News).[11]

It was not until March 1940, after Wang Jingwei formally established his regime, the Reformed Nationalist Government, in Nanjing, with a Propaganda Bureau headed by Lin Bosheng (a fellow Cantonese and long-time aide), that a more aggressive publication drive was launched in the foreign settlements. In November 1940, the Wang group took over control of the "Shanghai Press Censorship Bureau" on Nanjing Road from the Japanese army. The bureau continued to coax the Chinese press into submission and itself put out a total of six newspapers and eight magazines, such as *Sanmin zhoukan* (Three Peoples' Weekly) and the writer of love stories Zhang Ziping's *Wenxue yanjiu* (Literary Studies).[12] Fearing a boycott, however, none of these new publications dared advocate armistice openly. Instead, they pretended to be either popular magazines or Shanghai tabloids, giving major coverage to social scandals, nightlife guides, and pornography in order to cover up their political intent. They likewise tried to confuse their readers by publishing editorials and op-ed comments under pen names similar to those of famous resisters or by printing pro-Japanese news items side by side with patriotic statements by Nationalist or Communist leaders.[13]

Still, these publications had few subscriptions and many were beset by Nationalist-inspired violence. In the war of terror between No. 76 and the underground GMD secret service from 1939 through 1940, which operated on the basis of "an eye for an eye," the lives of pro-Japanese journalists and resisters were equally at risk. For example, the two young editors of a recently published newspaper sponsored by Ding Mocun, Mu Shiying and Liu Naou, both short-story writers noted for their Japanese-inspired modernist style (Xiandai pai) in the early 1930s, were assassinated one after another on Nanjing Road in 1940 in retaliation for the killing of two Nationalist newsmen.[14] At the same time, after it was bombed and raided four times in the fall of 1940, the office of another collaborationist paper, *Ping bao* (Peace News), which was located in the same neighborhood as all the other foreign-published newspaper offices, had to be protected with barbed wire and iron plate and guarded around the clock by a force of 36 armed No. 76 agents. All its editorial staff were compelled to live inside the offices, and when the editor in chief, Jin Xiongbai, had to attend his mother's funeral, he was protected by 100 heavily armed police sent by Zhou Fohai, who literally encircled the funeral home.[15]

The Peace Movement, then, proceeded with great difficulty in this atmosphere of militant nationalism. Until the complete occupation of Shanghai in 1941, few intellectuals were willing to join. According to Cheng Kuanzheng, a high-school principal who fled to Chongqing in 1940 to avoid collaboration, those who did join the movement, pejoratively dubbed *xiashui* (the drowning), were divided into the "compliant" and the "voluntary."[16] The former were people driven by the need for personal survival. The high cost of living in the Solitary Island propelled some writers and journalists who had lost their jobs under the Occupation to join the Wang group, which promised a steady, if not spectacular, income. Persuasion by friends (what the Chinese call *renqing*, human relationship) or threats against their physical safety by No. 76 coerced the compliance of others. On the one hand, for example, an introduction from friends brought Qin Shouou, a popular writer and the father of six, an invitaion to join the editorial staff of Jin Xiongbai's *Zhong bao* (China News) in Nanjing in early 1940 after his job (as assistant to Wang Tongzhao) was terminated by the forced closure of the Resistance newspaper *Daying yebao*. (He was soon dismissed because of his failure to write a "satisfactory editorial.") On the other hand, the educator Cheng Kuanzheng and the principal of East China Middle School were forced to pledge allegiance to the Peace Movement in exchange for their safety and that of their families.[17]

The "voluntary" collaborators were, however, mostly personally connected to Wang Jingwei and his entourage and/or shared their pessimistic view of Chinese resistance. They were different from the "compliant" ones in that they actively propagandized for the Peace Movement and persuaded friends to join it. Indeed, many of them, following Wang Jingwei, saw collaboration as "jumping into the living hell" (*tiao huokeng*) of negotiating peace with Japan in order to save the country from total collapse. For instance, Jin Xiongbai, the editor of *Ping bao* and later the chronicler of the Wang regime, had been friendly with Zeng Zhongming, who had financed his news agency in the mid 1930s, and very close to Zhou Fohai. Jin and Zhou had visited Shanghai and Nanjing brothels together since 1928. Because of their friendship, Jin helped to find a printer for *Zhonghua ribao* in 1939 and became one of Zhou's first recruits. The ideologues Liu Shike and Guo Xiufeng, who edited the Wang group's official organ, were former classmates of the editor Lin Bosheng's in Guangzhou.[18] And the Japan-trained economist Yuan Yuquan was persuaded by his colleague Gu Baoheng, a close friend of Zhou Fohai's aide Mei Siping's, to see Wang Jingwei, whose follower he soon became.[19] There were also some Japanese-educated Taiwanese intellectuals, such as the writer-editor Liu Naou (assassinated in 1940) who had built up a pro-Japanese cultural circle prior to the war.[20] These close-knit relations during a time of social and political isolation helped engender militant pro–Wang Jingwei rhetoric among the intellectual collaborators before 1941.

Aimed at justifying Wang Jingwei's stance, the intellectual collaborators' ideology was in effect a discursive response to the resisters' popular equation of appeasement with treachery and their charge of

loss of integrity (*shijie*). Echoing the official rhetoric of national liberation, these supporters of Wang's sought to redefine the discourse of
patriotism so as to place the Peace Movement in the nationalist tradition of the Chinese revolution. To this end, they turned to Sun
Yatsen's vision of "Greater Asianism" (Da Yazhou zhuyi) for a language of self-justification. Outlined in a 1924 lecture given by Sun
Yatsen in Yokohama, this vague concept suggested, on the assumption of "similiar languages and similiar cultures," an "obligation" of
Japan to help its "elder brother" China regain autonomy (rather than
to exploit it, as it had in the 1910s). On this basis the two "broth-
erly" countries would join forces in building an independent Asia,
free of Anglo-American imperialism. This idealistic perception of
Sino-Japanese cooperation set the tone for the Wang group's ideology of collaboration.

Conjuring up the images of a "dying wolf" and an "injured
tiger" respectively, the collaborators asserted that China was far too
weak to defend itself, whereas Japan was not strong enough to win
the war alone. Indeed, the war, as the Wang group liked to say,
"started as a mistake [*yincha yangcuo*] and was fought in a mess [*tuoni
daishui*]." Peace was thus not only possible but also essential—the
only way to save China as well as Japan. The Konoe declaration regarding a "New Order in East Asia" then affirmed the prophetic in-
sights inherent in Sun Yatsen's vision of "Greater Asianism." In this
view, it was the resisters who were the traitorous "others," for continued resistance could only lead China to disaster. It was appeasement that was the heroic cause of national salvation—heroic because
it challenged the timidity of the Nationalist leaders, who lacked the
courage to distinguish fact from illusion, and the irrationality of
the masses, who had fallen prey to the "chauvinistic war rhetoric"
of the CCP. In pushing the country to war, the Communists conspired to take advantage of the national disaster for their partisan ends.

The collaborators drew on the same cultural symbols and patriotic language as the resisters to define their motives. Long Muxun,
who joined Wang Jingwei because of personal connections and the
need to support his big family, for example, extended the Confucian
definition of *ren* (benevolence) as *airen* (love of one's fellow men)[21]
to include the will to *jiuren* (save others). The *Lunyu* story of Guan
Zhong (?–645 B.C.), who served the usurping duke of Huan, became

to him a prototypical expression of *chengren* (self-sacrifice for the sake of benevolence). As such, Wang Jingwei's struggle to negotiate peace between China and Japan was a righteous cause, born out of natural sympathy (*ceyin zhi xin*).[22] At the same time, some collaborators resorted to such May Fourth clichés as "enlightenment," "independent thinking," "devotion to scientific truth," "anti-dogmatism," and "alienation" to portray themselves as a rational and idealistic minority of "patriots," comparable to the martyrs of the 1911 Revolution who risked social ostracism and even death to speak the truth. As the ideologue Tao Xishen proclaimed: "[We] do not echo what others say [*suisheng fuhe*]. We oppose militant and dogmatic nationalism.... We champion science."[23]

Wang Jingwei, who had narrowly escaped death in 1910 after a failed attempt to assassinate a Manchu prince, was hailed as exemplifying this spirit of self-sacrifice.[24] And all the 52 victims of Nationalist violence from March 1939 to July 1940, among them Zeng Zhongming, Liu Naou, and Mu Shiying, were eulogized as "martyrs" who had sacrificed themselves to save China at what Chen Gongbo, Wang's most trusted lieutenant, called the "critical juncture" (*weinan guantou*).[25]

But the Peace Movement had its own heroic images of the past. Negotiators, rather than warriors (as in the case of the resisters), were its heroes. Dwelling upon the recurrent historical debates about militant as opposed to pacifist responses to foreign invasions from the Song (A.D. 960–1279) to the Qing (1644–1911) dynasties, collaborators took issue with the resisters in glorifying the virtues of survival and skillful negotiation. Thus the Song champion of appeasement, Qin Gui (not General Yue Fei), and the Qing statesman Li Hongzhang, who signed peace treaties with Western powers (not the militant Black Flag leader Feng Zicai), were lauded, along with Wang Jingwei, as "true patriots" for having had the courage and good sense to "save the lives of their fellow countrymen" by arranging armistices. As Jie Yi concluded, Chinese history's so-called traitors, *hanjian*, were merely "victims of bigotry," and the term should be discarded once and for all from the political discourse in order to restore justice to peace negotiators.[26]

Despite these patriotic claims to be an "enlightened" minority, the Peace Movement made little headway in Shanghai between 1939 and 1941. It never outgrew the political stigma of treason and terror. And the defection in 1940 of two of Wang Jingwei's top aides (Tao Xisheng and Gao Zhongwu), who had exposed Wang's secret accommodations with Japan and the brutality of No. 76 in suppressing resistance only darkened its image. The movement remained isolated. One propaganda official lamented, for example, that "despite our efforts there is no peace literature [heping wenxue]. All the writers who are any good choose to remain in the Resistance camp, and we are in dire need of manpower."[27]

The Japanese government, now under Prime Minister Yonai Mitsumasa, was apparently annoyed by Wang Jingwei's failure to gain popular support. Accomplishment of his earlier pledge to bring half the Chongqing officials and army into the Peace Movement seemed as remote as ever. Japan showed its displeasure by refusing to recognize the Nanjing regime until November 1940 (eight months after its inauguration); the Japanese now saw it as more a liability than the route to a speedy peace. Hence, despite protests from the Wang regime, they continued to seek direct peace negotiations with the Chiang Kaishek government.[28]

For their part, the Wang Jingwei group attributed its lack of popular support to the high-sounding rhetoric of the resisters, as well as to Japan's "bad faith." For example, Zhou Fohai and Chen Gongbo complained repeatedly in 1939-41 about the Japanese army's highhanded treatment of the occupied areas and its sense of superiority in dealing with the Wang regime, which it saw as no different from other puppet regimes elsewhere in China. They were particularly upset by the inconsistency of Japan's China policy and conflicts within the Japanese power structure, as evident in the change from the Konoe declaration in 1938 to the Basic Treaty in 1940, which aimed to reduce China to a Japanese military colony. This behavior was blamed for damaging the integrity of the Peace Movement in the Shanghai public's eyes.[29]

The problem of isolation ceased to trouble the collaborators when the Japanese occupied the foreign settlements in December 1941. In the four years ahead, the collaborators were, then, no longer a "minority revolt," but rather an established political power in the "peace area" (i.e., Central China). The Wang regime was beset by social and economic problems, however, and its political legitimacy was at best precarious. In Shanghai, which it strove to make a center of the "Greater East Asian Cultural Renaissance," many writers joined the movement; yet few of them propagandized for the New Order. Instead, they bemoaned the demise of the "good old days" and indulged in nostalgic reminiscence. The alienation prevalent among these intellectuals was largely a result of the social and economic chaos in Shanghai between 1942 and 1945, which affected everyone there.

The Quality of Life under Complete Japanese Occupation

The Pacific War started in Shanghai at almost the same time as the attack on Pearl Harbor. At 10 A.M. on December 8, 1941, following the bombing of the British gunboat *Petrel* in the Huangpu River, three Japanese Imperial Army divisions marched with tanks and motorcades into the foreign areas and set up road blocks along all the major roads. Within just a few hours, the Solitary Island disappeared. Japan tried to legitimate its military occupation in terms of "New Order" rhetoric. Proclaiming the war a struggle to liberate East Asia from Anglo-American imperialism, the Japanese converted the racecourse on Nanjing Road, symbolic of Western domination in Shanghai, into army headquarters, and renamed the Hong Kong and Shanghai Bank Building on the Bund, another British landmark, the Xingya (Promote Asia) Building. Huge photographs of American warships sunk at Pearl Harbor were posted at every busy intersection, while all the cinemas were required to show such newsreels as *Asia for the Asiatics* and *The Co-Prosperity Sphere*. The occupying force also took over all foreign-owned businesses, including banks and public utilities, as "enemy properties" and placed them under "military management." Westerners (except Germans, Vichy French, and Italians), hitherto Shanghai's masters, were ordered to wear red armbands, and, with their bank deposits liquidated, they now had to line up for food and petty cash and bow to Japanese sentries like everyone else. They were also prohibited from visiting restaurants, clubs, and movie houses. Beginning in February 1943, moreover, batches of Westerners were sent to concentration camps in the suburbs.[30]

Under the pretext of eradicating "enemy culture," the Japanese army closed down all the theaters, foreign-published newspapers, and major publishing houses (a total of seven) such as the Commercial Press and Enlightenment Bookstore. Over five million books and magazines charged with being anti-Japanese, anti-Manchukuo blasphemies were confiscated. On February 12, 1942, a decree was promulgated prohibiting possession of materials containing any reference to the CCP or the northeast, as well as prefaces or calligraphy by Chongqing officials.[31] All radio stations were banned except the German XGRS and the Japanese XQHA and XGOI; short-wave radios had to be turned in. In addition, printing shops were required to submit even commercial posters and placards for approval.[32] At the same time, rumors of a purge of blacklisted intellectuals were widespread. In fact, despite announcements of amnesty for "terrorists" who surrendered voluntarily in December 1941, many writers were arrested or disappeared.[33]

In an effort to ensure "public security," martial law and a curfew were declared in December 1941 (rescinded in late 1942). All businesses except restaurants and nightclubs had to close at 9 P.M. Barbed-wire barricades with Japanese guards were set up at major intersections; Chinese who passed by had to bow and to show their papers to avoid humiliation or even death. Moreover, the traditional *baojia* surveillance system was reinstituted, with each *baozhang* taking charge of ten households. In January 1942, after a census was taken of the foreign settlements, which recorded a population of 2.44 million, the Japanese announced division of the areas into 1,435 *bao* and 9,269 *jia*, with a total of over 101,747 households. Within each neighborhood, every member was instructed to report on others.[34] From these local control units, "volunteer corps" were also organized among adults between the ages of 20 and 45. Besides policing in around-the-clock shifts, their main duty was to encircle their respective areas with ropes during political emergencies (e.g., bombings or assassinations). People inside were not to be allowed to leave, and the areas would remain closed until suspects were caught. For instance, on February 14, 1942, the Chinese New Year's Eve, when the Sun Company on Nanjing Road was bombed, the whole block of offices and residences between Henan Road, Xizang Road, and

Avenue Edward VII was sealed off for two weeks; several children were reported to have starved to death during this blockade.[35] By the summer of 1942, as a result of all these measures, a Japanese official declared the "collapse of hostile Shanghai" (*tekisei Shanhai no ketsumatsu*) and the birth of a "New Shanghai."[36]

Throughout the four years of complete occupation from 1941 to 1945, the "New Shanghai" constituted a major economic resource for Japan within the "Daitōa Kyōeiken" ("Greater East Asian Co-Prosperity Sphere"); its wealth was to be expropriated to fuel the Japanese military machine's "southward" expansion into the Pacific. The Wang Jingwei regime, which had nominal control of the city, was hard-pressed to fulfill the Japanese demands. The task was impossible. As a port city, Shanghai was a commercial center whose wealth derived largely from trade with both the outside world and the hinterland. Now, cut off from foreign trade, it became a consumer city competing with the Japanese army for foodstuffs and raw materials from the Yangzi Basin (the area the Japanese Central China Expeditionary Forces designated as its economic base, from which "the war can be fed by the war itself" [*issen yōsen*]).[37] This competition became ever more intense after the Battle of Midway Island in June 1942, when Japan suffered repeated military setbacks at the hands of the United States in the Pacific and accordingly intensified its demands for war materials from China. The Nanjing government, which was compelled officially to declare war on the Allies in January 1943, was thus caught in the dilemma of either meeting Japanese demands (as the "rear base of the Greater East Asia," as Wang Jingwei described it)[38] or feeding the city. Almost invariably, of course, the former prevailed.

Along with political suppression, the scarcity of goods dragged Shanghai into what was currently known as the "dark world." It was a world of constant fear, poverty, uncertainty, and misery. During the 45 months of total occupation, Shanghai became a hell on earth. The economy collapsed and inflation went wild. Hoarding and black-marketeering thrived; massive unemployment was accompanied by widespread hunger. Anxiety about survival became a way of life in Shanghai. As one survivor aptly wrote, "Everything here is expensive except human life."[39]

Beginning in the summer of 1942, the hottest summer in Shanghai in 30 years (temperatures reaching 103° F), which brought with it widespread typhoid and cholera, the city was plagued by an uncontrollable upward spiral of prices. The economic difficulties of the Solitary Island period now seemed trivial by comparison. With 1936 as the reference point, the index of commodity prices witnessed a dramatic jump from 1,500 in December 1941 to 2,910 in June 1942 and 400,000 in July 1944, with a high of 660,000 in August 1945, when Shanghai was liberated.[40] Toward the end of the Occupation, for example, it cost Ch. $10,000 for hot water for a bath and $8,000 for one Beijing opera ticket.[41] Yet these were "luxuries." The greatest threat for the majority of Shanghai people was the sharp rise in food prices. In 1944 and 1945 respectively, according to one statistic, food was priced at 600 and 65,000 times the prewar cost.[42]

The exorbitant price of rice epitomized the precariousness of life during the Occupation. In July 1942, in order to ensure sufficient supplies of rice for the Japanese army in China,[43] the occupiers prohibited transportation of rice from the hinterland into the city. Instead, they decreed a ration system allowing holders of ration cards to buy 1.5 *sheng* (about 2.7 lbs.) of rice each from one of 400 licenced rice shops once a week for CRB $4.20. Long lines were formed in front of these shops hours before they opened at 9 A.M.[44]

Adults consumed an average of 0.88 lb. (about three bowls) of rice a day, however, so a week's ration, consisting in any case of stale and rotten rice mixed with stones and hulls, was enough for only three days. Worse still, in September the ration was reduced to 1.5 *sheng* every ten days, and in January 1943 to two such rations a month. Often, too, supplies failed to appear on time. Thus between 1942 and 1945 only 74 rations (125 *sheng* of rice) per person were dispensed. The total rice obtained between 1942 and 1945 was therefore enough for less than one year's consumption![45]

The only alternative source of rice was the black market, which accounted for about 70 percent of rice consumption in Shanghai.[46] The black market in rice started in 1940. As imports of foreign rice dwindled owing to the war in Indo-China, peasants in Shanghai's suburbs smuggled in rice to sell at rice shops for a higher price than that set by the foreign municipal councils. After July 1942, however,

Japanese military posts were set up around the city and "economic police" were sent around to monitor rice shops in order to enforce the rationing system. But each day about 8,000 smugglers, with rice bought in the suburbs hidden in their clothes, tried to venture through the blockades (guarded by soldiers and police with dogs permitted to kill on the spot) to peddle it secretly in back streets and crowded alleys.[47] Because of the danger, the price of black-market rice was high and fluctuated violently. It jumped from CRB $170 per picul (about 133.33 lbs.) in December 1941 to $450 in July 1942, for example, and to a new high of $1,220 in February 1943.[48] Except for late March 1943, when the ban on rice trafficking was relaxed, leading to an instant drop in price to $700, the cost of rice increased unabated until the very last day of the Occupation. On July 6, 1944, under the combined pressures of a halt in the flow of provisions and a renewed effort at curbing the black market, the price of smuggled rice jumped from CRB $6,800 in the morning to $8,000 in the afternoon and to $10,000 by nighttime. As 1944 ended the price approached $50,000, and in May 1945, with U.S. B-29s bombing Shanghai, it had reached the all-time high of $1,000,000 (over against rationed rice, which sold for $6,500).[49] As a result of this high cost and the uncertain supply of rice, rumors of cannibalism sprang up, and the standard daily greeting in Shanghai was: "How much is rice today?" Shanghai seemed to lose itself in a frenzy for food; rice became a citywide obsession.[50] Even male intellectuals, who might otherwise have denigrated domestic chores, indulged in constant complaints to each other about the lack of food and helped their wives in lining up for rations.[51]

This exorbitant cost of living was compounded by an economic depression during the Occupation. Despite various restrictions on the use of power, like cutbacks on public transport and limited allowance of domestic use of electricity,[52] the expropriation of coal and other raw materials by the Japanese army caused an appalling drop in industrial productivity. Many factories closed down. The lack of coal, for example, reduced electric power for industrial use in 1944 to 20 percent of the prewar level, and the water supply to about 30 percent. Thus at least 55 percent of the textile factories were closed.[53] Moreover, because of a great reduction in the supply of wheat from Wuhan, only 27 percent of the flour mills continued production.[54] In this gloomy economy, unemployment was tremendous. Some of these unemployed laborers, as instructed by the Japanese government, were recruited by the Wang regime to work in Japan. The fortunate few who managed to keep their jobs had an average monthly income of CRB $1,000, which was short of the price of one picul of black-market rice (a family of five or six consumed 7.5 piculs monthly) in 1943.[55] Many high-school teachers who made only $672 a month, teaching 56 hours a week, for instance, were only too happy to join the ranks of street peddlers, masseurs in public bathhouses, or rice smugglers, if they had the right connections or capital.[56]

While smuggling and hoarding were the only way to survive the Occupation for some, a few took advantage of the economic crisis to make quick profits. Between 1942 and 1945, as a result of Japanese commandeering and the corruption of the Nanjing regime, there were a total of 300 banks (a 50 percent increase over 1936) in the city, with some Ch. $75 billion in idle capital.[57] Much of the money was either connected to high-ranking collaborators (notably Chen Bijun, Wang Jingwei's wife, Zhou Fohai, the finance minister, and Li Shiqun) or belonged to Chongqing leaders being "protected" by top Nanjing officials.[58] They invested in hoarding and gold. In the tight economy practically all commodities, including toilet paper, medicine, and oranges, could be hoarded. The gold market, which was technically illegal, witnessed an enormous upturn from Ch. $11,286/500g in January 1942 to $193,760 in October 1943 and $25,000,000 in July 1945 (110,000 times the 1936 rate).[59] This speculation added to the already ferocious spiral of inflation in occupied Shanghai. Never in the city's history had there been such social and economic polarization.

If life meant misery for the majority, it was a carnival for a few. While most people in Shanghai struggled to make ends meet, with the result that begging, petty corruption, and crime became a part of the city's landscape,[60] the few parvenus who had made quick fortunes in speculation indulged themselves in a decadent life of luxury, promiscuity, and hedonism. Casinos, high-priced restaurants, high-class brothels, and opium dens opened everywhere. Life in Shanghai seemed fixed on the present; every moment was borrowed time. This social and moral chaos failed to inspire faith in the integrity and competence of the occupying force. The people of Shanghai had little confidence in the current social and political order. They looked nostalgically back to the good old days before the war and cared for nothing but "food or money."[61]

The Japanese and their puppets were acutely aware of the loss of popular confidence. Chen Gongbo, the mayor of Shanghai from 1940 to 1944, expressed his frustrations at a municipal meeting, groaning: "I cannot remain in office as long as the rice problem remains unresolved."[62] Yoshida Tōsuke, an outspoken Japanese official, remarked with acrimony that most Shanghainese "are not interested in the liberation of Asia, but rather in how much rice has cost ever since Shanghai's liberation."[63]

Dissension arose within the leadership over who was to be blamed for the dismal state of affairs. The Wang regime complained that the constant Japanese commandeering of Chinese economic materials was creating the inflation in Shanghai, and the Japanese army decried the collaborators for their hopeless impotence and incompetence in running the rationing system. Unlike its counterparts in Japan and Germany, they argued, the Shanghai government had fallen prey to vested interests, corruption, and inefficiencies. The press became the covert battleground for these bitter exchanges.[64] For most Shanghainese, however, the Nanjing regime and the Japanese Imperial Army were indistinguishable. Both of them belonged to the same "gang of robbers" who had turned the city into a virtual "hell." Thus, long before Japan's surrender to the Allies in August 1945, as Yuan Yuquan, deputy minister of the interior in the Wang regime, acknowledged, the people of Shanghai prayed in silence for liberation.[65]

The Rise of the "*Gujin* Group"

In such an atmosphere of political and economic pressure, many writers felt forced to collaborate. Unlike collaborationist intellectuals in Europe, such as Robert Brasillach, Pierre Drieu la Rochelle, and Paul de Man, who glorified the youthful vitality of "Homo Fascista" created by the fascist revolution and sense of community in the "New Order,"[66] literary collaboration in Shanghai was in most cases expressed in the form of nostalgia and in a state of alienation. Seeing and portraying themselves as *yilao* and *yishao*, old and young remnants of another age, totally at odds with the times, these intellectuals were encouraged by some ranking collaborators to indulge in a sentimentality of nostalgia. Contrary to the official call for "militant realism," they championed what I call a literature of *yimin*, a genre of lyrical essays that sought to blend remembrance with penitence and history with remorse, as a personal testimony to human tragedy. The banality of survival was celebrated as an inexorable law of human nature that mocked moral assertions. This philosophy of shame and self-pity was embodied by a group of men of letters centered around the bimonthly *Gujin* between 1942 and 1944.

Gujin was the first literary magazine published in Shanghai after its complete occupation. In the first months of 1942, the city's cultural world was dreary. All major writers had either fled to the interior or withdrawn into silence. The mass media were filled with Japanese propaganda or hack romances. In mid December 1941, *Shen bao* and *Xinwen bao*, the city's largest newspapers, were ordered republished under "military supervision." Along with them were some 40 tabloids and several collaborationist and Japanese papers, including *Zhonghua ribao* and *Xin shen bao*. Over half of the 60 pre–1941 journals were closed down. Among the few that survived Japanese censorship were *Wanxiang* (Phenomena) and *Xiaoshuo yuebao* (Fiction Monthly), two popular magazines that featured Mandarin Duck and Butterfly stories.[67] Thus the publication of *Gujin* in March 1942, with its informal essays devoted to historical anecdotes, was welcomed by the literate class. The first issue of about 1,500 sold out in five days. As the number of copies printed increased, *Gujin*'s popularity remained unabated until it was shut down by the Japanese army in October 1944.[68]

The publisher of *Gujin* was Zhu Pu. Born in 1902 to a landlord family in Wuxi (Jiangsu), Zhu was a veteran propagandist of the Peace Movement who had known Wang Jingwei since 1928, when he was a CC Clique–sponsored visiting scholar in Paris. Since then he had become involved in directing all of Wang's cultural projects, such as the *Nanhua ribao* (South China Daily) in Hong Kong and *Zhonghua ribao* in Shanghai. Although he was originally close to Lin Bosheng, from 1940 on he joined the inner circle of Zhou Fohai's faction, and played an important part in the organization of the

Wang regime. But after losing his wife and eldest son to illness in 1941, Zhu by his own account became so melancholic that in early 1942 he resigned from all ministerial posts in the Nanjing government and withdrew to Shanghai. Taking up advisory posts in both the China Bank (under Wu Zhenxiu) and the Central Reserve Bank, which was headed by Zhou Fohai, he indulged in the genteel life of a bibliophile and art connoisseur, while patronizing young artists. In March 1942 he launched *Gujin*, presumably as a psychological substitute for his family.[69] Actually, his personal misfortunes only exacerbated the profound frustration he felt over repeated humiliation at the hands of the Japanese army. This frustration in turn intensified his sense of moral guilt, an anxiety resulting from acting in violation of one's conscience and feeling oneself constantly judged, and accordingly stimulated a need to justify and repent.[70]

These guilt-ridden anxieties, according to Jin Xiongbai, were prevalent among the Wang leadership after the founding of the collaborationist regime in March 1940. They coincided with the signing of the "Basic Treaty" that formalized Japan's absolute control of the occupied territories and unfolded in full its policy of military domination. Jin vividly remembered that day, November 4, 1940, years later:

The treaty was signed inside the Wang government building....Before the arrival of the Japanese special representative, [General] Abe Nobuyuki, [Wang] was standing on the stairs in front of the auditorium, looking sad and gloomy. He stood there motionless, watching the clouds curling up on top of the distant Zijin Hill; then, he could no longer hold back the tears, which rolled down along his chins. All of a sudden he grasped his hair with his two hands, pulling up, pulling it out like crazy. Then he lowered his head....His whole face was covered with tears. All the people around [him] were stirred by Wang's sorrow, and thought about the fate of the country as well as themselves. The eyes of many of them also became red.[71]

The consequent economic and social turmoil further compromised the Nanjing government's claims to political legitimacy in the eyes of the public. It brought an end to the easy illusion of an imminent "just" peace. Unable to assert the Wang government's autonomy, while the national Resistance became increasingly formidable after the United States's entry into the war, the ranking collaborators were pervaded by a mood of pessimism and penitence. This mood found expression in widespread corruption and hedonism among officials, both high and low.[72] Despite his heart problem, for instance, Zhou Fohai, the powerful finance minister, later mayor of Shanghai (1944–45), took refuge in alcoholism and sexual adventures to assuage his deep sense of remorse. He regretted making the wrong choice, but felt compelled to stick to it. "Japan will certainly be defeated...but in the event that Japan were to win the war, China would certainly become its colony," he wrote in his diary shortly after the outbreak of the Pacific War, about which he was informed by his Japanese advisors only after the foreign areas of Shanghai had been occupied. "I had no way at all in the past to anticipate that the situation would become so chaotic and difficult after [March 30, 1940]. I lose heart just thinking about this right now. The circumstances are becoming such that I'm riding a tiger [*shizheng qihu* (i.e., a situation in which one cannot dismount)]."[73]

Indeed, once having made the wrong choice, one had to stay with it, for the choice, like a trap, had limited one's future options by firmly situating one against those who had chosen to resist. The resulted feelings of remorse found direct expression in the nihilistic philosophy of *Gujin*. In its premier editorial, Zhu Pu proclaimed that the magazine was to be dedicated to remembrance as well as connoisseurship, a literary act to ease the angst arising from the futility of the human condition. As a matter of self-justification, he drew on the rich tradition of philosophic pessimism in classical Chinese literature (e.g., Tao Yuanming, Du Mu, Su Shi) to point out the incongruity between morality and history. History was perceived, like the change of seasons, as a cycle of meaningless tragicomic recurrences, in which human striving was at the mercy of brute chance. Nothing but fate counted; political failure had nothing to do with moral failure. By the same token, moral choice was but a sham of political fortune. With a touch of sentimentality, Zhu quoted the famous observation of the Jin calligrapher Wang Xizhi (A.D. 321–379): "If in time future we see time present, it is like our seeing time past in time present; human life is but a vicissitude of ups and downs [*hou zhi shi jin ru jin zhi shi xi; shishi cangsang*]. We can but sigh in futility." This became a catchphrase for *Gujin*. Everyone, it was said, merely played a "leading or a supporting role in a certain comedy or tragedy" prearranged for them.[74]

Consonant with this state of mind, the self-image *Gujin* projected was that of a magazine of "unconventional scholars" (*mingshi*) and "eremitism" (*yinyi*).[75] *Mingshi* had traditionally been associated with famous scholars preferring a reclusive existence. Starting in the Wei-Jin period, *mingshi* were literati whose moral idealism alienated them from society at large. They defied social conventions and moral dogma and indulged in an eccentric, libertarian life-style free from formalities. Although some *mingshi* (e.g., Tao Yuanming, A.D. 365–427) actually went into seclusion to escape the "cage" of official duty imposed by the orthodox tradition entirely, most of them opted for the life of a *chaoyin* (hermit at court; e.g., the Ming essayist Yuan Hongdao, 1568–1610), which was distinguished by what Wolfgang Bauer calls an "internalization of anchoretical ideals," while still serving in government. Beneath their public personas, they were reputed to relish nature or its substitutes (e.g., landscape painting, poetry) as both expressive of their true selves and symbolic of self-purification. In a culture that stressed public service, then, *mingshi*, like *yinyi*, were decried by the Confucian public as narcissistic and immoral.[76]

In projection of its *mingshi* image, the cover of the first issue of *Gujin* featured a Late Song *chaoyin* poem whose first and last couplets are said to have suggested the title to Zhu Pu:

> I have been longing to withdraw from office
> because my strength is not adequate to its task.
> Traveling like a floating cloud
> I enjoy my freedom in my poor hut.
>
> Everything in the world is just traces and remains,
> Standing futilely in the West Wind,
> I contemplate the past.[77]

In November 1942, when the magazine switched from monthly to biweekly, its cover changed to a painting by the eccentric Qing artist Shitao (1630–1707) of two recluses sitting drinking and apparently sharing their reflections about time past on a mountain, under which floated a small boat. Meanwhile, the back cover of the first issue displayed several intimate photographs of the Nanjing leadership, including one of Zhou Fohai and his family taken in the garden of his house.

In Chinese political culture, photographs and calligraphy carry symbolic meaning. Thus the family picture of Zhou Fohai served as his signature of support for *Gujin*. Its close connection to the Nanjing leadership was further indicated by regular contributions from Zhou Fohai and political associates of his, such as Chen Gongbo, Liang Hongzhi, and Zhao Shuyong, the secretary of the Shanghai municipal government. Wang Jingwei also occasionally contributed essays and poems to grace its covers.[78] Thus even uninitiated readers, who might not know that Zhu Pu belonged to Zhou Fohai's inner circle, would have little problem in identifying *Gujin* with the latter's patronage.[79]

The juxtaposition of *mingshi* painting and poems and political photographs signified their symbolic connections. This explained the official sanction of *Gujin*. The two Shitao recluses suggested the ranking collaborators seeking to alleviate their remorse by identifying themselves with *mingshi*, in particular the *chaoyin* type. Thus Zhu Pu was fond of describing himself as "lonely and asocial," interested only in self-cultivation, while Chen Gongbo projected the romantic self-image of a carefree, aesthetic, and Don Juanesque political leader. Zhou Fohai, likewise, was quoted in an interview published in the first issue of *Gujin* as having no interests in "appearance, money, and the social life."[80]

Why such identification? As shown above, *mingshi* as a cultural archetype has two levels of suggestive meaning that appealed to the collaborators' yearning for self-justification. First, the "internalization of anchoritical ideals" (i.e., love of nature, wine, landscape painting, and poetry) represented a "symbolic purgative" that served to cleanse, to "purify" collaborators of their "contaminated selves": their bad consciences.[81] Second, and more significant, analogous to their pre-1941 rhetoric of minority revolt, the Nanjing leaders were pleased to exploit the cultural image of the misunderstood, and perhaps misplaced, idealism of Wei-Jin and late Ming eccentrics. From this perspective, their collaboration with Japan was simply an unconventional way of serving the country. The failure of their movement for peace notwithstanding, their "true selves" were no less patriotic than the resisters who denounced and defamed them. Now, although peace on their own terms seemed an increasingly remote prospect, they were helping to shield the Chinese people from far greater adversity at the hands of the Japanese (a stance comparable to Vichy France's post-1942 rhetoric of *éviter le pire*).[82]

Thus *Gujin* gave these political collaborators a "personal" space, contrary to their official personae, for "patriotic self-expression." Their writings were devoted entirely to self-revelatory reminiscences and memoirs; many (especially those of Wang Jingwei and Zhao Shuyong) were dedicated to the memory of friends martyred in the Chinese revolutions of 1911 and 1927. The tone of all these works was invariably self-justifying, confessional, remorseful, and dejected, exhibiting a deep anxiety for atonement. Zhou Fohai's oft-quoted essay in *Gujin*, "Shengshuai yuejin hua cangsang" ("Talking about human vicissitude after witnessing all the ups and downs"), for example, is revealing:

I am now only a little over 40 and have been involved in politics for just 16 or 17 years. Yet I have experienced all the tragedies and comedies of up and down, unity and disunity, rise and fall....I cannot but feel that everything personal is empty, and my thinking grows passive. If success does not bring us happiness, then why be sad if we lose?...However the situation we are in right now is like that when the duke of Zhou was fearful of rumors and when Wang Mang [45 B.C.–23 A.D.] was courteous to his subjects. Right and wrong have yet to be decided, and the question of merit or mistake is still unclear. If we gave up halfway, we would end up like Wang Mang [whose Xin dynasty was toppled and attacked by all official historians], although we actually have the duke of Zhou's intention [i.e., helping King Cheng of the Western Zhou dynasty (ca. 1122–771 B.C.) to pacify all the Eastern barbarians].[83]

The intended effect of all these historical allusions and this mixture of philosophical nihilism and political urgency, as Zhu Pu pointed out, was to evoke empathy for the author's misunderstood idealism. If he had made a wrong choice, his intentions were nonetheless good, and he was strongly committed to them. He was, in sum, a *guchen niezi* (lone official and illegitimate son) rather than a *luanchen zeizi* (disloyal official and unfilial son), as both the Communists and Nationalists called him.[84]

Yet underneath this literary facade of *chaoyin* yearning for empathetic understanding lurked a reality of brutality, cupidity, and political intrigue. Power and money held sway over the Wang regime; its leadership was torn apart by incessant factionalism. Since 1940 Zhou

Fohai, in particular, had created a powerful clique around himself, which included Zhu Pu. The group helped to expand his political and financial influence within the government. In 1943, for example, aiming to take over its military side, Zhou engineered a series of mafia-style factional wars that involved the cooperation of the Kempeitai and led to the assassination of the Secret Service head Li Shiqun, his former ally. The Zhou clique was also known for its extravagant life-style and open involvement in speculation and black-marketeering in the occupied areas. Moreover, although Zhou became the strongest man in the Nanjing regime, second only to Wang Jingwei, he had at the same time since 1941 established secret communications with the Chongqing Guomindang (with both Gu Zhutong, the chief commander of the Third War Zone, and Dai Li, head of the Military Bureau) and helped protect clandestine GMD leaders in Shanghai (including Jiang Bocheng and Wu Kaixian) as well as finance the Nationalist guerrillas around the Yangzi Delta. This political opportunism represented a sharp contrast to the *chaoyin* image and rhetoric in *Gujin*.[85]

Literature of Anachronism as a Mode of Collaboration

If it had been left to Zhu Pu alone, whose experience was in propaganda, *Gujin* would certainly not have achieved its literary success. Indeed, the fame of *Gujin* as a magazine of informal essays during the Occupation owed much to the editorship of Tao Kangde and, especially, Zhou Lian.

Zhou Lian was born in 1916 in Zhenghai (Zhejiang) to a merchant family but raised by his grandmother in Suzhou. After receiving his high-school education in Shanghai, he returned home, living a genteel life of tea drinking and sightseeing. He was famous among his friends for his passion for wine and Ming-Qing history. Soon he started writing essays and came to be marginally associated with the *Lunyu pai* (Analects group) and *Yuzhou feng pai* (Cosmic Wind group), both of which revolved around Lin Yutang in the mid 1930s.[86] These groups championed a literature of grace, leisure, and humor modeled on the late Ming Gongan school, as opposed to the prevalent political literature. In late 1936, Zhou moved to Shanghai and started a small magazine with Tao Kangde, the famous co-editor of *Yuzhou feng* (Cosmic Wind). The magazine was a failure and folded when the war broke out. Zhou was at the time enjoying his summer vacation in Zhenghai, but when it was attacked in November 1937, he returned to Shanghai. In 1940, after being briefly involved in Resistance journalism from 1938 to 1939, Zhou helped Tao Kangde, then under fire from the press as sympathetic to the Wang group for having arranged for the printing of its organ *Shidai wenxuan*, to publish *Yuzhou feng yuekan* (Cosmic Wind II), a magazine devoted largely to lyrical essays on subjects only indirectly related to the war. This dubious political behavior, along with his disdain for war propaganda, alienated Zhou's friends. One of them, the *zawen* writer Tang Tao, ridiculed him in 1941 as "a political clown" (*tu shang fenlian*). After Shanghai fell to the Japanese in December 1941, Zhou chose to stay behind, and, as most of the city's publications were closed down, planned with Tao Kangde, who had also remained in the city, to republish their magazine.[87]

According to Zhu Pu, who was then living a semi-reclusive life in Shanghai, Tao Kangde approached him in late December 1941 for support for the publication plan. In order to relieve his personal as well as political distress, Zhu agreed. But instead of helping them to republish *Yuzhou feng yuekan*, he got their help in launching a new magazine, *Gujin*, in March 1942. With Zhu's patronage, Zhou and Tao were both given sinecures at the Central Reserve Bank.[88] Following the tradition of *Lunyu*, the new magazine espoused a literature of simplicity (*gumao*), blandness, and refined taste (*chongdan yongrong*). It was in particular devoted to historical anecdotes and lyrical essays (*xiaopin wen*).

As David Pollard points out, the lyrical essay as a literary form is analogous to casual conversation that rambles along and wanders freely through different commonplace subjects. With its stress on sincerity and scorn of contrivance, it is a vehicle of untrammeled self-revelation, without the sophisticated requirements of poetry.[89] Originating in the *mingshi* literature of the Wei-Jin eccentrics and the late Ming Gongan literati, *xiaopin wen* was popularized by Zhou Zuoren in the mid 1920s with the aim of maintaining a safe distance from politics. In contrast to Lu Xun's fiery *zawen*, which lent itself to revolutionary commitment, *xiaopin wen* gave vent to individual feelings of alienation at a time of social upheaval, and to an attendant sense of guilt. As if to justify their resignation, writers of *xiaopin wen*, like their Wei-Jin predecessors, satirized moral dogmas, which in their view served to deny human needs through irrational sublimation for the sake of society. Instead, they preferred naturalness, seeking a "private space" for decent, quietistic existence by taking up the timeless theme of the commonplaceness of human nature— as summed up in Zhou Zuoren's catchphrase *renqing wuli* (human feelings and the natural order of things), that is, food, pleasure, local customs, and reminiscences of childhood. Thus most *xiaopin wen* exhibited within their simple, conversational style a gracious touch of penitence, bittersweetness, and masochistic self-indulgence that gave this subgenre a strong confessional tone.

Since Zhou Lian was adept at lyrical essays and a devotee of Ming-Qing history, he took on the job of editor-in-chief. The board of editors also included Zhu Pu (the publisher) and Tao Kangde, but Tao soon moved on to edit the Nanjing regime's official organ, *Zhonghua zhoubao* (China Weekly). The major problem facing Zhou in the early days was a lack of writers. During several months in early 1942, he managed to solicit manuscripts only from an engineering student (using many pen names) in exchange for quick cash.[90] Thus out of a total of eleven essays in the first issue, for example, all devoted to personal reminiscence and Ming-Qing anecdotes, seven were written by Zhou, Zhu, and the young student.[91]

After the Japanese completed their occupation of Shanghai in December 1941, in the apt words of an editorial in the now Japanese-run *Shen bao*, the literary world of Shanghai was thoroughly "stagnant," dominated only by "hackneyed peace pieces" (*heping bagu*) and "government-subsidized literature" (*baoxiao wenxue*).[92] Thus, the personal, reclusive tone and nostalgic, scholarly orientation of *Gujin*, along with Zhou Fohai's patronage, helped ease Zhou Lian's editorial problems. Indeed, it may well be that, despite Zhu Pu's persistent claim that his magazine was a "private venture," *Gujin* had the official mission of alleviating the "cultural stagnation" of Shanghai. The influence of Zhu Pu (who got Zhou Fohai to start writing for *Gujin* in early 1942) and Zhou Lian's gift of persuasion thus combined to create a literary network around the magazine.[93] Beginning with publication of the ninth issue (October 16, 1942), they had attracted enough contributions from occupied regions in both the north and south to switch the magazine from a monthly to a bi-weekly format. Notable among the contributors were some old literati who had survived different rounds of political turbulence since 1895, including Gong Xinjian (a descendant of the early Qing official Gong Dingzi, and himself a Qing imperial Hanlin Academy scholar), Lin Haosheng (Qing *jinshi* [presented scholar] and great grandson of the anti-opium imperial commissioner Lin Zexu), and the famous classicist Mao Heting (descendant of the famous Ming loyalist Mao Xiang and father of the Resistance playwright Mao Shuyan). After fleeing to Shanghai from the hinterland, these old literati sought solace in nostalgia, and they found a sense of worth in the frequent visits of Zhou Lian and the publication of their own reminiscences.[94] But the core writers of *Gujin* were a loosely organized group of young and middle-aged essayists from Shanghai and Nanjing who, like Zhou Lian, had in different ways identified or associated themselves with the apolitical and aesthetic style of the *Lunyu pai*.

Although generalization about literary collaborators is risky, as biographical materials are scarce and sketchy, some common features may be adduced about them. These writers were mostly in their late twenties and mid thirties, frail, timid, mediocre, and scholarly in disposition, well versed in classical texts, and only recent arrivals in Shanghai (or Nanjing) from the hinterland. Aloof from politics and secluded in their own world of private concerns, except for Tao Kangde, all of them had been obscure in the politicized world of prewar Chinese letters. They might—like Zhou Lian, the minor novelist Pan Yuqie, and the woman novelist Su Qing, who in the 1940s became famous for her uninhibited portrayal of sex—at times have contributed to *Yuzhou feng* or other small magazines; but all of them were outsiders to literary Shanghai.

After the eruption of the war, however, some of these writers were catapulted to sudden visibility in the literary world for their impassioned *zawen* against the Japanese invasion. Yet the total occupation of Shanghai confronted them with another reality altogether. Jin Xingyao, who was better known by the pseudonym Wen Zaidao, becoming *Gujin*'s leading writer, was a good example. Wen was born in 1916 to a wealthy merchant family in Dinghai, Zhejiang. He had originally come to Shanghai in 1930 to work for a relative, but his real interest was literature. So he left his job and, while studying classics with a private tutor, began to dabble in radical culture. Although marginal to the city's literary set, he had annotated some late Ming anthologies for a small publisher, and became close to the Communist A Ying, who was impressed by his classical knowledge. Soon he married Wu Guifang, a radical writer slightly older than himself, and their first child was born around the time the war broke out. It was probably through his wife as well as A Ying that Wen began to get involved in the Resistance. Living with his parents in a nice neighborhood in the French Concession, he did not need to work, but devoted all of his time to writing. Furious in style and couched in historical clichés, his *zawen* appeared in all the major foreign-published newspapers. In 1939, with Ba Ren, Ke Ling, and other leftists, he published the journal *Lu Xun feng* (Lu Xun Style). But it closed a year later because of internal dissension, which arose mainly because of Wen's acceptance of Tao Kangde, whom he perhaps knew through Zhou Lian, into the group. This episode aroused much animosity among Wen's comrades, and they were soon to hate him even more.[95]

In December 1941, Wen and his wife were arrested. In order to escape torture and to save his wife's life (she was threatened with attack dogs), Wen named names to No. 76 and, after his release, tried to coax his friends, including Ke Ling, to change sides. The guilt of having survived at the cost of betraying his friends and country haunted him throughout the Occupation. Why could he not endure torture as others did? Why had he given in so fast, so readily? After 1941, doubtless ashamed at his compromise, he started calling his study "Ru zhai" ("Studio of Shame").[96] And when he was asked by a friend about his condition in 1943, he replied in a defensive tone: "I am fine. As I examine myself in the dark of night, I somehow feel that my idealism has not died out completely.... Yet no one seems to forgive me."[97]

If Wen compromised reluctantly, the collaboration of some intellectuals seems to have been less accidental. Unlike Wen, they made their choice in a far less demanding and ambiguous situation; and they played a much more active role in the Wang regime. In 1943 Zhou Lian had become a director of the Shanghai chapter of the Zhongri wenhua xiehui (Sino-Japanese Cultural Association).

Liu Yusheng (Tsun-jen), a Cantonese writer who had returned to Shanghai (where he had edited magazines and been associated with *Yuzhou feng pai* in the 1930s) after the fall of Hong Kong in 1941 (where he was the colonial government's censor), joined the Nanjing government's Propaganda Ministry. He was also the bureau chief of the Zhongri wenhua xiehui, responsible principally for organizing public lectures for high-school students. In 1943 Liu and Tao Kangde, the editor of *Zhonghua zhoubao*, founded the Peace Bookstore with the Japanese army's backing.

Like Wen Zaidao, Zhou and Liu also agonized over their compromise. Writing in memory of his grandmother, Zhou, for example, expressed remorse at having made the wrong choice: "I am now in a situation of seeing no way out [*wuke naihe*]. For the sake of my own life or because of that one person [probably his future wife, Mu Lijuan, Mu Shiying's sister], I have sacrificed everything. But I feel no qualms. Except [for] the dead [his grandmother]....I hope she can forgive me and go on blessing me." Like Wen, too, he renamed his study, calling it "Jiu zhai" ("Studio of Remorse").[98]

But most writers were "softer" in their collaboration. They were both reluctant and did not "harm" others. They collaborated only to the extent of economic survival. Tan Zhengbi and Pan Yuqie, both high-school teachers and fathers of seven, and Bao Tianxiao and Qin Shouou, both prolific popular writers, for example, felt compelled to write for the collaborationist press after 1941 in order to support their families. In an ambiguous situation where inconsistency and confusion reigned, they tried to see themselves as merely fulfilling the demands of everyday life, holding necessary jobs, like those of postmen or clerks. Still they were at times ashamed of their failure to put up moral resistance. The essayist He Zhi spoke for these writers when he lamented: "[I am] a despicable man living in a despicable world. Everyone wants to live; yet everyone now lives in shame [*gouhuo*] while struggling to survive. Living in shame is but an expression of degeneration."[99]

It was mainly among the former two types of writers that moral guilt engendered a profound sense of remorse and an anxiety for atonement, for constant self-justification. Wen Zaidao, who was still living off his family fortune, felt the strong urge to write despite himself: "[After being humiliated] the best and most intelligent thing one can do...is to keep absolutely silent. Yet man is after all bound to contradict himself and is bound to be a pitiful being. In the end we fail to remain silent." Indeed, after a brief visit from Zhou Lian, who gave him a hint that he was publishing a magazine in the style of *Lunyu*, he sent in an essay to *Gujin*.[100] So *Gujin* lent an institutional voice as well as psychological support to these guilt-driven men of letters. Thus like the passivists and resisters, literary collaborators had their own groupings, which served to meet their emotional need for mutual support. Rather than reinforcing their will to rebel, as in the case of the Enlightenment Bookstore group or the Resistance theater, the writers around *Gujin* sought to justify themselves, to seek sympathy to alleviate their guilt.

The homes of Zhu Pu (named "Puyuan," or "Garden of Simplicity") on Jessfield Road and Zhou Lian ("Zhouzhuang," or "Villa of Zhou") and the office of *Gujin* in a huge Spanish-style townhouse on the quiet Avenue du Roi Albert (close to Wen Zaidao's and Liu Yusheng's houses on Bubbling Well Road) became the sites of literary gatherings whose rituals served as a "symbolic purgative" for the collaborators.[101] As if to display their attachment to China, most of them wore traditional gowns (rather than Western-style suits) and grew the goatees typical of Chinese literati.[102] They took pride and pleasure in their refined, humane taste. Their meetings were "elegant gatherings"(*yaji*), as Wen Zaidao self-congratulatingly called them, "free and easy but serious." With disheveled hair and cigarettes constantly in hand, the participants indulged in gossip, discussed classical art and literature, authenticated rare texts and paintings, exchanged anecdotes about Ming-Qing history, enjoyed wine and local delicacies, and comforted one another with tales of traditional and modern *mingshi*, such as the Qing essayist Li Ciming (1830–1894) and the May Fourth rebel Chen Duxiu (1879–1942), whose lives were flavored with eccentric behavior and ended tragically. Also, and significantly, more formal gatherings of *Gujin* writers, involving Zhou Fohai and other Nanjing leaders close to him, were often held on days celebrating the memory of tragic loyalist figures, such as Qu Yuan (?–ca. 265 B.C.), a statesman-poet who drowned himself after being banished from the court because of his staunch uprightness, on the day of the Dragon Boat festival (a festival that originated as a symbolic effort to save Qu).[103]

This atonement through identification with the cultural past found expression in *Gujin*. While unable to redeem their past or to completely dissociate themselves from the occupying forces, the *Gujin* group were anxious to justify their compromise, as well as to create a safe distance from politics as far as possible. In other words, they acknowledged the de facto reality of Japanese domination but tried to avoid legitimizing its coercive power. *Gujin*'s devotion to the *xiaopin wen* provided them with a fitting literary vehicle for expiation while maintaining an apolitical stance. Hence, unlike the political collaborators, who were patronizing them and took on the image of *chaoyin* in order to proclaim their patriotic "true selves," these writers identified themselves with *yimin*.

To the *Gujin* writers, *yimin* meant in particular *mingshi* who had survived a period of political and social turbulence and either adopted a wandering existence (e.g., Du Jun, 1611–1687) or quit their official posts in pursuit of a carefree life (e.g., the Jin literatus Zhang Han).[104] This explained their fascination with literary figures in the Wei-Jin, Late Ming, and Late Qing eras. Unlike the Shanghai resisters, who saw themselves as heroes fighting for the loyalist cause, these writers projected their feelings onto eccentrics who found themselves totally at odds with their times. Thus instead of glorifying the morality of revolt (as did Li Jianwu, A Ying, and Ke Ling), or the ethics of perseverance (like Wang Tongzhao, Geng Jizhi, and Zheng Zhenduo), the *Gujin* writers indulged in remembrance, bemoaning the loss of innocence. Nostalgia with a strong repentant and purifying undertone became the dominant motif of these collaborators' writings.[105]

In the collaborators' world, where lives were seen as being shaped by irrevocable choices and by fortuitous events, where everything occurred in meaningless cycles, existence became what Milan Kundera aptly calls "an unbearable lightness of being." It was a life left adrift, floating about without an anchor, light but strangely oppressive. There people were afflicted with a profound sense of helplessness and hopelessness. As one author lamented: "This is an abnormal age: killings, bombings, hoarding, and inflation. We who are starving and are impotent to change....feel superfluous, becoming slaves to mere existence."[106]

Thus nothing but mere existence itself, in the double sense of tangibility and physicality, counted. Ideals or abstractions were denied as empty; morality was but a sham of hypocrisy and the present was devoid of meaning. So, unlike the critic Paul de Man, who tried to "deconstruct" his collaborationist past by reducing physical existence to "poetic language" and history to "texts" that defy objective "readings,"[107] the *Gujin* essayists found solace in everyday existence in the past. As He Zhi put it, "the future is too distant and vague, and the present is beyond control. Both are meaningless. Only remembrance of time past can be redeeming."[108] The past became, then, both death-denying and self-defining. In recollecting the past, both personal and cultural, and translating it into art, one clung to the very existence one found worthless. Wen Zaidao captured the mood when he wrote:

The world has changed as days go by. Looking at all kinds of historical relics would only give rise to a vain and strange feeling of melancholy....But the more melancholic we are, the more difficult we find it to forget them, and the more passionate our attachment to them, as to our own lives. I have experienced what people with pain felt like under similar conditions. So in the senseless days that remain, I want only to browse in some old books, to talk about some old stories, and to remember some old friends.[109]

Ji Guoan, a Nanjing educator and cultural official who was another leading *Gujin* essayist, agreed: "In the past few years, because of my sadness about human life, I have begun to get interested in history. I feel that all knowledge is empty and senseless; only history can tell us something both credible and useful."[110]

Gujin was indeed filled with memories, the kind that served to assuage the angst that flowed from the "unbearable lightness of being." In a typically Freudian reaction formation, perhaps unconsciously opposed to their own compromise, the *Gujin* writers gave undue emphasis to sincerity and "genuine feeling" (*zhen*) in remembering the past. In fact, all of their memories were impregnated with clichés of self-denigration and self-pity drawn from the lyrical lexicon of Zhou Zuoren, the patron saint of *Gujin*. Although he lived in Beijing, Zhou contributed regularly to *Gujin* (often the leading articles) and, with his elegant style, political ambiguity, and quiet wisdom, inspired a literary school among the Shanghai collaborators, very much as Lu Xun did among the resisters. All the *Gujin* writers claimed to be or tried to become his disciples.[111]

Like Zhou Zuoren, these writers wove their pasts and passion for local customs and anecdotes (*fengtu renqing*) into nostalgic elegies. They juxtaposed their free, if unhappy, childhoods (they were weak and timid and thus subject to constant abuse) with bucolic idylls of country life. As Wen Zaidao remembered:

In the summer and autumn twilight, we did not have to go to school. We moved toward the rose-tinted setting sun through the lonely woods refreshed by the night wind. Some wild birds...sang us fragmentary songs, chirping and flying about. Then we all took off our clothes and hung them along the stone bridge, and when we saw that there was no one around, we quickly jumped into the small creek, which whispered as though in intimate conversation. [We soon started fighting, drifting into a fantasy of knights-errant.] As usual, I was afraid to join this kind of brawl. Although at times I was beaten up, I never dared speak out; rather I urged the others to stop....So what I got in the end was only contempt and ridicule...."You not only have no guts, you even try to sap other people's strength!"—This may be precisely the cause of my timidity and wavering in later life.[112]

This memory evoked a bittersweet melancholy, a mood at once nostalgic and self-justifying: if someone was too timid to defend himself even in times of harmony, what else could he do in the face of death if not compromise? Should he be blamed just because he was too weak to resist pressure? The image was also expressive of a yearning for a quietistic existence. Bewailing the strain of survival during the war, the *Gujin* writers declared themselves totally out of place in the present age of "passion and blood." "I am hopelessly gullible; therein lies my tragedy," grieved Ji Guoan. "I want a normal life, and I am mortally afraid of confronting choices. I should have lived in an age of peace and stability; I live in the wrong place and at the wrong time."[113]

"Living in the wrong place," they longed for a rustic life of quiet joys. Indeed, it became a cliché for all the *Gujin* writers, especially Zhu Pu and Ji Guoan, to preface their memoirs with phrases such as "I am a rustic through and through" and "All I want is a few acres of land, four to five thatched huts, and to be a farmer the rest of my days."[114] They complained of the war-induced restrictions and the high cost of living in Shanghai that made such dreams impossible to fulfill. As one writer parodied the reclusive Jin poet Tao Yuanming, "Because of the exorbitant rice price today, it is impossible 'to pick chrysanthemums by the eastern hedge.'"[115] Instead, they sought psychological compensation in travelogues, anecdotes of local customs, landscape paintings, and reclusive poetry; they sentimentalized these little amusements (*xiao quwei*) as alleviating the existential pains of life.

"Living at the wrong time," the *Gujin* writers transferred their feeling of estrangement to identification with *yimin*. Chen Xulun, a former university professor now living a reclusive life around Wuxi, quoted the Wei prince-poet Cao Zhi (A.D. 192–232) to explicate the identification mechanism: "Living in the closing years of a dynasty, scholar-officials found themselves in great distress with respect to making choices.... That's why as we study their works now we feel so attached to them. As Cao [Zhi] once said, 'Our memories of the dead/are but our thoughts of ourselves' [*ji shang shizhe/xing zinian ye*]."[116] Especially appealing to the *Gujin* group, as mentioned above, were the *yimin* of the Wei-Jin period (notably the "Seven Sages of the Bamboo Grove") and the Ming-Qing transition, such as Wu Weiye (1609–1672), Qian Qianyi (1582–1664), and Zhang Dai (ca. 1597–ca. 1676). All these literati were now remembered and represented by the *Gujin* writers as having been steeped in pain and the despair of failure to resist, yet having clung anxiously to their lives amid the social and political turbulence of their times. Zhang Dai's *Taoan mengyi* (Taoan dream memories) was in particular hailed as epitomizing the pathos of *yimin*—"anachronisms": a passionate attachment to an existence that evoked both guilt and shame. Wen Zaidao spoke for the group when he sentimentalized Zhang's text (echoing Zhu Pu's comment on Zhou Fohai) as a revelation of the torment of a "lone official and illegitimate son": "He had no hope; his life was reduced to a remorseful existence of 'dream memories.' His heart was gnawed at by a certain thing as long as he lived." And as if pleading his own case, he continued: "That seeking to survive despite contempt [*hangou tucun*], dragging out an ignoble existence by bearing humiliation [*renru tousheng*], clinging to life until the last breath, might well deserve our sympathy."[117]

As with the Wei-Jin and late Ming eccentrics, these self-styled "anachronisms" perceived themselves as nonconformists, ultrarational, independent, and cynical. They ridiculed the defenders of the Confucian orthodoxy of fidelity and chastity in times of crisis as hypocrites (*xiangyuan*) and sycophants (*mei*).[118] As if to counter the resisters who espoused integrity through noncooperation and self-sacrifice, the *Gujin* group tended to relativize or discredit morality by pointing up the human instinct for survival. They claimed that humanity was defined by the will to live, not the willingness to die for some abstract ideal. Politics was a dirty business, any claim of morality was just a lie, a cover-up for brutal manipulation. "The demand for self-sacrifice is nonsense," Ji Guoan proclaimed. "[I agree with the writer Su Qing's view on morality:] whereas dignitaries will flee with funds in a crisis, we commoners are asked to kill ourselves for the sake of the country. What an outrage! So morality is nothing but a selfish sham on the part of a minority."[119]

Whereas the Confucian orthodoxy of duty and public service was a political fiction, the Daoist heresy of freedom and withdrawal was truly human. "Gentlemen are dangerous. If you are loyal you will most likely be killed," wrote one author. "And if you are disloyal you will certainly be condemned.... That is why Daoism is so appealing."[120] But no *Gujin* writers had ever tried to discuss Daoist philosophy in a systematic fashion; rather they chose to express their minds through historical projections.

Wen Zaidao was particularly apt in finding symbolic parallels between men of letters in Wei-Jin times and in occupied Shanghai. His writings, rambling between the past and the present, convey the troubled psychology of the literary collaborators. Their art of nostalgia was just a means of distancing themselves from politics, and their tendency to self-pity and self-indulgence was a way to escape the full burden of collaboration. Living under foreign domination, they tried to be irrelevant, to be free of the duty of legitimizing the coercive power, as well as safe from political dangers. Thus, identifying himself with the Jin eccentrics Qi Kang (A.D. 223 – 262) and Zhang Han (who was reputed to have renounced his high office in search of personal freedom), Wen lamented:

All the abnormality of the literati of that time was caused by political oppression. They were disgusted with the political darkness, and they saw through the hypocrisies and stupidities of politics.... In a dark age every man finds himself in a dilemma. This is especially true of famous literati, who have always been pressed into the center of politics. In order to stay out of trouble and to stay clean, they have to hide their sincerity by feigning insanity and indulgence; otherwise they will end up serving to uphold the official orthodoxy [*lifa*]. [And equally stupid is when you choose to be too loyal.] It is as though you see someone you loathe suffering from malignant boils. If you tell him to his face that he stinks, he may kill you; if, on the other hand, he listens to you and takes steps to cure his boils, won't this do him good and yet be harmful to ourselves?... [Thus] self-preservation comes first.[121]

Echoing the Qing eccentric painter Zheng Banjiao (1693–1765), his advice to his readers was to "play the fool"(*hutu*).[122]

Moreover, through the representation of an idealized, decontextualized past, when food was supposed to be cheap and the incomes of literary men high, these writers highlighted the poverty, misery, and distress of the present condition. Economic survival was at stake. Any talk of moral idealism was empty and shallow without material support. Thus the author Yao Gong attacked the notion of female chastity, a typical Neo-Confucian metaphor of integrity, which, along with the concept of the loyal official, constituted a potent motif of Resistance literature, and defended remarriage: "To behave contrary to human desires is perhaps respectful but surely not to be emulated. To die of starvation is no small matter.... Except for the rich, who can afford to be chaste, ordinary women are dependent on men for their livelihood. They should be allowed to remarry."[123] Here the parallel between remarriage and political compromise was only too obvious. Apparently alluding to such passivists as Wang Tongzhao and Geng Jizhi, who portrayed themselves as the symbolic equivalent of "chaste women" and withdrew to preserve their patriotic ideals after 1941, He Zhi was more blatant: "To be a hermit one needs at least a few *mu* of land. It is therefore sheer nonsense to remind a starving man of integrity or to discuss chastity with a prostitute."[124]

This theme of survival amid turbulence, in contrast to a hero's death, was further elaborated by some literary collaborators in an attempt to redefine patriotic discourse. They sought to justify their compromise as an act of cultural nationalism.[125] Unlike the resisters, who equated collaboration with treason, the *Gujin* group reinterpreted patriotism to mean the struggle to save Chinese culture from demise as a result of the war and foreign occupation. Thus instead of celebrating the Japanese "New Order" in East Asia, these writers prided themselves on being the perpetuators of China's "Old Way." They were, in other words, loyalists in a cultural sense.

Echoing Zhu Pu's cyclical view of history, for instance, Zhou Lian described literary remembrance as mainly an endeavor to link the past and future by bearing witness to the present.[126] Indeed, to remember was to be remembered; survival became a means of continuing Chinese civilization. "In the midst of war, all the virtues of the old society have been destroyed," Zhou asserted. "Our task today is [to live on] so that we can perpetuate the wisdom of the past sages and to inaugurate a new era of peace for posterity."[127] Long Muxun, now teaching Chinese in Nanjing's Central University and editing a poetry magazine, resorted to biological analogy in attempting to unite the themes of personal and national survival: "[What distinguishes] man from the animal is his struggle to sustain the life of his race, to sustain the life of his nation.... Since a nation's life derives from its culture, the chief purpose of a man [of letters] is to [live on] so as to perpetuate bit by bit the cultural life of his nation."[128]

Gujin, then, provided a forum for this expression of cultural nationalism. In an effort to "preserve the Chinese identity," to borrow Wen Zaidao's phrase,[129] its writings were filled with allusions to and long quotations from classical texts, its dating followed the lunar calendar, and its columns were lined with discussions of the traditional life-style and local customs. This endeavor was applauded by Zhou Zuoren, who praised it as the organ of a "self-sacrificial struggle to preserve Chinese culture from destruction" while most intellectuals stood by in silence.[130]

Zhou Zuoren's criticism of resisters who withdrew to preserve their patriotic ideals was taken up by some Gujin writers as a statement of self-vindication. Tao Kangde for one claimed that passivity was at once selfish and self-righteous, and continuing to write a show of cultural loyalty. "[The passivists] mistake the purpose of writing. We should know by now that cultural products are beneficial to our nation and our race as a whole regardless of who happens to rule. So there's no reason for us to stop writing under this or that person's rule."[131] But what Tao seemed to overlook was that it was they alone, not the resisters, who chose to acknowledge the loss of China and subsequent Japanese rule. Only with this assumption could they claim cultural nationalism.

The ambiguity of Shanghai collaboration did not end here. The *Gujin* writers were all apparently enjoying the privileges and fame brought by their collaboration. Few of them played an active part in the Nanjing regime after contributing to *Gujin*, except Su Qing and Pan Yuqie, but their sudden elevation to the status of literary celebrities whose writings were solicited by all major editors in the occupied regions overwhelmed these hitherto obscure men of letters. Similarly they were overjoyed with their intimate contact with Nanjing leaders like Zhou Fohai, Chen Gongbo, and Zhu Pu who patronized their literary skills. For the first time in their lives, they were invited to important parties and treated with measured courtesy at social events. Self-congratulation and even sycophancy became obvious in many of them. Wen Zaidao, for one, while complaining of the political darkness that drove intellectuals to feign *hutu*, in his writings relished the "elegant gatherings" of *Gujin* and praised Zhou Fohai and Zhu Pu as the examplars of "sincerity" (*shuaizhen*) and "free spirit" (*satuo*)—the "Wei-Jin unconventionality" (*fengliu*).[132]

The political ambiguity, anachronistic motif, and self-justifying tone of *Gujin* captured the mood of occupied Shanghai. The nostalgia for prewar life, the lack of a serious magazine devoted to scholarship, and a desire for atonement (in varying degrees) among intellectuals made *Gujin* a success;[133] most issues are said to have gone through several reprints, each consisting of from 1,000 to 2,000 copies. *Gujin*'s fame helped galvanize Shanghai's cultural world.

Beginning in 1943, then dubbed "the year of the magazine," many publications modeled on the *xiaopin wen* of *Gujin*'s style emerged. Between 1943 and 1944, the year the publishing industry collapsed because of paper shortages and political suppression, over twenty magazines were launched, most of them literary ones devoted to personal reminiscences and historical anecdotes. The more famous among them were Su Qing's *Tiandi* (Universe) and Liu Yusheng's *Fengyu tan* (Talks amid Hardships), who drew on the same writers as *Gujin*.

At the same time, with government-subsidized journals and newspapers (except for the official organs *Zhonghua zhoubao* and

Zhonghua ribao) closing one after another (with an average life span of only three months), all the major commercial newspapers in Shanghai competed to preempt the improving market by giving considerable space to lyrical essays, memoirs, and love stories. Moreover, several publishing houses—such as the Gujin Press, Liu Yushen and Tao Kangde's Peace Bookstore, and Pan Yuqie's Zhixin Press—devoted mainly to publishing personal memoirs, essays, and historical anecdotes or biographical sketches (including such bestsellers as Zhou Fohai's *Wangi ji* and Chen Gongbo's *Hanfeng ji* (Bitter wind), which constituted 60 percent of all publications at the time, were established in 1943.[134]

Despite its contribution to the cultural world of occupied Shanghai, the backward-looking, self-justifying themes of *Gujin* came under increasing attack by the Nanjing regime. Under Lin Bosheng, a stalwart follower of Wang Jingwei's who was in conflict with Zhou Fohai's faction, the Central Propaganda Department strove to strengthen and unify the Reformed Nationalist government rule by forging a personal cult of Wang.[135] Through a series of mass campaigns between 1942 and 1944 featuring Wang Jingwei as the absolute leader of "New China," such as the "Xin guomin yundong" (New Citizens' Movement), it promoted a collectivist, forward-looking outlook defined by an amalgam of the Confucian virtues of "loyalty" and "propriety" and Western scientism. Never clearly defined, this eclectic outlook was meant to effect a spiritual transformation of China, enabling it not only to get through the "critical juncture" of the war but to join Japan in realizing Sun Yatsen's dream of "Greater Asianism." In particular, the propaganda drives were aimed at combating the "Anglo-American culture of egoism, nihilism, and decadence" and at creating a new culture of self-sacrifice and co-operation. All these efforts were subsumed under the ideal of a "Greater East Asian Renaissance" (Da Dongya wenyi fuxing).[136]

Yet literary developments in Shanghai exhibited the exact opposite. Wang regime ideologues were offended by the "escapist" and "individualistic" thrust of Occupation literature. They regretted that the age of committed literature, represented (ironically) by Lu Xun and other revolutionary writers like Guo Moruo and Cheng Fangwu (all of them, incidentally, educated in Japan). In its stead a decadent generation of writers who had no set ideology, no concern for life, and no respect for collective goals, but wrote only for money and fame, had arisen.[137] Apparently referring to the *Gujin* writers, for instance, Yue Xiuliang, a young propagandist, railed against the popular *xiao pinwen* in intolerant language comparable to that of the young Paul de Man chastising Robert Brasillach for his lack of political sense: "The cultural world of Shanghai is so despondent! Nothing but sorrow and recondite topics like nature and plants.... Today, when our society is afflicted by war scarcity, the age of literati indulging in poetic melancholy is gone! Literature is an instrument of mass mobilization.... So all the writers should stop complaining at once about loneliness or sorrow and go down instead to the crossroads to write about the masses."[138]

Liu Yusheng, both a cultural official and a *Gujin* associate, chose rather to lament the failure of the cultural exchange programs with Japan he commanded: "Politically speaking, our relationship with Japan is unprecedently good today, yet our effort to introduce Japanese literature is appalling.... [Both in quantity and quality] our Japanese translations are much worse than in the late Qing period, not to say the 1930s." He went on to blame this bleak situation on the lack of active writers in occupied areas who were versed, or even interested, in Japanese culture.[139]

Indeed, few literary journals in Shanghai carried Japanese translations; and those that did, notably Liu's own *Fengyu tan* and Tao Kangde's *Dongxi* (East and West) published mainly short stories and essays by such apolitical writers as Kawabata Yasunari and Tanizaki Jun'ichirō, whose sensuous, emotive works had long been familiar to Chinese readers.[140] Even the few Shanghai editors and writers who were sent to Japan on exchange programs (e.g., Tao Kangde, Liu Yusheng, and Zhou Yueran, a professor of English famous for his large pornography collection) knew no Japanese; their reports on their experiences in Japan read more like tourist guides than political propaganda. Written in a sketchy, impressionistic style, they were all personal reminiscences about geishas, sake, sushi bars, or Shinto shrines. Or else, as with Tao Kangde and Liu Yusheng, they were displays of self-importance—interviews with literary big names.[141]

Even more disconcerting to the Nanjing regime was the lack of active participation by writers. Beginning in 1943, the Central Propaganda Department under Lin Bosheng attempted to adopt the model of the 3,100-strong Nihon bungaku hōkokukai (Japan Literary Patriotic Association)[142] in building up a unified literary movement in the "peace areas" to help further the propaganda drive. Yet all such efforts were futile; throughout the Occupation, Shanghai writers (unlike their counterparts in Beijing) did not even have a formal citywide association.[143]

In November 1944, moreover, when the Wang regime organized a national literary conference in preparation for the upcoming Dai-tōa bungaku taikai (Third Greater East Asian Writers' Congress) to be held in Nanjing, only 40 people attended, and of these only one-third were writers. The two delegates from Shanghai were Tao Jingsun, a Japan-educated minor writer who was more fluent in Japanese than in Chinese, and the editor Zhou Yuren. Worse still, the meeting soon became a forum for pleas for more government funding and financial aid in support of literature and education.[144] "At no time have politics and culture gone in such opposite ways as now," one official complained. Writers who indulged in anachronistic sentimentality, he continued, with the aid of a Wei-Jin metaphor, were decadent, selfish devotees of qingtan (pure conversation); they must be held accountable for the problems besetting the Wang regime, just as their Wei-Jin counterparts had traditionally been blamed (by Confucian scholar-officials) for dynastic troubles, qingtan wuguo.[145]

The Japanese army, too, was displeased with the political apathy and pessimism expressed in literary Shanghai. From 1942 on, when the Japanese were repeatedly frustrated by the Allies in the Pacific, Japan began to switch to a "New China Strategy," essentially a policy of "strengthening the Nanjing regime." In order to free up more manpower and resources in the China theater for deployment in the South Seas, the new policy was designed to help the puppet administration stand on its own feet. Hence, when Prime Minister Tōjō Hideki visited China in 1942 and 1943, he repeatedly exhorted the Japanese authorities there to be more sensitive to the Chinese sense of national pride; and the press in Shanghai was filled with Japanese talk of "Japan's self-examination." Furthermore, apart from supporting the Wang regime in the consolidation of its military power in central China through the "Cleansing of Villages Movement" (qing-xiang yundong) in 1942–44, Japan made a few political and economic concessions to Nanjing, including the return of the erstwhile foreign settlements to Wang's nominal rule in August 1943.[146]

Yet the display of goodwill came too little and too late. By 1944 the Japanese authorities in Shanghai found that the Chinese intellectual community remained passive and skeptical of the Greater East Asian War that was supposed to liberate Asia from Anglo-American imperialism. Acknowledging Japanese failure to convert the Chinese to their ideology, the writer Toyoshima Masao denounced all Chinese intellectuals as "world citizens" who had forsaken their East Asian obligations. While many writers refused to write, those who did, he observed, were hacks, producing works of no relevance to the "liberation of East Asia." Another critic Yoshida Tōsuke was even more despondent: "Chinese intellectuals are without exception pro-China."[147]

On the other hand, most Japanese officials chose to shift the blame by railing against the "authoritarian rule" of the Wang regime and its hopeless incompetence at reducing inflation. The regime had alienated the Shanghai public, they charged. Intellectual discontent was thus only a symptom of political corruption. "In the past three or four years, not only have people in the unoccupied territories not supported Nanjing, but even within the peace areas there has been seething popular discontent," one Chinese critic concurred. "All government propaganda has been invariably divorced from reality, and it has also prohibited people from criticizing it. As General Morigaki has said, the first and foremost thing now is to gain public trust."[148]

Ironically, many *Gujin* writers justified their writings and answered their critics in the same terms as the Japanese authorities. They attributed the sorry state of Shanghai culture, or *wenhua shuailuo* (where the most popular magazine, *Zazhi* [Miscellany] had a circulation of only 15,000 copies), to political suppression and economic hardship. They bitterly complained about government censorship, which invariably equated social comments with political attacks. They complained equally harshly about the inverse ratio between income and inflation. For example, as Tao Kangde reported at a 1943 literary conference, while rice prices had risen over 100,000 percent over the prewar figure, writing fees had gone up only 12,000 percent. Hence most writers had had to give up writing; the few who could continue their craft had little time left for serious creation.

They were thus forced into hack writing and to take on extra jobs, such as teaching and clerking, in order to feed their families. How, Tao asked, was a "great" literature of "ideals" and "brightness" possible in a state of constant anxiety about survival? Indeed, the government should strive to enlist more writers by relaxing the censorship and improving their economic conditions.[149] Ji Guoan was even more pungent in defense of nostalgic essays, using the same metaphor his critic employed. "As long as there are people, there will be human nature. And we cannot get rid of people who speak the truth.... *Qingtan* is important because we, after fulfilling all the demands of life, have to say something from our hearts....All beings work because they need food, so we who spare no effort in fulfilling our duty in order to get food should have no qualms before our ancestors."[150]

All these criticisms added to the frustration of the Nanjing regime and its hostility toward the Shanghai intellectual community. *Gujin* became a ready target. Under the combined pressure of the Japanese military and the Ministry of Propaganda, Zhou Fohai felt pressed at times to advise Zhu Pu to dilute the nostalgic flavor of *Gujin*. Discuss current affairs more, he counseled, and publish some Japanese translations. But his suggestions were in vain.[151] In October 1944, about the same time that Wang Jingwei died in Japan after twice undergoing surgery, and ten months before the collapse of the collaborationist regime, *Gujin* was forced by the Japanese navy (which was close to the Lin Bosheng faction) to cease publication.[152] With a touch of self-mockery, Zhu Pu bid farewell to his readers, noting that *Gujin*, as a magazine of "old and new anachronisms," was itself out of place in the "new age of Greater East Asian Culture."[153]

Needless to say, this new age never came about. The occupying force's days were numbered. In the ten months ahead, the increasing factional struggles after Chen Gongbo took over the leadership, coupled with the imminent defeat of Japan, paralyzed the Nanjing regime. Many ranking collaborators, notably Zhou Fohai, who was now instructed by Dai Li to prepare the Lower Yangzi region for Nationalist takeover, were busy looking for "Chongqing connections," hoping to "expiate their crime by good deeds" (*jianggong shuzui*).[154] Amid U.S. bombing and rumors of an Allied landing, the economy of Shanghai virtually collapsed; political repression became ever more savage. Most newspapers and magazines were closed, including *Fengyu tan* and *Tiandi* (both in early 1945), because of increasing censorship and paper shortages. Those still publishing became frequent victims of *kai tianchuang* (blanks in publication) and had to pay over CRB $10,000 per ream of rationed paper (compared to Ch. $3, or CRB $1.5, in 1936), forcing them to cut coverage by over two-thirds. For example, the popular newspaper *Shen bao* published only two pages three times a week; *Zhonghua ribao*'s literary supplements changed from daily to monthly.[155]

After the demise of *Gujin* in mid 1944, Zhu Pu left for Beijing and Zhou Lian lapsed into silence. The *Gujin* group vanished; yet its brand of anachronistic essays remained the dominant literary form and taste in occupied Shanghai. As the city's liberation approached, the meek desire for atonement became an increasingly fervid search for forgiveness. Liu Yusheng's *Fengyu tan* and Su Qing's *Tiandi*, which was reputed to be patronized by both Chen Gongbo and Yang Shuhui, Zhou Fohai's wife, now provided the literary forum for their confessions. Ji Guoan and Wen Zaidao saw themselves again as spokesmen of the "degenerates" pleading desperately for clemency. Blaming the "turbulent age" of war, which forced "ordinary people" into a "demeaning survival," they sought to explain away their compromise by pointing out that they had been feigning *hutu*, indulging only in irrelevant nostalgia. Thus, Wen argued, "Everyone's life is made up of a totality of merits and demerits....So when we want to evaluate others, we should relax and trim our yardstick. Especially since there has been no perfect man since the [mythical, utopian] Three Ages, we should not deny someone completely just because he has made certain mistakes."[156]

This anachronistic stance provoked a postwar controversy over the extent of their treason. Immediately after Shanghai's liberation in August 1945, debates about the identification and punishment of collaborators erupted. In line with its moralistic outlook on China's national reconstruction, the left-leaning Zhonghua quanguo wenyi jie kangdi xiehui (All-China Association of Literary Resistance) lauded among other Resistance intellectuals Xu Guangping, Ke Ling, Wang Tongzhao, Li Jianwu, and Zheng Zhenduo as paragons of "patriotic integrity," while lumping together all the writers associated with the Wang Jingwei government as "traitorous men of letters" (*funi wenren*). It called for public ostracism of these collaborators and entreated the returning GMD government to put them all on trial.[157] Challenging this indiscriminate identification of literary collaborators as unfair, some intellectuals instead proposed making a fine distinction between writers who had willingly served the enemy and those, apparently referring to the *Gujin* essayists, who had cooperated in order to survive and written little of political importance. Hence "one's writings" should be the principal criteria for judgment.[158]

Both sides, in historical perspective, won to some extent. In order to focus its resources on the upcoming Civil War against the Communists, who were also involved in the debate, calling for blanket retribution, and affected by its own widespread corruption, the Nationalist government favored a general policy of "clemency" toward collaborators. Of the *Gujin* editors and writers, in accordance with a formula analogous to the more tolerant proposal, it tried only Liu Yusheng and Tao Kangde, whose leading roles in directing the Wang regime's cultural affairs got them two and three years' imprisonment respectively.[159] All the others were left alone. Although their anachronistic stance absolved them from conviction of treason, their collaboration during the Occupation nonetheless stigmatized them. Their moral and political ambiguity earned them the fate of permanent anachronisms.

Along with some ranking collaborators who fled overseas to escape persecution, living mostly in silence until their deaths, all the *Gujin* writers were practically ostracized from the Chinese world of letters after 1945. Starting in 1987, however, after 42 years of enforced silence, Wen Zaidao (under the new pseudonym Dao Zaiwen) took advantage of "liberalization" in China to contribute nostalgic essays on eccentrics in Chinese history to the Hong Kong-based, Shanghainese-run *Da cheng* (Panoramic), an anachronistic magazine devoted to nostalgia and reminiscences.[160]

Epilogue

•

The intellectual world of Nazi Europe, James Wilkinson observes, was one "in which moral choices were simplified to exclude all but two alternatives....[Resisters and Fascists] alike dealt in stark and simple alternatives, choices for and against."[1] Occupied Shanghai seemed to be a similarly Manichean world.

In the face of Japanese terrorism, intellectuals in Shanghai experienced the war as a dilemma of choosing between private and public morality: a choice of survival or patriotic commitment. This moral anxiety was exacerbated by a sense of shame. Unlike the Paris of occupied France or the Oslo of Quisling Norway, where Nazi dominance was complete, Shanghai was long a Solitary Island cut off from (but nonetheless in important senses part of) the vast land of "Free China." The exodus of intellectuals into the interior after the fall of Greater Shanghai in November 1937 left the few who remained with troubled consciences. Living under foreign rule rather than joining the national Resistance in unoccupied regions, they felt increasingly compelled to prove their commitment to China. They tended to equate justice with patriotism and human dignity with national identity (a tendency evident in the mid 1930s). Thus the theme of occupation as a trial of humanity (men versus beasts) shaped the literary discourse of Shanghai. Literature became a hegemonic field of self-affirmation and condemnation of the "other."

Underneath this Manichean rhetoric, however, was a complex tissue of responses to the moral dilemma. Intellectual choices in occupied Shanghai were fraught with moral and political ambiguities. Contrary to the freedom of nationalistic expression in Chinese-ruled territory, where, despite frequent Japanese air raids and prevalent GMD corruption and repression, clamor for resistance remained a way of cultural life,[2] occupied China was a China of ethical uncertainty. Patriotic defiance brought risk of death; compromise seemed to many inevitable, yet morally questionable. There were no easy, clear-cut solutions. In this situation, history provided a structure of meaning in terms of which Shanghai writers could define and textualize their stance. Appeal to the past served also to foster a sense of national pride, while for safety's sake creating a "hidden transcript" against oppression.

Chinese history was replete with moral-political crises analogous to the present condition. The experience of traditional literati during dynastic disjunctures (e.g., the Wei-Jin and Ming-Qing) and foreign occupation (e.g., the Yuan and Qing) endowed the culture with certain archetypal responses to the dilemma of choosing between public and private concerns: eremitism, loyalism, collaboration. While these categories derived their language and symbolism from the Confucian discourse of social responsibility, as Frederic Wakeman has recently shown, collaborators were distinguished by their "romantic" exaltation of individual sentiments. Eremitism (perhaps comparable to the European concept of the internal émigré), with its stoic resilience in withstanding cooptation, had been recognized ever since the Zhou dynasty (eleventh century B.C.–221 A.D.; e.g., Bo Yi and Shu Qi) as a legitimate and admirable avenue of moral revolt.[3] As Edward Said points out, culture is a socially symbolic system of evaluation and exclusion that (in a neutral sense) gives order and common values to society. Social behavior, in other words, is culturally determined.[4] Hence these cultural archetypes of moral and political choice shaped the minds and psyches of Shanghai intellectuals.

For most literary intellectuals in occupied Shanghai, then, the alternatives available in confronting the moral dilemma were the three modalities of cultural behavior: passivity, resistance, collaboration. Wang Tongzhao typified the group of passivists who sought social withdrawal as a symbolic protest to harmonize the conflicting demands of private and public concerns. He hoped to survive without losing his patriotic integrity. Resisters like Li Jianwu revolted against the threat of compromise by creating a dramatic language of tenacious defiance. As Li quoted Confucius on the front page of his play *Qingchun* (Youth), "[He is one] who knows what is impossible and yet attempts it; who does not know what is possible and yet attempts it" (shi zhi qi bu kewei erwei zheye; shi buzhi qi kewei erwei zheye). Haunted by their guilt over betrayal, on the other hand, the *Gujin* essayists sentimentalized their feelings of alienation in an aesthetics of nostalgia. Their attachment to the past was a way to assuage their melancholy at living a demeaning life and to rediscover their humanness. Wen Zaidao spoke for his fellow collaborators when he wrote: "Thinking in silence of the past and of the present encompassing distress, peace eludes me....Hopeless, helpless, I mourn inexpressibly our indifference to personal self-expression. Everything human is meaningless."[5]

It is nonetheless a mistake simply to read the past into the present. On the contrary, the tripartite mode of cultural behavior merely provided a strategic framework within which Shanghai writers defined and articulated their moral-political situation. Their responses were formulated in connection with the existential actualities of post–May Fourth Chinese society and politics. Indeed, a critical reading of literary texts produced during the Japanese Occupation reveals significant tensions between history and present reality, between collective commitment and individual concern; and in these tensions lay the ambiguity of intellectual choices in wartime Shanghai.

After the May Fourth movement, the recurring themes of critical reason, individual freedom, and humanitarianism coalesced into a powerful configuration of ideas that rendered the Neo-Confucian philosophy of loyalty and submission obsolete in the eyes of the educated elite. Yet the War of Resistance, like most other wars in the world, gave rise to a mood of militant nationalism that was conducive to the growth of authoritarian rule. Exploiting the situation, the Nationalist and Communist leaderships celebrated the traditional virtues of collectivist moralism in their respective campaigns against political dissent. The ideological boundary between resistance and collaboration became a dogma with which the two regimes could impose orthodoxy on the intellectuals who flocked to the interior after 1937. The result, as Leo Ou-fan Lee shows, was that an oppressive and conformist atmosphere reigned in the patriotic literary world of unoccupied China. "Hackneyed Resistance pieces" (*kang-zhan bagu*), a genre that portrayed patriotic heroism in a highly stereotypical and formulaic fashion, prevailed. The individualist ethos that was so much a part of the May Fourth discourse subsided.[6]

Paradoxically, without the protection of a Chinese government, writers in Shanghai enjoyed more creative options and freedom of initiative (but not necessarily greater success). Especially after 1941, Shanghai literature was characterized by a diversity of approaches, styles, and subject matter. Conversely, living in danger and shame under foreign domination, these writers were left largely to their own devices and inner resources and forced to grapple with the dilemma between private and public morality. It was in this context that the culturally inspired tripartite modes of intellectual response were formulated.

In his effort to harmonize the conflicting demands of patriotic ideals and self-preservation, Wang Tongzhao was also conscious of the accompanying tension between collective moralism and the May Fourth ideal of individual autonomy. Couched in a grotesque and idealistic language, his vision of Resistance enlightenment was in effect a minimal defense of individuality in a troubled time. In this light, his withdrawal after 1941 was a result both of his concern for personal safety and of his disillusionment with the moral quality of the war. The vindictive violence, authoritarian orientation, and ideological orthodoxy of the Chinese Resistance made Wang realize that self-cultivation was perhaps the only alternative left for the defenders of enlightenment. Private concerns became to him a source of shame, but at the same time a legitimate field of social defiance. Thus more than the traditional recluses who went into hiding in order to maintain their dynastic loyalty while saving their skins, Wang invested in passivity a symbolic meaning of intellectual autonomy. Yet this independence was preserved at the price of social impotence; and passivity in the face of an enemy capable of brutal suppression smacked of moral weakness. Was his commitment to individual reason a genuine conviction, was it self-deception and bad faith, serving to rationalize his intimidation, or was it both? And was his withdrawal an act of modern critical reason or merely a continuation of traditional eremitic escapism?

The existential irony contained in these questions explains why all of Wang's wartime writings reveal a profound sense of frustration and uncertainty, agonizing over the defeat of his moral vision. As projections of his ideas, the private and public realms of his fictional characters invariably collapse into a labyrinth of unresolved ambivalence. For example, in his very last novel written under the Occupation, *Shuangqing* (The two virtues), a story about a chaste prostitute searching for enlightenment during the early 1920s, the narrative breaks off abruptly in a mood of dread and anxiety. After rejecting revolutionary violence as a means to national unification, and having being driven out of idyllic escapism by warlords, the heroine of the story, Xiaoqian, finds that her work in a Catholic orphanage, although spiritually fulfilling, leads nowhere in a time of political turmoil. The incompleteness of the text only illuminates the moral ambiguity inherent in Wang's passive stance.

The Resistance theater of Li Jianwu exhibited yet another blend of individual freedom and national liberation. The Japanese Occupation created in Shanghai a *guantou*, or critical juncture, where all Chinese were subject to the test of loyalty in the face of terror and hunger. The lure of compromise was overwhelming. Like Sartre and other *écrivains résistants* in occupied Paris, Li conceived of himself as part of a moral elite, vowing to awaken the city's populace from the "iron house" of selfishness and timidity to resist. To him political engagement was also a moral choice. The courage to fight injustice presupposed an inner freedom. In this way, individual moral assurance was as crucial as esprit de corps in liberating China.

Hence in contrast to most Resistance playwrights of both the left and the right in Shanghai, who espoused a collectivist ethic of national loyalty through the medium of historical symbolism, Li insisted on the virtue of individual integrity. He openly defended individualism, which he redefined as a set of humanistic values including social justice and moral commitment, against the restrictive orthodoxy of collectivism. The true "individualists," as he called them, were those like Lu Xun or Balzac, who, defiant and fiercely independent, "refused to compromise with the establishment whatever it was." They fought to the death for what they believed (rather than were told) to be good for society.[7]

True to his belief, Li Jianwu shared Wang Tongzhao's ambivalent attitude toward the Resistance. Throughout the Occupation he joined no political groups (even remaining on the fringes of the Shanghai juyishe, which he had helped found); nor did he write historical dramas celebrating the cult of loyalism or female chastity. Instead, all his dramatis personae are lone warriors who pursue their ideals (romantic or political) with uncompromising zeal and a fierce sense of individual defiance. Thus in his most successful wartime play, Qingchun, the hero, Xier, holds the audience's imagination not with the familiar theme of troubled love in a feudal context but with his complete devotion to the girl he loves, Xiang, and his inspiring self-confidence, resilience, and audacity in defying the established order. The eventual romantic fulfillment—melodramatic as it is—underscores the dialectic between history and morality. Moral conscience transcends historical limits; and in this sense national liberation is contingent upon inner freedom. So, unlike Wang, Li revolted against both the alien reign of terror and organized resistance through individual engagement, a dedication to fight for justice all alone. (Still, for survival's sake, he joined dramatic troupes of politically dubious background—although he perhaps did not know this—and wrote and directed many plays of only commercial appeal; this somewhat compromised his moral idealism.) From this ideal of personal commitment sprang his moralistic outlook. He tended to place and textualize political action in a delimited morally charged universe of Right against Evil, Us against Them. His resultant conception of government was morally determined. Hence when patriotism ceased to be a unifying force in postwar China, when corruption and self-interest became the new national priorities, he lost all hope for a "reborn China." Unable to change the postwar world himself, he could only embrace (and willingly put himself at the service of) the new regime in 1949, which was believed to be of relative "honesty" and had a proven anti-imperialist record, living a quiet, scholarly life (except when under periodic attack during political campaigns) until his death in 1982. Herein lie the limitations of Li's humanistic ethic of "individualism."

In contrast to Wang and Li, the Gujin group dismissed the moral dilemma in justifying their collaboration. In spite of their repeated contention that personal survival was basic to human nature and morality a sham of social oppression, these guilt-ridden essayists felt that their existence was a misery, debased and meaningless. They perceived and expressed themselves in the tradition of yimin, a term that historically carried the meaning of "remnants" loyal to the previous dynasty. But during the Occupation the Gujin group gave a new, defensive overtone of "anachronism" to this traditional concept. They tended to equate *yimin* with eccentrics in the chaotic Wei-Jin period and the Ming-Qing transition. Bemoaning their loss of innocence, they looked at their survival with a deep sense of alienation. The past was forever gone, and gone with it also was the chance to make another choice. Economic crises in Shanghai and the political impotence of the Wang Jingwei regime made their compromise all the more remorseful. The present became to them a constant burden of despair. Life seemed to offer little hope for redemption; some relief might nevertheless be sought through the floating world of remembrance.

It is no wonder that the writings of the *Gujin* group were suffused with images and motifs of nostalgia. Under these essayists' pens, their childhoods were steeped in a mood of tender sentimentality. And China, as evoked by its landscape and unchanging local customs, became frozen in an age of idyllic romance, where everyone was able to live in peace and self-gratification. This attachment to a symbolic, rather than political, past betrays the anachronistic orientation of the literary collaborators' self-conception as *yimin*. They were not remnants of, or as such loyal to, any specific Chinese (or foreign) regime; rather, they were committed to an abstract notion of cultural China, which was now collapsing under Japanese conquest. To them, unlike the passivists and resisters, China as a nation had lost to Japan.

The *Gujin* group rationalized their physical survival after the "demise" of China as an act of cultural nationalism. They looked backward rather than, as the Japanese preached, forward to the "Greater East Asian Order." Their literary remembrances were to them living testimony of the Chinese identity. But in contrast to the Confucian cultural ideal of fidelity espoused by the Resistance, the group found in the heresy and romantic self-indulgence of *yimin* the embodiment of Chinese culture. These essayists ridiculed and deplored the Neo-Confucian exaltation of public morality as an unnatural, irrational means of suppressing private yearnings. The restoration of a cultural China must therefore be based on the unorthodox *yimin* culture, which they identified as a celebration of human desires, a recognition of human weaknesses. Herein lay the ambiguity of the *Gujin* group. They were afflicted with guilt over their compromise, they accepted foreign domination, they hobnobbed with the Nanjing leaders, and they indulged in their celebrity privileges. Still their writings during the Occupation revealed little pro-Japanese sentiment or propagandistic concern. They might be useful to the occupiers, who were desperate for "literary talent" to give Shanghai a veneer of normality, yet they made themselves irrelevant to their struggle for legitimacy. Nostalgia represented to them, in this connection, both an escape from the existential pain of collaboration and a refuge from political involvement.

These three modes of response to the dilemma between private and public morality reveal to us the complexity of intellectual choices in occupied Shanghai. The moral ambivalence of Wang Tongzhao's passivity, the anti-establishment "individualism" of Li Jianwu's resistance theater, and the anachronistic escapism of the *Gujin* group's collaboration add up to a historical mosaic more nuanced and more ambiguous than most conventional portrayals of life and thought during the War of Resistance, which were most often written from the vantage points of Chongqing and Yan'an. Hereafter any generalization about the wartime intellectual and literary situation in China should take into account the moral dilemmas that haunted people of political consciousness in the occupied areas. (Here a systematic comparison of Shanghai with other occupied areas such as Beijing, Guangzhou, Hong Kong, or the countryside is also called for.)[8] Ambiguity and complexity must be restored to the false clarities of the Japanese Occupation if we are to rediscover the multiplicity of voices in our history.

Similarly, any effort to theorize about the human condition under foreign occupation, which has been based largely on the complex history of Nazi Europe, should also incorporate the experience of Chinese intellectuals (as well as those of other Asian countries) during the war. To what extent was the "ambiguous situation" of occupied Shanghai similar to that of, say, Paris or Brussels or Oslo? Were the Chinese and the Europeans different in their approaches to the moral and political dilemmas that confronted them? Did Europe witness a rise of drama and occasional essays similar to that in China? What were the optimum roles of literature and intellectuals in a politicized world under foreign domination? And can we use the notion of a tripartite mode of response as a point of reference for the comparison?[9] In sum, any inquiry into the universal question of

Occupation experience needs to transcend the present Eurocentric tendency.

In retrospect, reading the eight years of war from the perspective of Shanghai history, the Occupation marked the beginning of the end for Shanghai. From being a small market town when Western enclaves were first created there in the 1840s, Shanghai had by the turn of the century become a bustling metropolis (with all its glaring social inequities and imperialist abuses) that commanded China's commercial economy. Furthermore, given their cosmopolitan lifestyles and the Western claim of extraterritoriality, the foreign areas had become the haven of a Chinese counterculture. Especially after the "White Terror" of 1927, radical intellectuals flocked to the city in search of freedom of expression and new sources of information. They took advantage of their "borrowed" liberty to voice criticism of the Chinese government, which otherwise tolerated no ideological insubordination. From this dissent the cultural vitality of the 1920s and 1930s emerged. Shanghai before the war, then, represented the limited "social space" to which what Marie-Claire Bergère calls the "other China" of bourgeois and radical cultures owed its survival.[10]

The Japanese invasion in August 1937 set in motion a sequence of events that finally changed all this. Political terrorism, criminal tyranny, and economic difficulties in the Gudao seriously compromised the autonomy of the governments of the foreign areas. Even this circumscribed autonomy was destroyed when the Japanese occupied the foreign zone in 1941 and the whole city was placed under the Wang regime's nominal control. Without Western "protection," the city soon found itself in the grip of runaway inflation, while political suppression became ever more savage. As this study shows, however, some Chinese intellectuals clung to their severely circumscribed "social space" and persevered in the fight for freedom, both national and personal, throughout the Occupation. In recognition of China's contribution to the anti-Fascist struggle, the Western powers relinquished their treaty rights in Shanghai in 1943 and 1944.

When the war was over, the Nationalist government thus returned to rule a Shanghai without foreign areas. It was a triumph of Chinese nationalism. The GMD's incompetence and corruption soon pushed the city's war-torn economy to virtual collapse, however, and the political situation became brutally repressive as the Civil War intensified, multiple layers of censorship were formed, and schools and university campuses were inundated with spies. As a result, liberal publications such as Ke Ling's *Zhoubao* (Weekly) and Zhu Anping's *Guancha* (The Observer) were banned, and young Communists were massacred. All these measures crushed liberal hopes for the creation of a humane, democratic postwar China by rational means. Only continued Western influence and the GMD's inefficiency and unpopularity checked the savagery of suppression. Without the freedom and vitality that went with its "borrowed" liberties and vibrant prewar economy, moreover, Shanghai was only a once-glamorous city that had lost its raison d'être. What remained was the bizarreness, the greed, the bestial poverty, and the half-baked Westernization of old Shanghai. Gone was the haven of the dissenting countercultures.

The city's erstwhile glamor evaporated into a memory after the Communist takeover. The CCP's feat in establishing an independent China was achieved at the expense of cultural diversity. By freeing China from the bondage of imperialism, the new government appropriated and confiscated the claims to nationalism that had been the rallying point for a variety of intellectual dissenters since the 1920s. As the foremost symbol of imperialist privileges in China, Shanghai was now deprived not only of its "borrowed" liberty but also of its "enforced" openness to world cultures. Intellectuals associated with its liberal, cosmopolitan past (including Ba Jin and Ke Ling), in spite of their nationalistic commitment during the Occupation, were chastised, while the city became the capital of anti-Western "radicalism" during the Cultural Revolution. Shanghai, in this regard, was no different from other great modern cities under Communist rule; as Marshall Berman describes it, the "radical solution seems to be dissolution: tear down the boulevards, turn off the bright lights, expel and resettle the people, kill the sources of beauty and joy that the modern city has brought into being." [11]

After many years of isolation and neglect, the city is still pervaded by a sense of its past glory, although decay, dinginess, dilapidation, and shabbiness are everywhere. The *lao Shanghai* (old Shanghainese) are itchingly nostalgic for the glamorous past—Zhou Xuan and Marlene Dietrich, Edgar Snow and Silas Hardoon, Lu Xun and

Du Yuesheng, the Uchiyama Bookstore and the Paramount Night-club, the Jade Buddha Temple and the Cathedral of St. Ignatius, the Lone Battalion and Bloody Saturday—a half-unreal, almost hallucinatory past they cannot hope to relive elsewhere (except, perhaps, in Hong Kong).[12] What these people seem to forget, however, is that, as the Japanese Occupation demonstrated, the freedom and economic vitality of old Shanghai rested on shaky ground and lived on borrowed time. Republican Shanghai's experience with modernity was full of ambiguity: it represented a new commodity culture offering rich possibilities for individual development on the one hand and an imperialist regime of terror and exploitation on the other. An important legacy of the resistance intellectuals discussed here lies in their desperate struggle to liberate the Chinese capacity for freedom, resolving that historical irony. Thus, rather than restoring the vanished world of the prewar era—especially after the "June Fourth massacre" of 1989, which violently stripped the CCP of its halo and nationalist myth—the major challenge ahead is how to create a truly modern, free, and cosmopolitan Shanghai that is also politically integrated into an independent, democratic China.

Reference Matter

Notes

Complete authors' names, titles, and publication data for works cited in short form are given in the Bibliography, pp. 221–40.

Preface

1. The best-known study of the Wang Jingwei regime in English, with special emphasis on the Japanese perception of and relationship to it, is Boyle. See also Gerald Bunker, *The Peace Conspiracy: Wang Ch'ing-wei and the Chinese War* (Cambridge, Mass., 1972). The political sensitivity of collaboration and the relationship between the Wang regime and the Communists made serious historical research in China impossible until after 1980. The Department of History at Fudan University in Shanghai has played a vital role in creating the new field of "Wangwei zhengquan yanjiu" (Wang regime studies). Since 1984, under the energetic editorship of Professor Huang Meizhen, three volumes of a planned seven-volume collection of archival materials on the Wang regime, *Wangwei zhengquan ziliao* (Selected materials of the Wang collaborationist regime), which includes the two volumes edited by Huang and Zhang, have been published. Based on these materials and personal interviews with surviving collaborators in Shanghai and Nanjing, a number of important books on the Wang regime appeared in the 1980s, e.g., Huang, Shi, and Jiang, *Wangwei*. In Taiwan, however, there have thus far been no collective research efforts or books devoted to the problem of collaboration during World War II. For an article that reflects Taiwanese scholarship on the Wang regime, see Lu Baoqian, pp. 939–60.

2. It is owing partly to Gunn's formalistic approach and partly to the fact that many of the major sources for this book—memoirs and economic data—were not available or easily accessible to him (see *Unwelcome Muse*) that I come up with a quite different interpretation of cultural life under the Occupation. In Shanghai, parallel to the new interest among historians in

collaboration, literary critics have started to pay attention to Occupation literature. The Literary Research Institute of the Shanghai Academy of Social Sciences has been the major force behind this new line of research. Although no systematic study of the literary development of occupied Shanghai has as yet appeared, two immensely useful collections of research materials, *Shanghai Gudao wenxue huiyilu* and *Shanghai Gudao wenxue xuanbian,* constituting volumes 2 and 3 respectively of a multivolume project entitled *Shanghai Gudao wenxue ziliao congshu* (Shanghai Solitary Island literary materials series), have come out. These materials cover only resisters who were either "comrades" (e.g., A Ying and Yu Ling) or "friends" (e.g., Zheng Zhenduo and Ke Ling) of the Chinese Communist Party; writers with few connections to it have been overlooked. In Taiwan, on the other hand, the northeastern literary scholar Liu Xinhuang has published two books on literary collaborators and resisters in wartime China. They are basically compilations of materials classified along a narrowly defined "patriotic" line and, although very informative, are highly moralistic and ideological in tone.

3. For discussion of Chinese writers' social role, see Rudolph Wagner, "The Chinese Writer in His Own Mirror: Writer, State, and Society—the Literary Evidence," in *China's Intellectuals and the State,* ed. Merle Goldman, Timothy Cheek, and Carol Harmin (Cambridge, Mass., 1987), pp. 183–232; and Ezra Vogel, "The Unlikely Heroes: The Social Role of the May Fourth Writers," in *Modern Chinese Literature in the May Fourth Era,* ed. Merle Goldman (Cambridge, Mass., 1977), pp. 145–60.

4. For the term "grey zone," see Levi, particularly pp. 36–69.

5. The pattern is masterfully evoked in Frederic Wakeman's *Great Enterprise,* a study of the Ming-Qing transition.

6. Said, p. 39. For a poststructuralist approach to the issue of wartime collaboration, see Vicente Rafael, "Anticipating Nationhood: the Philippines Under Japan" (unpublished paper, 1990). Despite my disagreement with the apolitical orientation of poststructuralism, I do not mean to disparage it in toto. Especially helpful for critical research is its "cosmopolitan" stance rejecting theoretical overtotalization (with its accompanying notion of transcendental ego). Also, in its defiant affirmation of particularity and specificity of being, poststructuralism reconstitutes the notion of "truth" as a discourse of multiple meanings and cultural expressions. See Poster on the subject; and see, too, Anthony Giddens, "Structuralism, Post-Structuralism and the Production of Culture," in *Social Theory Today,* ed. A. Giddens and J. Turner (Stanford, 1987), pp. 195–223.

7. See Jameson, pp. 1–82.

8. See Said, esp. pp. 1–53 and 158–225.

9. See Scott, who bases his excellent study on non-elite groups around

the world and draws his evidence from such popular cultural activities as grumbles, prayers, carnivals, folk songs, and folklores. My study of Shanghai intellectuals concurs with many of his findings.

Prologue

1. On the December Ninth Movement, see Israel, *Student Nationalism*.

2. The quotation is from Van Slyke, pp. 68–69; for an insider's view of the movement, see Sha, pp. 1–15. See also Coble, ch. 8.

3. Sha, pp. 30–35. See also Tang Zhenchang, ed., pp. 717–26; and *Yierjiu*.

4. Van Slyke, pp. 92–180.

5. Many contemporaries have testified that the "Marco Polo Bridge Incident" on July 7, 1937, the date now officially accepted as the beginning of the War of Resistance against Japan, was at the time perceived as merely another local incident, similar to the "Mukden Incident." It was only when sustained fighting broke out in Shanghai that observers came to the conclusion that the War of Resistance had started. For this testimony, see, e.g., Zhang Yiwang, pp. 1–58.

6. Farmer, pp. 42–43.

7. Ibid., p. 46.

8. Sergeant, p. 301.

9. Many scholars believe that (as rumors within a small circle of foreigners at the time had it) the bombings were no mere coincidence. Rather, the pilot was ordered by Chiang Kaishek to bomb the foreign areas especially in order to bring the United States—which did not want to get involved in the Sino-Japanese conflict, beyond condemning the unprovoked Japanese aggression—into the War of Resistance. See, e.g., Sergeant. On the attitudes of the foreign powers, see Akira Iriye, *The Origins of the Second World War in Asia and the Pacific* (New York, 1987). The foreign areas had acquired a reputation for invulnerability, inasmuch as it survived intact and even prospered during all China's major national crises, such as the Taiping Rebellion of the 1850s, the first influx of Chinese into the area, and the 1911 Revolution. Even on the eve of the Battle of Shanghai, the foreign business community still assumed that the war, if it ever happened, would be restricted to the Chinese areas. See Bergere.

10. This description of the war is based on Song Ruike, "Bayisan Songhu kangzhan jishi" (A true account of the Battle of Shanghai), and Gu Gaodi, "Wo suo zhidao de Bayisan zhanyi pianduan" (A fragment of the Battle of Shanghai from my own perspective), in *Kangri,* 2: 34–73 and 74–90; *Bayisan*; Farmer, pp. 34–95; and *Bayisan kangzhan*, pp. 3–89. As Farmer relates, a Japanese communique reported in 1937 that on the two days

between October 25 and 27, "850 planes had dropped 2,526 bombs on the battlefront, leaving millions of refugees on the run" (p. 78). When the Japanese marines entered Jinshanwei, they terrorized the town in a murderous orgy, with three days of burning and massacre, and as they passed through the neighboring village of Luojin on their way to Nanshi, they killed 2,244 civilians.

11. Ba Jin, *Kongsu*, p. 45.

12. The board of the SGJ was composed of nine members, two of whom, Pan Gongzhan and Tong Xingbai, were Shanghai GMD unit chiefs. The other seven were business leaders affiliated with the Chinese Chamber of Commerce and the Federation of Shanghai Areas, who included Du Yuesheng and Qian Xinzhi. See *Dangan yu lishi* (Archive and history) 1, no. 3 (Mar. 1986): 2.

13. All member groups had to complete an application form before their registration. The form contained questions like: Number of members? Registered with any party or official organs? See Shanghai Municipal Police Files, no. 7994 (Nov. 1937). For the organizational structure and political significance of the SGJ, see also Wu Kaixian, pp. 15–16.

14. Jiang Hao, "Shanghai shi gejie houyuanhui gailüe" (A brief history of the SGJ), in *Kangri*, 1: 239.

15. Shanghai Municipal Police Files, no. 7994A (Nov. 1937).

16. Ibid.

17. Xia Yan, "Ji Jiuwang," p. 32.

18. Tang Zhenchang, p. 782.

19. For a vivid description of such "street dramas," see Du, p. 44.

20. Tian Han, "Zhongguo huaju yishu fazhan de jingli he zhanwang" (The history and prospects of the artistic development of Chinese theater), *Zhongguo huaju* 1: 3–12. For the text of the play, see *Shenghuo zhishi* 2, no. 9 (Sept. 1936). This play had many versions with slight differences, variations were usually made at each performance.

21. Yu Ling, "Modui," p. 21.

22. *Jiuwang*, Oct. 19, 1937.

23. Examples of this category were the Cyclists' National Salvation Corps (with 45 members), whose members were students adept at cycling, and the People's Lecture Party to Save the Country (with 31 members), whose members were mostly high-school teachers and college students. See Shanghai Municipal Police Files, no. 8039A (Oct. 1937). At the same time there were the Shanghai Educational Circles National Salvation Association, which had a membership of over 800, and the Shanghai Student Circles National Salvation Association, with 40 group members. See Tang Zhenchang, p. 784.

24. *Jiuwang*, Oct. 19, 1937.

25. Ibid. See also Tang Zhenchang, p. 783.

26. Shanghai Municipal Police Files, no. 8039A (Sept. 1937).

27. *Jiuwang*, Oct. 15, 1937.

28. Shanghai Municipal Police Files, no. 8038A (Nov. 1937).

29. Shanghai Municipal Police Files, no. 7994A (Nov. 1937).

30. *Jiuwang*, Oct. 11, 1937.

31. For examples of this formulation of the idea concerning the 1911 Revolution, see Zheng Zhenduo "Wuchang qiyi de gushi" (The story of the Wuchang uprising), and Pan Hannian.

32. Yang Dongchun, pp. 9–11.

33. See *Jiuwang*, Oct. 18, 1937. For a systematic study of the official creation of the Lu Xun cult by the CCP during the war, see Holm, "Lu Xun," pp. 152–79.

34. *Jiuwang*, Oct. 18, 1937.

35. For an example of the use of this term, see Qian Junrui.

36. Zhang Wozhou, p. 7.

37. See, e.g., Min Ren and Qian Junrui.

38. See, e.g., Zou, "Yinian."

39. Zou, "Duanjian."

40. Hu Ziying.

41. Qian Junrui, "Xie ge yaoqiu jiuwang de pengyou men" (To friends who want to take part in national salvation), *Kangzhan sanrikan*, Sept. 13, 1937. This radical characterization of wartime political corruption can be seen as the earliest formulation of a theme that soon became prominent in all genres of literature. The most successful work capturing this phenomenon was Zhang Tianyi's famous wartime novel *Huawei xiansheng* (Mr. Huawei).

42. Qian Junrui, p. 5; see also Hu Sheng and Ai Siqi.

43. Hu Sheng; Jin Ding; Qian Juntuan, p. 6.

44. Yu Ling, "Modui," p. 21; *Jiuwang*, Sept. 1937.

45. "Yi ge baogao" (One Report), *Kangzhan sanrikan*, Sept. 6, 1937, p. 11.

46. *Wenhua zhanxian*, no. 3 (Sept. 21, 1937), p. 8.

47. Bruce, pp. 64–74.

48. "Wei baowei da Shanghai yundong gao shimin shu" (Manifesto for the movement to defend Greater Shanghai), *Jiuwang*, Nov. 3, 1937.

49. Shanghai Municipal Police Files, nos. 8039A and 8002A (both Nov. 1937).

50. Shanghai Municipal Police Files, no. 8039A (Oct. 1937).

51. *Jiuwang*, Oct. 30, 1937.

52. For firsthand accounts of the "Lone Battalion," see *Bayisan Songwu*;

Bruce, pp. 64–66; *Shanghai Gudao wenxue zuopin xuanbian*, 3: 18–40. According to other sources, the flag Yang smuggled to the Gujun was too small; the larger flag raised above the warehouse was sent later, along with six trucks of food and clothes contributed by the people of Shanghai. The Boy Scouts War Service Corps was responsible for this smuggling. See Tang Zhenchang, p. 785. For an account by one of these boy scouts, see Yu Wensheng, "Wei Gujun songliang" (Transporting foodstuffs for the Lone Battalion), in *Shanghai yiri* (Shanghai, 1939).

53. Bruce, p. 66.

54. Yu Wensheng; Sergeant, p. 308.

55. "Zai Gujun fenzhan zhong jinian Huang Keqiang xiansheng" (The commemoration of Huang Keqiang during the courageous fight of the Lone Battalion), *Jiuwang*, Oct. 30, 1937.

56. Shanghai Municipal Police Files, no. 7994A (Nov. 1937).

57. Chen Chunren, p. 23.

58. See *Shen bao*, Nov. 12, 1938.

59. The term *wangguo nu* ("conquered people") was much used in 1938 and 1939 by people who felt ashamed about staying behind; see, e.g., Zhong Wangyang, "Wangguo nu," *Shanghai Gudao wenxue zuopin*, 3: 74–78.

1. Passivity: Wang Tongzhao and the Ideal of Resistance Enlightenment

1. Kong Lingjing, ed., p. 42.

2. The biographical information on Wang's prewar life is drawn, except as otherwise stated, from Feng and Liu, eds., pp. 12–39, and Wang Tongzhao, *Wang Tongzhao duanpian*, pp. i–vii.

3. See, e.g., Zheng Zhenduo, "Dao Wang Tongzhao xiansheng" (Mourning Mr. Wang Tongzhao); Zang Kejia, "Jiangsan jin hezai" (Where is Jiangsan now); Zang Yunyuan, "Ji shiren Wang Tongzhao" (In memory of the poet Wang Tongzhao), in Feng and Liu, eds., pp. 68–108. For a collection of photographs of Wang, see Feng Guanglian and Liu Zangren, eds., *Wang Tongzhao* (Hong Kong, 1985), pp. i–vi.

4. See Wang Tongzhao's "Huiyi," pp. 244–52.

5. Lucien Bianco, *Origins of the Chinese Revolution*, trans. Muriel Bell (Stanford, 1971), pp. 42–43. For a study of the May Fourth Movement along the theme of enlightenment, see Schwarcz. On the European humanist tradition, see Bullock.

6. The theme of disillusion and surrender is a common motif of post–May Fourth literature. For two famous examples, see Lu Xun's "Pang-

huang" (Hesitation), in *Lu Xun quanji* (Beijing, 1981), and Wang Tong-zhao's *Chunhua* (Spring Flower) (Shanghai, 1934).

7. Wang Tongzhao, *Wang Tongzhao wenji*, 1: 179.

8. See ibid., 5: 216–18.

9. For an excellent study of May Fourth literature, see Lee, "Romantic Individualism," pp. 239–58.

10. See, e.g., "Taigeer de sixiang yu qi shige de biaoxian" (The thought of Tagore and its poetic expression), and "Meiyu de mudi" (The object of aesthetic education), in *Wang Tongzhao wenji*, 4: 315–22 and 438–61; and Qu Shiying, "Chunyu zhi ye xu" (Preface to *Chunyu zhi ye*), in Wang Tongzhao, *Wang Tongzhao duanpian*, pp. 455–57.

11. My view of the liberal notion of war is based on Howard and Walzer.

12. Feng and Liu, eds., p. 15.

13. Wang Tongzhao, *Wang Tongzhao wenji*, 4: 523.

14. Wang Tongzhao, *Wang Tongzhao duanpian*, p. 5.

15. Feng and Liu, eds., p. 18.

16. Wang Tongzhao, "Shuanghen" (Frost stains), in *Wang Tongzhao wenji*, 1: 180.

17. See Bauer, pp. 164–66.

18. Wang Tongzhao, *Wang Tongzhao duanpian*, pp. 3–5.

19. "A record of the northeastern trip" (Dongbei jixin), in Wang Tongzhao, *Wang Tongzhao duanpian*, p. 6. Wang's experiences in the northeast were represented in his anthology of essays, *Beiguo zhi chun* (Spring in the north), which is collected in *Wang Tongzhao wenji*, 5: 3–102.

20. For Wang's trip and comments on his publications during this period, see Feng and Liu, eds., pp. 28–33, 188–445.

21. Ibid., pp. 700–702. On the Federation of Chinese Writers and Artists, see *Zuoyi wenyi yundong shiliao* (Historical materials on the leftist literary movement) (Nanjing, 1980), pp. 254–55.

22. For the "Two Slogans" Debate, see Tsi-an Hsia, *Gate of Darkness: Studies on the Leftist Literary Movement in China* (Seattle, 1971).

23. Wang Xiyan, "Huiyi Tongzhao xiansheng" (In memory of Mr. Tongzhao), in Feng and Liu, eds., pp. 77–79.

24. Zheng Zhenduo, "Dao Wang Tongzhao," pp. 67–69. For some samples of Wang's appeal to the *Wenxue* contributors, see *Wang Tongzhao wenji*, 6: 530–44. And for not revealing his address, see Wang's letter to Zhao Jingshen in *Zhongguo xiandai wenyi ziliao congkan*, no. 6 (Apr. 1981), pp. 220–21.

25. See Mao Dun, "Fenghuo," p. 9.

26. Zhang Jinglu, *Zai chubanjie*, p. 191.

27. Mao Dun, "Zhangshang," p. 1. *Fenghuo* was jointly published by four recently folded journals: *Wenxue* (Literature), *Yiwen* (Translation), *Zhongliu* (Midstream), and *Wenji* (Literary Season).

28. *Shanghai Gudao wenxue huiyi*, 1: 33.

29. Wang Tongzhao, "Ye"; for Mao Dun, see "Xie yu shensheng de baosheng zhong" (Writing amidst the gunfire of the holy war), *Fenghuo*, no. 1 (Aug. 25, 1937): 1; for Ba Jin, see his "Gei Shanchuan," pp. 82–86; and see Jing Yi, pp. 10–11.

30. See Wang Tongzhao, "Chongdong," p. 20. For similiar views among other *Fenghuo* editors, see, e.g., Ba Jin and Tian Jian.

31. Wang Tongzhao, *Wang Tongzhao wenji*, 6: 545–47.

32. See "Zhanshi zhanhou wenyi jiantao zuotanhui" (A symposium on wartime and postwar literature), *Shanghai Wenhua*, no. 6 (July 1946), p. 187.

33. Wang Tongzhao, " 'Zhe shidai' xu" (Preface to *Zhe shidai*), in *Wang Tonzhao shixuan*, p. 183.

34. Wang Tongzhao, "Chongdong." See also his "Kangzhan zhong de wenyi huodong" (The literary movement during the war), in *Wang Tongzhao wenji*, 6: 554–59.

35. Wang Tongzhao, "Yi Jinsiniang," p. 204.

36. For various rumors and Japanese harassment in Shanghai, see Yao Sufeng et al., pp. 70, 76. For Japanese abuses on the Garden Bridge, see Tao Juyin, *Gudao*, ch. 3.

37. Yao Sufeng et al., pp. 70–72. See also Mao Dun, "Fenghuo." Rather typical of these intellectuals was the essayist Lu Danlin, who had helped manage a refugee center during the battle of Shanghai. Though a man of apolitical temperament, after repeated exhortation from friends, and news of political intimidation, he decided he no longer had the freedom "to let out [his] anger in Shanghai." Lu soon left for Hong Kong and helped found the magazine *Da feng* (Great Wind), which became one of the most popular wartime literary periodicals. It provided Shanghai émigrés in Hong Kong with a forum for airing patriotic ideas. See Yao Sufeng et al., pp. 77–78.

38. Feng and Liu, eds., p. 40.

39. "Largely unoccupied" because the part of the International Settlement called Hongkou, which lay north of Suzhou Creek, was in fact occupied by the Japanese army. Nicknamed "Little Tokyo," this area had long been dominated by Japanese residents of the city. Only that part of the International Settlement south of Suzhou Creek and the French Concession remained unoccupied. For two succinct accounts of this situation, see Jones, pp. 57–72 and Barnett, chs. 1–3.

40. Calvocoressi and Wint, p. 265. On European resistance movements, see also Rings; Kedward, *Resistance in Vichy France*.

41. Statement by Sterling Fessenden, then chairman of the Shanghai Municipal Council of the International Settlement, on November 13, 1937; quoted from Xu Zhucheng, p. 225.

42. *Shanghai Municipal Council Annual Report*, 1937, p. 244; Yi Ren, p. 131.

43. Shanghai Municipal Police Files, no. 8039A (Mar. 1941).

44. Shanghai Municipal Police Files, no. 3019 (Dec. 1937).

45. Ibid.; see also Xu Zhucheng, p. 268, and Tao Juyin, *Jizhe*, p. 184.

46. Shanghai Municipal Police Files, no. 3019 (Dec. 1937); see also Ke Ling and Ren Jiarao.

47. The sales of the *Damei wanbao* rose from 2,000–3,000 to 40,000–50,000 in late 1937; see Zhang Zhihan, p. 43.

48. The term is borrowed from Ke Ling. See his "Wenhua huangyuan" (Cultural wilderness), in *Ke Ling zawen*, pp. 94–101.

49. For Shanghai residents' refusal to buy the Japanese-sponsored newspaper, see Shanghai Municipal Police Files, no. 3019 (Dec. 1937); and on the boycott of Chinese papers, see Ke Ling and Ren Jiarao. The declining sales of the preeminent *Xinwen bao* (Daily News), from 180,000 prewar to fewer than 10,000 in the first month after its submission to Japanese censorship, are one example of this boycott; see Xu Zhucheng, p. 272. For the term "armchair resisters," see Kedward, *Occupied France*, pp. 53–55.

50. For a comprehensive account of the founding of *Wenhui bao*, see Xu Chiheng, pp. 263–66; see also Xu Zhucheng, pp. 281–83.

51. Xu Chiheng, p. 266. According to Xu Zhucheng, moreover, H.M. Cumine's monthly salary was Ch. $300, plus allowances, which was impressively high when compared to that of top-level Chinese staff. For example, the monthly salary of the editor-in-chief of the *Xinwen bao* was Ch. $200–300, while that of chief reporter of the *Dagong bao* was $150–200; see Xu Zhucheng, pp. 263, 282.

52. For this figure, see Xu Chiheng, p. 270. At the same time the famous *Xinwen bao* had a sale of only 50,000 copies. The decrease in subscriptions was owing in part to its compromise and in part to the restriction of its sales route.

53. Ba Ren, "'Lu Xun feng' huajiu" (Remembering *Lu Xun feng*), in *Ba Ren*, p. 143.

54. Ke Ling, "Yangbao," p. 341.

55. The eminent *Shen bao*, after repeated failures to gain a profitable foothold in Hankou and Hong Kong, returned to Shanghai to resume publication on October 10, 1938, under the nominal management of the

U.S.-registered Columbia Publishing Company, which was headed by an American lawyer, N.F. Allman.

56. Kong Yuanzhi, "Huangpu," p. 456; and "Wuyue," p. 307. This observation was probably not an exaggeration. According to one source, there were 23 newspapers and 109 journals registered with the Shanghai Muncipal Council in 1936; in 1937-38, the number jumped to 89 and 258 respectively (Yi Ren, p. 131). See also the Japanese-published *Shanhai yoran,* pp. 71-72, which lists 26 prominent newspapers with average daily sales of over 25,000 copies in 1939.

57. Rhetorical devices were improvised to cover Chinese defeats in ways that were both patriotic and "honest." Thus "change of battle zone" or "moves into a new zone" signaled retreat.

58. Xu Zhucheng, p. 271.

59. There has thus far been no publication of primary materials or systematic study of GMD involvement in wartime Shanghai's cultural activities, or in particular in its press industry. This study is based on personal memoirs by Xu Zhucheng, Bao, and Li Qiusheng.

60. Wang Yaoshan, pp. 57-58; see also Liu Xiao.

61. The editorial appeared in May 1938. There is a translation in Shanghai Municipal Police Files, no. 3019 (Sept. 1938).

62. See Kubota, pp. 9-19. Nonetheless, through postal workers seeking to "elude the Japanese censors," a limited number of copies of these foreign-published newspapers were secretly hoarded in occupied areas near Shanghai; like other blackmarket goods, they sold for 70 to 100 percent more than their original price (2.5 cents). For the resistance of postal workers, see Powell, p. 34. And for the black-marketeering, see Kong Yuanzhi, "Wuyue," p. 307.

63. Shanghai Municipal Police Files, no. 8039A (July 1938).

64. For a vivid description of the horror of Bridge House, see Collar, ch. 6.

65. Tao Juyin, *Gudao,* pp. 30-32. See also Zhu Menghua, pp. 152-54.

66. Zhu Menghua, p. 154.

67. Ibid. Altogether, according to one source, there were over 42 murders and 148 reports of threats received in 1938, compared to 22 cases and 82 reports in 1937; see *Shanghai Municipal Council Annual Report,* 1939, pp. 237-347.

68. Kong Lingjing, ed., p. 325.

69. For example, the essayist Kong Lingjing wrote: "At this time of national crisis, the intellectuals who have moved to the interior are bravely fighting the enemy. We who remain here are marked as cowards, so we should not complain about a dangerous life....As long as we can move, we

should try our best to create troubles for the enemy." See Kong, "Hua-guang juzhuan huiyilu" (Reminiscing about Huaguang Dramatic College), in *Shanghai Gudao wenxue huiyi*, 2: 394. Another writer, Wen Zaidao (Jin Xingyao), asserted that both love and individual life should be sacrificed to the freedom of the nation. See his "Chuhan suibi" (An essay in early winter), in Kong Lingjing, ed., pp. 117–20.

70. Tang Tao, "Jijiu cacao" (Random notes), in Kong Lingjing, ed., pp. 277–78.

71. Wilkinson, pp. 42–50.

72. Zheng Zhenduo, "Da shidai wenyi congshu xu" (General preface to *Da shidai wenyi congshu*), in Kong Lingjing, ed., p. i. The quotation is from a famous poem by the Song statesman Fan Zhongyan (989–1050).

73. The term "beating war drums from the sidelines" is from Ba Ren—see *Shanghai Gudao wenxue huiyi*, 1: 119; the quotation is from Kong Lingjing, ed., p. 395.

74. Correspondence with Ke Ling, June 21, 1987.

75. Wen Zaidao, "Qiang yu bi" (Gun and pen), in Kong Lingjing, ed., p. 139.

76. For a general description of *zawen* in occupied Shanghai, see Gunn, *Unwelcome Muse*, pp. 59–69.

77. For a memoir of the *Shiji feng*, see Ke Ling, *Zhuzi*, pp. 34–36; see also Xu Kailei, "*Shiji feng*," pp. 32–44. On Smedley's report on Communist areas, see Janice and Stephen MacKinnon, *Agnes Smedley* (Berkeley, 1988), pp. 182–232.

78. Zhu Lang, "Wang Tongzhao xiansheng zai Qingdao" (Mr. Wang Tongzhao in Qingdao), in Feng and Liu, eds., p. 60. For the Communist student movement at Jinan University, see *Shanghai Gudao wenxue huiyi*, 1: 140–48 and 2: 20–29 and 316–32.

79. The first quotation is from Yuan Yalu, "Jinan si jiaoshou" (The four professors at Jinan), in Feng and Liu, eds., pp. 56–58; the second from Xu Kailei, "Huainian," pp. 73–77.

80. Wang Jicheng, "Xu" (Preface), in Feng Guanglian and Liu Zengren, eds., *Wang Tongzhao*, pp. i–iii.

81. Qin Shouou, "Wang Tongzhao yu 'Daying yebao' fukan" (Wang and the *Daying yebao* supplement), in *Shanghai Gudao wenxue huiyi*, 1: 131–33.

82. See, e.g., "Liuzai Shanghai ne haishi dao waidi qu" (Should we stay in Shanghai or go to the interior), *Jiangnan xinwen*, no. 7 (Nov. 1940).

83. See, e.g., his "Bianhou hua" (Editor's notes), *Wenxue*, 9, no. 2 (Aug. 1937).

84. Wang Tongzhao, *Wang Tongzhao wenji*, 4: 52.

85. *Shanghai Gudao wenxue huiyi,* 2: 23–24; and Xu Kailei, p. 75.

86. See, e.g., Wilkinson, pp. 37–40.

87. Wang Tongzhao, *Fanci,* p. 43. *Fanci* is the collection of Wang's prose poetry serialized in *Shiji feng.* Unless otherwise stated, this whole section is based on analysis of this book, and the page numbers given parenthetically in the text refer to it.

88. Ba Jin, *Jia* (Family) (Hong Kong, 1989), pp. 16–17.

89. Ke Ling, *Ke Ling zawen,* p. 184. See Chapter 2 for more discussion of the intellectual resistance in occupied Shanghai.

90. Wei Zheng, p. 439.

91. On the theoretical problems involving moral systems, see Gert.

92. Barnett, pp. 25–28. Shanghai city's rice came mainly from Qingpu, Songjiang, Changshu, Kunshan, and Wuxi. Rice from these five regions was known collectively as "native rice" in Shanghai.

93. The phrases "deformed prosperity" and "the loose sand" (of cheap labor) were popular in descriptions of Shanghai at the time. See, e.g., Kong Yuanzhi, "Huangpu." For a discussion of Shanghai's wartime industry, see Tang Zhenchang, pp. 801–5.

94. See Liu Tiesun, p. 880; *Shangye zazhi* (Commerce magazine) 1, no. 2 (Oct. 1940): 53, and Confidential U.S. State Department Reports, Apr. 1939–Dec. 1940. According to the latter source, the cost of living index rose from 118.15 percent in 1937 to 203.25 percent in 1939, 579.70 percent in 1940 and 732.79 percent in April 1941. This is a slightly conservative estimate, cf. Wan Ren, p. 283.

95. For an interesting report of "cheap rice" in the foreign settlements, see Confidential U.S. State Department Reports, no. 00725 (Feb. 1940). As for the price of "cheap" and black-market rice, see ibid., no. 00697 (Jan. 1940), and Shanghai Municipal Police Files, no. 8039A (Aug. 1941). In 1940, each person was allowed to buy one *dou* (17.6 lbs.) of *yangmi,* but in 1941 the quota dropped to only one *sheng* (1.76 lbs.); see Tao Shiping, chs. 5–7.

96. Quoted from Barnett, p. 52. According to Shanghai municipal government statistics, the lowest cost of living in 1941 was Ch. $167.84; the average income of lower-middle-class white-collar workers was Ch. $150, and that of apprentices, Ch. $40; see *Shanghai zhoubao* 3, no. 7 (Feb. 1941): 197.

97. *Zhiye yu xiuyang* (Vocation and cultivation) 1, no. 2 (July 1939): 56. The editors were Ye Xinan and the famous nutritionist and collector Ding Fubao.

98. The increases in the crime rate, rice riots, and strikes after 1938 are a clear indication of this. There were, for example, 75 rice riots in December 1939 alone (Barnett, p. 54) and according to the annual reports of the

Shanghai Municipal Council, there was a great increase in strikes, from 21 in 1938 to 124 in 1939 and 152 in the first half of 1940 (to July); see Wan Ren, p. 284. As for thefts, there were 139 reported cases in July–Dec. 1939, compared to 342 in 1940 (Zhou Huaren, *Shanghai*, pp. 104–5).

99. See *Shanghai zhoubao*, 3, no. 12 (Mar. 1941): 366–67; and Tang Zhenchang, p. 804.

100. See Ge, who provides a vivid account of these speculative activities. Publications of the time were filled with public outcries against speculation, particularly against the rice profiteers. For a literary depiction of these phenomena, see Luo.

101. For literary portrayal of the problems of opium and gambling in occupied Shanghai, see Zheng Dingwen, pp. 86–94; "Life's Show-window," in Randall Gould Papers; Chen Chunren, pp. 156–77 and 214–80. See also Su Shan.

102. Interview with Liu Yichang, Hong Kong, July 1986.

103. *Shanghai shenghuo*, 3, no. 2 (Feb. 1939): 76, and 3, no. 5 (May 1939): 90.

104. See the excellent account of the activities of the "Shanghai District Office" by its chief from 1939 to 1941, Chen Gongshu, pp. 2–40, 106–286. According to the Shanghai Municipal Police Files, no. 4685 (Nov. 1941), the "Shanghai District Office" had slain 107 Japanese military and Chinese and Taiwanese collaborators in 1940.

105. See Huang, Shi, and Jiang; and Yeh. For a memoir by No. 76 leaders, see Ma Xiaotian and Wang Manyun, *Wangwei tegong neimu* (The inside story of the Wang regime's secret services) (Henan, 1986).

106. These descriptions are from Confidential U.S. State Department Reports, no. 00114–00118 (May 1941).

107. Xu Chiheng, pp. 31–36.

108. Xu Kailei, p. 104.

109. For accounts of such security measures, see Zhang Zhihan, pp. 48–49, and Zhao Junhao, pp. 1–85.

110. Bao, p. 83.

111. See a summary of this propaganda endeavor in Shi Ying, p. 186.

112. See, e.g., Lin Zemin, p. 280.

113. Ke Ling, *Shilou*, p. 34.

114. Ba Ren, "Lun *toujijia*," pp. 473–74.

115. Wen Zaidao, "Saochu yimin qi," p. 110.

116. Ke Ling, "Shimo zhiyu" (Beyond vilification), in Wen Zaidao et al., p. 351.

117. Wang Tongzhao, *Qu lai jin*, pp. 131–33.

118. Ibid., pp. 113–17.

119. See Barthes, esp. pp. 15–17.

120. See Ferguson, pp. 460–68. See also Anderson.

121. The title of the collection is *Huating he*. The other three stories collected here were "Huating he" (discussed later), "Muai" (Motherly love), and "Xinsheng" (A rebirth). These three, unlike "Lei yu yi," had appeared in journals published in Shanghai or in Chongqing. The heroes of the latter two are a Catholic nun and a priest respectively. They both, in different representative ways, but with similar religious symbols, attempt despite great adversity to bring spiritual salvation to China. Their endeavors are futile— the nun fails to save an orphaned child, the priest is forced by illness and the church's order to discontinue his service in China. Thus the failure of "enlightenment." But the endings of these stories are similarly artificial, unlike that of "Lei yu yi," giving false hope of future changes totally at odds with the natural course of the narrative. This ambivalent structure was per- haps a result of Wang's intention to add a sense of optimism, however dim and vague, in order not to alienate or discourage the reading public. All these stories have been republished in Zheng, Wang, and Geng.

122. Zheng, Wang, and Geng, p. 50.

123. For the painting and a discussion of Brueghel (ca. 1525–1569), see Keith Roberts, *Brueghel* (Oxford, 1971), plate 10.

124. Wang Tongzhao, "Zhuinian Tongxuan laoren" (Remembering Old Gentleman Tongxuan), in *Qu lai jin*, pp. 40–46.

125. Zheng, Wang, and Geng, pp. 102, 109–10.

126. Ibid., p. 112.

127. This poem is collected in Zheng, Wang, and Geng, front page.

128. The metaphor of the "dark world" was so popular that it appears in almost every contemporary book or article written by Shanghai authors other than collaborators and Japanese. See, e.g., Tao Juyin, *Tianliang*, pas- sim. For an interesting account of the metaphor and its connotations, see Chen Chunren, pp. 226–30.

129. Kubota, p. 32; *Shanghai Gudao wenxue huiyi*, 1: 121.

130. Correspondence with Ke Ling, June 21, 1987.

131. There is no exact figure for the victims of this persecution. Thus far we know of over 30 cases of arrest, most of them involving leftist writ- ers. The victims included Xia Minzun, Ke Ling, and Kong Lingjing. See Zhao Jingshen, *Wentan*, pp. 86 and 136. See also *Shanghai Gudao wenxue huiyi*, 2: 196–205.

132. *Shanghai Gudao wenxue huiyi*, 2: 404.

133. For example, the writer and painter Qian Juntao stopped publish- ing anti-Japanese magazines and closed his publishing house after December 1941, devoting himself to the study of oracle bones and ancient Chinese art

throughout the Occupation (see Qian Juntao). Tao Juyin left his editorial job at the *Xinwen bao* to compose a collective biography of the participants in late Qing Hundred Days Reform and care for his sick wife and infant son (see Tao, *Tianliang*). The author Zhang Duosheng hawked rice to support his family, but most writers-turned-merchants chose to open secondhand bookstores (see Tang Tao, "Wo he," p. 77).

134. See Mote, esp. pp. 279–90. The resemblances between recluses under the Japanese Occupation and during dynastic changes in Yuan or Ming times, as will be discussed in detail in the Epilogue, were in some significant ways only formal. Yet Mote's distinction between devotion to the political authority and commitment to principle itself (p. 283) and his view that the main instrument of most Confucian loyalists was their "restraining force" (p. 286) are particularly well-taken. For slightly different use of the term "symbolic resistance" with respect to Nazi-dominated Europe, see Rings, pp. 153–61; Wilkinson, pp. 112–26.

135. This is a famous quotation from the Song Neo-Confucian philosopher Zhu Xi (1130–1200); see Zhu Xi, p. 177.

136. As the playwright Li Jianwu expressed the thinking of the Shanghai recluse: "It is for [our] moral conscience and for our nation" (Li, "Wan Sange").

137. Jiang Kanghu, "Shijie shi gengda," pp. 101–2.

138. For a succinct exposition of modern images of the traditional recluse, see Jiang Xingyu. On the historical evolution of the terms for hermit, *yinshi* and *yinyi*, see Bauer.

139. Tang Tao [Mo Ran], "Chenmo," pp. 14–16.

140. As Geng Jizhi's wife recalled fondly, "The similar goal of anti-Japanese resistance brought [Geng] into a much closer relationship with his few friends like Wang Tongzhao and Zheng Zhenduo in the Solitary Island." See Qian Fuzhi, "Zhuihuai zheju shiqi de Geng Jizhi" (A recollection of the secluded life of Geng Jizhi in the Solitary Island), in *Shanghai Gudao wenxue huiyi*, 1: 354.

141. This translation is from Watson, p. 76.

142. See Scott. For a very interesting account of this kind of group discussion, see Tao Juyin, *Tianliang*, passim; and Chen Chunren, pp. 222–39.

143. During the Solitary Island period, the Shanghai office was charged with sending new manuscripts or galley proofs of old publications—both high school textbooks and literary works—to the interior (via two sea routes from Shanghai to Chongqing or Guilin: one through Ningbo or Wenzhou; another from Haiphong in Vietman to Kunming) to be printed. Each editor in the Shanghai Kaiming office had a monthly income of Ch. $20. This was, of course, not enough to live on in Shanghai, so most of

the editors took other jobs on the side, such as teaching. See *Wo yu kaiming*, pp. 291–303.

144. Kaiming's editorial board included such May Fourth intellectuals as Xia Mianzun, Xu Diaofu, Gu Junzheng, and Zhou Zhenpu, all of them natives of Zhejiang or Jiangsu. The new editors employed after 1941 included the historian Zhou Yutong, the literary historian Guo Shaoyu, who fled Beijing after being forced to accept a teaching job at the Japanese-occupied Beijing University, and the bibliographer Chen Naiqian. The feeling of the Kaiming community of recluses was epitomized by a couplet composed by Guo, which was hung on the office door: "Smoke from the cooking fire ascends outside the window/Running water sounds before the house." Its bucolic tone ameliorated the miserable working and living conditions of the ramshackle, leaky bookstore, evoking a world of cozy eremitism. See *Wo yu Kaiming*, pp. 108–70.

145. Ibid., pp. 168–73; Correspondence with Ke Ling, Feb. 1, 1983.

146. Xu Kailei, "Huainian," p. 76, see also Yuan Yalu, "Jinan si jiaoshou," p. 58.

147. Feng and Liu, eds., pp. 42–43.

148. Xu Kailei, "Huainian," pp. 73–77.

149. See Chen Fukang, pp. 208–22.

150. Wang wrote in 1946 that he had known Xia Mianzun in the early 1920s, but that they did not become good friends until the Occupation. See his "Mianzun xiansheng."

151. Xia's conversion to Buddhism was also his way of resisting pressure to collaborate. As he was a returned student from Japan in the 1910s and spoke excellent Japanese, many Japanese army officers came to press him to join the Wang Jingwei regime. Xia's overt devotion to Buddhism was a way to express his apathy toward politics. Despite this, he was arrested, together with six other publishers (two from Kaiming) and professors, by the Kempeitai in November 1943 and detained for three weeks. After his release, Geng was more committed to his Buddhist translation. For his life under the Occupation, see Lou Shiyi, "Huainian Xia Mianzun" (Remembering Xia Mianzun), *Renwu*, no. 4 (July 1981): 152–59. On *jushi* as a mode of Chinese eremitism, see Bauer, pp. 172–75.

152. See Qian Fuzhi, "Zhuihuai zheju," 1: 354; and Zhao Jiabi, "Huainian Geng Jizhi" (In memory of Geng Jizhi), in *Shanghai Gudao wenxue huiyi*, 1: 359–72.

153. The *Collected Works of Lu Xun* was complied and published for the first time, a project initated by Xu Guangping, Zheng Zhenduo, and Ba Ren. The publication of this 20-volume work occurred at the Fu she headquarters, Hu Zhongchi's house on 2 Rue Ratard, and the compilation and copyediting of the collected works, a job that had involved over ten people,

including Xu Guangping, Tang Tao, and Ke Ling, were done at Xu's house at 64 Joffre Lane. Edgar Snow's book was translated by eleven people, including Hu Zhongchi and the young Communist writers Mei Yi, Feng Binfu, and Lin Danqiu, each working on one chapter. For intimate and interesting accounts of the Fu she and its publications, see *Shanghai Gudao wenxue huiyi*, 1: 24–65.

154. For Zheng's activities during the Occupation, see his *Jiezhong* and the various memoirs by Wu Wenqi, Zhou Yiping, and Zheng Erkang in *Shanghai Gudao wenxue huiyi*, 2: 140–88. See also the memoirs of the poet Xin Di and the writers Wu Yan, Shi Tuo, and Tang Tao in *Yi Zheng Zhenduo* (Remembering Zheng Zhenduo) (Shanghai, 1988); and, especially important, Chen Fukang, ed., *Zheng Zhenduo nianpu* (The chronology of Zheng Zhenduo) (Beijing, 1988), pp. 285–328.

155. For two intimate memoirs on sharing food and wine, see Xu Diaofu, "Yi Geng Jizhi xiansheng" (Remembering Mr. Geng), and Zhou Yutong, "Dao Jizhi xiansheng" (Condoling Mr. Jizhi), *Wenyi fuxing* 3, no. 3 (May 1947): 275–76 and 277–78.

156. Wang Tongzhao, "Mianzun xiansheng." For a sample of Wang's poems at this difficult time, see Feng and Liu, eds., p. 110.

157. Wang Tongzhao, "Mianzun xiansheng."

158. For this community of connections, see, e.g., Fan Quan, "Wo renshi de Wang Tongzhao xiansheng" (The Mr. Wang Tongzhao that I know), *Xin wenxue shiliao*, no. 2 (1990): 120–22; *Shanghai Gudao wenxue huiyi*, 1: 352–71.

159. Correspondence with Ke Ling, June 21, 1987.

160. Ibid., Feb. 1, 1988.

161. For a general study of *Wanxiang*, see Yang Yousheng, pp. 21–28. Ke Ling recalled that he frequently went to Kaiming for contributions and for information about other writers in Shanghai and in the interior (correspondence with Ke Ling, Feb. 1, 1988).

162. Wang Tongzhao, "Mianzun xiansheng."

163. "Xia Mianzun yangmao hun changhe shi," pp. 55–58. Such use of private occasions for political purposes is common in Chinese history. In May 1989, for example, the celebration of the famous Beijing University philosopher Zhang Dainian's long teaching career was turned by his students and colleagues into a public statement of their moral commitment to a freer, more humane China. See Vera Schwarcz, "Memory, Commemoration, and the Plight of China's Intellectuals," *Wilson Quarterly*, Autumn 1989, pp. 128–29.

164. See Ke Ling, *Zhuzi*, pp. 44–51 and 257–80; correspondence with Ke Ling, Nov. 15, 1990.

165. Correspondence with Ke Ling, Feb. 1, 1988.

166. See, e.g., Takahashi, pp. 4–9; Zhou Huaren, "Dongya," pp. 2–5.

167. Indeed, the connection between women as social victims and symbolic resisters as political prey was a common literary device in occupied Shanghai. For example, Geng Jizhi published three stories in *Wanxiang* during 1942–43 describing the victimization of women by society—widow, rape victim, and prostitute—as a metaphor for symbolic resistance under Japanese occupation. See his "Gu dasao" (Aunty Gu), "Chongfeng" (Reunion), and "Baomu" (Nanny), all collected in Zheng, Wang, and Geng, pp. 113–45.

168. For a study of such perceptions, see Chow, chs. 3–4.

169. The term is borrowed from Frederic Wakeman's analysis of the Ming loyalists; see his *Great Enterprise*, 2: 1084–85.

170. Wang Tongzhao, *Wang Tongzhao wenji*, 4: 317.

171. For a vivid description of the rumor and the evacuation, see *Chunqiu* 2, no. 4 (Apr. 1945).

172. "He has grown bald....All his teeth are gone. It is hot, but he puts on a padded cotton overcoat. Underneath he wears an old brownish cloth gown. Gone are the years when he wore a stylish Western-style suit. Eight years of hard life have left their mark on him," his friend Zhu Lang noted (Feng and Liu, eds., p. 60).

173. See Feng and Lui, eds., p. 43.

2. Resistance: Li Jianwu and the Theater of Commitment

1. Ke Ling, *Ke Ling*, p. 109.

2. Li's childhood has been reconstructed from his own account; see "Li Jianwu zizhuan," pp. 26–29.

3. Wang Tongzhao was at the time the literary editor of the famous *Chen bao* (Morning Post). He helped Li revise many of his writings and gave him a lot of encouragement, and most of Li's early works were published in *Chen bao*. Li liked to call Wang his "unofficial teacher" (ibid).

4. For a general study of French neoromantic criticism, see Albert Thibaudet, *French Literature from 1795 to Our Era*, trans. Charles Lam Markmann (New York, 1967).

5. For Li's experiences in Paris and Beijing, see Xu Shihu, pp. 87–90.

6. Li Jianwu, *Qiemeng*.

7. Li Qishan was remembered as an especially stern and demanding father, even in the Chinese context. When his son forgot to bow to him on his birthday, for example, he slapped him repeatedly in the presence of prison guards. See Li Jianwu, *Li Jianwu chuangzuo*, p. 272. Li would not have been allowed to become involved in acting, one of the most disgrace-

ful vocations, which would bring shame to a family. For a description of a pioneering actor's experience in this regard, see Xu Banmei.

8. The description of Li's early life and his father's career is based on "Zizhuan," pp. 335–37, and *Li Jianwu chuangzuo*, p. 264.

9. The cultural and social objectives of the early *huaju* were reflected in the original appelation of *huaju* and names of the earliest dramatic groups and the plays they chose to stage. The original term for modern drama was *xin wenming ju* (new civilized drama); the name *huaju* was coined by Tian Han in the 1920s. Among the earliest groups were the Xinmin she (Society of New Citizens) and Kaiming she (Enlightenment Society); and the first plays to be put on were *Chahua nü* (1907), adapted from Alexandre Dumas *fils*'s *La Dame aux Camélias*, and *Heinu yutian lu* (1908), a version of Harriet Beecher Stowe's *Uncle Tom's Cabin*. Other favorite Western playwrights included Ibsen, Shaw, and Romain Roland. For a brief history of modern Chinese drama, see *Zhongguo huaju yundong* and Mackerras.

10. For some excellent discussions of the problems of *huaju* in the 1920s and 1930s, see *Zhongguo huaju yundong*.

11. Li Jianwu, *Liang Yunda*, p. i.

12. Li Jianwu, *Yi shen zuo ze*, (setting personal example) (Shanghai, 1948) p. i.

13. Ibid, p. ii.

14. Quoted in Li Jianwu, *Juhua*, p. 47.

15. See Li Jianwu, *Li Jianwu chuangzuo*, pp. 223–33.

16. See Li Jianwu, *Zhe buguo* and *Shisan nian*.

17. See *Shisan nian*, p. 37. A translation of the two plays and their postscripts can be found in Li Jianwu, *It's Only Spring and Thirteen Years*. For two fine analyses of Li's early plays, with a different emphasis from mine, see Takeda, pp. 54–59, and Pollard, "Li Chien-wu," pp. 364–88.

18. Shi Tuo, "Ji yiwei," p. 85.

19. Li Jianwu, *Qiemeng*, pp. 32–33.

20. Chen Fukang, ed., *Zheng Zhenduo nianpu*, p. 267.

21. Almost all the intellectuals who remained in Shanghai after the start of the Occupation cited problems of physical disability and family obligations (e.g., Ke Ling, Tang Tao, Wang Tongzhao). These became a stereotyped pattern of self-justification. In fact, Li, like other intellectuals, may simply have been unwilling to leave his secure, comfortable life and fine collection of books behind in Shanghai to move to the backward and unknown interior. For a description of Li's house, which was reportedly lined with expensive books in both Chinese and English, see Shi Tuo, *Shanghai*.

22. For some interesting accounts of trips into the interior, see Bao,

and Zhu Wen. Prominent among those who died were Ye Zi and Lu Yan, whose fate was widely publicized in Shanghai.

23. See Shanghai Municipal Police Files, no. 8039A (Dec. 1937). This group was affiliated with the now underground SGJ, which planned to organize a demonstration of patriotic will on New Year's Day by boycotting Japanese goods, having Chinese shops hoist national flags, and sending people into residential areas to distribute patriotic leaflets. According to another police report, Zuan Hua Co. printed New Year cards with national salvation messages and sold 6,400 cards within a week (no. 8039A, Jan. 1938). For the Japanese victory parade, see Sergeant, pp. 308−9.

24. Furuyama, p. 81.

25. Ke Ling, *Ke Ling*, p. 42.

26. Liu Xiao, pp. 37−40 and 51−58. See also *Shanghai renmin*. The Shanghai CCP was divided into six committees (labor, cultural, employee, education, women, and refugees and students) and two special branches (customs office and police office). The cultural committee was subdivided into three branches, drama, journalism, and literature.

27. Bentley, *Playwrights*, and *Thinking*.

28. Sartre, *Sartre*, p. 39.

29. For interesting studies of Resistance theater in occupied Europe, see Myrsiades, pp. 99−106, and Marsh, pp. 199−369.

30. The Shanghai Association of the Theatrical Circle for National Salvation was dissolved in early 1938 after its move to Wuhan, then the headquarters of the Nationalist government, becoming the larger Chinese Federation of Theatrical Circles. The Shanghai Municipal Government Chinese Employees' Club, which was open to all Chinese white-collar workers in the Shanghai municipal government, was organized shortly before the war; it had become very active in rear echelon work and, after Shanghai's fall, was involved under Li Bolong in the amateur theater movement that flourished from 1938 to 1940.

31. Cheng Zhongyuan, pp. 93−95.

32. Gu Zhongyi was scheduled to direct the first show, but he was forced to decline and go into hiding after receiving a death threat. This provided the French municipal government with a reason to disband the group. See *Zhongguo huaju yishujia*, 3: 30−70 and 311−34.

33. Ibid., p. 59; Yu Ling, "Modui," p. 1: 21; Gu Zhongyi, pp. 143−45. Chu Minyi, an in-law of Wang Jingwei's, soon joined the "Peace Movement." Zhao Zhiyou, special representative in charge of army finance of Chen Cheng, commander-in-chief of the Third War Zone in Anhui, served as nominal head of the society.

34. Ren Yongliang, ed., H: 10−14.

35. Gu Zhongyi, p. 146.

36. Yu Ling, "Modui," p. 22.

37. Xu Shihu; *Li Jianwu wenxue*, p. 328. Besides academic research during 1935−37, Li published some pieces of literary criticism in Shen Congwen's literary supplement, anthologized in 1936 as *Juhua ji* (Appreciation). But, like all of his prewar plays, this was largely ignored by the literary world until Li became famous during the war.

38. Ke Ling, *Ke Ling*, pp. 182−85.

39. Owing in large part to overcrowding and bad sanitation as a result of the influx of war refugees in 1938−40, epidemic diseases were rife in the foreign areas, including cholera, scarlet fever, and meningitis. Children were particularly vulnerable to these diseases. Indeed, the sons of two Communist writers, Ba Ren and Shi Ling, died of high fever, and two children of Tang Tao's of tuberculosis, all in 1938.

40. Li Jianwu, *Qie meng*, pp. 39−40.

41. The motive for resistance is a complex and complicated issue. As with most resisters, Li's decision had never been fully articulated, probably not even to himself, and was certainly representative of those of many liberal Shanghai intellectuals of the time. For a sensitive study of French resisters' motives, see Kedward, *Resistance in Vichy France*, pp. 75−81.

42. Li Jianwu, "Xibo xiansheng" (Mr. Xibo), "Shijian" (Time), and "Pifu" (The ordinary people), in *Li Jianwu chuangzuo*, pp. 222−33. The quotation is from "Pifu," p. 230.

43. Ba Ren, *Ba Ren*, p. 151. For the term "versus habit," see Fussell.

44. On intellectual collaborators, see, e.g., Ke Ling, *Ke Ling*, p. 305.

45. Ke Ling recapitulated the Resistance discourse with similar disease symbolism: "Before the mirror of history, the distinction between man and beast is sharp. This is in the final analysis a matter of human dignity. Our war is a surgery. It cuts away decayed flesh, allowing new muscle to grow. [China] will soon grow stronger. Through the trial of time, all national trash is being eliminated" (*Ke Ling*, p. 266).

46. The romanticization of the peasantry as a symbol of tenacity was reinforced by the firsthand experience of Chinese intellectuals who traveled to and from the interior. "In this trip [from Shanghai to Chongqing, I realized] how great the Chinese power to survive is," one Shu Zhao observed, for example. "The majority of our countrymen have very simple needs, and they are accustomed to harsh lives. Several times when we went up into the mountains, we saw a few peasant families. They lived in straw sheds barely able to shelter them from the wind and rain, they ate only brown rice, crude tofu, and soup made of pepper powder....This is the Chinese power

to survive. A nation with such strength is unconquerable" (Shu, "Neidi tongxun" [Letter from the Interior], *Shanghai zhoubao* 1, no. 19 [March 1940]: 558–59). See also Yang Gang, "Xing" (Star), in *Shanghai Gudao wenxue zuoping*, 2: 16–18.

47. See Cao. For a general introduction to literary activities and thought in the interior, see Lee, "Literary Trends," pp. 421–91.

48. Japan had a parallel view of the war as a vehicle of national purification. See Dower, esp. pp. 203–92.

49. The CCP in Shanghai, for example, maintained very close contacts with the New Fourth Army in the hinterland. Between 1938 and 1941, over 20,000 people were organized to join the Communist guerrillas, and a total of Ch. $1.3 million was raised in Shanghai for the base. See *Shanghai renmin*, pp. 3–23.

50. For Huang Zuolin, see *Zhongguo huaju yishujia*, 3: 241–72; for *Wenzhen*, see *Shanghai Gudao wenxue huiyi*, 1: 392.

51. See "Li Jianwu zizhuan."

52. See Li Jianwu, "Yi Zhenduo"; "Li Jianwu zizhuan," pp. 40–70; and *Shanghai Gudao wenxue huiyi*, 1: 277–89.

53. The very first play was Gu Zhongyi's translation of *Topaze* by Marcel Pagnol, directed by Wu Renzhi, which ran for three days, commencing September 23, 1938. Li's play was performed October 27–30, 1938. Since the provision of relief for war refugees created tremendous problems for the two foreign area authorities, permits for public performances were easier to obtain if organizers made them into charity shows. The French Municipal Council made it clear that performances in its famous auditorium had to be related to the promotion of French interests. Hence the strategy of the Shanghai Dramatic Arts Society. See Ren, H: 9–16.

54. Li Jianwu, "Ai yu si," pp. 24–25.

55. Li Jianwu, "Wo wei shenme." Roland's play had been translated in the early 1920s. It was other members of the society who suggested the play to Li. Li decided to retranslate it because, as he said, he loved the play so much and was so elevated by its moral message that he felt intolerant of the awkard translation available.

56. Li Jianwu, "Wo wei shenme." Li quotes Mencius 2.1.2 in stressing the power of moral engagement: "If, on self-examination, I find that I am upright, I will go forward against thousands and tens of thousands" (trans. James Legge, *The Chinese Classics* [Oxford, 1895], 2: 187–88).

57. "In order to become a free Chinese citizen, every one of us should have a complete change of consciousness. We should cleanse ourselves of [moral evils]...and follow our consciences to [write and produce]...to inspire our people," declared the critic Cai Chusheng 4 (Jan. 1939): I: 4.

Since the most popular form of art at that time was cinema, the main thrust of the Resistance assault was aimed at movie producers. With the blessing of the Nationalist government, a "cleansing movement" in Hong Kong (which became the "Hollywood of China" after Shanghai's fall) sought to redirect the Chinese movie industry toward national Resistance and away from apolitical commercial goals. This movement was widely publicized in Shanghai and was used to reinforce the attack on all apolitical art there. See *Wenxian* 6 (Apr. 1939): H: 5. The CCP organized two groups of critics, one for cinema and the other for literature, to orchestrate a "cleansing movement" in Shanghai. One of its results was a collective appeal co-signed by 51 writers, who included Yu Ling and A Ying, "Shanghai gebao fukan bianzhe zuozhe jinggao Shanghai dianying jie" (An appeal to the Shanghai cinema circles from editors and writers of all the Shanghai literary supplements), *Wenxian* 6 (Apr. 1939): H: 14–15.

58. Ke Ling, *Ke Ling*, p. 131.

59. Li Jianwu, "'Ai yu si,'" p. 25.

60. Nonetheless, the Shanghai juyishe restaged the play again in February 1940, for seven shows, owing to popular demand.

61. In 1938–39 there were about 40 cinemas and over 100 opera houses in Shanghai. Because most Chinese movie companies were destroyed during the battle of Shanghai, no more than 20 percent of the films shown locally were Chinese. (The most popular movie ever was *Gone with the Wind*, which ran for six weeks to full houses in Shanghai in 1940.) Even with three shows a day, all the Shanghai cinemas were overcrowded, according to Gong Mingdao (p. 227). The dominance of Hollywood movies is evident in a list of those being shown in March 1939: out of 25 films, only 8 were Chinese-produced; 17 were from the United States, among them *If I Were King* (1938), *Young at Heart, Paris Honeymoon* (1939), and *Charlie Chan in Honolulu* (1938). See *Wenxian* 1 (Apr. 1939): H: 43–44. Chinese opera, either Beijing or Shaoxing, emphasizing music and martial arts and the traditional romantic theme of *caizi jiaren* (gifted scholars and beauty), remained popular among the older generation, both rich and poor. Famous Beijing opera performers then in Shanghai included Qilin Tong (Zhou Xinfang). Under the influence of leftist writers like Tian Han, Zhou's repertoire during the war included several patriotic plays, such as *Mingmo yihen* (Eternal sorrows of the late Ming era) and *Hui yin er di* ([Song] Emperors Hui and Yin).

62. See Chen Chunren, chs. 11–12.

63. Some drama critics also criticized the internal weakness of *huaju*. The theater journal editor Hu Songqing, for example, enumerated five main defects found in most amateur groups: rashness, superficiality, carelessness,

awkward movement, and clumsiness of reading. He blamed these for the failure of *huaju* to attract an audience and to maintain their interest. "Before every show, we have tried very hard to drag the audience into the halls, but the poor performances on stage made them leave in bitter disappointment....[Thus] we should strengthen our study [of drama] and should be more serious and careful in our attitude toward theater arts," he lamented. See Hu Songqing, pp. 7–8.

64. For the historical context and literary significance of the idea of "Chinese Style," see Wylie; and see also Holm, "Literary Rectification."

65. Yi Li, p. 44. For the appropriation of popular culture into high culture in pre-modern China, see Tanaka, pp. 148–60.

66. See Scott.

67. For example, the marriage of the essayist Kong Lingjing in November 1938 provided the first meeting for all patriotic intellectuals since the fall of Shanghai, a forum for discussion on what to do to inspire resistance. Indeed, the supplement of *Shiji feng* (Century Wind) and the journal *Lu Xun feng* (Lu Xun Style), in both of which Kong was involved, in part owed their inception to this meeting. The Communist critic Ba Ren was especially famous for his zeal in playing mah-jongg, despite his harsh attacks on popular entertainments, and there were stories about some of his essays being written during games, with his editors waiting at his side. See *Shanghai Gudao wenxue huiyi*, 1: 389–402. For birthday parties, see Gu Zhongyi, p. 143. It was at such a party that Gu first met all the members of the Qingniao jushe and was invited to join the society. For funerals, see *Yuzhou feng*, no. 91 (Oct.–Nov. 1941). As for study groups, which were mostly Communist-led, see, for example, *Shanghai Gudao wenxue huiyi*, 1: 254–76 and 2: 316–32. Luncheon clubs were formed mainly by professors, entrepreneurs, financers, and other professionals. Some of them were organized by the underground CCP. The most famous of these clubs were the Xinger jucanhui and Xingsi jucanhui, so named because they met, respectively, every Tuesday and Thursday. Among the regular members of the former were Xu Guangping, Liu Shaowen, and Zhang Zhonglin. The latter was composed largely of former SWH leaders such as Zheng Zhenduo and Liu Zhanen, the president of the Baptist Hujiang University, who was assassinated by Yellow Way terrorists in 1938. See Gu Zhizhong, "Baohai zayi" (Random reminiscence of the journalistic world), *Wenshi ziliao xuanbian*, no. 24 (1985).

68. For theater prices, see advertisements in *Juchang yishu*; for movie prices, see Guo Peng, p. 474.

69. Sartre, *Sartre*, pp. 3–6. On the form of *nanxi*, see Zbikowski.

70. See Li Jianwu, *Li Jianwu juzuo*, pp. 233–328.

71. Ba Jin later remembered that he might have introduced the play for publication in Guilin. But he was not sure. So *Fanma ji* remained an unpublished manuscript, circulated only among close friends, until 1980. See ibid., p. 569.

72. Li Jianwu, *Li Jianwu juzuo*, pp. 250–328.

73. For an interesting study of this literary practice in the context of late imperial China, see Robert Hegel, *The Novel in Seventeenth-Century China* (New York, 1981), ch. 3.

74. Shu Yan. There was a similar flourishing of prose ostensibly about history and historical figures. The essayist Zhou Lian, who later collaborated, ascribed this popularity to a tendency to draw parallels between resisters and collaborators of the past and the present (Zhou Lian, *Qingming*, p. 15). The Communist playwright Yu Ling recalled that censorship rules for drama in historical form were much less strict than those for modern writing (see his "Modui," p. 24). According to one anecdote, Yu was praised by Guo Moruo in 1942, when he fled to Chongqing, as correctly and brilliantly employing the technique of using the past to satirize the present to dodge political suppression by both the Japanese and foreign areas police (see Cheng Zhongyuan, p. 97).

75. For a discussion of metaphor and language, see Lakoff and Johnson.

76. The dance hall was probably co-owned with one Wu Bangfang, a dance instructor at the Sino-French Dramatic Institute, who was well connected with the Shanghai GMD. See Cheng Zhongyuan, p. 96; Yu Ling, "Modui," p. 23. For the names of the plays and rates of attendance, see Gu Zhongyi, p. 156. According to Tu Guangqi, then a new actor and later in the 1960s a famous director in Hong Kong, the majority of the Shanghai juyishe's artists received a monthly allowance of only Ch. $32, while the daily cost of living was Ch. $1.20 per person. Poverty was a part of their lives. See Tu Guangqi, p. 44.

77. Gu Zhongyi recorded that the play ran 35 days (Gu, p. 156). Yu Ling, on the other hand, claimed that it played to a full house for over two months and recalled suggesting to A Ying that he adopt the title *Mingmo yihen* to give the censors the impression that his costume play was a rendition of the Beijing opera, enabling it to be approved easily ("Modui," p. 23).

78. Tu Guangqi, pp. 46–47.

79. The opera *Mingmo yihen*, based on *Taohua shan* (The peach blossom fan), was written by Ouyang Yuqian, one of the greatest modern Chinese playwrights, and performed in December 1937 by the famous actor Zhou Xinfang. Ouyang was instrumental in mounting an effort in 1937 to reform

Beijing opera. He was helped in this direction by his friend Zhou Xinfang. His experimentation was, however, cut short by his departure to the southwest in early 1938 because of repeated threats against his life.

80. Along with other historical dramas, A Ying's *Bixue hua* has been systematically studied by Edward Gunn, but Gunn chooses to focus on the "propagandistic" aspect of such plays rather than the symbolic significance of history in them and the need for historical camouflage in the teeth of foreign domination. So he argues that their "exploration into historical materials" was a manifestation of the "resurgence of tradition" corresponding to their "anti-Romanticist" ethos. See *Unwelcome Muse*, chs. 2–3.

81. See Ke Ling, *Juchang*; and Tu Guangqi, p. 48. On suppression, see Yu Ling, "Modui," pp. 23–24.

82. There were other professional companies performing in 1939–41. For example, the short-lived Zhongfa jushe (Sino-French Dramatic Society), organized by the Sino-French Dramatic Institute in June 1939, and disbanded in August of the same year, staged Xu Xingzhi's adaptation *The True Story of Ah Q* and Cao Yu's *Empress Yang* among other plays. There was also the famous Zhongguo luxing jutuan (Chinese Traveling Drama Company), a professional group founded before the war, which returned to Shanghai in late 1939 after a stay of two years in Hong Kong. This company's members were close to A Ying and were especially good at costume plays. Perhaps because the company was much less political and polemical than the others, and was therefore less hesitant in giving priority to entertainment values, its shows enjoyed great popularity. Moreover, in mid 1940, A Ying and Wu Yonggang followed the CCP's instruction to establish another group, named Xinyi she (New Arts Society), mainly to stage A Ying's own plays, in order to divert the Japanese and foreign area authorities' attention from the Shanghai juyishe. Its repertoire included *Nü dianzhu* (Woman shopkeeper), *Mulan congjun* (Mulan joins the army), and A Ying's *Hong Xuanjiao*. See *Shanghai Gudao wenxue huiyi*, 1: 293–98; Gu Zhongyi, pp. 149–50 and 161–62; and Gunn, "Shanghai's Orphan Island."

83. Gu Zhongyi, pp. 157–59. The author acknowledges that the list is incomplete, based only on his memory. These historical plays included *Chen Yuanyuan*, Yu Ling's *Daming yinglie quan* (Heroes and faithful women of the Ming dynasty) and Gu's *Liang Hongyu*. Not included in this list, for example, were Zhou Yibai's *Wen Tianxiang*, Shu Yan's *Yue Fei*, and A Ying's *Yang O zhuan* (The story of Yang O), *Haiguo yingxiong* (The hero of a maritime nation), and *Hong Xuanjiao*, which formed his famous cycle of late Ming dramas. A Ying was helped in the collection of material and scholarly advice by the famed revolutionary poet Liu Yazi. For A Ying's

activities and his working relation with Liu, see *Shanghai Gudao wenxue huiyi*, 1: 302–14.

84. Gu Zhongyi, pp. 159–60. The most popular play was Ba Jin's *Jia* (Family), which ran for three months. Both Wu Zuguang and Yang Han-sheng were leftists living in the southwest. In order partly to show that Shanghai was "Gudao bu gu" (Solitary Island is not solitary) and partly to have more original plays, Shanghai theater chose to perform plays written by writers in the interior. The Shanghai juyishe, with its connections, commis-sioned leftist playwrights in unoccupied China to write plays about Shang-hai. At the same time, the flourishing theater in the southwest also staged plays written by writers in Shanghai; see Xia Yan, *Choucheng*, pp. i–iii.

85. Peng Ziyi's *Wen Tianxiang* exemplifies the first category. It portrays the Song loyalist Wen's martyrdom as a realization of *ren* and *yi*, which defines and distinguishes man in Confucian terms. See *Wen Tianxiang* (Shanghai, 1940). The representative work of the second category is Tang Na's *Chen Yuanyuan*. Dedicated to his "loyal and chaste mother," the play is intended to reinterpret Chen Yuanyuan's role in the fall of the Ming dynasty in order to contrast her fidelity to the greed and immorality of her husband, General Wu Sangui, who joined the Manchu conquerors. To achieve this goal, Tang acknowledges, he "altered many recorded facts of history." The message of the play is evident in Chen's exhortation to Wu not to join the Manchus: "I have known since I was a child that a good man should be loyal to his country, whereas a *lienü* [faithful woman] should die for her husband." See Tang Na.

86. See Tang Tao, pp. 370–73; Hui, pp. 56–57. See also the summary of the debate in Gunn, *Unwelcome Muse*, ch. 3; and Dong, p. 208.

87. Li Jianwu, *Juhua*, pp. 104–9. Li was demanding with respect to the art and craft of costume plays; he thought they should be historically authentic and careful about facts. He was unhappy with A Ying's *Bixue hua* because it adopted formulaic language from Beijing opera while appropriat-ing modern clichés like "love, freedom and struggle." He found such his-torical dramas, with their eagerness to be "realistic," simply grotesque.

88. Ouyang Wenpu is quoted from Li Jianwu, *Juhua*, pp. 159–63.

89. See, e.g., Li Zhongshao, pp. 26–27.

90. For Ba Ren's comments on Li, see Li Jianwu, *Zhe buguo*; Yu Ling, "Yinian," p. 55. *Xiju yu wenxue*, a journal edited exclusively by Yu Ling, pub-lished many essays in defense of Li in 1940, including one by Li Zhongshao.

91. Quoted from Li Zhongshao, p. 24.

92. Li Jianwu, *Li Jianwu chuangzuo*, p. 249.

93. Li Jianwu, *Li Jianwu wenxue*, p. 215.

94. As Simone de Beauvoir observed of Sartre in 1940: "[I am] quite

taken aback by the vigor of his moralism....Did I buy things on the market? A little tea occasionally, I told him. Even this was too much....Sartre had always asserted his ideas, not to mention his likes or dislikes, in a most dogmatic fashion, whether verbally or through his personal actions. Yet he never formulated them as universal maxims....The first evening [after his release from prison] he gave me yet another surprise. He had not come back to Paris to enjoy the sweets of freedom, he told me, but to act. How? I inquired, taken aback. We were so isolated, so powerless! It was precisely this isolation that had to be broken down, he said. We had to unite, to organize a resistance movement." For a brilliant account of Sartre's life in Nazi-occupied Paris, see Cohen-Solal, especially pp. 129–244. And for a lovingly sensitive study of the great historian March Bloch in Vichy France, see Fink, esp. pp. 205–324.

95. Li Jianwu, *Li Jianwu wenxue*, pp. 221–36.

96. Ibid., pp. 220–22; see also *Juhua*, pp. 161–63.

97. Wang Wenxian was very poor but refused to sell himself to the enemy. Li Jianwu translated his play *Peking Politics*, which was originally written in English and first performed at Yale University when Wang was studying there in 1927, and introduced it to theaters. Every time the play was performed, he took a collection and gave the proceeds to Wang. Li apparently also did his best to help Zhu Ziqing's wife and children survive the eight years of Occupation; Mrs. Zhu still talked of his help at the hardest time with gratitude in the 1980s. See Wang Weiguo and Qi Zhong, p. 173.

98. *Shanghai Gudao wenxue huiyi*, 1: 227–90; Gu Zhongyi, pp. 150–55. The quotation is from Song Qing, "Zhe yiyue" (This month), *Juchang yishu*, no. 10 (Aug. 1939). According to Wu Shaoshu, the leading GMD official in occupied Shanghai, who was concerned mainly with military intelligence and maintaining loyalty among the wealthy and public figures, praised the Shanghai juyishe for its success in inspiring Shanghai youth to continued resistance. He even attempted to buy off the society through its sponsor and nominal director, Zhao Zhiyou, but the attempt failed. So the Nationalists had to start their own professional company instead—the Tianfeng jutuan (Heavenly Wind Company), which was led by the playwright Yao Ke and the director Fei Mu. It specialized in historical drama and was particularly famous for Yao's hit *Qinggong yuan* (The malice of the Qing court). See Wu Shaoshu, p. 90. See also *Shanghai renmin*, pp. 187–89.

99. Li Jianwu, "Ai yu si," p. 25.

100. Ke Ling, *Juchang*, p. 92.

101. For a detailed, vivid account of the first week of complete Japanese Occupation, see Tao Juyin, *Tianliang*, ch. 2.

102. Zheng Zhenduo, "Xunshu rilu" (Daily record of book seeking), *Dagong bao*, Nov. 1945.

103. Huai Jiu, pp. 223.

104. Li wrote two essays, one on Wang and another on a Mr. Li, a hermit who devoted all his time to music and scholarship and was supported throughout the Occupation by his brother, the writer Ba Jin, in a tone of respect and envy. He used the term *junzi ren* (gentleman) of them, reminiscent of the Confucian ideal, and praised their withdrawal as a tenacious fight against "the ultimate trial," expressing thereby their lonely virtues. See his "Wan Sange," and "Huai Wang Tongzhao" (For Wang Tongzhao), in *Qiemeng*, pp. 88–93.

105. The Fudan professor and fellow traveler Zhu Duanjun was said to have been persuaded by a Communist literary organizer, who had remained in Shanghai after 1941, to enter the theater industry in order to bring some progressive elements to the Shanghai theater. See *Zhongguo huaju yishujia*, 2: 96–120.

106. Carey, pp. 73–74.

107. Chen Chunren, ch. 14; Gu Zhongyi, pp. 163–67; and Wang Jun.

108. Many of these intellectuals had no prior experience of dramatic art. For example, Ke Ling, the embattled editor of *Shiji feng*, first joined a movie company after the occupation of the foreign areas was completed. When Japan seized control of the film industry, he quit and worked for a short time as a salesman, but soon lost all his savings. Then he was brought into the Kugan jutuan (Struggle Theater Group), a leftist company, as playwright and stayed on until the end of the war. Correspondence with Ke Ling, June 21, 1987.

109. Ke ling, *Juchang*, p. 24. See also Luo, p. 89.

110. Quoted from "Wo dui huaju jie de xiwang" (My wish for the theater circle), *Wanxiang* 3, no. 4 (Oct. 1943): 110–12, 142–47. For representative criticism from collaborators, see Bing, pp. 162–67. For an account of the general reaction to the Shanghai theater, see Ke Ling, "Shanghai lunxian qijian," pp. 1–18.

111. Zhou Yuren, "Zhongguo," pp. 110–14.

112. Some political plays in occupied Shanghai also managed to be performed through political manipulation. In 1943, according to Shu Yan, some Chinese in a paramilitary organization suggested that the Japanese army sponsor a performance of their new play on the Song loyalist Yue Fei, saying that they hoped to change the public's perception of peace by completely reversing the historical significance of Yue and his rival Qin Kuei. They then submitted a copy of their play for examination, which had Yue portrayed as a brute warlord and Qin as a patriot. The play was approved

and was sponsored by the Imperial Army's Chinese mouthpiece, *Qingnian bao* (Youth News). For the performance, the script was changed to Shu Yan's patriotic play *Yue Fei,* which had been written in 1940 but never performed. On stage, Qin was made to speak of the necessity for peace in Cantonese, which immediately led the audience to think of Wang Jingwei. The play ran to a full house from its third day on but was banned on the fifth day. See Shu Yan, "Yue Fei," pp. 90–93.

113. For a vivid account of the fear of Japanese suppression among Chinese writers, see Gu Zhongyi, pp. 165–66. See also Zheng Zhenduo, *Zheju.*

114. Some literary magazines such as Ke Ling's *Wanxiang* and Chen Dieyi's *Chunqiu* (both discussed in Chapter 1) also declared themselves commercial ventures in order to evade political suppression. Although they mainly published love stories and historical novels, these journals also printed plays and reports on performances and performers.

115. Quoted from Zhao Jingshen, "Yi Shanghai," p. 126. See also Zheng Zhenduo's speech on Shanghai's intellectual resistance at the same meeting.

116. Li then joined the C.Z.C. Entertainment Company, set up by a group of businessmen and theater enthusiasts, which claimed a capital of CRB $50,000, but it closed after three months. In late 1943, after working briefly for the Chinese Arts Company and the Shanghai Arts Lights Theater, he switched to the newly established Shanghai United Arts Company, founded by the movie tycoons Liu Zhonghao and Liu Zhongliang, the owners of the Jincheng, Jindu and Shijie theaters and the Guohua Movie Company, who (allegedly with intimate connections with the Chongqing government) refused to turn their cinemas over to Japanese control. It boasted an operating capital of CRB $100,000. At the same time, using his personal connections, Li wrote and introduced plays, mostly by writers of the interior, for many other companies. While he had written no more than three plays in 1937–41, he completed no fewer than ten, all of them adaptations from French and English texts, in the period after the Japanese occupied the Solitary Island.

117. Gu Zhongyi, p. 175.

118. Li Jianwu, "Yu youren," pp. 28–29. The life of Li Guinian was immortalized in a poem by the famous Tang poet Du Fu, "Meeting with Li Guinian in Jiangnan."

119. Li Jianwu, "Yu youren," pp. 28–29.

120. Li Jianwu, "Yu youren"; Yang Jiang, *Xiju erzhong* (Two comedies) (Fuzhou, 1982), p. 1. See also *Shanghai Gudao wenxue huiyi,* 1: 213–14. Yang Jiang got her inspiration for her play *Chenxin ruyi* (Gratification) from

a mutton lunch with Li Jianwu and Chen Linrui in late 1942. The first draft of the play was first commented on by Chen and then sent to Li for further comments. But Li immediately introduced it to the director Huang Zuolin for performance. Li later also played the role of Xu Langzhai in 1943. At that time Qian Zhongshu was always hiding in his study writing his famous novel *Weicheng* (The besieged city), which became known only after the war. For a fine study of Qian's life and works, see Theodore Huters, *Qian Zhongshu* (Boston, 1982).

121. Li Jianwu, "Yu youren," p. 29.

122. Li Jianwu, *Qiemeng*, p. 102.

123. Quoted in Wang Weiguo and Qi Zhong, p. 178. The critic was a certain Dong Shi, and the article appeared in Ke Ling's *Wanxiang*.

124. Li Jianwu, *Fengliu*, p. 1.

125. See Gu Zhongyi for titles of some of these plays.

126. See, e.g., Xu Guangsheng, pp. 66–70.

127. Li Jianwu, *Hua xin feng*. My reading of Li's adaptations of Sardou is different from that of Edward Gunn, who chooses to give more stress to the French playwright's display of "suspense and escapism," as an indication of the prevalent "cynicism toward the theatre." See *Unwelcome Muse*, p. 104. The quotation is from "Liuyue xiju yanchu" (Theaters in June), *Zazhi* 11, no. 4 (July 1993): 190–91.

128. See Tony Hyder's excellently researched "Translator's Afterword," in *It's Only Spring*, pp. 119–20. See also Ke Ling, "Xuyan" (Preface), in *Li Jianwu juzuo*, pp. 1–17; and "Shanghai lunxian."

129. *Qingchun*, p. 126. The translation is by David Pollard; see his "Springtime," p. 216.

130. See, e.g., Shi Tuo's *Da maxituan* (Big circus), Ke Ling's *Henhai* (Sea of grief), and Kong Lingjing's *Li Taibai*.

131. *Qingchun*, p. 159; the translation is from Pollard, "Springtime," p. 222.

132. See Ienaga, chs. 8–9 and 11; see also Kisaka.

133. For the effect of the devastating Ichigo campaign on the Nationalist government and the interior, see Lloyd Eastman, "Nationalist China During the Sino-Japanese War," in *The Cambridge History of China*, ed. John King Fairbank and Albert Feuerwerker, vol. 13, pt. 2 (Cambridge, 1981), pp. 580–601; for the condition of Shanghai, see Tao Juyin, *Tianliang*, pp. 235–322; and Boyle, ch. 15.

134. Ke Ling, *Henhai*, p. 98.

135. Li Jianwu, "Zuian" (Evidence), in *Li Jianwu chuangzuo*, pp. 255–57.

136. Amery, esp. pp. 21–40. This is a touching and brutally sensitive memoir of the author's inhuman experience in Breendonk at the hands of the Nazi SS. Amery's description of the tortured, who usually regarded

their torturer with a mix of helplessness and "wretched admiration," can be applied almost word for word to Li: "In torture does the transformation of the person into flesh become complete. Frail in the face of violence, yelling out in pain, awaiting no help, capable of no resistance, the tortured person is only a body, and nothing else besides that" (p. 33). Also: "A slight pressure by the tool-wielding hand is enough to turn the other—along with his head, in which are perhaps stood Kant and Hegel, and all nine symphonies, and the World as Will and Representation—into a shrilly squealing piglet at slaughter" (p. 35).

137. The reconstruction here of Li's torture and experience in the Kempeitai station is reconstructed from his moving essays "Qiuyuan dayu" (Hagiwara Daikyoku), "Zuian," "Xiao lan benzi" (A little blue notebook), in Qiemeng, pp. 65–87. For two moving and terrifying accounts of torture and the condition of Japanese prisons, see Xu Guangping; and Situ, pp. 151–85.

138. Xu Shihu, p. 98. In 1966, during the Cultural Revolution, Li, who was then working at the Foreign Literature Research Institute of the Chinese Academy of Social Science in Beijing, was visited by two Red Guards from Shanghai, who accused him of treason in the Japanese prison and subjected him to violent interrogation. Inasmuch as it had been such a self-redeeming event, and the most honorable of his life, Li was outraged by the fabrication. He would have killed himself if he had not been stopped by his wife, who said to him—quietly but firmly: "I have been with you for the whole life, I know who you are. I do," and by his colleagues and good friends Qian Zhongshu and Feng Zhi. See Wang Weiguo and Qi Zhong, pp. 184–85.

139. After the war, Li discussed the martyrdom of the editor Lu Yi, who was killed after going to the Shanghai Municipal Police office to protest against the Japanese suppression of his Wenhua shenghuo chubanshe (Cultural Life Press), with an autobiographical tone: "[Lu Yi symbolized] moral transcendence that made human human....In ordinary times he had never shown us any heroic deeds, but when crisis came, he was the bravest....He [personified] the kind-natured Chinese people, he was the young, defiant voice of our age-old nation." See his "Lu Yi de sanwen" (Lu Yi's essays), in Lu Yi sanwen ji (Taibei, 1979), pp. 212–13.

140. See Ke Ling and Yang Yingwu, pp. 345–53.

141. The play was serialized after the war in the leftist literary journal Wenzhang, nos. 1–4 (Jan.–July 1946).

142. Li was not only regarded as the "leader of Shanghai theater" between 1942 and 1945 but became actively involved and widely respected in the postwar literary world. For example, aside from being selected to give a keynote speech on behalf of the Shanghai theater at the inaugural

meeting of the Shanghai branch of the Zhongguo quanguo wenyi xiehui (Chinese National Association of Literature and Arts) in December 1945, he became the associate editor, along with Zheng Zhenduo, of the influential journal *Wenyi fuxing* (Renaissance), whose contributors included literary heavyweights like Guo Moruo, Ba Jin, and Mao Dun, and where Qian Zhongshu's *Weicheng* was first serialized. Together with Gu Zhongyi and Xiong Foxi, he also founded the Shanghai shili shiyan xiju xueyuan (Shanghai Municipal College of Experimental Theater)—the predecessor of today's prestigous Shanghai College of Theater. See Wang Weiguo and Qi Zhong, pp. 179–80; Zhao Jingshen, "Ji Shanghai wenxie."

143. For these writers' views and their involvement with the famous postwar magazine *Zhou bao* (Weekly), see Ke Ling, *Zhuzi*, pp. 76–117. Along with Chen Xihe, Chen Linrui, Tang Tao, Qian Zhongshu, Xu Jie, Shi Tuo, Xia Mianzun, Zhou Jianren (Lu Xun's young brother), and Xu Guangping, they co-signed a public letter in October 1945 urging that there be a trial of cultural collaborators as a way to "cleanse China of its national shame." See *Wenhui bao*, Oct. 20, 1945.

144. Li Jianwu, *Zuihua*, pp. 133–34. For an interesting study of the postwar literary scene in Shanghai, see Huters, pp. 54–80.

145. Lin Ling, 4: 504–8. On the last days of Japanese rule in Shanghai, see Tao Juyin, *Gudao*, ch. 20.

146. Li Jianwu, *Li Jianwu chuangzuo*, p. 253.

147. Xu Shihu, pp. 95–96; Wang Weiguo and Qi Zhong, p. 179. For the smuggling network, see Lloyd Eastman, "Facets of an Ambivalent Relationship: Smuggling, Puppets, and Atrocities During the War, 1937–1945," in *The Chinese and the Japanese: Essays on Political and Cultural Interactions*, ed. Akira Iriye (Princeton, 1980), pp. 275–303.

148. Li Jianwu, *Li Jianwu chuangzuo*, p. 253.

149. The intellectual impact of the War of Resistance on the Civil War (1945–49) and the eventual Communist victory has received little attention by historians. For example, Suzanne Pepper's excellent *Civil War in China* explains the downfall of Chiang Kaishek mainly in terms of the corruption and impotence of the Nationalist regime and the ways (mainly) liberal-minded intellectuals responded to it. This is certainly valid. Yet, as shown here, the idealized perception of the war as a spiritual revolution and the self-conception among resistance writers of a morally chosen few destined to re-create China also shaped their responses to the postwar situation. Their hopes and disillusionment, in other words, should be traced to their wartime experiences. In Li's case, as shown above, he joined many writers in 1946, all of whom had lived through the Occupation with dignity and integrity (including Zheng Zhenduo, Ke Ling, and Xia Mianzun), in

pleading for the reestablishment of the ethical imperative of moral integrity in building a free, humane, and independent China. Yet his hopes were soon shattered by runaway inflation, bureaucratic corruption, and ever-widening social inequality.

3. Collaboration: The "Gujin Group" and the Literature of Anachronism

1. The term *yimin* has been conventionally translated as "remnants" or "relics," referring to literati who refused to serve new dynasties. But in the case of the Shanghai literary collaborators, as I shall show later, their self-proclaimed *yimin* stance smacked of a sentimental, defensive, and self-indulgent sense. Hence my translation, "anachronisms."

2. For a discussion of this phase of the war, see Wang Pei and Yang Weihe, *Zhongguo kangri zhanzheng shigao* (History of the Chinese War of Resistance) (Hubei, 1983), ch. 1.

3. For detailed analyses of the political exchanges between the Wang group and the Japanese army that led to the "Peace Movement," the consequent founding of the Nanjink regime in March 1940, and the political problems of the regime until the end of the Occupation, see Boyle; and Huang and Zhang, eds, *Wang Jingwei jituan panguo*. See also Jin Xiongbai's classic, *Wang zhengquan*. For a historical study of the "Reorganization Clique," see Wang Ke-wen, "The Kuomintang in Transition" (Ph.D. diss., Stanford University, 1985).

4. This study is devoted to intellectual collaborators; only marginal attention will be given to Wang Jingwei and his political followers—notably Zhou Fohai, Chen Gongbo, and Lin Bosheng. For biographical studies of these collaborators, see Huang, ed., *Wangwei*; and Susan Marsh, "Chou Fo-hai," pp. 304–27. And on Wang Jingwei, see Cai Dejin, *Wang Jingwei*; and Wen Shaohua.

5. "Heping yundong xunnan tongzhi zhuanye" (Special issue on martyrs of the Peace Movement), *Zhongyang daobao* 1, no. 5 (Sept. 1940): 1–14; see also *Xin shen bao*, Sept. 1, 1940.

6. Zhou Fohai, "Huiyi yu qianzhan" (Memory and projection), originally published in July 1939, reprinted in Huang and Zhang, eds., *Wang Jingwei jituan toudi*, p. 3.

7. Jin Xiongbai, *Wang zhengquan*, 1: 38–39.

8. See "Zhongguo Guomindang diliuci quanguo daibiao dahui xuanyan" (The manifesto of the Sixth Congress of the Guomindang) and "Jueding yi fangong wei jiben zhengce" (A resolution to establish anticommunism as the basic policy), in Huang and Zhang, eds., *Wang Jingwei guomin,*

pp. 324–32 and 337–39. For an official version of the "New Order," see the proclamation of Matsuoka Yōsuke, then Japan's foreign minister, "The New Order in East Asia," *Contemporary Japan* 3, no. 1 (Mar. 1939): 1–9. For a discussion of the self-justifying propaganda of Vichy France, see Kedward, *Occupied France*, pp. 17–45; and Paxton, chs. 1–3.

9. For a theoretical elaboration of this, see Zhu Zhujun, pp. 312–37.

10. See Huang, Shi, and Jiang. For an interesting study of the emotional and cultural world of No. 76 leaders, see also Yeh Wen-hsin, pp. 545–62.

11. "Zhai Shanghai Wang Jingwei yipai de huodong" (The activities of the Wang group in Shanghai), classified Japanese intelligence report, and Qian Junrui et al., "Wang pai zhai Shanghai gejie huodong zhenxiang" (Activities of the Wang group among various Shanghai circles), in Huang and Zhang, eds, *Wang Jingwei guomin*, pp. 172–76 and 242–56. Wang Jing-wei's lack of success led the authors of the Japanese report to conclude that "the masses had lost confidence in him. Disappointment and suspicion are being intensified." The publisher of the *Huamei wanbao*, Zhu Zuotong, a casino boss cum newsman, friendly to both Nationalist and Communist journalists, agreed to sell his paper to the Wang group and betrayed his friend, the GMD agent and *Shen bao* reporter Jin Huating to No. 76, which led to his assassination in front of a nightclub (see Chapter 1). In retaliation Zhu was soon killed by the Nationalist servicemen. See Shanghai Municipal Police Files, no. 3019 (Mar. 1938); Jin Xiongbai, *Wang zheng-quan*, 1: 66–76.

12. On newspapers, see Liu Qikui, "Wangwei hanjian wenhua lun-shu" (On the Wang regime's traitorous culture), in *Wang Jingwei hanjian*, pp. 217–62; and Shanghai Municipal Police Files, no. 3019 (Jan. 31, 1941). On magazines, see *Dongya xinwen*, p. 96. The Propaganda Bureau had a staff of 96 people.

13. Jin Xiongbai, *Jizhe*, pp. 100–104; and *Wang zhengquan*, 1: 172–76.

14. The paper was published after Ding bought the famous anti-Japanese newspaper *Wenhui bao* from its foreign publisher for over Ch. $50,000. For stories of the two victims from a collaborationist per-spective, see *Xin shen bao*, June 29–30 and Sept. 4–8, 1940. For a Japanese account, see Matsuzaki, pp. 183–202, 226–90.

15. Jin Xiongbai, *Jizhe*, pp. 103–7. *Ping bao* was edited by Jin under the sponsorship of Zhou Fohai; its office was at the intersection of Fuzhou and Shackloo roads, close to all the foreign-published newspaper offices.

16. Cheng Kuangzheng, "Cong heshui zhong yuedeng pian" (A leap ashore from the troubled water), in Huang and Zhang, eds., *Wang Jingwei guomin*, pp. 373–82.

17. Jin Xiongbai, *Jizhe*, pp. 93–95. For Cheng and his colleague, see Huang and Zhang, eds., *Wang Jingwei guomin*, pp. 172–74, 373–80.

18. Jin Xiongbai was introduced to Zhou Fohai by Chiang Kaishek during the Northern Expedition when Jin worked as a military reporter for the famous *Shih bao* (Times Daily). Along with other high-ranking GMD officials, mostly with backgrounds in journalism, such as Chen Bulei, Jin and Zhou indulged themselves together in gambling and nightlife. See Jin Xiongbai, *Wang zhengquan*, 1: 1–6, and *Jizhe*, 1: 24–42; and Guo Xiufeng, pp. 165–67.

19. Yuan Yuquan, "Jinglizhe de huiyi" (A survivor's memory), in Zhu and Chen, eds., p. 134.

20. Liu Naou was born in Taiwan and went to high school and university in Japan. He came to Shanghai in the late 1920s, where his wealth soon enabled him to become financier to and leader of the Japanese-inspired modernist school. When the war broke out in 1937, he helped the Japanese to recruit performing artists and to establish the Central China–based China Movie Company for propaganda purposes. For his life, see Matsuzaki, pp. 226–78.

21. "Fan Ch'ih asked about benevolence, The Master said, 'Love your fellow men.'" *Lunyu*, ch. 12, line 22. See Confucius, *Analects*, p. 116.

22. Long, pp. 4–5. The story of Guan Zhong as quoted by Long is from *Lunyu*, ch. 14, line 16: "Tzu-lu said, 'When Duke Huan had Prince Chiu killed, Shen Hu died for the Prince but Kuan Chung failed to do so.' He added, 'In that case, did he fall short of benevolence?' The Master said, 'It was due to Kuan Chung that Duke Huan was able without a show of force, to assemble the feudal lords nine times. Such was his benevolence. Such was his benevolence.'" See Confucius, *Analects*, p. 126. Long had to teach 33 hours a week at five universities in order to support his wife and seven children after 1937. As a result his stomach problem recurred, becoming so serious that at times he could not even swallow water. It was perhaps at this time that Wang Jingwei approached him and he accepted the offer. See Long, "Muxu shengya."

23. Wang Yun, pp. 45–48.

24. See, e.g., Zhang Zhijian, pp. 31–32; Xu Yishi, pp. 5–7; Wang Yun, pp. 45–50. During the First Congress of East Asian Journalists, held in 1941 in Canton, all participants paid tribute to the Statue of the Seventy-Two Martyrs, built to commemorate the Yellow Flower Mound uprising against the Manchus in April 1910, pleading commitment to the peace cause. Comparing themselves to the martyrs of the Yellow Flower Mound Uprising, they described the "Peace Movement" as a self-sacrificial struggle for righteousness and liberty. See *Dongya xinwen*, pp. 1–22.

25. See *Xin shen bao*, Sept. 3, 1940.

26. Jie Yi, pp. 8—15. See also Jiang Kanghu, "Shijie shida."

27. Shen Yifan, pp. 15—16. Xu Zhuyuan, an obscure writer, defined Peace literature as a literature devoted to the propagation of "Greater East Asianism," championing mutual assistance and permanent peace between China and Japan. See Xu Zhuyuan, pp. 5—9. The most famous figure in the Peace Movement was certainly Zhang Ziping, a Japan-returned writer who was best known among young readers in the 1920s for his sentimental portrayal of triangular love affairs. But his serialized novel in *Zhong bao* was so unpopular that the editor, Jin Xiongbai, had to stop its publication in the middle. See *Jizhe*, p. 95.

28. For Japan's various efforts in seeking peace talks with Chongqing, see Boyle, ch. 14.

29. See Zhou Fohai, "Liangyao," pp. 32—32; and Chen Gongbo, "Zenyang," pp. 34—36; for the negotiations and harsh terms of the Basic Treaty, see *Zhongyang daobao* 1, no. 9 (Dec. 1940): 1—29.

30. See *Xin shen bao*, Dec. 8—22, 1941; "Shanghai Repercussions as War Spreads to the Pacific," *Shanghai Calling* 2, no. 1 (Dec. 23, 1941); Carey, pp. 1—78. Tao Shiping, pp. 84—85; and *Shanghai Gudao wenxue huiyi*, 2: 388—90. Despite all these restrictions, Shanghai was one of the very few places that was open to Jews during World War II. Japan seems not to have shared in the anti-Semitism of its ally, Nazi Germany (and its puppet Vichy France). As a result, tens of thousands of European Jews found refuge in Shanghai. Most of these refugees were able to find only low-paying manual work and were obliged to live in squalor in Hongkou, which soon became known as the Jewish town. See Kranzler.

31. Zhang Jinglu, ed., *Zhongguo chuban*, 5: 402; Tao Juyin, *Tianliang*, pp. 56—60.

32. Shanghai Municipal Police Files, no. 8149 (Mar. 1942); *Shanghai Calling* 1—3 (1941—43). XGRS broadcast every day from 7:00 A.M. to midnight, mainly news (in English, Mandarin, Cantonese, Italian, Russian, German, and French) and classical music. XQHA was on the air from 7:00 A.M. to 21:50 P.M., and was devoted to news (Japanese as relayed from Tokyo, Chinese from Shanghai, and English), military programs, light music, and the Japanese soldiers' hours. XGOI broadcast special programs, such as foreign music and Japanese lessons for Chinese, from 10:00 A.M. to 21:00 P.M.

33. *Xin shen bao*, Dec.—Mar. 1941—42, passim; Tao Juyin, *Tianliang*, chs. 2 and 6.

34. Tao Juyin, *Tianliang*, p. 87; Tao Shiping, p. 87.

35. Chen Chunren, pp. 238—40.

36. See Azuma, pp. 1–55.

37. Quoted from Li Da, p. 2.

38. See Gu Fengcheng, p. 15. See also Wang Jingwei's speeches during 1942–44, collected in Yu Zidao et al., eds., pp. 2–13 and 20–31, 87–93.

39. Tao Juyin, *Tianliang*, p. 49.

40. Li Shiqi, pp. 4–7; Ke Lun, pp. 15–17. All the figures quoted in this chapter, unless otherwise stated, are based on Guomindang Chinese dollars (*fabi*), which ceased to circulate in Shanghai after March 1943, when the Wang Jingwei government decreed that the only official currency was the Central Reserve Note (*zhongchu juan*), or CRB, printed by Zhou Fohai's Central Reserve Bank. The value of the CRB was set at two *fabi*. There were no official statistics for commodity prices in 1945. This figure was compiled retroactively in the late 1950s. See *Shanghai jiefang*, p. 335. See also Tang Zhenchang, p. 843.

41. *Dazhong* 3, no. 7 (May 1946): 106. In December 1941, a Beijing opera ticket cost from Ch. $ 0.40 to $18. *Xin shen bao*, Dec. 1–25, 1941, passim.

42. Tang Xinyi, ed., p. 59. Like all statistics compiled during and after the Occupation, these figures take 1936 as 100 percent. The Chinese Academy of Social Science calculated that by August 1945, food prices had undergone a 8,165,177 percent increase since 1936. See *Shanghai jiefang*, pp. 330 and 335.

43. According to Yuan Yuquan, deputy minister of industry in the Nanjing government, by 1942 the productivity of all rice-producing areas in the lower Yangzi decreased to about 20–30 percent of the prewar level. This low productivity was a result both of war devastation and Japanese exploitation. Aside from widespread corruption of the local gentry and Wang regime officials, the Japanese army commandeered agricultural produce at below-market prices. Accordingly, the peasants refused to grow crops for or sell their produce to the Japanese, trying instead by any means to take their rice to Shanghai, where they could make a better profit. The rationing system was thus devised to curb buying rice directly from peasants and to limit the rice consumption of Shanghai. Of the limited amount of rice exacted from the lower Yangzi peasantry, the Japanese army got the lion's share. In 1944, for example, out of 250,000 tons of rice acquired, 220,000 tons were allocated to the Japanese army and the remaining 30,000 tons were distributed among the Wang regime's police and army and the people of both Shanghai and Nanjing. See Yuan Yuquan, no. 1, pp. 100–102.

44. Pan Zaixin, pp. 21–25; Tao Juyin, *Tianliang*, pp. 160–250. The rationing system was soon expanded to include matches, coal, flour, edible

oil, sugar, and soap. In March 1943 rationing was put under the control of the newly founded Quanguo shangye tongzhi zonghui (National Commission on Commerce Control), operated jointly by the Japanese consulate in Shanghai and the Ministry of Industry of the Wang regime as a device to strengthen the Nanjing government's role in running its precinct. As a result of the government's involvement in the "Greater East Asian war," the committee was charged with centralizing distribution of all economic goods in the Yangzi Basin and provisioning Shanghai and Nanjing while ensuring military supplies for the Japanese army. The only systematic studies of this important economic organization and its significance for the collaborators' relations with the Japanese are Yuan Yuquan, no. 1; and Li Da, pp. 1–12. On the commission, see Wang Ke-wen.

45. Tang Xinyi, ed., p. 147; and Chen Yingchuan, pp. 48–52.

46. Cang Hai, p. 12.

47. There was an average profit margin of about CRB $300 to $400 per picul in black-market rice. See Tao Juyin, *Tianliang*, pp. 22–28 and 173–75; and see also Pan Zaixin, p. 24.

48. Pan Zaixin, p. 23.

49. Tao Juyin, *Tianliang*, pp. 264–312; Li Shiqi, p. 4; Tan Xinyi, ed., p. 119; Mao Xunsheng, pp. 42–50; Feng Sheng, pp. 72–74. On rationed rice, see Tang Xinyi et al., p. 147.

50. See, e.g., Cang Hai, pp. 1–14.

51. Queueing for necessities before they were gone or their price rose was a part of life in occupied Shanghai. For example, in November 1943, coal briquets were priced at CRB $51 per *jin* (0.5 kg.), and each person was rationed $10 worth once a week (the black-market price was over CRB $100). Long lines waited in front of coal stores. In December, all briquets were gone, and the black-market price jumped to CRB $350. The price of rationed flour in 1945 had also jumped 486 times over 1936. See Tao Juyin, *Tianliang*, pp. 240–48; Tang Xinyi, ed., p. 147. Men had to help their wives because there were so many things to line up for, and for some especially precious goods—like rice and coal—waiting in line was a social Darwinian jungle. It got very rough. Women were always abused by the police and thugs, who made a living by extorting from the weakest. See Chen Chunren, pp. 196–98.

52. In early 1942, the schedules of buses and tramcars in the International Settlements were cut to peak hour services only: 7:30–9:30 A.M., 12:30–1:30 P.M., 4:30–6 P.M., and all traffic lights were turned off. Beginning in June 1942, moreover, households and commercial premises were allowed only 45 percent of the electricity they had consumed in 1941, and in December 1943 supplies for domestic use were further cut to 65 percent

of 1942's consumption; neon lights in the city, which had won Shanghai the reputation of being "the Paris of the Orient," had to be turned off at 7 P.M. In early 1945 electricity was supplied to individual households only between 7 and 10 P.M. Shanghai literally became a "dark world." See Tang Zhenchang, p. 853.

53. Ke Lun, pp. 7–16. In 1936 a total of 3 million tons of coal a year was needed to fuel the manufacturing sector; after 1941 an average of only 600,000 tons was available annually. Owing to power shortages in 1944, for example, every household in Shanghai had water supplies only between 9 A.M. and 4 P.M. daily and 7 kwh of electricity per month, and all shops were instructed to close by 7 P.M. in order to save energy. See *Zhongguo jingji* 2, no. 10 (Oct. 1944): 16.

54. The shortage of wheat supplies was owing to war damage and the low rate of collection from peasants. In 1943, for example, the National Commission on Commerce Control planned to acquire 540,000 tons of wheat from Wuhan, but only 220,000 tons were collected. Moreover, only 10 percent of this was allocated for public consumption in Shanghai; the remaining 90 percent was set aside for the military and shipped to Manchukuo and North China. See Yuan Yuquan, no. 2, pp. 99–100.

55. In January 1943, Japan began seeking the help of the Wang regime in enlisting Chinese laborers, especially skilled shipbuilders, to work there. Nanjing complied, and between 1943–44, at least 2,500 laborers, some of them women, were shipped to Japan and the Philippines. See Tang Zhenchang, pp. 842–43; *Riwei Shanghai*, pp. 265–75. See also Si Wei, "Meiyue," pp. 9–12; Zhou Zhen, pp. 8–11. See also Zhu Yanling, pp. 49–54.

56. Because of the lack of space, classes in occupied Shanghai averaged 90–108. Jiang Feng, pp. 118–19; Tao Juyin, *Tianliang*, p. 205. There were many stories in contemporary publications about intellectuals who joined rank with unemployed workers, displaced small businessmen, and housewives to become involved in the rough business of smuggling. There were at any given time a total of over 100,000 smugglers of all kinds of goods along the Shanghai-Hangzhou and Shanghai-Nanjing rail lines.

57. Yuan Yuquan, no. 1, pp. 86–87; and Shi Yu, pp. 4–11.

58. For example, Liang Hongzhi, the head of the defunct "Reformed Government" puppet regime, and now director of the Wang government's Supervisory *Yuan* (branch), was allegedly asked by Kong Xiangxi, the Nationalist government's finance minister, to "protect" his properties in Shanghai, as well as those of his brother-in-law, T. V. Song. See Yuan Yuquan, "Jinli zhe de huiyi," p. 139.

59. Tang Xinyi, ed., p. 55.

60. Reports and complaints of petty corruption and crime constituted

the bulk of writing under the Occupation. Several examples will suffice to indicate the prevalence of these social problems. Pickpockets were at work every day at bus stops and on buses, which were invariably overcrowded, and at night many passersby were stripped of their clothes in the less crowded alleyways. People often had food in hand snatched away by beggars on the street. But few victims reported these crimes to the authorities, because they were bound to lose even more in the process. Along with postmen, who demanded tips for their services, and bus conductors, who refused to make change, policemen charged a small fee for every case reported. They also extorted "protection money" from people lining up for rations and carrying goods home. Firefighters expected victims to pay them extra too; the famed exquisite "Aili Garden," built by the Jewish millionaire Silas Hardoon, was almost destroyed because the present residents were too poor to bribe firefighters when it was on fire. Travelers also had to pay hundreds of dollars to attendants and luggage carriers in order to get on a train. See Shen Cheng, "Shehui tuihua zhi xianxiang yu duice" (Social degeneration and its solutions), *Shen bao yuekan* 3, no. 1 (Jan. 1945): 58–62; Tao Juyin, *Tianliang*, pp. 260–64; *Zhongguo jingji* 2, no. 10 (Oct. 1942): 16. See also Li Siji, *Aili yuan menguing lu* (A dream record of the Aili *yuan*) (Beijing, 1984).

61. Shen Cheng, pp. 1–8.

62. Quoted from Feng Sheng, p. 72.

63. Quoted from *Shen bao*, Aug. 1, 1943. See also Yoshida, pt. 1.

64. *Shen bao*, *Wenyou*, and *Xin zhongguo bao* (New China Daily) were the main proponents of Japanese views; *Zhonghua ribao* (China Daily), *Zhengzhi zhoubao* (Politics Weekly), and *Zhonghua zhoubao* (China Weekly), the organs of the Nanjing government, represented the collaborators' ideas. For two representative articles, see Shen Cheng and Lin Wenru.

65. Yuan Yuquan, no. 1.

66. For a fine study of Fascist writers in Vichy France, see Kaplan; see also Robert Wohl, *The Generation of 1914* (Cambridge, Mass., 1979) for a historical exploration of intellectual Fascism in Europe.

67. *Shen bao* and *Xinwen bao* were the only newspapers allowed to published again after being closed down on December 8, 1941. The major newspapers circulating in occupied Shanghai from 1942 to 1945 were *Xin zhongguo bao*, *Zhonghua ribao*, *Guomin xinwen* (Citizen News), *Ping bao*, and *Xin shen bao*, with an average circulation of 40,000 apiece; all of them started publication in 1939 and 1940. See Azuma, pp. 66–67; and Yang Xiuqing, pp. 87–100.

68. Zhu Pu, "Mantan," p. 40, and "*Gujin* liangnian," pp. 46–47.

69. Zhu had been editor of *Shidai wenxuan* (Times Selection) and

Shidai wanbao (The Times Evening News), both organs of the Wang group, and after 1940 the vice minister of organization and propaganda of the Nanjing regime. He was later appointed to a ceremonial post on the Committee on the National Economy. See "Sishi zishu," pp. 20–24.

70. See Carroll, pp. 9–32. For an interesting discussion of the Chinese concept of guilt, see Eberhard.

71. Jin Xiongbai, *Wang zhengquan*, 1: 113–14.

72. See, e.g., ibid., 2: 101–36, 151–68.

73. Cai Dejin, ed., *Zhou Fohai*, 1: 620 (Dec. 11, 1941), and 2: 667 (Mar. 21, 1942).

74. *Gujin*, no. 1 (Mar. 1942): 2.

75. Wei Yan, p. 53.

76. See Mather; and Bauer.

77. Zhu Pu, "Mancheng fengyu," p. 32. The poem is by the Song poet Zheng Zhen (Jushan, 1199–1262).

78. Most of Wang Jingwei's writings for *Gujin* were sentimental works reminiscing about his comrades who had sacrificed themselves in the anti-Manchu 1911 Revolution. See, e.g., his "Guren gushi" (Old friends and old stories), *Gujin*, no. 19 (Mar. 1943): 2–4.

79. For Zhou's patronage of *Gujin*, see Zhu Pu, "Mengtan," p. 40, and "*Gujin* yinian," pp. 24–26.

80. On Zhu Pu, see his letter to his second wife, whom he married in 1944, "Puyuan duanjian" (A brief note from Puyuan), *Gujin*, no. 40, (Feb. 1944): 4; on Zhou Fohai, see Zuo Bi, pp. 5–6. On Chen Gongbo's self-image, see his "Shanghai," pp. 1–3 and "Wo de shi," pp. 1–10.

81. The terms are borrowed from Chou Ch'ih-ping in his analysis of the Ming Gongan school's obsession with nature and travel. See Chou.

82. For a well-articulated, almost classical exposition of this position, see Jin Xiongbai, *Wang zhengquan*, vols. 1–2. Marshal Pétain liked to say: "If I could not be your sword, I tried to be your shield." For a study of Vichy France's rhetoric, see Paxton.

83. "Shengshuai yuejin," pp. 17–18. Zhou's "Bing hou" (In recovery), recording his feelings while recovering from pneumonia and a heart attack in 1943, is also revealing: "Actually it is not clear whether it is fortunate or not that I do not die now. Perhaps heaven will not let me escape [so] easily from the sea of bitterness, but rather subject me to more sufferings and disasters before letting me off from these chaotic times.... [So] from now on I will not belong to myself. I will not care about success or failure, profit or loss. I will just do what I think is right for the country and for the race" (*Gujin*, no. 3 [May 1943]: 4). Both these serialized essays later appeared in *Wangyi ji* (The past is gone), a bestseller published by the Gujin Press.

84. Zhu Pu, "Wangyi ji," p. 14. Chen Gongbo's self-pitying remark was also a reaction formation, indicative of the anxiety that resulted from guilt, "How can I expect others to understand me when at times I don't even understand myself. I don't think anyone in the world can understand me."

85. On Zhou's factional politics, see Jin Xiongbai, *Wang zhengquan*, 1: 128–45 and 2: 69–73; and Huang and Zhang, eds., *Wang Jingwei guomin*, pp. 276–324; on Zhou's secret relations with the Guomindang, see Tang Shengming.

86. Zhou Zuoren was the spiritual father of the Analects group. Its philosophy was articulated by the prolific writer and translator Lin Yutang, who echoed Zhou's view that composition should be "centered on one's own self, written in a gracious and graceful tone." The group had at different times published *Lunyu, Renjian shi* (Universe), and *Yuzhou feng* (Cosmic Wind), all edited by Lin and Tao Kangde. After the outbreak of the war in 1937, *Yuzhou feng* was moved to Guangzhou and then to Guilin. See Lee, "Literary Trends," pp. 421–91 on the Analects group; on the Gongan School, see Chou. The account of Zhou Lian's early life given here is based on his *Huafa* and "Yuzhou feng," pp. 155–58.

87. Zhou Lian, "Yinian lai," pp. 61–64; and also his *Huafa*, pp. i–vi. As for Tao Kangde, see his "Jiantao," p. 350; and Zhang Jiying, p. 72. For Tao's involvement with the Wang group, see Qian Junrui et al., "Wang pai zhai Shanghai gejie huodong zhenxiang." Tao was said to have arranged for the Science Company on Avenue Foch, one of the two largest printers in Shanghai, to print *Shidai wenxuan*, edited by Zhu Pu, whom Tao and Zhou Lian had known since the early 1930s, when the "Reorganization Clique" was active in building a cultural network in Shanghai. After a trip by Tao to Hong Kong in 1938, the contact seems to have been renewed, as evidenced by the essays Zhu and several other senior members of the Wang group wrote for Tao's *Yuzhou feng* in 1939. For Tang Tao's attack on Zhou Lian, see "Dao Muzhai" (Condoling Muzhai), *Yuzhou feng yuekan*, no. 51 (Oct. 1941): 2–3.

88. Zhu Pu, "Mancheng fengyu," p. 32.

89. Pollard, *A Chinese Look at Literature*, pp. 121–38.

90. Zhou Lian, "Yinian lai."

91. Ibid., pp. 61–62. The remaining four included serialized personal notes (*biji*) by Liang Hongzhi, the former head of the Reformed Government in Nanjing (1938) and Zhu Pu's future father-in-law; an unpublished previous contribution to *Yuzhou feng yuekan*; and a reprint of a 1910 essay of Wang Jingwei.

92. *Shen bao sheping*, 2: 105. For descriptions of the literary world in 1942, see also Su Qing, p. 150.

93. Zhou was known for his warmth, genteel courteousness, and historical erudition; and he was keen to insist that *Gujin* was no different from *Yuzhou feng,* and that contribution to it thus had little political import. See Wen Zaidao, "Jiegu lunjin," pp. 39-45.

94. Many old scholars had collaborated since 1937 and held government posts in the Wang regime. They included the famed historian Qu Duizhi, who was responsible for persuading Zhou Zuoren to join the Japanese-controlled North China Political Committee, and the famous journalist and opera critic Xu Yishi.

95. See Wen Zaidao, *Fengtu,* pp. 189-260. See also *Shanghai Guda wenxue huiyi,* 1: 117-30, 389-402; 2: 154-55. *Yuzhou feng yuekan,* no. 51 (Oct. 1941): 4-12.

96. Wen Zaidao, *Fengtu,* p. 69.

97. On Wen Zaidao's collaboration, see my correspondence with Professor Qian Jinxi, Feb. 8, 1987; on Wen's coercion of Ke, see correspondence with Ke Ling, June 21, 1987. The quotation is from Wen's letter to Chen Dieyi, editor of the popular magazine *Chunqiu* (Annals); see "Zuojia shujian" (Writers' correspondence), *Chunqiu* 2, no. 1 (Dec. 1944): 99.

98. For Liu Yusheng, see *Wenhui bao,* May 17, 1946; *Gujin,* no. 10 (Nov. 1942): 16. Although not powerful, the Sino-Japanese Cultural Association, founded in July 1940 and headed by Wang Jingwei, was one of the most important official cultural organizations in Shanghai, charged with cultural exchange with Japan, with its head office in Nanjing. The Shanghai chapter was established in September 1941 and reorganized in March 1943. Chen Gongbo and Chu Minyi headed the Advisory Board, and other board members, in addition to Zhou Lian, included Fu Shishuo (the former Hangzhou university president), Fan Zhongyun (president of Central University in Nanjing), Zhao Shuyong, Jin Xiongbai, Tao Kangde, and, after 1943, Liu Yusheng. While bureau chief, Liu had, for instance, arranged for the famous woman writer Zhang Ailing and others to speak on Japanese literature and read from their own works. For Zhou Lian's statement, see "Mingxin," pp. 41-45. When Zhou Lian later married Mu Lijuan in March 1943 many prominent figures in the Wang regime (including Chen Gongbo, Liang Hongzhi, Fan Zhongyun, and, of course, Zhu Pu) and such important *Gujin* writers as Wen Zaidao, Liu Yusheng, and Tao Kangde attended the wedding banquet. See *Zazhi* 11, no. 1 (Apr. 1943): 96-97.

99. The concept of "soft collaboration" is developed in Jankowski, chs. 6-9. On Tan Zhengbi, see his "Dao yige wuzhi de linghun," pp. 64-69. For Bao Tianxiao and Qin Shouou, see their essays in *Fengyu tan,* 1943-44. The situation of these writers who collaborated for money came out in an interview I had with Zheng Yimei (Shanghai, Jan. 23, 1986). There

were differences in the behavior of these "soft" collaborators after they were forced to compromise. Whereas Tan Zhengbi's and Bao Tianxiao's cooperation was limited, extending only to writing, and they mainly produced historical and popular works that had little bearing on the present, Pan Yuqie enjoyed intimate relations with ranking collaborators because of his skill in palm reading and geomancy, which Zhou Fohai and Zhu Pu in particular believed in with a passion. Besides joining the Sino-Japanese Cultural Association as a director, Pan was also given the Award for Greater East Asian Literature for a short story anthology containing impressionistic sketches of the Shanghai lower middle class. See Pan Yuqie, pp. 49–50. Su Qing, the best-selling novelist of sexual experience, started writing full-time after her divorce. Through the offices of Tao Kangde and Liu Yusheng, whom she knew because of her contributions to Gujin, she got to know Zhou Fohai and Chen Gongbo, and with her diplomatic skills, she climbed fast. Through Zhou's and Chen's patronage, she obtained a sinecure in the Shanghai Municipal Government, and in 1944 she also started her own magazine, Tiandi, modeled on Gujin. Su's most famous work was Jiehun shinian (Ten years of marriage). For her life, see Ouyang, p. 70.

More difficult to categorize are the Communist writers. The woman novelist Guan Lu, for example, was sent by the CCP to infiltrate the Wang regime's cultural establishment and became the editor of Nüsheng (Woman's Voice). Another Communist, Lu Feng, edited the popular Zazhi (Magazine), published by Yuan Shu, probably one of the most enigmatic secret service agents in Chinese history. Yuan was said to be a Communist agent, but he worked closely with the GMD intelligence service in Shanghai, and he had been actively involved with the Kempeitai before joining the Wang regime in 1940. In 1942, he became the chief of the Jiangsu Provincial Bureau of Education.

Zhang Ailing, arguably the most famous and most interesting woman novelist of the time, started writing in 1942 after returning from Hong Kong. She wrote not for money but for self-expression, as well, probably, as fame. Besides living for a while with the Wang regime's talented propaganda chief, Hu Lancheng, Zhang wrote for Gujin, Zazhi, and other publications. She must have known by then that these magazines had collaborationist backing, but her literary achievement and unconventionality placed her above the fray. For a sensitive comment on Zhang's wartime life, see Ke Ling, Juchang, pp. 149–64; on her life with Hu Lancheng, see Hu's Jinsheng jinshi (This life, this age) (Taibei, 1976); and see also Gunn, Unwelcome Muse, ch. 5, for a general discussion of her literary works.

100. Wen Zaidao, "Jiegu lunjin," pp. 39–45.

101. The huge townhouse at 2 Avenue du Roi Albert, with its ten

acres of land, belonged to Jin Xiongbai; it was originally used as the Shang-hai office of his Nanjing Xingye Bank, and later as his own private club. Many important literary events, such as a roundtable discussion in 1945 with Zhang Aling and the *Zazhi* editors, were held there. See Jin Xiongbai, *Jizhe*, p. 126.

102. For a group picture of *Gujin* writers, including Zhou Fohai and Zhu Pu, see the back cover of *Gujin*, no. 25 (June 1943).

103. See, e.g., Wen Zaidao, "Puyuan yaji," pp. 8-10.

104. See, e.g., Shen Erqiao, "Mingmo shiren Du Chacun xiansheng" (The late Ming poet Du Chacun), *Gujin*, no. 43/44 (Apr. 1944): 15; and Wen Zaidao, *Fengtu*, pp. 1-8.

105. For an excellent study of remembrance and nostalgia as a motif in classical Chinese poetry, see Owen, pp. 80-141.

106. Qian Sui, pp. 2-3. For the term, see Kundera.

107. For Paul de Man's works on this theme, see particularly his *Blind-ness and Insight: Essays in the Rhetoric of Contemporary Criticism* (Minneapolis, 1983); and *The Resistance to Theory* (Minneapolis, 1986). As for interpreta-tions of de Man's theory of deconstruction in light of his newly disclosed journalistic works in the Belgian paper *Le Soir*, see Hamacher, Hertz, and Keenan, eds., *Responses*.

108. He Zhi, pp. 4-7.

109. Wen Zaidao, "Jinghai," p. 22. As he concisely put it in another instance: "Nothing in this world but the 'past' is meaningful; although it is gone, it is after all 'factual' and it can never be changed" (*Fengtu*, p. 17).

110. Ji Guoan, "Gujin yu wo," p. 33.

111. When Zhou Zuoren toured Nanjing and Suzhou in 1943, many Shanghai writers and editors, including Liu Yusheng and Tao Kangde, went there to see him and to associate with him, and his trip became a major lit-erary event, from which a spate of essays and reports emerged. See, e.g., Ji Guoan, "Zhitang xiansheng nan lai yinxiang zhuiji" (A recollection of Zhi-tang's trip to the south), *Gujin*, no. 20/21 (Apr. 1943): 5-8. For discussion of Zhou Zuoren's collaboration and critical analysis of his wartime writings, see, e.g., Lou Shiyi et al., pp. 2-53; see also Li Jingbin, *Zhou Zuoren pingxi* (A critical analysis of Zhou Zuoren) (Xian, 1986).

112. Wen Zaidao, *Fengtu*, pp. 79-80.

113. Ji Guoan, "Zhi ji," pp. 15-17. *Tiandi* was published in October 1943 by Su Qing, with the patronage of her alleged lover, the Shanghai mayor Chen Gongbo, in imitation of *Gujin*. After *Gujin*'s demise in Octo-ber 1944, *Tiandi* became its successor, championing the cause of anachronis-tic literature.

114. See, e.g., Zhu Pu, "Puyuan suitan," pp. 1-4; and Ji Guoan, "Hai shang," pp. 23-27.

115. Ji Guoan, "Lun sheshen chudi," pp. 18–20. Tao Yuanming's poem, which was frequently quoted at the time, is translated by Burton Watson as "Drinking Wine No. 5," in *The Columbia Book of Chinese Poetry* (New York, 1984), 1: 135. See also Yao Gong, "Tan Mingmo," pp. 17–19; and Zhou Lengjia, "Tan shanju," p. 2.

116. Chen Yulun, "Wu Meicun," pp. 25–29.

117. Wen Zaidao, *Fengtu*, pp. 6, 80. For a scholarly study of *Taoan Dream Memories*, see Owen, pp. 134–41.

118. See Ji Guoan, "Lun congrong jiushi," pp. 20–24; Liu Ping, pp. 19–22. See also Zhou Lengjia, "Qinggao," p. 2; and Wen Zaidao, *Fengtu*, p. 117.

119. Ji Guoan, "Lun congrong jiushi," p. 22.

120. Ji Guoan, "Lun sheshen chudi," pp. 18–20.

121. Wen Zaidao, "Wei-Jin renwu," pp. 15–19. The story of Zhang Han as narrated in *Shishuo xinyu*, a favorite allusion of Wen and other *Gujin* writers, deserves full quotation here: "Zhang Han was summoned to serve as an aide in the administration of the prince of Qi, Sima Jun. While he was in Luoyang, and saw the autumn winds rising, it was then that he longed for the wild rice, the water-lily soup, and the sliced perch of his old home in Wu [Suzhou]. He said, 'What a man values in life is just to find what suits his fancy, and nothing more. How can he tie himself down to an official post several thousand *li* from home in pursuit of fame and rank?' Whereupon he ordered his carriage and proceeded to return home. Shortly thereafter the prince of Qi was defeated and killed. His contemporaries all claimed Zhang was clairvoyant." Liu Yiqing, *Shishuo xinyu jiaojian* (Beijing, 1984), ch. 7, line 10, p. 317; my translation, based on that in Liu I-ch'ing, *Shih-shuo hsin-yu: A New Accounts of Tales of the World*, trans. Richard Mather (Minneapolis, 1976), p. 201.

122. Wen Zaidao, *Fengtu*, p. 36.

123. Yao Gong, "Furen qizhu," pp. 15–17.

124. See He Zhi.

125. Popularized by the "National Essence school" (*guocui pai*) during the early 1920s as a conservative reaction to the May Fourth espousal of cultural enlightenment, cultural nationalism denoted an identification with traditional culture as the defining characteristic and ultimate identity of China as a nation-race. See Laurence Schneider, "National Essence and the New Intelligentsia," in *Limits of Change*, ed. Charlotte Furth (Cambridge, Mass., 1976), pp. 57–89.

126. In a note on the Qing novel *Niehai hua* (Flower in the sinful sea), which was republished by *Gujin* as a poetic evocation of late Qing eccentrics, Zhou Lian wrote: "For us to look back on those who lived in the Tongzhi and Guangxu eras is no different from men of those times looking

back on literati in the times of Qianlong and Jiaqing" ("*Niehai hua* renwu," pp. 20–22).

127. Zhou Lian, "Bianji houji" (Editor's note), *Gujin*, no. 54 (Sept. 1944), p. 12.

128. Long Muxun, "Fu Li Jianqing shu," pp. 31–32.

129. Wen Zaidao, *Fengtu*, p. 37. Ji Guoan said that his fondness for following Zhou Zuoren's style of quoting long passages from classical works was to make sure that no one in the occupied areas would "forget about China." See his "Wo yu Liandu ji" (*Liandu ji* and I), *Tiandi*, no. 15 (Jan. 1945), pp. 19–22.

130. Zhou Zuoren, "Wenchao," pp. 14–15.

131. Tao Kangde, "Lun chuban wenhua," pp. 80–81.

132. See, e.g., Wen Zaidao, "Puyuan yaji."

133. Even Zheng Zhenduo was an avid reader of *Gujin*; see his diary entry of Apr. 1, 1944. Chen Fukang, p. 220.

134. These publishing houses included the Gujin Company, Tiandi Press, and Peace Bookstore. All of them belonged to the Japanese-controlled Zhongguo lianhe chuban gongsi (United China Publishing Company), which also included such large publishing houses as the Commercial Press and Enlightenment Bookstore (the last two published only reference works and Chinese history, such as *The Twenty-Four Histories*, however). Yang Shouqing, p. 387.

135. The Propaganda Department was known among the collaborators as the "Cantonese Guild" because most of its leading personnel were former classmates of Lin Bosheng's from Canton. Even its Japanese advisor, the famed poet Kusano Shinpei, who represented the Press Bureau of the Japanese Expeditionary Army Headquarters, was a graduate of Canton's Lingnan University and a good friend of Lin's. Among other things, the Propaganda Department was in charge of censorship in all occupied regions and formulating theoretical rationalizations for the Nanjing regime's policies. See Zhang Runsan, pp. 1–81.

136. See, e.g., Zhou Huaren, "Dongya," pp. 2–5, and "'Wenxie' fakanci" (Foreword to *Wenxie*), *Wenxie* 1, no. 1 (Nov. 1943): 1–2; and Feng Jie, "Jianli Dongfang benwei wenhua," pp. 1–2. See also Takahashi. For the text of the propaganda outline, see *Shen bao nianjian* (Shanghai News Almanac) (Shanghai, 1943). See also Yu Zidao et al., eds., pp. 368–408.

137. See, e.g., He Gang, p. 21; and Yang Yiming.

138. Yue Xiuliang, pp. 144–46. See also Zhang Yu, "Shuo beiai" (On melancholy), *Zazhi* 3, no. 2 (May 1944): 27–29. For Paul de Man's essay on Robert Brasillach (*Le Soir*, Aug. 12, 1941), see Hamacher, Hertz, and Keenan, eds., *Paul de Man's Wartime Journalism*, pp. 130–31. For a partial translation, see id., *Responses*, pp. 22–24.

139. Liu Yusheng, "Huaixiang," p. 157.

140. For an account of the wartime literary activities of these prominent Japanese writers, see Keene, "Japanese Writers," pp. 209–15; and "Barren Years," pp. 67–112.

141. See, e.g., Zhou Yueren, "Zai Riben," pp. 129–31; Tao Kangde, "Xixing," pp. 132–35, and "Dongxing," p. 14. See also Liu Yusheng, "Huaixiang."

142. The Nihon bungaku hōkokukai was founded in May 1942 under the auspices of the Japanese Intelligence Agency, and its officers included many eminent writers, such as Kikuchi Kan. For Japan's propaganda work and cultural activities during the war, see Shillony, pp. 110–56.

143. Liu Yusheng, "Da Dongya zhanzheng," pp. 12–16. For Beijing's literary situation, an understudied subject that calls for immediate attention from historians, see Liu, *Kangzhan shiqi lunxianqu wenxue shi*. See also Gunn, *Unwelcome Muse*, ch. 1. There was a "national" literary organization in Beijing called the Zhongguo lianyi zuojia hui (Association of Chinese Writers), but it consisted only of minor writers, such as Chen Dabei, Li Jianwu's former drama coach, Ding Ding, Zhou Yuren, and Lin Weiyin. It had very little influence in the literary world of the Occupation.

144. *Wenxie* 2, no. 12 (Dec. 1944): 10–11. The Greater East Asian Writers' Congress held three meetings during the war: in Tokyo in November 1942 and August 1943 and in Nanjing in November 1944. The Nanjing meeting was dedicated to cultural cooperation among Japan, China, Manchukuo, Mongolia, and Taiwan.

145. Gu Fengcheng, "Wenhua jie," p. 97. See also Ji Guoan, "Tan qingtan," pp. 18–22.

146. See Boyle, ch. 15; Yuan Yuquan, no. 1, pp. 82–85. For an example of the talk of "Japan's self-examination," see "Juantou yu" (Editorial) in *Wenyou* 3, no. 1 (May 1944): 1. On the "Cleansing of Villages Movement," see Yu Zidao et al., eds.

147. The first quotation is from Tao Jingsun, "Tixie," pp. 9–10. The second is from Yoshida, pp. 73–79; see also his "Riben de zhengyi" (The true intent of Japan), *Wenyou* 2, no. 17 (Jan. 1944): 8–10.

148. See, e.g., "Juantou yu," p. 1. *Wenyou* (Literary Companion) was published and edited by the Press Office (Shimbunhan) of the Japanese Expeditionary Army in China. Similar views were also expressed by *Shen bao*, which was also under the direct control of the Press Office. The quotation is from Gao Xiang, pp. 7–9.

149. Tao Kangde, "Lun chuban wenhua," p. 81. Actually, besides having an appointment at the Central Reserve Bank (together with Zhou Lian), Tao himself wrote prolifically and edited several magazines at the same time. Essayists like Long Muxun and Tan Zhengbi wrote extensively and

taught at hourly rates at different colleges or at several high schools in order to make ends meet. See Jiang Chun et al., "Chuban wenhua zhi wenti" (Problems of the publishing culture), *Zazhi* 11, no. 5 (Aug. 1943): 24–28. Hourly rates for college teaching in 1943 were, to give some examples, CRB $10 at Jiaotong University , CRB $22.50 at St. John's University, and CRB $60 at the Shanghai Medical School. See "Shanghai gaodeng jiaoyu gaikuang" (A survey of Shanghai higher education), *Wenxie* 2, no. 2 (Mar. 1944): 41–48. At the well-publicized Third Conference of the Nihon bungaku hōkokukai, the novelist Ishikan Totsuzo called for a great literature devoted to a "Liberated Asia" and criticized trivial autobiographical fiction. See Keene, "Japanese Writers," p. 308. This theme was taken up by many Japanese cultural officials in Shanghai, who called for a "romantic" literature dedicated to the realization of Peace in Asia. See "Zhongguo wenxue zhi xianzhuang" (The current Chinese literary scene), originally published in *Dairoku shimpō* and translated into Chinese in *Zazhi* 13, no. 2 (May 1944): 172–76.

150. Ji Guoan, "Tan qingtan," pp. 18–22.

151. Shu Sheng, pp. 4–5.

152. Zhu Pu, "Houji" (Postscript), in *Zhou Fohai riji* (The diary of Zhou Fohai) (Hong Kong, n.d.).

153. Zhu Pu, "Xiaoxiu," p. 1.

154. See Jin Xiongbai, *Wang zhengquan*, 2: 59–94; Yuan Yuquan, "Jinglizhe de huiyi."

155. See Su Qing, pp. 67–151; and Yang Shouqing.

156. Wen Zaidao, "Zhiren lunshi," p. 79. See also id., "Shihuang," pp. 22–26; Ji Guoan, "Wo yu *Liangdu ji*," pp. 19–22.

157. *Wenhui bao*, Oct. 1, 1945.

158. "The issue is not whether one collaborated or not; but rather whether one was evil or not," the famed movie directors Shi Dongshan and Cai Chusheng argued, for example (*Wenhui bao*, July 14, 1946).

159. For the trial of Liu and Tao, see *Wenhui bao*, May 17 and June 1, 1946. The two were arrested with the voluntary aid of their former protégé Su Qing. In October 1945, the special emissary of the Guomindang Central Propaganda Department, Zhan Wenhu, announced that "with the few exceptions of national scum who willingly propagandized for the enemy and the puppet regime, and are therefore subject to prosecution, all those who were forced to make such a stupid move [serving the Wang regime] in order to survive deserve our pardon" (*Wenhui bao*, Oct. 15, 1945). So it was those intellectuals who had official posts in the collaborationist regime (like the propaganda official Dai Yingfu and Fu Shishuo, governor of Zhejiang) or who had edited mainly political newspapers and journals for them who

were prosecuted. Long Muxun, who was marginally associated with *Gujin* because of his close relationship with Wang Jingwei, was also imprisoned for his service in the Wang regime's cultural and educational realms. See Yi Jun, "Wo de biming" (My pen name), *Shijie ribao*, Jan. 5, 1992. In fact, the highly complicated politics of prosecuting collaborators, which involved the issues of whom to indict and how and when to do so, and its relationship to the Civil War, awaits systematic study. Among the top leaders of the Wang regime executed in 1946 were Chen Gongbo, Chen Bijun, Chu Minyi, Mei Siping, and Lin Bosheng; Zhou Fohai's death sentence was commuted by Chiang Kaishek for his aid to the Nationalist guerrillas in Central China (the "Loyal and Patriotic Army"), but he died of a heart attack in prison in 1946. A few prominent collaborators, such as the publisher of the Japanese-run *Shen bao*, Chen Binhe, fled to Hong Kong. Zhu Pu also miraculously found refuge in Hong Kong after the war, while Zhao Shuyong went to teach in Southeast Asia. As for Jin Xiongbai, he served two years in a GMD prison before pursuing a freelance writing career in Hong Kong and Japan, where he later died. In 1977, shortly before his death, he was still striking a typically *Gujin* note, writing, for example: "The stuff we call politics has no right or wrong; nor does it have good or bad. What matters is whether you win or you lose" (*Jizhe shengya wushi nian*, p. 135). After serving two years in a Shanghai prison, Liu Yusheng left to teach in Hong Kong; he is now professor emeritus of Chinese literature at the Australian National University.

160. See, e.g., Dao Zaiwen, "Yang Du hanmo," pp. 9–16.

Epilogue

1. Wilkinson, p. 264.
2. See, for example, Israel, "Random Notes."
3. Wakeman, "Stoics, Romantics, and Martyrs," pp. 631–66.
4. Said, pp. 5–16.
5. Wen Zaidao, *Fengtu*, p. 1.
6. Lee, "Literary Trends." In both the Nationalist- and Communist-controlled areas, because of the rhetoric of patriotic heroism, eremitism as a cultural mode of symbolic protest was condemned rather as treasonable escapism. See Jiang Xingyu.
7. Li Jianwu, "Geren zhuyi" (Individualism), in *Li Jianwu wenxue*, pp. 220–22.
8. For two studies of occupied areas, see Sophia Lee, "Social Order in Beijing Under Japanese Occupation"; and Peter Seybolt, "Patriotic War of

National Liberation? Collaboration Between Chinese and Japanese During the War of Resistance, 1937–45: A Case Study of Neihuang County, Henan Province" (papers presented at the 43d Association for Asian Studies, April 1991).

9. For a somewhat similar view, see Kedward, *Vichy France and the Resistance*, pp. 1–10. However, Kedward's plea for a comparative study of foreign occupation is aimed mainly at deepening understanding of the French experience.

10. See Bergère.

11. See Berman, pp. 154–55.

12. For a typical piece of nostalgia, see "Shanghai rengzai fou" (Is there still a Shanghai now?), *Shijie ribao*, May 8–9, 1991.

Bibliography

A Ying. *Bixue hua* (Flower in blood). Beijing, 1962.

———. *Haiguo yingxiong* (The hero of a maritime nation). Fujian, 1985.

Ai Siqi. "Wenhua zai kangzhan zhong" (Culture in the midst of the War of Resistance). *Kangzhan sanrikan*, Sept. 6, 1937.

Amery, Jean. *At the Mind's Limits: Contemplations of a Survivor on Auschwitz and Its Realities.* Trans. Sidney and Stella Rosenfeld. Bloomington, Ind., 1980.

Anderson, Marston. "The Morality of Form: Lu Xun and the Modern Chinese Short Story." In *Lu Xun and His Legacy*, ed. Leo Ou-fan Lee. Berkeley, 1985.

Azuma Hideo. *Shanhai wa tachi agaru* (The rise of Shanghai). Tokyo, 1943.

Ba Jin. "Gei Shanchuan xiansheng" (To Mr. Yamakawa). *Fenghuo*, no. 4 (Sept. 1937).

———. *Kongshu shu* (Denunciation). Fujian, 1985.

Ba Ren. *Ba Ren zawenji* (Collected miscellaneous essays of Ba Ren). Beijing, 1985.

———. "Lun *Toujijia*" (On *Toujijia*). *Shanghai zhoubao* 1, no. 16 (Feb. 1940).

Ballard, J.G. *Empire of the Sun.* New York, 1984.

Bao Mingshu. *Kangri shiqi dongnan dihou* (The southeast interior during the War of Resistance). Taibei, 1974.

Barnett, Robert. *Economic Shanghai: Hostage to Politics, 1937–1941.* New York, 1941.

Barthes, Roland. *Writing Degree Zero.* Trans. A. Lavers and C. Smith. New York, 1980.

Bauer, Wolfgang. "The Hidden Hero: Creation and Disintegration of the Ideal of Eremitism." In *Individualism and Holism in Confucian and Taoist Values*, ed. Donald Munro. Ann Arbor, Mich., 1985.

Baum, Vicki. *Shanghai '37.* 1939. Reprint. Hong Kong, 1986.

Bayisan kangzhan shiliao xuanpian (Selected historical documents on the August 13 Battle of Resistance). Shanghai, n.d.

Bayisan Songhu kangzhan (The August 13 Shanghai-Wusong Battle of Resistance). Beijing, 1987.

Becker, Ernest. *The Denial of Death.* New York, 1973.

Bentley, Eric. *Playwrights as Thinkers.* San Diego, 1987.

———. *Thinking About Playwrights.* Evanston, Ill., 1987.

Bergère, Marie-Claire. "'The Other Shangahi': Shangahi from 1919 to 1949." In *Shanghai: Revolution and Development in an Asia Metropolis,* ed. Christopher Howe. Cambridge, 1981.

Berman, Marshall. *All That Is Solid Melts into Air: The Experience of Modernity.* New York, 1988.

Bing Du. "Shanghai jutan manbu" (A visit of the Shanghai theater). *Zazhi* 9, no. 8 (Aug. 1942).

Boyle, John. *China and Japan at War, 1937–45: The Politics of Collaboration.* Stanford, 1972.

Bruce, George. *Shanghai's Undeclared War.* Shanghai, 1937.

Bullock, Alan. *The Humanist Tradition in the West.* London, 1985.

Cai Chusheng. "Zhanhou de Zhongguo dianyin dongtai ji muqian de gaijin yundong" (The trend of postwar Chinese cinema and its reform movement). *Wenxian* 4 (Jan. 1939).

Cai Dejin. *Wang Jingwei pingzhuan* (Biography of Wang Jingwei). Sichuan, 1988.

———, ed. *Zhou Fohai riji* (The diary of Zhou Fohai). 2 vols. Shanghai, 1986.

Calvocoressi, Peter, and Guy Wint. *The Total War.* London, 1985.

Camus, Albert. *The Rebel.* Trans. A. Bower. New York, 1956.

Cang Hai. "Lun zhanshi guomin shenghuo" (On wartime national life). *Wenyou* 2, no. 4 (Jan. 1944).

Cao Yu. *Tuibian* (Metamorphosis). Shanghai, 1948.

Carey, Arch. *The War Years at Shanghai: 1941–45–48.* New York, 1967.

Carroll, John. *Guilt: The Grey Eminence Behind Character, History and Culture.* London, 1985.

Chen Chunren. *Kangzhan shidai shenghuo shi* (A history of wartime life). Hong Kong, n.d.

Chen Fukang, ed. "Zheng Zhenduo yijiu sisi nian riji" (The 1944 diary of Zheng Zhenduo). *Xin wenxue shiliao,* no. 2 (1990).

Chen Gongbo. "Shanghai de shizhang" (The mayor of Shanghai). *Gujin,* no. 11 (Nov. 1942).

———. "Wo de shi" (My poetry). *Gujin,* no. 24 (June 1943).

———. "Zenyang cai dedao Zhongri yongjiu heping" (How to achieve permanent Sino-Japanese peace). *Shidai wenxuan* 2, no. 1 (Feb. 1940).

Chen Gongshu. *Kangzhan houqi fanjian huodong* (Espionage during the later period of the War of Resistance). Taibei, 1986.

Chen Yingchuan. "Shanghai shi wupin peiji gaikuang" (A survey of Shanghai's ration system). *Xinwen yuekan* 1, no. 3 (July 1945).

Chen yulun. "Wu Meicun yu Huishan heshang" (Wu Meichun and Monk Huishan). *Gujin*, no. 50 (July 1944).

Cheng Zhongyuan. "Ji geming xijujia Yu Ling" (Remembering the revolutionary dramatist Yu Ling). *Xin wenxue shiliao*, no. 12 (May 1983).

Chou Ch'ih-ping. *Yuan Hung-tao and the Kung-an School*. Cambridge, 1988.

Chow, Rey. *Women and Chinese Modernity: The Politics of Reading Between East and West*. Minneapolis, 1991.

Coble, Parks, Jr. *Facing Japan: Chinese Politics and Japanese Imperialism, 1931–1937*. Cambridge, Mass., 1991.

Cohen-Solal, Annie. *Sartre: A Life*. Trans. Anna Cancogni. New York, 1987.

Collar, Hugh. *Captive in Shanghai: A Story of Internment in World War II*. Hong Kong, 1990.

Confidential U.S. State Department Reports. Microfilm reproduction. 1937–41.

Confucius. *The Analects*. Trans. D.C. Lau. London, 1979.

Dao Zaiwen [Jin Xingyao]. "Yang Du hanmo jiqi youguang renwu" (The calligraphy of Yang Du and all those involved). *Dacheng*, no. 168 (Nov. 1987).

Des Pres, Terrence. *The Survivor: An Anatomy of Life in the Death Camps*. New York, 1980.

Dongfang Xi [Kong Lingjing]. "Lun Gudao wenyi de fajian" (On the development of Solitary Island literature). *Lu Xun feng*, no. 15 (June 1939).

Dongya xinwen jizhe dahui shilu (Record of the Congress of East Asian Journalists). Nanjing, 1941.

Dower, John. *War Without Mercy: Race and Power in the Pacific War*. New York, 1986.

Du Yunzhi. "Huiyi kangzhan shiqi Shanghai de huaju" (My memory of theater in wartime Shanghai). *Da cheng*, no. 3 (Feb. 1973).

Eberhard, Wolfram. *Guilt and Sin in Traditional China*. Berkeley, 1967.

Farmer, Rhodes. *Shanghai Harvest: A Diary of Three Years in the China War*. London, 1945

Fei Xichou. *Shanghai xin zhinan* (A new guidebook of Shanghai). Shanghai, 1939.

Feng Guanglian, and Liu Zangren, eds. *Wang Tongzhao yanjiu ziliao* (Research materials on Wang Tongzhao). Ningxia, 1983.

Feng Jie. "Jianli Dongfang benwei wenhua" (The establishment of our own Eastern culture). *Dongfang wenhua* 1, no. 6 (Nov. 1942).

Feng Sheng. "Meiyue Huazhong jingji" (Central China's economy in months). *Zhongguo jingji* 2, no. 8 (Aug. 1944).

Ferguson, Suzanne. "Defining the Short Story: Impressionism and Form." In *Essentials of the Theory of Fiction*, ed. M. Hoffmann and P. Murphey. Durham, N.C., 1988.

Fink, Carole. *Marc Bloch: A Life in History.* Cambridge, 1989.

Frye, Northrop. *Anatomy of Criticism.* Princeton, 1957.

Furuyama, Tadao. "Nitchū sensō to Shanhai minzoku shihon" (The Sino-Japanese War and national capitalism of Shanghai). In *Dentō-teki keizai shakai no rekishi to tenkai,* ed. Hayama Teisaku, vol. 2. Tokyo, 1983.

Fussell, Paul. *The Great War and Modern Memory.* New York, 1977.

Gao Xiang. "Bawo minxin diyi" (It is paramount to win popular confidence). *Shen bao yuekan* 1, no. 3 (Nov. 1944).

Ge Zizheng, ed. *Mingguo ershijiu nian Shanghai zhi jingji yu shangye* (The economy and commerce of Shanghai in 1940). Shanghai, 1941.

Gert, Bernard. *Morality: A New Justification of the Moral Rules.* New York, 1988.

Gong Mingdao. "Shanghai tongxun" (Correspondance from Shanghai). *Yuzhou feng,* no. 91 (Jan. 1940).

Gould, Randall. Randall Gould Papers. Box 5. Hoover Institution Archives, Stanford.

Gu Fengcheng. "Wenhua jie xiaochen de yuanyin" (Reasons for the despondence of the cultural circle). *Shen bao yuekan* 1, no. 3 (Mar. 1943).

———. "Xianjieduan Zhongguo de jingji wenti" (China's economic problems in the present stage). *Wenyou* 2, no. 4 (Jan. 1941).

Gu Zhongyi. "Shinian lai de Shanghai huaju yundong" (The Shanghai dramatic movement in the last ten years). In *Kangzhan shinain lai Zhongguo de xiju yundong yu chiaoyu,* ed. Hong Shen. Shanghai, 1948.

Gunn, Edward. "Shanghai's Orphan Island and the Development of Modern Drama." In *Popular Chinese Literature and Performing Arts in People's Republic of China,* ed. Bonnie McDougall. Berkeley, 1984.

———. *Unwelcome Muse: Chinese Literature in Shanghai and Peking, 1937–1945.* New York, 1982.

Guo Peng. "Gudao fengjingxian" (Special features of the Solitary Island). *Yuzhou feng,* no. 110 (Dec. 1940).

Guo Xiufeng. "Wangwei shiqi de Zhonghua ribao" (*Zhonghua ribao* during the Wang regime period). *Wenshi ziliao,* no. 5 (Aug. 1980).

Hamacher, Werner, Neil Hertz, and Thomas Keenan, eds. *Paul de Man's Wartime Journalism, 1939–1943.* Lincoln, Neb., 1989.

———. *Responses: On Paul de Man's Wartime Journalism.* Lincoln, Neb., 1989.

Hashikawa, Bunsō. "Japanese Perspectives on Asia: From Dissociation to Coprosperity." In *The Chinese and the Japanese,* ed. Akira Iriye. Princeton, 1980.

He Gan. "Wentan sici" (Four defects of the literary world). *Wenyou* 3, no. 11 (Oct. 15, 1944).

He Zhi. "Feihua eryi" (Sheer nonsense). *Tiandi,* no. 9 (June 1944).

Henriot, Christian. "Lone Island: Shanghai Under Japanese Occupation (1937–1945)." Paper presented to the Conference on Cities in the Second World War, Geneva, 1989.

Hinder, Eleanor. *Life and Labor in Shanghai: A Decade of Labor and Social Administration in the International Settlement.* New York, 1944.

Holm, David. "Lu Xun in the Period of 1936–1949: The Making of China's Gorki." In *Lu Xun and His Legacy*, ed. Leo Ou-fan Lee. Berkeley, 1985.

———. "The Literary Rectification in Yenan." In *Essays in Modern Chinese Literature and Literary Criticism*, ed. Wolfgang Kubin. Bochum, 1982.

Honig, Emily. *Sisters and Strangers: Women in the Shanghai Cotton Mills, 1919–1949.* Stanford, 1986.

Howard, Michael. *War and the Liberal Conscience.* New Brunswick, N.J., 1977.

Hu Sheng. "Kangzhan shiqi de wenhua" (Wartime culture). *Kangzhan sanrikan*, Aug. 29, 1937.

Hu Songqing. "Tan Gudao biaoyan yishu" (On the performing arts in the Solitary Island). *Juchang yishu*, no. 4/5 (Mar. 1939).

Hu Ziying. "Zai huoxian de houmian" (At the rear of the battlefront). *Kangzhan sanrikan*, Aug. 29, 1937.

Huai Jiu. "Yi Lu Yi" (Remembering Lu Yi). In *Lu Yi sanwen ji*, ed. Qin Xianci. Taibei, 1979.

Huang Meizhen, Shi Yuanhua, and Jiang Yihua. *Wangwei qishiliu hao tegong zongbu* (The No. 76 secret service headquarters of the Wang regime). Shanghai, 1984.

Huang Meizhen, ed. *Wangwei shi hanjian* (The ten traitors of the Wang regime). Shanghai, 1986.

Huang Meizhen, and Zhang Yun. *Wang Jingwei jituan panguo toudi ji* (The traitorous collaboration of the Wang clique). Henan, 1987.

———, eds. *Wang Jingwei guomin zhengfu chengli* (The founding of the Wang nationalist government). Shanghai, 1984.

———. eds. *Wang Jingwei jituan toudi* (The collaboration of the Wang clique). Shanghai, 1984.

Hui Tang. "Lishi yu xianshi" (History and reality). *Shanghai zhoubao* 1, no. 2 (Nov. 1939).

Hung, Chang-tai. "Female Symbols of Resistance in Chinese Wartime Spoken Drama." *Moder China* 15, no. 2 (1989).

Huters, Theodore. "Critical Grounding: The Transformation of the May Fourth Era." In *Popular Chinese Literature and Performing Arts in People's Republic of China*, ed. Bonnie McDougall. Berkeley, 1984.

Ienaga, Saburō. *The Pacific War: World War II and the Japanese, 1931–1945.* New York, 1978.

Israel, John. "Random Notes on Wartime Chinese Intellectuals." *Republican China* 9, no. 3 (Apr. 1984).

———. *Student Nationalism in China, 1927–1937*. Stanford, 1966.

Jameson, Frederic. *The Political Consciousness: Narrative as a Socially Symbolic Act*. Ithaca, N.Y., 1981.

Jankowski, Paul. *Communism and Collaboration: Simon Sabiani and Politics in Marseille, 1919–1944*. New Haven, 1989.

Ji Guoan. "*Gujin* yu wo" (*Gujin* and I). *Gujin*, no. 19 (Mar. 1943).

———. "Hai shang jixing" (A trip to Shanghai). *Gujin*, no. 30 (Sept. 1943).

———. "Lun congrong jiusi" (On heroic death). *Gujin*, no. 7 (Sept. 1942).

———. "Lun sheshen chudi" (On putting oneself in another's situation). *Gujin*, no. 38 (Feb. 1942).

———. "Tan qingtan" (On pure conversation). *Tiandi*, no. 2 (Nov. 1943).

———. "Wo yu *Liangdu ji*" (*Liangdu ji* and I). *Tiandi*, no. 15 (Jan. 1944).

———. "Zhi ji pian" (Self-understanding). *Tiandi*, no. 13 (Oct. 1944).

Jiang Chun. "Chuban wenhua zhi wenti" (Problems of publishing culture). *Wenxie* 2, no. 2 (Mar. 1944).

Jiang Feng, ed. "Jiaoyu zuotan" (A symposium on education). *Shen bao yuekan* 1, no. 3 (Mar. 1943).

Jiang Kanghu. "Shijie shida" (It is a grave matter to lose one's integrity). *Zhonghua ribao*, May 5, 1941.

———. "Shijie shi gengda" (Losing one's integrity is a much graver matter). *Zhengzhi yuekan* 1, no. 5 (May 1941).

Jiang Xingyu. *Zhongguo yinshi yu Zhongguo wenhua* (Chinese eremitism and Chinese culture). Shanghai, 1944.

Jie Yi. "Jianghe yu hanjian" (Appeasement and traitors). *Shidai wenxuan*, no. 3/4 (June 1939).

Jin Ding. "Wenyi zuojia yingyou de renshi yu renwu" (Knowledge writers should have and their mission). *Jiuwang ribao*, Sept. 12, 1937.

Jin Xiongbai. *Jizhe shengya wushi nian* (My fifty years as a journalist). Hong Kong, 1977.

——— [Zhu Zijia]. *Wang zhengquan de kaichang yu shouchang* (The beginning and end of the Wang regime). 6 vols. Hong Kong, 1984.

Jing Yi. "Wo de hua" (My words). *Fenghuo*, no. 1 (Aug. 1937).

Jones, F.C. *Shanghai and Tientsin*, San Francisco, 1940.

Kangri fengyun lu (A record of the War of Resistance). 2 vols. Shanghai, 1985.

Kangzhan jianguo shi yantaohui lunwen ji (Collected papers of the symposium on the history of the War of Resistance and national construction). 2 vols. Taibei, 1985.

Kaplan, Alice Yaeger. *Reproductions of Banality: Fascism, Literature, and French Intellectual Life*. Minneapolis, 1986.

Ke Ling. *Henhai* (Sea of grief). Shanghai, 1947.

————. *Juchang ouji* (Random notes on theater). Tianjin, 1983.

————. *Ke Ling zawen ji* (Selected miscellaneous essays of Ke Ling). Beijing, 1985.

————. "Shanghai lunxian qijian xiju wenxue guankui" (My partial view of the dramatic literature in occupied Shanghai). *Shanghai shifan xueyuan xuebao*, no. 2 (Apr. 1982).

————. *Shilou duchang* (A lone voice in a city room). 1940. Reprint. Shanghai, 1984.

————. "Yangshang bao bian" (A defense of foreign-published newspapers). In *Biangu ji*. Shanghai, 1938.

————. *Zhuzi shengya* (A life of making words). Shanxi, 1986.

Ke Ling, and Ren Jiarao. "Ji yangshang bao de xingshuai" (On the rise and fall of foreign-published newspapers). *Renmin zhenqxie bao*, Jan. 1–Feb. 1, 1984.

Ke Ling and Yang Yingwu. "Huiyi Kugan" (Remembering Kugan). In *Zhongguo huaju yundong wushi nian shiliao ji*, vol. 2. Beijing, 1985.

Ke Lun. "Meiyue Huazhong jingji dashi" (Monthly economic events in Central China). *Zhongguo jingji* 2, no. 10 (Oct. 1944).

Kedward, H.R. *Occupied France: Collaboration and Resistance, 1940–1944.* Oxford, 1985.

————. *Resistance in Vichy France: A Study of Ideas and Motivation in the Southern Zone, 1940–1942.* Oxford, 1978.

Kedward, Roderick [H.R.], and Roger Austin, eds. *Vichy France and the Resistance: Culture & Ideology.* London, 1985.

Keene, Donald. "Japanese Writers and the Greater East Asian War." *Journal of Asian Studies* 23, no. 2 (Feb. 1964).

————. "The Barren Years: Japanese War Literature." *Monumenta Nipponica* 33, no. 1 (Spring 1978).

Kirchheimer, Otto. *Political Justice: The Use of Legal Procedure for Political Ends.* Princeton, 1961.

Kisaka Junichiro. *Taiheiyō sensō* (The Pacific War). Tokyo, 1982.

Kong Lingjing, ed. *Hengmei ji* (Angry eyebrows). Shanghai, 1939.

Kong Yuanzhi. "Huangpu tantou" (The shore of Huangpu River). *Dafeng*, no. 15 (Aug. 1938).

————. "Wuyue de Shanghai" (Shanghai in May). *Dafeng*, no. 10 (June 1938).

Kranzler, David. *Japan, Nazis and Jews: The Jewish Refugee Community of Shanghai.* New York, 1976.

Kubota Chiseki. *Shanhai Kempeitai* (Japanese military police in Shanghai). Tokyo, 1956.

Kundera, Milan. *The Unbearable Lightness of Being.* Trans. Michael Heim. New York, 1984.

Lakoff, George, and Mark Johnson. *Metaphors We Live By.* Chicago, 1980.

Lan Hai. *Zhongguo kangzhan wenyi shi* (A history of Chinese Resistance arts and literature). Shandong, 1984.

Lee, Leo Ou-fan. "Literary Trends: The Road to Revolution, 1927–1949." In *The Cambridge History of China*, ed. John King Fairbank and Albert Feuerwerker, vol. 13, pt. 2. Cambridge, 1981.

———. "Romantic Individualism in Modern Chinese Literature: Some General Explorations." In *Individualism and Holism in Confucian and Taoist Values*, ed. Donald Munro. Ann Arbor, Mich., 1985.

Levenson, Joseph R. *Confucian China and Its Modern Fate.* 1958–65. Reprint. Berkeley, 1968.

Levi, Primo. *The Drowned and the Saved.* Trans. Raymond Rosenthal. New York, 1989.

Li Da. "Shanghai jingji de dongtai" (The recent development of the Shanghai economy). *Shen bao yuekan* 2, no. 8 (Aug. 1944).

Li Jianwu. "'Ai yu si de bodou' zai Gudao shiqi de zhengshi yanchu" (The official performance of *Le Jeu de l'Amour et de la Mort*). *Shanxi shiyuan xuebao*, no. 4 (1981).

———. *Fengliu zai* (Debt of love). Shanghai, 1946.

———. *Hua xin feng* (Fernande). Shanghai, 1947.

———. *It's Only Spring and Thirteen Years.* Trans. Tony Hyder. Oxford, 1989.

———. *Juhua erji* (Appreciation II). Shanghai, 1942.

———. *Li Jianwu chuangzuo pinglun xuanji* (Selected creative and critical works of Li Jianwu). Beijing, 1984.

———. *Li Jianwu juzuo xuan* (Selected dramatic works of Li Jianwu). Beijing, 1985.

———. *Li Jianwu wenxue pinglun xuan.* (Selected literary criticism of Li Jianwu). Yichuan, 1983.

———. "Li Jianwu zizhuan" (Autobiography of Li Jianwu). *Shanxi shiyuan xuebao*, no. 4 (1981).

———. *Liang Yunda.* Shanghai, 1934.

———. *Qiemeng dao* (A knife for cutting dreams). Shanghai, 1948.

———. *Qingchun* (Youth). Shanghai, 1948.

———. *Shisan nian* (Thirteen Years). Shanghai, 1939.

———. "Wan sange" (An elegy for the Third Brother). *Wenhui bao*, Nov. 29, 1945.

———. "Wang Deming." *Wencong*, nos. 1–4 (Jan.–July 1946).

———. "Wo wei shenme yao chongyi 'Ai yu si de bodou'" (Why I retranslated *Le Jeu de l'Amour et de la Mort*). *Shen bao*, Oct. 27, 1938.

———. "Yi Zheng Zhenduo" (In memory of Zheng Zhenduo). *Shouhuo*, no. 4 (July 1981).

————. "Yu youren shu" (A letter to a friend). *Shanghai wenhua*, no. 6 (July 1946).

————. *Zhe buguo shi chuntian* (This is only spring). Shanghai, 1937.

————. "Zizhuan" (Autobiography). In *Zhongguo xiandai zuojia zhuanlue*. Sichuan, 1981.

Li Ling. "Huiyi Sushang Shidai chubanshe" (Remembering the Russian-run Times Publishing House). In *Zhongguo chuban shiliao*, vol. 4. Beijing, 1958.

Li Qiusheng. "Shanghai Gudao baoye douzheng shi" (The history of the struggle of Shanghai Solitary Island journalism). *Zhuanji wenxue* 45, no. 2 (Aug. 1984).

Li Shiqi. "Yierba hou zhi Shanghai wujia" (Shanghai's commodity prices after December 8). *Zhongguo jingji* 2, no. 6 (July 1944).

Li Zhongshao. "Yinian lai Gudao juyun de huigu" (A review of the Solitary Island's dramatic movement in the past year). *Xiju yu wenxue* 1, no. 1 (1940).

Lin Wenru. "Liangyue lai Huazhong jingji dashi" (Economic events in Central China in the past two months). *Zhongguo jingji* 1, no. 2 (Jan. 1944).

Lin Zemin. "Ganqing jueding lizhi" (Passion determines reason). *Shanghai zhoubao* 1, no. 10 (Jan. 1940).

Liu Ping. "Mingmo renwu" (Personages in the late Ming era). *Gujin*, no. 6 (Aug. 1942).

Liu Tiesun. "Cong tongji shuji shang guancha Shanghai wujia" (The observation of Shanghai's commodity prices through statistics). *Riyong jingji yuekan* 3, no. 6 (June 1941).

Liu Xiao. "Shanghai dixiadang huifu he chongjian qianhou" (The restoration and reconstruction of the underground party). *Dangshi congkan*, no. 1 (1979).

Liu Xinhuang. *Kangzhan shiqi lunxianqu dixia wenxue* (Underground literature in wartime occupied areas). Taibei, 1985.

————. *Kangzhan shiqi lunxianqu wenxue shi* (A history of the wartime Occupation literature). Taibei, 1980.

Liu Yusheng. "Da Dongya zhanzheng yu Zhongguo wenxue de dongxiang" (The Greater East Asian War and the trend of Chinese literature). *Wenxie* 1, no. 2 (Dec. 1943).

————. "Huaixiang ji" (Nostalgia). *Fengyu tan*, no. 6 (Oct. 1943).

Long Muxun. "Fu Li Jianqing" (A reply to Li Jianqing). *Gujin*, no. 34 (Nov. 1943).

————. "Muxun shengya guo ershi nian" (Over twenty years of a teaching career). *Gujin*, nos. 19–23 (Mar.–May 1943).

————. "You jinian Kongzi dao women heping yundong zhe de zeren"

(From commemorating Confucius to our mission as Peace Movement activists). *Zhongyang daobao* 1, no. 6 (Sept. 1940).

Lou Shiyi et al. "Diwei shiqi Zhou Zuoren sixiang chuangzuo yantaohui ziliao huibian" (Conference on Zhou Zuoren's thought and creation during the Occupation). *Lu Xun yanjiu dongtai*, no. 1 (1987).

Lu Baoqian. "Lun Wang Shaoming zhi panguo shijian" (On Wang Shaoming's treason). In *Kangzhan jianguo shi yantaohui lunwen ji*. Taibei, 1985.

Lu Chuan. "Xiju yinian" (Theater of one year). *Xin Dongfang* 9, no. 1 (Sept. 1943).

Luo Hong. *Gudao shidai* (The age of the Solitary Island). Shanghai, 1947.

Mackerras, Colin. *The Chinese Theatre in Modern Times*. Amherst, Mass., 1975.

Mann, Susan. "Widows in the Kinship, Class and Community Structure of Qing Dynasty China." *Journal of Asian Studies* 46, no. 1 (Feb. 1987).

Mao Dun. "Fenghuo liantian de rizi" (In those wartime days). *Xin wenxue shiliao*, no. 4 (Nov. 1983).

———. "Zhangshang gezi de gangwei" (To stand on each other's station). *Fenghuo*, no. 1 (Aug. 1937).

Mao Xunsheng. "Huazhong jingji bingtai zhi kaocha" (A study of the economic problems of Central China). *Shen bao yuekan* 3, no. 1 (Jan. 1945).

Marsh, Patrick. "The Paris Theatre During the German Occupation." *Rev. d'hist. du theatre* 33, no. 3 (1981).

Marsh, Susan. "Chou Fo-hai: The Making of a Collaborator." In *The Chinese and the Japanese,* ed. Akira Iriye. Princeton, 1980.

Masui Koichi. *Sabakareru O-seiken* (The Wang regime on trial). Tokyo, 1948.

Mather, Richard. "Individualist Expression of the Outsider During the Six Dynasties." In *Individualism and Holism in Confucian and Taoist Values,* ed. Donald Munro. Ann Arbor, Mich., 1985.

Matsuzaki Keiji. *Shanhai jinbun-ki* (Shanghai literature and arts). Tokyo, 1941.

Metzger, Thomas A. *Escape from Predicament: Neo-Confucianism and China's Evolving Political Culture*. New York, 1977.

Min Ren. "Minzhong dongyuan wenti" (The problem of mass mobilization). *Wenhua zhanxian*, no. 4 (Oct. 1, 1937).

Mote, Frederick. "Confucian Eremitism in the Yuan Period." In *Confucianism and Chinese Civilization*, ed. Arthur Wright. Stanford, 1964.

Myrsiades, Linda. "Greek Resistance in World War II." *Drama Review* 2, no. 1 (1977).

Ouyang Hui. "Su yi Qing lihun shimo" (The divorce of the traitor Su Qing). *Duzhe*, no. 2 (Dec. 1945).

Owen, Stephen. *Remembrances: The Experience of the Past in Classical Chinese Literature*. Cambridge, Mass. 1986.

Pal, John. *Shanghai Saga*. London, 1963.

Pan Hannian. "Cong Xinhai yilai de kangri yundong dao jintian de quanmin kangzhan" (Anti-Japanese movements from the 1911 Revolution to the present national Resistance). *Jiuwang ribao*, Oct. 10, 1937.

Pan Ling. *Old Shanghai: Gangster in Paradise*. Hong Kong, 1984.

Pan Yuqie. "Wo yu Gujin" (*Gujin* and I). *Gujin*, no. 19 (Mar. 1945).

Pan Zaixin. "Tantan Shanghai de shimi wenti" (On the problem of rice in Shanghai). *Zhongguo jingji liangyuekan* 1, no. 2 (Sept. 1943).

Paxton, Robert O. *Vichy France: Old Guard and New Order, 1940–44*. New York, 1972.

Pepper, Suzanne. *Civil War in China: The Political Struggle, 1945–1949*. Berkeley, 1978.

Pollard, David. *A Chinese Look at Literature: The Literary Values of Chou Tsojen in Relation to the Tradition*. London, 1973.

———. "Li Chien-wu and Modern Chinese Drama." *Bulletin of the School of Oriental and African Studies* 34, no. 2 (1976).

———, trans. "Springtime" In *Twentieth-Century Chinese Drama: An Anthology*, ed. Edward Gunn. Bloomington, Ind., 1983.

Poster, Mark. *Critical Theory and Poststructuralism: In Search of a Context*. Ithaca, N.Y., 1989.

Powell, John. *My Twenty-five Years in China*. New York, 1942.

Pryce-Jones, David. *Paris in the Third Reich: A History of the German Occupation, 1940–44*. New York, 1981.

Qian Junrui. "Huanxiang gongzuo yundong" (The movement to return to the countryside). *Kangzhan sanrikan*, no. 8 (Sept. 1937).

Qian Juntao. "Liuxia jinian de hengji" (Leaving traces of memory). *Wenyi chunchiu*, no. 5 (Sept. 1945).

Qian Sui. "Chang yu feichang" (Normality and abnormality). *Tiandi*, no. 5 (Feb. 1944).

Ren Yongliang, ed. "Shanghai juyishe yu Ren zhi chu de yanchu" (The Shanghai Dramatic Arts Society and the performance of *Topaze*). *Wenxian* 1 (Oct. 1938).

Ri Koran. *Watakushi no hansei* (The first half of my life). Tokyo, 1987.

Rings, Werner. *Life with the Enemy: Collaboration and Resistance in Hitler's Europe, 1939–1945*. Trans. J. Maxwell Brownjohn. New York, 1982.

Riwei Shanghai shi zhengfu (The Japanese puppet Shanghai Municipal Government). Shanghai, 1986.

Said, Edward. *The World, the Text, and the Critic*. Cambridge, Mass. 1983.

Sartre, Jean-Paul. *Sartre on Theatre*. Trans. Frank Jellinek. New York, 1976.
———. *Literature and Existentialism*. Trans. Bernard Frechtman. Secaucus, N.J., 1980.
Schwarcz, Vera. *The Chinese Enlightenment: Intellectuals and the Legacy of the May Fourth Movement of 1919*. Berkeley, 1986.
Schwartz, Benjamin. *The World of Thought in Ancient China*. Cambridge, Mass. 1985.
Scott, James C. *Domination and the Arts of Resistance: Hidden Transcripts*. New Haven, 1990.
Sergeant, Harriet. *Shanghai: Collision Point of Cultures, 1918–1939*. London, 1991.
Sha Qianli. *Manhua Jiuguohui* (An informal account of the National Salvation Federation). Beijing, 1983.
Shanghai dixiadang zhiyuan Huazhong kangri genjudi (The Shanghai underground party cell's assistance to the base areas of Central China). Shanghai, 1987.
Shanghai Gudao wenxue baokan bianmu (Catalogue of Shanghai Solitary Island literary supplements and journals). Shanghai, 1986.
Shanghai Gudao wenxue huiyilu (Memoirs of Shanghai Solitary Island literature). 2 vols. Beijing, 1984.
Shanghai Gudao wenxue zuopin xuanbian (Selected works of the Shanghai Solitary Island literature). 3 vols. Beijing, 1987.
Shanghai jiefang qianhou wujia ziliao huibian (Collected materials on pre-liberation Shanghai's commodity prices). Shanghai, 1958.
Shanghai Municipal Council Annual Report. Chinese edition. Shanghai, 1937–1941.
Shanghai Municipal Police Files. Microfilm reproduction. Shanghai, 1937–1943.
Shanghai renmin yu Xin sijun (Shanghai people and the New Fourth Army). Shanghai, 1989.
Shanghai shenghuo (Shanghai life). Shanghai, 1937–1941.
Shanhai yoran (A brief guide to Shanghai). Shanghai, 1939.
Shen bao sheping xuan. (Selected *Shen bao* editorials). Shanghai, 1943.
Shen Cheng. "Xin qingshi xia wujia wenti zai tichu" (A new look at the problem of commodity prices under the new circumstances). *Shen bao yuekan* 1, no. 9 (Sept. 1943).
Shen Yifan. "Heping wenyi de jianli yu xinjin zuojia" (The creation of peace literature and new writers). *Zhongyang daobao* 1, no. 30 (Feb. 1940).
Shi Tuo. "Ji yiwei waiyuan neifang de laoyou" (Remembering an old friend who was externally smooth but internally upright). *Xin wenxue shiliao*, no. 2 (May 1987).

————. *Shanghai shouzha* (Shanghai sketches). Shanghai, 1941.

Shi Ying. "Shilun peifu Wu Peifu de xinli" (On the popular admiration for Wu Peifu). *Shanghai zhoubao* 1, no. 7 (Dec. 1939).

Shi Yu. "Lun fangzhi tonghuo pengzhang zhengce" (On policies to prevent inflation). *Zhongguo jingji* 2, no. 10 (Oct. 1944).

Shillony, Ben-Ami. *Politics and Culture in Wartime Japan.* Oxford, 1981.

Shu, Sheng. "Zonglun wenhua ji" (A general discussion of culture). *Gujin,* no. 11 (Nov. 1942).

Shu Yan. *Dong Xiaohuan.* Shanghai, 1947.

————. "Yue Fei de zaoyu" (The vicissitudes of Yue Fei). *Dushu,* no. 1 (Jan. 1980).

Shu Zhao. "Neidi tongxun" (Correspondence from the interior). *Shanghai zhoubao* 1, no. 9 (Mar. 1940).

Si Wei. "Meiyue Huazhong jingji dashi" (Economic events in Central China by months). *Zhongguo jingji* 2, no. 4 (Apr. 1944).

————. "Yinian lai zhi Huazhong jingji" (The economy of Central China over the past year). *Zhongguo jingji* 2, no. 2 (Feb. 1944).

Situ Zhong. *Xue zhai* (Debts of blood). Fuzhou, 1985.

Song Qing. "Zhe yiyue" (This month). *Juchang yanjiu,* no. 10 (Oct. 1939).

Struve, Lynn. "Some Frustrated Scholars of the K'ang-hsi Period." In *From Ming to Ch'ing,* ed. Jonathan Spence and John Wills. New Haven, 1979.

Su Qing. *Tao* (Tide). Shanghai, 1945.

Su Shan. "Huxi duku xunli" (A visit to gambling dens in Huxi). *Huamei zhoubao,* no. 1 (June 1938).

Sugimura Hirozō. *Shina, Shanhai no keizai-teki shosō* (Various dimensions of the economy of China and Shanghai). Tokyo, 1943.

Takahashi Ryozo. "Jianli Zhongguo xin wenhua de jiben wenti" (The basic problem of creating a new Chinese culture). *Wenxie* 2, no. 1 (Jan. 1944).

Takeda Taijun. "Ri Kengo no kigeki ni tsuite: Chugoku no chisei" (On Li Jianwu's comedies: Intellect in Chinese literature). *Chūgoku bungaku geppō,* no. 40 (July 1938).

Tan Zhengbi. "Dao yige wuzhi de linghun" (Mourning an innocent soul). *Zazhi* 11, no. 3 (June 1943).

Tanaka Issei. "The Social and Historical Context of Ming-Ch'ing Local Drama." In *Popular Culture in Late Imperial China,* ed. D. Johnson, A. Nathan, and E. Rawski. Berkeley, 1985.

Tang Na. *Chen Yuanyuan.* Shanghai, 1940.

Tang Shengming. "Wo feng Jiang Jieshi ming cangjia Wang zhengquan de jingguo" (The course of my following Jiang Jieshi's order to join the Wang regime). *Wenshi ziliao,* no. 40 (1980).

Tang Tao [Mo Ran]. "Chenmo pian" (On silence). *Chunqiu* 1, no. 3 (Oct. 1943).

———. *Tang Tao zawen ji* (Selected miscellaneous essays of Tang Tao). Beijing, 1984.

———. "Wo he Xiangxian" (Xiangxian and I). *Xin wenxue shiliao*, no. 1 (Jan. 1985).

Tang Xinyi, ed. *Zhanshi Shanghai jingji* (The economy of wartime Shanghai). Shanghai, 1946.

Tang Zhenchang, ed. *Shanghai shi* (History of Shanghai). Shanghai, 1989.

Tao Jingsun. "Tixie shang xuyao de jichu jianjie" (Guidance requires basic understanding). *Wenyou* 2, no. 21 (Mar. 1944).

Tao Jingsun et al. "Zhongguo wenxue zhi xianzhuang" (The current scene of Chinese literature). *Zazhi* 13, no. 2 (May 1944).

Tao Juyin. *Gudao jianwen* (My experience in the Solitary Island). Shanghai, 1979.

———. *Jizhe shenghuo sanshi nian* (My thirty years as a journalist). Beijing, 1984.

———. *Tianliang qian de Gudao* (The Solitary Island before dawn). Shanghai, 1947.

Tao Kangde. "Dongxin riji" (Journey to the east). *Gujin*, no. 34 (Nov. 1943).

———. "Jiantao ziji" (Self-Examination). *Yuzhou feng*, no. 80 (June 1939).

———. "Lun chuban wenhua de ren yu wu" (On the personnel and materials of publishing culture). *Shen bao yuekan* 1, no. 3 (Mar. 1943).

———. "Xixin riji" (Journey to the west). *Dazhong* 2, no. 2 (Feb. 1944).

Tao Shiping. *Shanghai chunqiu* (A history of Shangahi). Hong Kong, 1968.

Tian Jian. "Wo zuzhou" (I swear). *Fenghuo*, no. 3 (Sept. 1937).

Tu Guangqi. "Gudao shiqi de huaju jie" (The theatrical circle during the Solitary Island period). *Da cheng*, no. 6 (May 1974).

Van Slyke, Lyman. *Enemies and Friends: The United Front in Chinese Communist History*. Stanford, 1967.

Wakeman, Frederic, Jr. "Stoics, Romantics, and Martyrs in Seventeenth-Century China." *Journal of Asian Studies* 18, no. 4 (Aug. 1984).

———. *The Great Enterprise: The Manchu Reconstruction of Imperial Order in Seventeenth-Century China*. 2 vols. Berkeley, 1985.

Walzer, Michael. *Just and Unjust Wars: A Moral Argument with Historical Illustrations*. New York, 1977.

Wan Ren. "Sinian lai Shanghai shimin shenghuo" (Shanghai people's life in the past four years). *Shanghai zhoubao* 4, no. 9 (Aug. 1941).

Wang Jingwei hanjian zhengquan de xingwang (The rise and fall of the traitorous Wang regime). Shanghai, 1987.

Wang Jun. "Yinian lai Shanghai jutan de bianqian he yanchu" (The performance and development of Shanghai theater in the past year). *Taipingyang zhoubao* (Dec. 1942).

Wang, Ke-wen. "Collaborators and Capitalists: The Politics of Economic Control in Wartime Shanghai." Unpublished paper.

Wang Manyun. *Wangwei tegong neimu* (The inside story of the Wang regime's secret service). Henan, 1986.

Wang Tongzhao. "Chongdong yu zhending" (Impulse and calmness). *Fenghuo*, no. 2 (Aug. 1937).

———. *Fanci* (Superfluous words). Shanghai, 1939.

———. "Huiyi Beijing xuesheng wusi aiguo yundong" (A memoir of the May Fourth student patriotic movement). In *Wusi yundong huiyilu*, vol. 2. Beijing, 1979.

———. *Ouyou sanji* (Random notes from the European trip). Shanghai, 1947.

———. "Mianzun xiansheng guhou zhuiyi" (Remembering Mianzun after his death). *Wenhui bao*, July 5, 1946.

———. *Qu lai jin* (Past, future, and present). Shanghai, 1940.

———. *Wang Tongzhao duanpian xiaoshuo ji* (Selected short stories of Wang Tongzhao). Shanghai, 1940.

———. *Wang Tongzhao shixuan* (Selected poetry of Wang Tongzhao). Beijing, 1958.

———. *Wang Tongzhao wenji* (Collected works of Wang Tongzhao). 6 vols. Shandong, 1981.

———. "Ye shenchen" (Deep night). *Fenghuo*, no. 1 (Aug. 1937).

———. "Yi Jinsiniang qiao" (Remembering Lady Golden-Threads Bridge). *Fenghuo*, no. 11 (Nov. 1937).

Wang Weiguo, and Qi Zhong. "Ta zai jiaohong yu julang jian: Li Jianwu de xiju shengya" (Between the burning sun and the rolling tide: The dramatic career of Li Jianwu). In *Zhongguo huaju yishujia zhuan*, vol. 3. Beijing, 1988.

Wang Yaoshan. "Guanyu dixiadang chongjian de jingguo" (Concerning the reconstruction of the underground party). *Dangshi ziliao congkan*, no. 1 (Nov. 1979).

Wang Yun. "Liangnian lai de guolei wenhua jie" (Chinese cultural circles in the past two years). *Shidai wenxuan*, no. 8/9 (Nov. 1939).

Watson, Burton, trans. *Chuang Tzu: Basic Writings.* New York, 1964.

Wei Yan. "Zhounian de hua" (On the anniversary). *Gujin*, no. 19 (Mar. 1943).

Wei Zheng. "Daode yu kangzhan" (The War of Resistance and ethics). *Yuzhou feng*, no. 82 (July 1939).

Wen Shaohua. *Wang Jingwei zhuan* (Biography of Wang Jingwei). Jilin, 1988.

Wen Zaidao [Jin Xingyao]. *Fengtu xiaoji* (Sketches of local customs). Shanghai, 1944.

———. "Jiegu lunjin" (Talking about the present by alluding to the past). *Gujin*, no. 19 (Mar. 1943).

———. "Puyuan yaji ji" (An elegant gathering at the Puyuan). *Gujin*, no. 25 (June 1943).

———. "Saochu yimin qi" (To eliminate the spirit of reclusiveness). In *Hengmei ji*, ed. Kong Lingjing. Shanghai, 1939.

———. "Shihuang" (Collecting scraps for living). *Tiandi*, no. 17 (Feb. 1945).

———. "Wei-Jin renwu ji" (Personages of the Wei and Jin dynasties). *Gujin*, no. 39 (Jan. 1944).

———. "Zhiren lunshi" (Knowledge of people and evaluation of time). *Fengyu tan* 1, no. 1 (Apr. 1943).

Wen Zaidao et al., eds. *Biangu ji* (War drums). Shanghai, 1938.

Wilkinson, James. *The Intellectual Resistance in Europe*. Cambridge, Mass. 1981.

Wo yu Kaiming (The Enlightenment Bookstore and I). Shanghai, 1985.

Wright, Gordon. *The Ordeal of Total War, 1939–1945*. New York, 1968.

Wu Kaixian. "Kangzhan shiqi de Du Yuesheng" (Du Yuesheng during the War of Resistance). *Da cheng*, no. 167 (Oct. 1973).

Wu Lanxi. "Wangwei zhengfu mori ji" (The Last Days of the Traitorous Wang Regime). N.p., n.d. Mimeo.

Wu Shaoshu. "Ji Shanghai tongyi weiyuanhui" (Remembering the United Shanghai Committee). *Wenshi ziliao xuanji*, vol. 9.

Wylie, Raymond. *The Emergence of Maoism: Mao Tse-tung, Ch'en Po-ta, and the Search for Chinese Theory, 1935–1945*. Stanford, 1980.

"Xia Mianzun yangmao hun changhe shi" (Poetry in celebration of Xia Mianzun's fortieth wedding anniversary). *Wanxiang* 3, no. 3 (Sept. 1943).

Xia Yan. *Choucheng* (City of distress). Shanghai, 1940.

———. "Ji Jiuwang ribao" (My memory of *Jiuwang ribao*). *Xinnwen yanjiu*, vol. 3 (May 1980).

Xu Banmei. *Huaju chuangshi qi huiyilu* (A memoir of the pioneering period of modern drama). Beijing, 1957.

Xu Chiheng. "Wenhui bao chuangkan chuqi shiliao" (Historical materials of the founding period of the *Wenhui bao*). *Xinwen yanjiu ziliao* 3 (Nov. 1981).

Xu Guangping. *Zaonan qianhou* (Before and after the calamity). Shanghai, 1950.

Xu Guangsheng. "Jutan wanglai" (Communications between dramatic companies). *Wanxiang* 4, no. 5 (Nov. 1944).

Xu Kailei. "Huainian Wang Tongzhao tongzhi" (Remembering Comrade Wang Tongzhao). *Renwu*, no. 3 (May 1981).

———. "*Shiji feng* fukan huiyilu" (A memoir of the supplement of *Shiji feng*). *Shanghai Gudao shiqi wenxue shiliao* (mimeographed newsletter issued by Shanghai shehui kexueyuan wenxue yanjiusuo), no. 12 (Dec. 1986).

Xu Shihu. "Li Jianwu de yisheng" (The life of Li Jianwu). *Xin wenxue shiliao*, no. 3 (Aug. 1983).

Xu Yishi. "Lingbu zhuyi" (No-ism). *Shidai wenxuan*, no. 3/4 (June 1939).

Xu Zhucheng. *Baohai jiuwen* (Old news from the sea of journalism). Shanghai, 1981.

Xu Zhuyuan. "Heping wenyi jianshe lun" (On the creation of peace literature). *Zhongyang daobao* 1, no. 17 (Nov. 1940).

Yang Dongchun. "Jinian Xinhai geming yu dangqian de kangzhan" (Commemoration of the 1911 Revolution and the present War of Resistance). *Wenhua zhanxian*, no. 5 (Oct. 1937).

Yang Jiang. *Xiju erzhong* (Two comedies). Fuzhou, 1982.

Yang Xiuqing. "Liangnian lai de chuban jie" (The publishing world in the past two years). *Wenyi chunqiu*, no. 1 (Oct. 1944).

Yang Yiming, ed. *Wentan shiliao* (Historical materials of the literary scene). Danian, 1944.

Yang Yinsheng. *Wen Tianxiang*. Shanghai, 1940.

Yang Yousheng. "Huiyi Ke Ling tongzhi bian Wanxiang" (Remembering Comrade Ke Ling editing *Wanxiang*). *Shanghai Shifan xueyuan xuebao*, no. 1 (Jan. 1981).

Yao Gong. "Furen qichu yu zaijia" (Women's divorce and remarriages). *Gujin*, no. 40 (Feb. 1944).

———. "Tan Mingmo shanren" (On Late Ming mountain recluses). *Gujin*, no. 15 (Jan. 1943).

Yao Sufeng et al. "Zuojia li Hu suoji" (Brief accounts of writers fleeing Shanghai). *Da feng* 1, no. 3 (Mar. 1938).

Yeh, Wen-hsin. "Dai Li and the Liu Geqing Affair: Heroism in the Chinese Secret Service During the War of Resistance). *Journal of Asian Studies* 48, no. 3 (Aug. 1989).

Yi Guan. "Babai zhuangshi kangzhan xin" (The resistance spirit of the eight hundred warriors). *Jiuwang ribao*, Oct. 31, 1937.

Yi Li. "Lu Wenlung." *Juchang yishu*, no. 4/5 (Mar. 1939).

Yi Ren. "Bayisan yilai Shanghai baojie de dongtai" (The press in Shanghai since August 13). *Shanghai zhoubao* 1, no. 5 (June 1940).

Yierjiu yihou Shanghai jiuguo hui shiliao xuanji (Selected historical materials on the Shanghai National Salvation associations after December 9). Shanghai, 1987.

Yoshida Tosuke. "Riben dui Hua zhengce yu Zhongguo zhishi jie" (Japan's China policy and Chinese intellectuals). *Shen bao yuekan* 1, no. 3 (Mar. 1943).

——. *Nikka mondai no zenmen-teki kaiketsu no tame ni* (For a total solution of the Sino-Japanese problem). Tokyo, 1944.

Yu Ling. "Modui yipian diao A Ying" (Condoling A Ying while reading his late works). In *A Ying wenji*, vol. 1. Hong Kong, 1979.

——. "Yinian du ju ji" (A year of reading plays). *Xiju yu wenxue* 1, no. 1 (1940).

Yu Wensheng. "Wei Gujun songliang" (Transporting foodstuffs for the Lone Battalion). In *Shanghai yiri*. Shanghai, 1939.

Yu Zidao, et al., eds. *Wang Jingwei guomin zhengfu "qingxiang yundong"* (The Wang Jingwei National government's "Cleansing of Villages Movement"). Shanghai, 1985.

Yuan Yuquan. "Rikou jiaqiang lüeduo Huazhong zhanlue wuzhi paozhi 'shangtong hui'" (The Japanese enemy's increased plundering of Shanghai's strategic materials and concoction of the National Commerce Control Commission). *Dangan yu lishi*, nos. 1–2 (Mar.–June 1987).

Yue Xiuliang. "Women xuyao youxue yourou de wenyi" (We need literature of flesh and blood). *Shen bao yuekan* 1, no. 8 (Aug. 1943).

Zbikowski, Tadeusz. *Early Nan-hsi Plays of the Southern Sung Period*. Warsaw, 1974.

Zhang Jiying. "Ji wenjian: Tao Kangde" (Tao Kangde: A cultural traitor). *Duzhe*, no. 2 (Dec. 1945).

Zhang Jinglu. *Zai chuban jie ershi nian* (My twenty years in the publishing world). 1940. Reprint. Shanghai, 1984.

——, ed. *Zhongguo chuban shiliao* (Historical materials on Chinese publishing). 6 vols. Shanghai, 1953–59.

Zhang Runsan. "Nanjing Wangwei ji ge zuzhi jiqi paixi huodong" (Some organizations of the Wang regime and their cliquish activities). *Wenshi ziliao xuanji*, vol. 40 (1981).

Zhang Wozhou. *Zhanshi de wenhua gongzuo* (Cultural work during the war). Shanghai, 1937.

Zhang Yiwang. *Lunxian qianhou de Shanghai* (Shanghai before and after the Occupation). Hankou, 1938.

Zhang Zhihan. "Zhuiyi kangri zhanzheng zhong Shanghai xinwen yimu douzheng shi" (Remembering an act of the history of the struggle of Shanghai journalism during the War of Resistance). *Da ren*, no. 31 (Nov. 1972).

Zhang Zhijian. "Kangzhan zhong de wenhua jie" (The cultural circle during the War of Resistance). *Shidai wenxuan*, no. 3/4 (June 1939).

Zhao Jingshen. "Yi Shanghai wenxie chengli dahui" (Remembering the inaugural meeting of the Shanghai Literary Federation). *Wenyi fuxing* 1, no. 1 (Jan. 1946).

———. *Wentan yijiu* (A recollection of the literary scene). Shanghai, 1948.

Zhao Junhao. *Shanghai baoren de douzheng* (The struggle of Shanghai journalists). Shanghai, 1945.

Zheng Dingwen. *Dajie* (Elder sister). Fujian, 1983.

Zheng Zhenduo. "Dashidai wenyi congshu xu" (Preface to the *Dashidai wenyi congshu*). In *Hengmei ji*. Shanghai, 1939.

———. *Jiezhong de shu ji* (The acquisition of books during the calamity). Shanghai, 1956.

———. *Zheju sanji* (Random notes from hibernation). Shanghai, 1946.

Zheng Zhenduo, Wang Tongzhao, and Geng Jizhi. *Yunhua ji* (Essence). Fujian, 1985.

Zhongguo huaju yishujia zhuan (Biographies of Chinese dramatists). 4 vols. Beijing, 1988.

Zhongguo huaju yundong wushi nian shiliao ji (Collected historical materials on the fifty years of the modern dramatic movement). 2 vols. Beijing, 1958.

Zhou Fohai. "Liangyao zhongyan" (Bitter medicine and sincere advice). *Shidai wenxuan* 2, no. 1 (Feb. 1940).

———. "Shengshuai yuejin hua cangsang" (Commenting on human vicissitudes after witnessing all the ups and downs). *Gujin*, no. 3 (May 1943).

Zhou Huaren. *Shanghai de gaizao* (The transformation of Shanghai). Shanghai, 1943.

———. "Dongya wenyi fuxing yundong" (The Greater East Asian Literary Renaissance Movement). *Wenxie* 2, no. 2 (Mar. 1944).

Zhou Lengjia. "Tan shanju" (On living in mountains). *Tiandi*, no. 5 (Feb. 1944).

———. "Qinggao buyi" (It is not easy to be aloof from material concerns). *Wenyou* 4, no. 1 (Nov. 1944).

Zhou Lian. *Huafa ji* (Gray hair). Shanghai, 1940.

———. "Mingxin de jinian" (A deeply engraved memory). *Fengyu tan* 1, no. 1 (Apr. 1943).

———. "*Niehai hua* renwu ji" (On a genealogy of personages in *Niehai hua*). *Gujin*, no. 37 (Dec. 1943).

———. "Qingming ji tiji" (Preface to *Qingming*). *Renshi jian* 1, no. 2 (Aug. 1939).

———. "Yinian lai de bianji zaji" (Random notes about my editorial life in the last year). *Gujin*, no. 19 (Mar. 1943).

———. "Yuzhou feng yu wo" (*Yuzhou feng* and I). *Yuzhou feng*, no. 100 (June 1940).

Zhou Yuren. "Zai Riben suojian" (My experience in Japan). *Dazhong* 1, no. 11 (Nov. 1943).

———. "Zhongguo juyun jinkuang" (Recent development of the Chinese dramatic movement). *Shen bao yuekan* 4, no. 4 (Apr. 1945).

Zhou Zhen. "Zenyang jiejue Shanghai de minshi wenti" (How to solve the food problem in Shanghai). *Shen bao yuekan* 1, no. 9 (Sept. 1943).

Zhou Zuoren. *Kukou gankou* (Bitterness and sweetness). Shanghai, 1944.

———. "*Wenchao* xu" (Preface to *Wenchao*). *Gujin*, no. 12 (Sept. 1944).

———. *Zhitang huixianglu* (Autobiography), Hong Kong, 1970.

Zhu Jinyuan, and Chen Zuen, eds. *Wangwei shoushen jishi* (A true record of the trial of Wang regime traitors). Hangzhou, 1988.

Zhu Menghua. "Riben junguo zhuyi zhe zai Shanghai de baoxing" (The brutality of Japanese militarists in Shanghai). *Shanghai difang shi ziliao*, no. 1 (Dec. 1982).

Zhu Pu. "*Gujin* liangnian" (Two years of *Gujin*). *Gujin*, no. 43/44 (Apr. 1944).

———. "*Gujin* yinian" (One year of *Gujin*). *Gujin*, no. 19 (Mar. 1943).

———. "Mancheng fengyu hua gujin" (Remembrance in the midst of prevailing turmoil). *Gujin*, no. 9 (Oct. 1942).

———. "Mantan *Gujin*" (Random notes about *Gujin*). *Gujin*, no. 2 (Apr. 1942).

———. "Puyuan suitan" (Random talks from Puyuan). *Gujin*, no. 29 (May 1943).

———. "Sishi zishu" (Autobiography at forty). *Gujin*, no. 1 (Mar. 1942).

———. "Wangyi ji xu" (Preface to *Wangyi ji*). *Gujin*, no. 15 (Jan. 1943).

———. "Xiaoxiu ci" (Farewell). *Gujin*, no. 57 (Oct. 1944).

Zhu Wen. *Fenggu ji* (War drums). Fuzhou, 1984.

Zhu Xi. *Reflections of Things at Hand.* Trans. Wing-tsit Chan. New York, 1967.

Zhu Yanling. "Jinri zhi minsheng wenti" (People's livelihoods today). *Shen bao yuekan* 2, no. 1 (Jan. 1944).

Zhu Zhujun. "Heping yundong yu xinli gaizao" (The peace movement and change of psychology). *Zhongyang daobao* 1, no. 23 (Jan. 1941).

Zou Taofen. "Yilianchuan de wenti" (A long series of problems). *Kangzhan sanrikan*, Aug. 26, 1937.

———. "Duanjian" (Short reply). *Kangzhan sanrikan*, Aug. 29, 1937.

Zuo Bi. "Ji Zhou Fohai xiansheng" (An interview with Mr. Zhou Fohai). *Gujin*, no. 1 (Mar. 1942).

Glossary

A Ying　阿英

airen (love of one's fellow men)　爱人

Ba Jin　巴金

Ba Ren　巴人

Bao Tianxiao　包天笑

Baoshan　宝山

Baowei da Shanghai yundong xuanchuan dagang (Outline of Propaganda
　for the Defense of Greater Shanghai)　保卫大上海运动宣传大纲

baoxiao wenxue (government-subsidized literature)　报销文学

bu tuoxie jingshen (uncompromising spirit; tenacious defiance)　不妥协精神

Cai Diaotu　蔡钓徒

Cao Yu　曹禺

Cao Zhi　曹植

ceyin zhi xin (natural sympathy)　恻隐之心

chaoyin (hermit at court)　朝隐

Chen Bijun　陈碧君

Chen Gongbo　陈公博

Chen Gongshu　陈恭澍

Chen Linrui　陈麟瑞

Chen Xihe　陈西禾

Chen Xulun　陈旭轮

chengren (self-sacrifice for the sake of benevolence)　成仁

chongdan yongrong (blandness and refined taste)　冲淡雍容

chujian (eliminating traitors)　除奸

Da dongya wenyi fuxing (Great East Asian Renaissance)　大东亚文艺复兴

Da Yazhou zhuyi (Greater Asianism)　大亚洲主义

Dachang　大场

Daitu (Badlands)　歹土

Damei wanbao (Great American Evening News)　大美晚报

daode de zilüxing (moral self-discipline)　道德的自律性

Daying yebao (Great Britain Evening News)　大英夜报

Ding Mocun　丁默邨

ersi shixiao shijie shida (to starve to death is a very small matter; to lose one's integrity is a grave matter)　饿死事小; 失节事大

Fan Quan　范泉

Fan Zhongyun　樊仲云

fei zhan (pacifism)　非战

Feng Youzhen　冯有真

Fenghuo (Beacon)　烽火

fengtu renqing (local customs and ancedotes)　风土人情

Fengyu tan (Talks amid Hardship)　风雨谈

Fu she (Restoration Society)　复社

funi wenren (traitorous men of letters)　附逆文人

Geng Jizhi　耿济之

gengxin de minyue (renewed social contract)　更新的民约

gouhuo (live in shame)　苟活

Gu Zhongyi　顾仲彝

guchen niezi (lone official and illegitimate son)　孤臣孽子

Gudao bu gu (Solitary Island was not solitary)　孤岛不孤

Gujin (Reminiscences)　古今

Gujun (Lone Battalion)　孤军

gumao (simplicity)　古茂

Guo Moruo　郭沫若

Guo Xiufeng　郭秀峰

guofang ju (theatre of national defense)　国防剧

guonan (national calamity)　国难

Hagiwara Daikyoku　萩原大尉

hanjian (traitor, collaborator)　汉奸

hangou tucun (seeking to survive despite contempt)　含垢图存

haoran zhengqi (natural spiritual elan)　浩然正气

heian shijie (dark world)　黑暗世界

heping bagu (hackneyed peace pieces)　和平八股

heping fangong jianguo (peace, anticommunism, and national construction)　和平反共建国

heping wenxue (Peace literature)　和平文学

heyu zhengyi zhi heping (a just peace)　合于正义之和平

Hong Mo 洪谟

Hong Shen 洪深

Hongkou 虹口

hongyi (inner strength) 弘毅

hou zhi shi jin ju jin zhi shi xi shishi cangsang (if in time future we see time
  present, it is like our seeing time past in time present; human life is but
  a vicissitude of ups and downs) 后之视今如今之视昔世事沧桑

huaju (spoken drama) 话剧

Huang Zongxi 黄宗羲

Huang Zuolin 黄佐临

Huangdao hui (Yellow Way Association) 黄道会

huanxiang (return to the countryside) 还乡

huoming (individual survival) 活命

hutu (play the fool) 糊涂

Huxi 沪西

Ji Guoan 纪果庵

ji shang shizhe xing zinian ye (Our memories of the dead/ are but our
  thought of ourselves) 既伤逝者行自念耶

jianai (universal love) 兼爱

Jiang Chunfang 蒋椿芳

jianggong shuzui (expiate the crime by good deeds) 将功赎罪

Jiangwan 江湾

jietou ju (street drama) 街头剧

Jin Huating 金华亭

Jin Xiongbai 金雄白

Jinan 暨南

Jinshanwei 金山卫

Jinsiniang qiao 金丝娘桥

Jiu zhai (Studio of Remorse) 疚斋

jiuguo wumen qiusheng wulu (no gate to save the nation, no path to survival)
  救国无门，求生无路

jiuwang gongzuo (national salvation work) 救亡工作

Jiuwang ribao (National Salvation Daily) 救亡日报

jiuwang yundong (national salvation movement) 救亡运动

junzi guqiong (gentleman being steadfast in hardship) 君子固穷

jushi (lay monk) 居士

Kaiming shudian (Enlightenment Bookstore) 开明书店

kangzhan ju (resistance plays) 抗战剧

kangzhan jianguo (Resistance and National Construction)　抗战建国

Kangzhan sanrikan (Resistance Triweekly)　抗战三日刊

Ke Ling　柯灵

kong hanjian bing (traitor paranoia)　恐汉奸病

Kong Lingjing　孔另境

Konoe Fumimaro　近衛文麿

Kugan jutuan (Struggle Company)　苦干剧团

laocheng (prison city)　牢城

Li Bolong　李伯龙

Li Dazhao　李大钊

Li Guinian　李龟年

Li Qishan　李岐山

Li Shiqun　李士群

lianchi (sense of shame)　廉耻

Liang Hongzhi　梁鸿志

lienü bu erfu zhongchen bu erzhu (faithful woman marries only one husband; loyal official serves only one master)　烈女不二夫 忠臣不二主

lifa (official orthodoxy)　礼法

Lin Bosheng　林柏生

Liu Naou　刘呐鸥

Liu Shaowen　刘少文

Liu Yusheng　柳雨生

Liuhe　浏河

Lu Yi　陆蠡

luanchen zeizi (traitorous ministers and unfilial sons)　乱臣贼子

Lunyu (pai) (Analects group)　论语（派）

Luodian　罗店

Mao Dun　茅盾

Mao (Shu Yan)　冒舒湮

mei (sycophant)　媚

mingshi (unconventional scholars)　名士

moshou (evil hand)　魔手

Mu Shiying　穆时英

Nanshi　南市

Ouyang Yuqian　欧阳予倩

Pan Gongzhan　潘公展

Pan Yuqie　潘予且

Paotaiwan　炮台湾

Ping bao (Peace News) 平报

Ping Jinya 平襟亚

Pudong 浦东

Puyuan (Garden of Simplicity) 朴园

Qi Kang 嵇康

Qian Junrui 钱俊瑞

Qian Zhongshu 钱钟书

qiao biangu (beating war drums on the sidelines) 敲边鼓

qijie (moral integrity) 气节

qimeng (enlightenment) 启蒙

Qin Shouou 秦瘦鸥

qingbai (morally pure) 清白

qingcao (sentiment) 情操

Qingniao jushe (Blue Bird Dramatic Society) 青鸟剧社

qingtan (Pure conversation) 清谈

Qingxiang yundong (Cleansing of Villages Movement) 清乡运动

Qiyue (July) 七月

Quangongting 全公亭

Quanguo gejie jiuguo hui xiehui (All-China Federation of National Salvation Unions) 全国各界救国会协会

renge (human dignity) 人格

renqing wuli (human feelings and the natural order of things) 人情物理

renru tousheng (dragging out an ignoble existence by bearing humiliations) 忍辱偷生

Ru zhai (Studio of Shame) 辱斋

satuo (free spirit) 洒脱

Sha Wenhan 沙文汉

Shanghai juyishe (Shanghai Dramatic Arts Society) 上海剧艺社

Shanghai shi gejie kangdi houyuan hui (SGJ) (All-Shanghai Federation for the Support of Armed Resistance) 上海市各界抗敌后援会

Shanghai shi wenhua jie jiuwang xiehui (SWH) (Shanghai Cultural Circles National Salvation Federation) 上海市文化界救亡协会

Shanghai xiju jiaoyishe (Shanghai Theatre Friendship Club) 上海戏剧交谊社

Shanghai xiju jie jiuwang xiehui (Shanghai Dramatic Circles National Salvation Association) 上海戏剧戏剧界救亡协会

Shanghai yishu juyuan (Shanghai Arts Theatre) 上海艺术剧院

Shen bao (Shanghai News) 申报

shensi guantou (juncture of life and death) 生死关头

shensi cunwang de zuihou guantou (critical juncture of life and death) 生死存亡的最后关头

Shi Hui 石挥

Shi Tuo 师陀

shi zhi qi bu kewei erwei zheye; shi buzhi qi kewei erwei zheye ([He is] one who knows what is possible and yet attempts it; who does not know what is possible and yet attempts it) 是知其不可为而为者耶; 是不知其可为而为者耶

shi zhi wei zhuang/shi chu wuming jun wu douzhi (An army with a just cause enjoys high morale/an army without one is devoid of fighting will) 师直为壮/师出无名军无斗志

Shiji feng (Century Wind) 世纪风

shijie shixiao shiye shida (loss of integrity is a small matter; loosing a job is exceedingly serious) 失节事小, 失业事大

Shitao 石涛

sicheng (city of death) 死城

Song Xilian 宋希濂

Su Qing 苏青

suisheng fuhe (echo what others say) 随声附和

Sun Ruihuang 孙瑞璜

Sun Yefang 孙冶方

Tan Zhengbi 谭正璧

Tang Tao 唐弢

Tao Jingsun 陶晶孙

Tao Kangde 陶亢德

Tegong zongbu (Secret Service Headquarters) 特工总部

tekisei bunka 敵性文化

Tiandi (Universe) 天地

tiao huokeng (jumping into the living hell) 跳火坑

Tōa shin'chitsujo (New Order in East Asia) 東亞新秩序

Tu Guangqi 屠光启

tuoni daishui (in a mess) 拖泥带水

Wang Jingwei 汪精卫

Wang Tongzhao 王统照

Wang Wenxian 王文显

Wang Xizhi 王羲之

wangguo nu (conquered people) 亡国奴

Wanxiang (Phenomena) 万象

wanzhi meihua bing (Twisted-branch Plum Syndrome) 弯枝梅花病

Wen Zaidao (Jin Xingyao) 文载道(金性尧)

Wenhui bao (The Standard) 文汇报

Wenxue (Literature) 文学

Wu Guifang 武桂芳

Wu Kaixian 吴开先

Wu Renzhi 吴仞之

Wu Yonggang 吴永刚

wuke neihe (seeing no way out) 无可奈何

Wusong 吴淞

Xia Mianzun 夏丏尊

Xia Yan 夏衍

xiangyun (hypocrites) 乡愿

xiao quwei (little amusements) 小趣味

xiaopin wen (lyrical essays) 小品文

xialiu (obscenity) 下流

xiashui (drowning) 下水

Xie Jinyuan 谢晋元

Xin guomin yundong (New Citizens' Movement) 新国民运动

Xin shen bao (New Shanghai News) 新申报

xingji you chi (self-consciousness of shame) 行己有耻

xinli gaizao (a revolution of national consciousness) 心理改造

Xu Diaofu 徐调孚

Xu Guangping 许广平

Xu Xingzhi 许幸之

yaji (elegant gathering) 雅集

Yandian (Twenty-ninth telegram) 艳电

Yang Dongchun 杨东纯

Yang Jiang 杨绛

Yang Shuhui 杨淑慧

yangshang bao (foreign-published newspapers) 洋商报

Yangshupu 杨树浦

Ye Shengtao 叶圣陶

yi (virtuous) 义

Yi bao (Translation News) 译报

yi gu yu jin (using the past as a metaphor for the present) 以古喻今

Yi she/dui (Ant Society/Troupe) 蚁社/队

yimin (anachronism) 遗民

yincha yangcuo (started as a mistake) 阴差阳错

yinjian (licentiousness)   淫贱

yinyi (eremitism)   隐逸

yi zhan (just war)   义战

Yoshida Tosuke   吉田東祐

You Shufen   尤淑芬

yu jiaoyu yu yule (placing pedagogy within entertainment)   寓教育于娱乐

Yu Ling   于伶

Yuan Hongdao   袁宏道

Yuan Yuquan   袁愈佺

Yue Xiuliang   乐秀良

Yuzhou feng (pai) (Cosmic Wind group)   宇宙风（派）

Zazhi (Miscellany)   杂志

Zhabei   闸北

Zhang Dai   张岱

Zhang Han   张翰

Zhang Ziping   张资平

Zhao Jiabi   赵家壁

Zhao Shuyong   赵叔雍

Zhao Zhiyou   赵志游

zheju (hibernation)   蛰居

zhen (genuine feeling)   真

zhenjie (chastity, fidelity)   贞洁

Zheng Zhenduo   郑振铎

zhicai (punish)   制裁

zhongchen lieshi (loyal ministers and martyrs)   忠臣烈士

Zhongfa lianyihui (Sino-French Friendship Club)   中法联谊会

Zhonghua quanguo wenyi jie kangdi xiehui (All-China Association of Literary Resistance)   中华全国民艺界抗敌协会

Zhonghua ribao/zhoubao (China Daily/Weekly)   中华日报（周报）

zhongxin (loyalty and sincerity)   忠信

zhongyi (loyalty)   忠义

Zhou Fohai   周佛海

Zhou Lian   周黎庵

Zhou Liangjia   周楞伽

Zhou Zuoren   周作人

Zhu Duanjun   朱端钧

Zhu Pu   朱朴

Zhu Xinggong   朱惺公

Zou Taofen   邹韬奋

Index

In this index an "f" after a number indicates a separate reference on the next page, and an "ff" indicates separate references on the next two pages. A continuous discussion over two or more pages is indicated by a span of page numbers, e.g., "57–59." *Passim* is used for a cluster of references in close but not consecutive sequence.

Ai yu si de bodou (Li Jianwu), 85–86
All-China Association of Literary Resistance (Zhonghua quanguo wenyi jie kangdi xiehui), 153
All-China Federation of National Salvation Unions (Quanguo gejie jiuguo hui xiehui), 2
All-Shanghai Federation for the Support of Armed Resistance, *see* Shanghai shi gejie kangdi houyuan hui
Anachronisms, *see* Yimin
Analects group, *see* Lunyu pai
Anhui, 96
Ant Society, *see* Yi she
Ant Troupe, *see* Yi dui
Arrests, 56, 63, 76, 96, 105–6, 137, 182n131, 184n151, 218n159
Ashina (Li Jianwu), 106
Asia for the Asiatics, 120
Assassinations, 30, 36, 48f, 79, 115, 133
Autonomy, 24, 45, 93–94, 163; individual, 21–23, 158
A Ying, 7, 37, 56, 77, 84, 137, 194–95nn82–83; and Shanghai juyishe, 78, 193n77; *Bixue hua*, 90–91

"Babai chuangshi kangzhan xin," 18
Badlands, 48

Ba Jin, 5, 12, 27, 39, 42, 63, 72, 164, 193n71; and Resistance theater, 89, 195n84
Banking and Finance Employees' Club, 74
Banks, 125
Baojia, 121–22
Bao Mingshu, 49
Bao Tianxiao, 138, 212–13n99
"Baowei da Shanghai yundong xuanchuan dagang," 17
Ba Ren, 7, 34, 37, 50, 56, 61, 82f, 93, 96, 189n39
Battle of Shanghai, xvi, 4, 28–29, 74; in foreign areas, 2–4, 171–72nn9–10
Beacon, *see* Fenghuo
Beaumarchais, Pierre-Agustin, 101
Begonia (*Qiuhaitang*), 98
Benighted Shanghai (*Ye Shanghai*), 90
Bian Zhilin, 74
Bitter Wind (*Hanfeng ji*), 148
Bixue hua (A Ying), 90–91
Black market, 123–24
Blockades, 46, 121–22
"Bloody Saturday," 4
Blue Bird Dramatic Society (Qingniao jushe), 77
Bo Li, 85
Bo Yi, 156

Bombings, 3–4, 49, 115, 121, 171n9
Books, 56, 61
Bruce, George, 17
Buddhism, 60, 184n151

Cai Diaotu, 36
Cai Ruheng, 91
Cai Shuhou, 78
Cai Yuanpei, 7
Call to Arms (*Nahan*), 27
Cao Yu, 84; *Thunderstorm*, 77; *Tubian*, 83, 96
Cao Zhi, 143
Carlton Theater, 95, 102
CC Clique, 49
CCP, *see* Chinese Communist Party
Censorship, 35, 63; GMD, 26, 164; Japanese, 32, 34, 56, 85, 121
Central News Agency (GMD), 7, 35
Central Propaganda Department (GMD), 34–35, 148, 149–50
Central Reserve Bank, 128, 134
Century Wind, *see Shiji feng*
Chang Yuqing, 35
Chastity, 145
Chen Bijun, 125, 218–19n159
Chen Dabei, 71
Chen Duxiu, 139
Cheng Fangwu, 148
Cheng Kuanzheng, 115f
Chen Gongbo, 119, 126, 131, 147f, 152f, 211n84, 212–13nn98–99, 214n113, 218–19n159
Chen Gongshu, 48
Chen Linrui, 94, 100, 201n143
Chen Liting, 8
Chen Wandao, 37
Chen Xihe, 78, 84f, 94, 100, 201n143
Chen Xulun, 143
Chiang Kaishek, xi, 2, 4, 12, 18, 25, 83, 119, 171, 218–19n159
China Bank, 128
China Daily, *see Zhonghua ribao*
China News (*Zhong bao*), 116
"China Problem," 111
China's Red Army Marches (Smedley), 38

China Weekly, *see Zhonghua zhoubao*
Chinese-American Evening News, *see Huamei wanbao*
Chinese Art Company (Huayi jutuan), 99
Chinese Communist Party (CCP), 1f, 7, 83, 96, 117, 164f, 190–91n57; propaganda of, 34, 50; activism of, 84f; committees in, 95, 188n26; guerrillas in, 111, 190n49
Chongqing, 19, 34, 58, 96, 104, 112
Chu Minyi, 78, 188n33, 212n98, 218–19n159
Civil war, 1, 67, 154, 164
"Cleansing of Villages Movement," 150
Collaboration, xivf, 32, 57, 110–11, 160–61, 218n158; terrorism and, 48–49; literary, 114–15, 126–27; symbolism of, 117–18
Collaborators, 82, 98–99, 125, 153–61 *passim*, 193n74, 201n143, 212n94, 212–13n99, 216n135, 218–19n159; support for, 112–13; intellectual, 115–17, 134–47; isolation of, 119–20; in *Gujin*, 131–32, 136–37; ambiguity of, 161–62
Collectivism, 83
Commercial Press, 121
Committee of United Coordination, 34
Communists, xi, 38, 76, 154, 157
Confucianism, 144, 156–57
Co-Prosperity Sphere, The, 120
Corruption, 129, 173n41, 208–9n60
Cosmic Wind, *see Yuzhou feng*
Cosmic Wind group, *see Yuzhou feng pai*
Cosmic Wind II, *see Yuzhou feng yuekan*
"Crane of hunting, The," *see* "Huating he"
Cui Wei, 8
Cultural Committee (CCP), 35
Cultural Front (*Wenhua zhanxian*), 12
Cumine, H. M., 33

Dachang, 4, 10, 16
Da cheng (magazine), 154
Dadao shi zhengfu, 32
Dai Li, 133, 152

Daitōa bungaku taikai, 150
Daitōa Kyōeiken ("Greater East Asian
    Co-Prosperity Sphere"), 122
Daitu, 48
Damei wanbao (newspaper), 32
Dan Ni, 102, 106
Daoism, 144
Dao Zaiwen, *see* Wen Zaidao
Dark world (*heian shijie*), xiii, 56, 122,
    182n128
"Dawn in rose shades" ("Meigui se
    zhong de liming"), 41
Da Yazhou zhuyi, see "Greater Asianism"
Daying yebao (newspaper), 39, 116
Death of Li Xiucheng, The (*Li Xiucheng
    zhi si*), 92
December Ninth Movement, 1
Demonstrations, 10–11
Didiao julebu, 111
Ding Mocun, 49, 113, 115
Dongxi (magazine), 149
Drama, 16, 71–77 *passim*, 190n53; street,
    8–9, 10; historical, 91–93, 194–
    95nn80,83,85,87. *See also Huaju*
Du Jun, 140
Du Mu, 129

East and West, *see Dongxi*
Economy: during occupation, 46–
    47, 122–25, 151–52, 161, 180–
    81nn92–96,98,100, 206–7nn40,43–
    44,51, 208n53–56; collapse of, 153,
    163–64
Eighth Route Army Office, 76
Elite, xii, 23, 36–37, 40
Encountering Sorrow (*Lisao*), 84
Enlightenment, 43, 53–54, 65–66; Re-
    sistance, 21–22, 40–46, 51, 158
Enlightenment Book Company, *see*
    Kaiming shudian
Eremitism, 50, 57, 130, 156, 219n6
Essays, xvi, 26, 134–35, 149
Extended-Settlement Areas, xiii

Factionalism, 132–33
Fangxia nide bianzi (Chen Liting), 8

Fanma ji (Li Jianwu), 88–89, 107–8,
    193n71
Fan Quan, 62
Fan Zhongyun, 114, 212n98
Farmer, Rhodes, 2–3
Federation of Chinese Writers and Art-
    ists (Zhongguo wenyijia xiehui), 26
Fenghuo (journal), 11, 27–29
Feng Youzhen, 35
Fengyu tan (magazine), 147, 149, 153
Feng Zhimo, 71
Feng Zikai, 50f, 63
Fernande (Sardou), 101
Film industry, 97f, 104, 190–91nn57,61,
    204n20
Fitch, William Clyde: *Truth,* 78
Five Dynasties, 106–7
Flaubert, Gustave, 70, 79, 100
Flower of blood (*Bixue hua*), 90–91
Foreign areas, xii, 3–4, 163, 171–
    72nn9,10; newspapers published in,
    31–34. *See also* French Concession;
    Gudao; International Settlement
France, Anatole, 93
Free China, 84, 108, 155
Freedom, 82, 108–9, 163f, 190n57;
    moral, 102ff
French Concession, xii, 19, 30, 35, 112;
    bombing of, 3–4; Jinan University
    in, 38, 74; Resistance theater in,
    78, 92
French Municipal Council, 86, 190n53
French Municipal Council Auditorium,
    85
French Municipal Government, 78
Fudan University, 79, 97
Fu Lei, 62
Fund-raising, 6, 10
Fu Rushan, 99
Fu she, 61
Fushen liuji, 98

Gaizu pai, 111
Gangsters, 48
Gao Da, 64–65
Gao Zhenyi, 88

Gao Zhongwu, 119
Ge Nenniang, 90–91
Geng Jizhi, xvi, 23, 59, 60ff, 145, 183n140, 186n167
GMD, *see* Guomindang
GMD Press Censorship Bureau, 32
Gnoisbois (French commissioner of education), 86
Gong Xinjian, 136
Gould, Randall, 32, 47–48
Great American Evening News (*Damei wanbao*), 32
Great Britain, 34
Great Britain Evening News, *see Daying yebao*
"Greater Asianism," 117, 148
"Greater East Asian Co-Prosperity Sphere," 122
"Greater East Asian Cultural Renaissance," 120
"Greater East Asian Renaissance," 148
Greater East Asian War, 151
Great Way Government (Dadao shi zhengfu), 32
Green Gang, 48
Guancha (journal), 164
Guan Zhong, 117–18, 204n22
Guangzhou, 111
Gu Baoheng, 116
Gudao, xiii, 30–31, 76, 84, 155, 163; newspapers in, 31–34; living conditions in, 46–47, 80
Guerrillas, 15, 133, 190n49
Guilin, 58
Gujin (journal), xvi, 110–11, 127–33 *passim*, 157, 212n93; editors of, 134f; contributors to, 135–47 *passim*, 160–62, 210n78; criticism of, 148, 152
Gujin Press, 148
Gujun, 17–19
Guomindang (GMD), xi, 1f, 6, 10, 13–14, 76, 83, 96, 107, 111, 133, 154, 157, 163–64, 196n98; propaganda, 7, 11, 50; suppression by, xiii, 26–27; secret services of, 48–49, 115

Guo Moruo, 7, 12, 19, 148
Guo Tianwen, 28–29
Guo Xiufeng, 116
Gu Zhongyi, 78f, 86, 90, 92, 188n32, 190n53, 193n77
Gu Zhutong, 4, 133

Hagiwara Daikyoku, 105–6, 108
Hanfeng ji (Chen Gongbo), 148
Hangzhou, 108
Hangzhou Bay, 4f
Hedonism, 47–48, 125–26, 129
Henhai (Ke Ling), 104
Heroism, 5, 75, 80, 81–82, 157; myth of, 71, 72–73; collective, 83–84; mythless, 103–4, 106
He Zhi, 138, 141, 145
Hoarding, 47, 125, 178n62
Hong Kong, 30, 47, 61, 84
Hong Kong and Shanghai Bank Building, 120
Hongkou, 2, 36, 176n39
Hong Mo, 78
Hong Shen, 16, 71
Horse trading, *see Fanma ji*
Huai Jiu, 97
Huaju, 71f, 74, 87, 95, 187n9, 191–92n63; companies performing, 77–79; patriotism through, 76–77, 84, 91; reemergence of, 97f, 100f
Huamei wanbao (newspaper), 32–33, 114
Huangdao hui, 35–36
Huang Jinrong, 99
Huangjin Theater, 95
Huang Tianli, 73, 80
Huang Xindi, 84
Huang Xing, 18
Huang Zongxi, 61
Huang Zuolin, 84, 96ff, 101, 106
Huanxiang, 15
"Huating he" (Wang Tongzhao), 54–56, 182n121
Hua xing feng (Li Jianwu), 101, 199n127
Huayi jutuan, 99
Humanitarianism, 21–22, 40, 45

Hu Sheng, 14
Huxi, 2, 28, 36, 48, 112
Hu Zhongchi, 61, 184–85n153

Ichigo offensive, 104
Idealism, 12, 23
Ideology: Japanese, 150–51
Individualism, 45, 159
Institute of Sino-French Studies, see
    Zhongfa yanjiusuo
Integrity, 82, 91
Intellectuals, 5–6, 7, 17, 30, 49, 75–76,
    151, 163, 187n21; resistance by,
    13–15, 36–37, 56–57, 153, 178–
    79n69, 192n67; flight of, 16, 155,
    176n37; collaboration by, 115–17,
    134–47
International Settlement, xii, 3, 6, 11,
    19, 77, 112
Investment, 98f
Isolation: of collaborators, 119–20
Iwane Matsui, 4

Japanese Expeditionary Army, 99
Japanese Imperial Army, 104
Japanese Thought Police, 56
Japan Literary Patriotic Association, see
    Nihon bungaku hōkokukai
Jeu de l'Amour et de la Mort, Le (Roland),
    85f, 94
Jiang Bocheng, 133
Jiangsu Provincial Party Committee,
    34, 76
Jiangwan, xii, 2, 15
Jietou ju, see Street drama
Jie Yi, 118
Ji Guoan, 111, 141, 142–43f, 153,
    216n129
Jilin, 25
Jinan University, 38–39, 70, 74, 79, 97
Jing Yi, 28
Jin Huating, 34
Jin Shan, 16
Jinshanwei, 5, 29, 171–72n10
Jinsiniang Bridge, 5, 29
Jin Xiaoyu (Li Jianwu), 101–2

Jin Xiongbai, 115f, 128, 203n15,
    204n18, 212n98, 213–14n101,
    218–19n159
Jiuwang ribao (newspaper), 7, 11, 18f, 27
Jiuwang yundong, see National salvation
    movement
Ji Yunqing, 114
Joint Savings Society Godown, 17f
Journals, see Magazines
July (Qiyue), 39

Kaifeng, 111
Kaiming shudian, 58–59, 63, 183–
    84nn143–44, 185n161
Kangzhan sanrikan (newspaper), 11–12
Kawabata Yasunari, 149
Ke Ling, xvii, 34, 36, 43, 50f, 62, 66,
    76, 86, 137, 164, 182n131, 184–
    85nn153,161, 187n21; as Shiji feng
    editor, 37–38; as Wanxiang editor,
    62–63, 198n114; resistance by, 68,
    153, 189n45, 197n108; on huaju, 91,
    101; Henhai, 104
Kempeitai, 35, 99, 102, 108, 113, 133;
    arrests and interrogation by, 63,
    105–6, 184n151
Kidnappings, 2, 49
Kong Lingjing, 56, 84, 182n131, 192n67
Konoe Fumimaro, 111
Kugan jutuan, 102, 106
Kwantung Army, 1

Lady Golden-Threads Bridge, see
    Jinsiniang Bridge
Lafayette Theater, 92, 95, 106
Lan Lan, 85
"Lei yu yi" (Wang Tongzhao), 52–54
Lemaître, Jules, 93
Liang Hongzhi, 32, 131, 208n58, 212n98
Liangyu zhong de huohua (Wang Tong-
    zhao), 41–42, 51, 55
Liberation, 104, 108, 113, 153
Li Bolong, 9, 95, 108, 188n30
Li Ciming, 139
Li Dazhao, 23, 73
Li Gongpu, 2

Li Guinian, 99–100

Li Hongzhang, 118

Li Jianwu, xvi, 79, 82, 162, 186–
    87nn3,7, 189n37, 197n104, 200–
    201nn139–40; resistance by, 68–
    69, 75, 81, 108–9, 153, 159–60,
    189n41, 201–2n149; father's death
    and, 70–71; *Zhe buguo shi chuntian*,
    72f, 80, 88, 90, 93; *Shisan nian*, 73,
    80, 93; *Sahuang shijia*, 78; in Re-
    sistance theater, 84f, 87, 93–97,
    99–101, 190nn53,55, 196n97, 198–
    99nn116,120; *Ai yu si de bodou*,
    85–86; *Fanma ji*, 88–89, 107–8,
    193n71; historical drama, 92–93,
    195n87; adaptations by, 101–2;
    Qingchun, 102–5, 156–57, 160;
    interrogation of, 105–6, 199–
    200nn136–38; *Wang Deming*, 106–7

Lin Bosheng, 114, 116, 127, 148f, 152,
    216n135, 202n4, 218–19n159

Lin Haosheng, 136

Lin Yutang, 133

Li Qishan, 69–70, 186n7

Lisao (journal), 84

Li Shiqun, 49, 113, 125, 133

Literary Front (*Wenzhen*), 84

Literary Studies (*Wenxue yanjiu*), 114

Literature (*Wenxue*), 26

Liu Changsheng, 76

Liu Naou, 115f, 118, 204n20

Liu Shaowen, 76, 78, 95

Liu Shike, 116

Liu Xiao, 76

Liu Xiwei, *see* Li Jianwu

Liu Yazi, 94, 194–95n83

Liu Yusheng (Tsun-jen), 138, 147ff,
    153f, 212–13nn98,99, 218–19n159

Li Xianjun, 90

Li Xiucheng zhi si (Yang Hansheng), 92

Li Zhen, 107

Locke, John, 42

"Lone Battalion," see Gujun

Long Muxun, 117, 146, 217–18n149,
    218–19n159

Lou Shiyi, 60

"Low-key Club" (Didiao julebu), 111

Loyalty, 82f, 89

Lu Ji, 55

Lunyu pai, 133, 136, 211n86

Luodian, 16

Lu Xun, 2, 11, 12–13, 28, 38, 134, 148;
    collected works of, 61, 184–85n153

Lu Xun feng (journal), 137, 192n67

Lu Xun Style, *see* Lu Xun feng

Lu Yi, 55–56, 200n139

Lyceum Theater, 78, 95

Macbeth (Shakespeare), 106

Magazines, 114–15, 127, 153, 178n56,
    198n114. *See also* by name

Mao Dun, 7, 11, 19, 23, 26f, 63, 84

Mao Heting, 136

Mao Zedong, 83

Martial law, 121

May Fourth Movement: ideas of, 21–23,
    42, 50, 53, 93, 157f, 174n6

May 30 Movement, 24

"Meigui se zhong de liming," 41

Mei Siping, 116, 218–19n159

Metamorphosis, *see* Tuibian

Military Bureau of Statistics and Investi-
    gation (GMD), 48

Military Special Services Section, *see*
    Kempeitai

Ming dynasty, 140

Ming Gongan school, 133f

Mingmo yihen (Ouyang Yuqian), 90,
    193–94n79

Mingshi, 130f, 139f

Ministry of Education (GMD), 61

Mobilization, 12–15 *passim*, 23

Moralism: collective, 93–94, 157

Morality, 24, 67, 82f, 104, 135; public
    and private, xiii–xiv, 43–44, 155,
    158–59; ambiguity of, xv, 156–57;
    defining, 42–43; and action, 45–
    46; self-righteous, 51–52; and poli-
    tics, 107–8; and collaboration,
    138–39

Morigaki, 151

Movies, *see* Film industry

Mukden Incident, 1
Mu Lijuan, 138, 212n98
Murders, 36, 49. *See also* Assassinations
Mu Shiying, 115, 118, 138

Nahan (journal), 27
Nanhua ribao (newspaper), 127
Nanjing, 16, 19–20, 91
Nanshi (Nantao), xii, 5, 19, 36, 48
Nanxiang, 16
National Central Library, 61
National Day, 10
Nationalism, 24, 40, 93, 117, 155, 163f;
    militant, 2, 115, 157; violence and,
    44–45; cultural, 145–46, 147,
    215n125
Nationalists, see Guomindang
National Salvation Daily, *see Jiuwang
    ribao*
National salvation movement, 5–6, 13f,
    188n23; organizations in, 6–10, 30,
    76, 172n23
National salvation unions, 1–2, 9
Neo-Confucianism, 82f, 91, 92–93,
    145, 157
New Asia Hotel, 35
"New China Strategy," 150
New Citizens' Movement (Xin guomin
    yundong), 148
New Fourth Army, 95, 190n49
"New Order in East Asia," 110–13 *pas-
    sim*, 117
"New Shanghai," 122
New Shanghai Daily, *see Xin shen bao*
Newspapers, 7, 49, 114f, 148, 153,
    177n49, 178nn56,62, 209n67; sup-
    pression of, 31–32, 56, 96, 121, 127;
    in foreign areas, 32–34. *See also by
    name*
Nihon bungaku hōkokukai, 150,
    217n142
1911 Revolution, 11–12, 19, 69, 88,
    113, 118
Niu Xiaoshan, 81, 106
Northern Expedition, 12, 73
Nostalgia, 26, 64, 110, 120, 126, 152,

154, 164–65; as collaborationist
    theme, 136, 140, 142–43, 161, 162,
    210nn78,83, 215–16n126
Novels, 26, 63–65
No. 76, 48–49, 56, 119; activities of,
    113–16
Nüzi gongyu (Yu Ling), 88

Observer, The (*Guancha*), 164
Occupation, xii–xiii, 61–62, 64; intel-
    lectual life under, xvi, 30, 162–63;
    living conditions under, 46–48,
    122–26, 189n39, 206–9nn44,51–
    56,60
Orphan son of Madam Zhao, The
    (*Zhaoshi guer*), 107
Othello (Shakespeare), 106
Outline of Propaganda for the defense
    of Greater Shanghai ("Baowei da
    Shanghai yundong xuanchuan
    dagang"), 17
"Outline of Propaganda in Commemo-
    ration of Lu Xun's Death" (SWH),
    12–13
Ouyang Wenpu, 93
Ouyang Yuqian: *Mingmo yihen*, 90,
    193–94n79

Pacific War, xiii, 120, 129
Pacifism, 113, 118
Pan Gongzhan, 7, 172n12
Panoramic (*Da cheng*), 154
Pan Yuqie, 136, 138, 147f, 212–13n99
Paotaiwan, 4
Passivity, xiv, xv–xvii, 197n104; as resis-
    tance, 21, 57–59, 66, 156, 158; criti-
    cism of, 145, 146–47
Patrie! (Sardou), 92
Patriotism, 1, 33, 36–37, 51, 84, 86f,
    112f, 117f, 155, 157; through writ-
    ing, 26–27, 39, 41–42, 76; through
    plays, 88, 91, 95f, 100–101; of *ming-
    shi*, 131–32; cultural nationalism
    and, 145–46
Peace Bookstore, 148
Peace Movement, 48, 110, 118–19,

188n33, 204n24; promotion of, 112–13; propaganda of, 113–14, 205n27; intellectuals in, 115–17

Peace News, *see Ping bao*

Periodicals, 31–32

Phenomena, *see Wanxiang*

Ping bao (newspaper), 115, 203n15, 209n67

Ping Jinya, 62f

Plays, *see* Drama

Poetry, xvi, 29, 41–42, 63

Promote Asia Building (Xingya Building), 120

Propaganda, 17, 79, 151, 216n135; GMD, 6f, 34, 50; in street drama, 8–9, 16; by national salvation organizations, 10–13; collaborationist, 32, 204n20; CCP, 34, 50; Peace Movement, 113–14, 116

Publishing industry, 27, 114, 153; under occupation, 30, 58–59, 121, 148, 216n134

Pudong, xiii, 2

Put down your whip (*Fangxia nide bianzi*), 8

Pu Yi, 1

Qian Junrui, 15

Qian Qianyi, 143

Qian Zhongshu, 94, 100, 201n143

Qi Kang, 144

Qingchun (Li Jianwu), 156–57; themes in, 102–5, 160

Qingdao, 25, 66

Qing dynasty, 140

Qinghua University, 70

Qingnian jiuguo fuwutuan, 10

Qingniao jushe, 77

Qin Gui, 118

Qin Shouou, 39, 116, 138; *Qiuhaitang*, 98

Qiuhaitang (Qin Shouou), 98

Qiyue (supplement), 39

Quangongting, 5

Quanguo gejie jiuguo hui xiehui, 2

Qu Yuan, 139

"Rape of Nanjing," 19–20

Red Star over China (Snow), 61, 87, 184–85n153

Reformed Nationalist Government, 114, 148

Reform Government (Weixin zhengfu), 32

Refugees, 2–4, 6, 9–10, 171–72n10, 205n30

Remarriage, 145

"Remembering Lady Golden-Threads Bridge" ("Yi Jinsiniang qiao"), 29

Reminiscences, *see Gujin*

"Reorganization Clique" (*Gaizu pai*), 111

Resistance, xivff, 19, 35, 68–69, 96, 128, 155, 183n140, 189n41, 193n74, 195–96n94; by intellectuals, 13–15, 36–37, 56–57, 178–79n69, 192n67; promotion of, 16–17, 29, 50, 104–5; of Gujun, 17–18; enlightenment and, 21–22, 40–46, 51, 158; by press, 31–32; passive, 57, 58–59; symbolic, 57–58, 186n167, 189n45; through theater, 76–79, 83–84, 102, 104, 159; role of, 82–83; freedom through, 108–9; types of, 156–57, 183n134, 184n151

Resistance Triweekly, *see Kangzhan sanrikan*

Restoration Society (Fu she), 61

Roland, Romain: *Le Jeu de l'amour et de la Mort*, 85f, 94

Rongwei Theater Company, 99

Sahuang shijia (Li Jianwu), 78

Sanmin zhoukan (magazine), 114

Sardou, Victorien, 92, 101

Scholars, *see Mingshi*

Seclusion, 59–60

Second Revolution, 69

Secret Service Headquarters, *see* No. 76

"Seven Sages of the Bamboo Grove," 143

SGJ, *see* Shanghai shi gejie kangdi houyuan hui

Shakespeare, William, 106
Shanghai Arts Light Theater (Shanghai yiguang jutuan), 99
Shanghai Arts Theater, see Shanghai yishu juyuan
Shanghai Cultural Circles National Salvation Federation, see Shanghai shi wenhua jie jiuwang xiehui
Shanghai Cultural Circles National Salvation Union (Shanghai wenhua jie jiuguo hui), 26
Shanghai Daily (Shanhai mainichi), 35
Shanghai Dramatic Arts Society, see Shanghai juyishe
Shanghai Dramatic Circles National Salvation Association, see Shanghai xiju jie jiuwang xiehui
Shanghai juyishe, 78–79, 85, 193n76, 194n82, 195n84, 196n98; discussion group, 87–88; as professional company, 89–90; performances of, 90–92; Li Jianwu in, 94, 96, 159
Shanghai Municipal Council, 6
Shanghai Municipal Police, 31–32, 49, 172n13
Shanghai Music Conservatory, 39
Shanghai Press Censorship Bureau, 32, 114
Shanghai Professional Company (Shanghai zhiye jutuan), 96
Shanghai shi gejie kangdi houyuan hui (SGJ), 6, 9, 10–11, 16–19 passim, 172n12, 188n23
Shanghai shi wenhua jie jiuwang xiehui (SWH), 15–19 passim, 28, 74f; activities of, 7, 9, 16; propaganda by, 10, 11–13
Shanghai Theater Friendship Club (Shanghai xiju jiaoyishe), 95
Shanghai Vocational Circles National Salvation Association (Shanghai zhiye jie jiuwang xiehui), 9
Shanghai wenhua jie jiuguo hui, 26
Shanghai xiju jiaoyishe, 95
Shanghai xiju jie jiuwang xiehui, 8, 74f, 77

Shanghai yiguang jutuan, 99
Shanghai yishu juyuan, 77–78, 85, 188n32
Shanghai zhiye jie jiuwang xiehui, 9
Shanghai zhiye jutuan, 96
Shang Zhen, 70
Shanhai godo shimbun (newspaper), 33
Shanhai mainichi (newspaper), 35
Shanyu (Wang Tongzhao), 26
Sha Qianli, 2
Sha Wenhan, 35, 76
Shehui ribao (newspaper), 36
Shen bao (newspaper), 34, 127, 135, 153, 177–78n55, 209n67
Shen Junru, 2
"Shengshuai yuejin hua cangsang" (Zhou Fohai), 132
Shidai wenxuan (magazine), 114, 211n87
Shi Hui, 102
Shi Liang, 2
Shi Tuo, 62, 201n143
Shiji feng (supplement), 37–38, 41, 192n67
Shimbunhan, 99
Shisan nian (Li Jianwu), 73, 80, 93
Shitao, 130
Shizilin, 4
Short stories, xvi, 149; by Wang Tongzhao, 52–56
Shu Qi, 156
Shu Yan, 89f
Shuanqing (Wang Tongzhao), 63–64, 159
Sino-American Daily (Zhongmei ribao), 29
Sino-French Friendship Club (Zhongfa lianyihui), 78, 85
Sino-Japanese Cultural Association, see Zhongri wenhua xiehui
Sister Moon, 52–53
Sixth National Congress, 112–13
Smedley, Agnes: China's Red Army Marches, 38
Smuggling, 125, 173–74n52
Snow, Edgar: Red Star over China, 61, 87, 184–85n153
Social contracts, 44–45

Society for Literary Research, *see*
    Wenxue yanjiu hui
Society News (*Shehui ribao*), 36
Solitary Island, *see* Gudao
Songjiang, 16
Song of uprightness (*Zhengqi ge*), 92
Song Xilian, 15
Song-Yuan, 88
Sorrow of the Late Ming, *see Mingmo
    yihen*
South China Daily (*Nanhua ribao*), 127
Sparks in Purgatory, *see Liangyu zhong de
    huohua*
Standard, The, *see Wenhui bao*
Statue of Peace, 52–54
Street drama, 8–9, 16
Struggle between Love and Death, The,
    see Ai yu si de bodou
Struggle Company, *see* Kugan jutuan
Study groups, 87–88
Sun Company, 121
Sun Kexian, 90–91
Sun Ruihuang, 61, 106
Sun Yatsen, 12, 112–13, 117
Sun Yefang, 35, 76
Su Qing, 136, 147, 153, 212–13n99,
    214n113
Surveillance, 121–22
Su Shi, 55, 129
SWH, *see* Shanghai shi wenhua jie
    jiuwang xiehui
Symbolism, xvii, 18–19, 55, 186n167,
    189–90nn45,46; cultural, 11–13,
    156; in Resistance theater, 87,
    88–89; collaborationist, 117–18,
    131, 142–45

Tagore, Rabindranath, 24
"Talking About Human Vicissitude
    After Witnessing All the Ups and
    Downs" ("Shengshuai yuejin hua
    cangsang"), 132
Talks amid Hardships, *see Fengyu tan*
Tang Ruoqing, 90
Tang Tao, 36f, 57, 62, 97, 134, 184–
    85n153, 187n21, 189n39, 201n143

Tan Zhengbi, 138, 212–13n99, 217–
    18n149
Taoan dream memories, *see Taoan mengyi*
Taoan mengyi (Zhang Dai), 143
Tao Jingsun, 150
Tao Kangde, 133–37 *passim*, 148f,
    211n87, 212–13nn98,99, 217n149;
    on passivity, 146–47; on economic
    hardships, 151–52; trial of, 154,
    218–19n159
Tao Xisheng, 119
Tao Yuanming, 129f, 143
"Tears and wing," *see* "Lei yu yi"
Tegong zongbu, *see* No. 76
Terrorism, xiiif, 115; Japanese, 35–36;
    under Wang Jingwei regime, 48–
    49; against theaters, 77, 79, 85; in
    Peace Movement, 113–14
Theater, xvi, 71, 74, 194n82; Resistance,
    69, 77–79, 85–95 *passim*, 159–60,
    193–94nn76–77,79, 195n84, 197–
    99nn105,108,112,120; amateur,
    94–95, 188n30; suppression of, 96,
    121; commercial, 97–98, 100
Third Area Army, 4
Third Greater East Asian Writers' Con-
    gress (Daitōa bungaku taiki), 150
Thirteen years, *see Shisan nian*
This is only spring, *see* Zhe buguo shi
    chuntian
Three Peoples' Weekly (*Sanmin
    zhoukan*), 114
Thunderstorm (Cao Yu), 77
Tiandi (magazine), 147, 153
Tian Han, 71, 108
Times Selection, *see Shidai wenxuan*
Tōa shin'chitsujo, *see* "New Order in
    East Asia"
Tōjō Hideki, 150
Tosca, La (Sardou), 101
Toyoshima Masao, 151
Translation News (*Yi bao*), 35
Treason, 153–54
Truth (Fitch), 78
Tsun-jen, *see* Liu Yusheng
Tu Guangqi, 90f, 193n76

Tuibian (Cao Yu), 83, 96
Tunxi, 108
"Twenty–ninth telegram," 112
"Twisted–branch Plum Syndrome,"
80, 86
Two virtues, The, see Shuangqing

United States, 32–34, 128, 171n9
Universe, see Tiandi

Violence, 44–45, 115. See also Terrorism

Wang Deming (Li Jianwu), 106–7, 109
Wang Jingwei, xif, 48f, 102, 116, 122,
152, 218–19n159; and Peace Movement, 110, 111–14, 118; regime of,
119–20, 132–33, 150–51, 161,
203n11, 212nn94,98; support for,
127–28, 148; in Gujin, 131f, 210n78
Wang Tongzhao, xvi, 59, 97, 153, 162,
183n140, 187n21; passive resistance
of, 21, 145, 156; May Fourth Movement and, 22, 23–24, 158; patriotic
writings of, 25–26, 158–59; as
Wenxue editor, 26–27; and Fenghuo,
27–29; at Jinan University, 38–39;
resistance enlightenment of, 40–41;
Liangyu zhong de huohua, 41–42, 51;
on morality, 42–46, 51–52; "Lei yu
yi," 52–54; "Huating he," 54–55;
Huating he, 55–56, 182n121; Shuan-
qing, 63–64, 159; as recluse, 66–67;
and Li Jianwu, 70, 84, 86, 186n3
Wang Wenxian, 70, 94, 196n97
Wang Xizhi, 129
Wang Zaoshi, 2
Wangyi ji (Zhou Fohai), 148
Wanxiang (magazine), 62–63, 99, 198n114
War-front service corps, 9–10
War of Resistance, xii, 2, 12–13, 14,
27f, 68–69, 107, 111, 157, 162,
171nn5,9, 201–2n149
"Wartime Mobile Dramatic Troupe
Number 2," 16
Weekly (Zhoubao), 164
Wei-Jin period, 140, 143, 144–45

Weixin zhengfu, 32
Wei Zheng, 43
Weng Shuaiping, 39
Wenhua zhanxian (newspaper), 12
Wenhui bao (newspaper), 33, 49, 114,
203n14
Wenxue (journal), 26
Wenxue yanjiu (magazine), 114
Wenxue yanjiu hui, 23–24, 25
Wen Zaidao, 37, 50, 147, 154; collabora-
tion by, 111, 136–45 passim, 153,
157
Wenzhen (journal), 84
White Terror, 25, 163
Woman's dormitory, see Nüzi gongyu
Wong-Quincy, John, see Wang Wenxian
Writers, xii, xiv, 30; as moral elite, 36–
37; seclusion of, 59–60; under
occupation, 61–62, 182–83n133;
for Wanxiang, 62–63; collaboration
by, 126–27, 134–47, 153–54, 212–
13n99; associations for, 144, 149–
50, 217nn143; economic hardships
on, 151–52, 217–18n149
Wu Guifang, 137
Wuhan, 19, 111
Wu Kaixian, 133
Wu Peifu, 50
Wu Rengzhi, 78, 90
Wusong, 4
Wu Weiye, 143
Wu Yonggang, 90, 194n82
Wu Zhenxiu, 128
Wu Zuguang: Zhengqi ge, 92

Xia Mianzun, 59–66 passim, 182n131,
184nn144,150–51, 201n143
Xi'an, 69
Xiang, 102–3, 104, 160
Xian Xinghai, 9
Xiaopin wen, 134–35, 140, 149
Xiaoqian, 64–65
Xia Yan, 7, 71, 84
Xie Jinyuan, 17
Xier, 102–3, 104, 160
Xinguang Theater, 77, 87–88, 95

Xin guomin yundong, 148
Xingya Building, 120
Xin shen bao (newspaper), 33, 114, 127, 209n67
Xinwen bao (newspaper), 127, 177nn49,51–52, 209n67
Xuangong Theater, 89
Xuanzhong, 99–100
Xu Diaofu, 62, 184n144
Xu Guangping, 56, 61, 96, 153, 184–85n153, 201n143
Xu Shenyu, 61, 84
Xu Xingzhi, 85
Xu Zhimo, 24
Xuzhou, 111

Yan'an, 34
Yangawa Heisuke, 16
Yang Dongchun, 12
Yang Hangsheng: *Li Xiucheng zhi si,* 92
Yang Huimin, 17–18, 173–74n52
Yang Jiang, 94, 100, 198–99n120
Yangshang bao, 34f
Yang Shuhui, 153
Yangshupu (Yangtzepoo), xii–xiii, 2, 4
Yang Zao, 89
Yan Xishan, 69–70
Yao Gong, 145
Yeats, W. B., 24
Yellow Way Association, *see* Huangdao hui
Ye Shanghai (Yu Ling), 90
Ye Shengtao, 23, 26, 50, 63
Yi bao (newspaper), 35
Yi dui, 9, 16
"Yi Jinsiniang qiao," 29
Yimin, 110f, 127, 140, 143–44, 160–61, 202n1
Yi she, 9–10, 74
Yonai Mitsumasa, 119
Yoshida Tōsuke, 126, 151
You Shufen, 70
Youths' National Salvation Service Corps (Qingnian jiuguo fuwutuan), 10
Yuan Hongdao, 130
Yuan Shikai, 69

Yuan Yuquan, 116, 126
Yue Xiuliang, 149
Yu Hongjun, 19
Yu Ling, 7, 65, 71–78 *passim,* 85f, 89, 93, 96, 193n74; *Nüzi gongyu,* 88; *Ye Shanghai,* 90
Yuzhou feng (magazine), 134, 212n93
Yuzhou feng pai, 133, 138
Yuzhou feng yuekan (magazine), 134

Zawen, 37–38, 136f
Zeng Zhongming, 111, 116, 118
Zhabei (Chapei), xii, 2, 4
Zhandi fuwutuan, see War-front service corps
Zhang Aiping, 76
Zhang Dai: *Taoan mengyi,* 143
Zhang Geng, 9
Zhang Han, 140, 144, 215n121
Zhang Henshui, 101
Zhang Jie, 85
Zhang Jusheng, 95
Zhang Ke, 85
Zhang Naiqi, 2
Zhang Wozhou, 13
Zhang Xisheng, 61
Zhang Yongni, 61
Zhang Ziping, 114, 205n27
Zhao Jiabi, 27–28, 54, 62
Zhao Junhao, 56
Zhaoshi guer, 107
Zhao Shuyong, 114, 131, 212n98, 218–19n159
Zhao Zhiyou, 78, 86, 188n33
Zhe buguo shi chuntian (Li Jianwu), 72f, 80, 88, 90, 93
Zhejiang, 96
Zheju, 57
Zheng Banjiao, 145
Zhengqi ge (Wu Zuguang), 92
Zheng Zhenduo, 12, 23, 27, 62, 66, 84, 97, 183n140, 184n153, 200–201n142; resistance by, 26, 39, 60–61, 153; on moral elitism, 36–37; at Jinan University, 38, 70
Zhenru, 38, 74

Zhixin Press, 148
Zhong bao (newspaper), 116
Zhongfa lianyihui, 78, 85
Zhongfa yanjiusuo, 79, 97
Zhongguo University, 22, 23–24
Zhongguo wenyijia xiehui, 26
Zhonghua quanguo wenyi jie kangdi
    xiehui, 153
Zhonghua ribao (newspaper), 114, 116,
    127, 148, 153, 209n67
Zhonghua zhoubao (newspaper), 135, 147
Zhongmei ribao (newspaper), 29
Zhongri wenhua xiehui, 137f, 212n98
Zhoubao (journal), 164
Zhou dynasty, 156
Zhou Fohai, xi, 112, 115f, 119, 125,
    133, 147, 152, 212–13n99, 218–
    19n159; and Zhu Pu, 127f, 135;
    hedonism of, 129, 204n18; in *Gujin*,
    130–31; "Shengshuai yuejin hua
    cangsang," 132; *Wangyi ji*, 148

Zhou Jianyun, 7
Zhou Lian, 111, 133–34, 136–39 *pas-
    sim*, 146, 153, 193n74, 212n98; as
    Gujin editor, 135, 212n93
Zhou Muzhai, 37
Zhou Yueran, 149
Zhou Yuren, 98, 150
Zhou Zuoren, 97, 134f, 141–42, 146,
    211n86, 214n111, 216n129
Zhuangzi, 58
Zhu Anping, 164
Zhu Duanjun, 78, 97, 197n105
Zhu Laoxian, 54–55
Zhu Pu, 114, 127, 139, 142–43, 146f,
    153, 209–10n69, 212n98, 212–13n99,
    218–19n159; as *Gujin* publisher,
    128–35 *passim*, 152
Zhu Qinglai, 114
Zhu Xinggong, 49
Zhu Ziqing, 63, 70, 94
Zou Taofen, 2, 11, 14, 19

Library of Congress Cataloging–in–Publication Data

Fu, Poshek, 1955–
Passivity, resistance, and collaboration : intellectual choices in occupied Shanghai,
    1937–1945 / Poshek Fu
p.   cm.
Includes bibliographical references and index.
ISBN 0-8047-2172-6 (cl.) : ISBN 0-8047-2796-1 (pbk.)
1. Shanghai (China)—History.   2. Chinese literature—China—Shanghai—History
    and criticism.   3. Sino-Japanese Conflict, 1937–1945—China—Shanghai—
    Literature and the War.   I. Title.
DS796.S257F8   1993
951'.132—dc20
                                                                    93-10239
                                                                    CIP

Original printing 1993
Last figure below indicates year of this printing:
05   04   03   02   01   00   99   98   97   96